# THE PALACE OF WESTMINSTER

## HOUSES OF PARLIAMENT

SIR ROBERT COOKE

# THE PALACE OF WESTMINSTER

## HOUSES OF PARLIAMENT

DISTRIBUTED IN THE UNITED KINGDOM & COMMONWEALTH
BY MACMILLAN LONDON LTD.

PUBLISHED BY
BURTON SKIRA LTD.

First published in the United Kingdom by
Burton Skira, Ltd.
110 St. Martin's Lane, London WC2N 4AZ


ISBN 2-88249-014-3 (Burton Skira, Inc.)

Distributed in the United Kingdom & Commonwealth
ISBN 0-333-459-237 (Macmillan London Ltd.)

Cooke, Sir Robert
The Palace of Westminster

Designed by Richard S. Papale

Printed and bound in Switzerland
BCK Graphic Arts SA
Geneva

Front cover: Detail of a ceiling panel in the Members' Dining Room (page 174)
Back cover: Central Tower of the New Palace by Barry (page 128)
Fly leaf: H.R.H. The Duchess of York
Photographed by H.R.H. Prince Andrew

*To the memory of*
*all those*
*Saints*
*Kings, Queens, Princes*
*Prime Ministers*
*Parliamentarians*
*and*
*Architects*
*who*
*in more than a thousand years*
*created*
*the living*
*Palace of Westminster*
*the*
*Houses of Parliament*

Sir Robert Cooke, December 1, 1986

# CONTENTS

*Portrait of The Prime Minister, the Rt. Hon. Mrs Margaret Thatcher, M.P., by Gilly Rayner (1984).*

**10 DOWNING STREET**

LONDON SW1A 2AA

THE PRIME MINISTER

It is a fair claim that the Palace of Westminster - beloved of so many Parliamentarians past and present and increasingly familiar in these days to the public at large - is in better order now than it has ever been. Those who have been at such pains over the years to maintain its fabric and perfect its adornments have given us the most tangible possible reminder of our debt to past generations for preserving the heritage of this country's historic buildings. The same constant care and vigilance are needed in our own day if we, too, are to be seen as faithful stewards by those who come after us.

The Palace of Westminster has no rivals as a symbol of our democratic institutions, and most Prime Ministers in the past have given a lead in encouraging the conservation and, where necessary, restoration of this priceless building. During my time as Prime Minister I have felt myself privileged to be able to carry on this tradition and a great deal of preservation work has been successfully completed. Much of it goes unseen, but among the more spectacular projects so far undertaken the greatest pleasure has come from restoring the magnificent ceiling of the chamber of the House of Lords and the exciting transformation of the State Rooms in the Speaker's House.

Barry and Pugin would be proud of their Palace today.

Margaret Thatcher

November, 1986

*Sir Robert Cooke*

# ACKNOWLEDGEMENTS

I would first of all like to thank H.R.H. The Duchess of York for initiating the book, the Prime Minister for writing the foreword, Mr. Richard Burton for publishing it, Dr. Penelope Hunting for her scholarly assistance, and Miss Linda S. Cook for typing it.

The Secretary of State for the Environment has been enormously supportive as have the Lord Great Chamberlain, The Lord High Chancellor, Mr. Speaker, the Officers of both Houses of Parliament and Parliamentarians generally. I am also grateful for the interest shown by General Secretary Mikhail Gorbachev and the co-operation of Mrs. Grishina, the Director of the Research Museum of the U.S.S.R. Academy of Arts.

The owners and custodians of the paintings, drawings, prints, documents and artifacts illustrated in this book are warmly thanked for their co-operation and for allowing material in their collections to be used.

The descendants of Sir Charles Barry have been generous in their interest and support, especially Mrs. P.B. Stanley-Evans, Mrs. Kathleen Adkins and Brigadier John Wolfe-Barry O.B.E. My own family has encouraged and assisted me throughout. This has been invaluable.

*Robert Cooke*
*December 1986*

The author died in January 1987. He had finished the text of this book but did not live to edit it. H.R.H. The Duchess of York, Dr. Hunting and myself have endeavoured to accomplish this task in accordance with his wishes.

*Jenifer Cooke*
*July 1987*

# INTRODUCTION

Queen Victoria's first Prime Minister, Lord Melbourne mocked the revival of the Age of Chivalry, but his successor, Sir Robert Peel, played a major part in the great Gothic adventure at Westminster in partnership with Albert, Prince Consort and his Royal Fine Arts Commission. Disraeli, even more deeply involved with the creators of the New Palace, distanced himself from them when the sun ceased to shine and recommended the Commons to hang an architect. It was the austere Gladstone who prevented a disastrous enlargement of the House of Commons' Chamber.

In more recent times, Winston Churchill insisted that a New House of Commons be a faithful echo of the old. He was quite convinced that any other shape or form would actually destroy the unique quality of the Parliament in which he sat for more than sixty years.

Changeless, yet subtly changing, Westminster contrives to meet each new challenge. The history of the New Palace is a story without an end.

*Sir Robert Cooke*

*Saint Peter consecrating the church on Thorney Island, from the thirteenth century manuscript "La Estoire de Seint Aedward le Rei."*

# I

## A ROYAL RESIDENCE

The Old and New Royal Palaces of Westminster, their Chapels and the nearby Abbey, all grew up upon a tiny island on the north shore of the River Thames. Thorney Island was an inhospitable place overgrown with briars and thorns, bounded by two streams of the Tyburn of immortal memory, which here discharged into the Thames. Near here have been found fossil remains from 120,000 years ago. The giant ox, narrow-nosed rhinoceros, the cave lion and the straight-tusked elephant all once existed at Westminster. There is evidence of an Iron Age settlement and remains of Roman dwellings. There was a Romano-British rubbish pit beneath where is now the courtyard of 10 Downing Street.

Flete, the fifteenth century historian, prior of Westminster, believed that there was a Roman temple to Apollo on Thorney Island, a temple which was destroyed by an earthquake.

Tradition has the first St. Peter's Church built by King Lucius in A.D. 184. The arrival of the Saxons once more left the Thorney Island a desolate place. By ancient tradition, supported by documents executed some time after the event, the Christian convert, King Sebert, was inspired to restore the ruined Church of St. Peter on Thorney Island. A miracle soon followed.

"The eve of the day fixed by Bishop Mellitus of London for the Hallowing and Dedication of the new St. Peter's was marked by flood and tempest. Edric, a fisherman, who lived in Thorney, was awakened by a loud voice calling him by name. It was midnight, he arose and went forth. The voice called him again from the opposite bank of the River, which is now Lambeth, bidding him put out his boat to ferry a man across the River.

Arrived in Thorney, the stranger directed his steps to the church, and entered the portal. Straightway the church was lit up as by a thousand wax tapers, and voices arose chanting psalms - sweet voices such as no man had ever heard before. The voices could be none other than those of angels come down from Heaven itself to sing the first service in the new Church. Then the voices fell, and he heard one voice loud and solemn: and then the heavenly choir uplifted their voices again. Presently all was still. The lights went out as suddenly as they had appeared and the stranger came forth. 'Know, O Edric,' he said, 'know that I am Peter. I have hallowed the church myself. Tomorrow I charge thee that thou tell these things to the Bishop, who will find a sign, and token in the church of my hallowing. And for another token, put forth again upon the river, cast thy nets, and thou shalt receive so great a draft of fishes that there will be no doubt left in thy mind. But give one tenth to this to my holy church.' He put forth as directed, and cast his net, and presently brought ashore a draft miraculous.

In the morning the Bishop with his clergy, and the King with his following, came up from London in their ships to hallow the church. They were received by Edric, who told them this strange story. And within the church the Bishop found the lingering fragrance of incense far more precious than any that he could offer; on the altar were the drippings of wax candles (long preserved as holy relics, being none other than the wax candles of Heaven), and written in the dust certain words in Greek character. He proclaimed the joyous news, he held a service of thanksgiving instead of a hallowing. And after the service they returned to London and held a banquet, with Edric's finest salmon lying on a lordly dish in the midst."[1]

The consecration of the church on Thorney Island was the prelude to the foundation of the Benedictine community nearby, usually attributed to King Offa of Mercia *circa* 785. Somehow the foundation survived the Danish invasions of the ninth century, as did an Anglo Saxon settlement situated slightly to the north, on the site of Treasury Green in Whitehall. King Edgar provided some stability by endowing the church and monastery at Westminster before another wave of Danish invasions devastated Thorney Island. Again, it was the King, this time King Canute, who revived the church on Thorney Island. Canute is reputed to be the first King to reside at Westminster, as the church and its immediate neighbourhood were by then known. If the historian John Nordern is to be believed, it was at Westminster that King Canute rebuked the waves of the tidal Thames, to prove the stupidity of his fawning courtiers; his name is still invoked by modern Parliamentarians given to flights of imagery.

Thus, first the Church was established at Westminster, later came the Royal Palaces and later still the Parliament.

Edward the Confessor, proclaimed King in 1042, devoted himself to the building of the Abbey at Westminster. King Edward's devotion to St. Peter is conveyed in the Bayeux Tapestry, where the words *hic portatur corpus Eadwardi regis ad ecclesiam Petri* record his burial in the Abbey, eight days after its consecration.

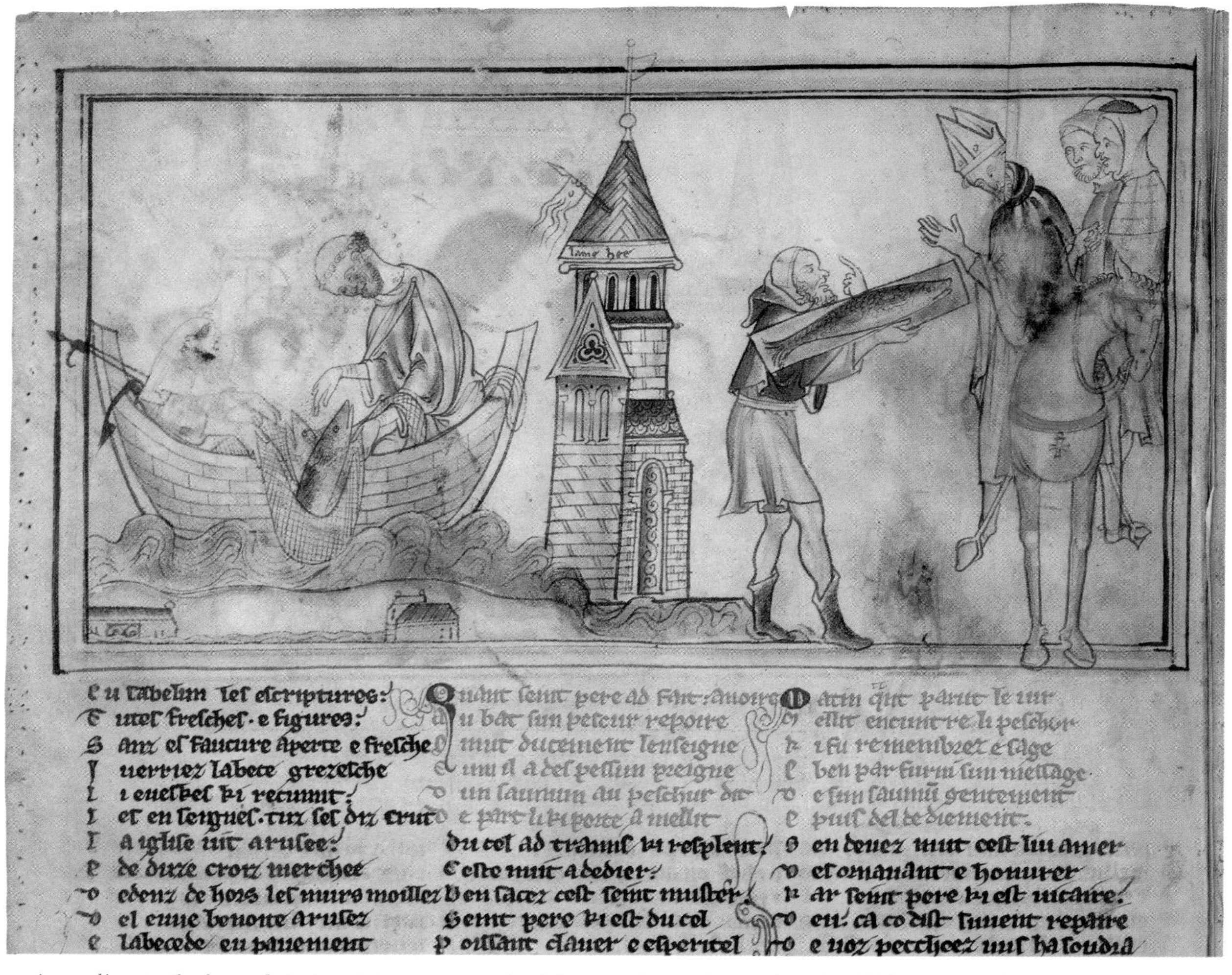

*According to the legend, Saint Peter was rowed to Thorney Island by Edricus the Fisherman, who later presented a salmon to the Bishop of London.*

## *Westminster Hall*

It is to the first Norman King William I (the Conqueror) that we owe the name New Palace of Westminster. He was determined to create a new and grander residence for himself than the Old Palace of his Saxon predecessors in which Edward had ended his days. William ordered fifteen ship-loads of Caen stone; but the only one to arrive in this country was diverted to the monks of St. Augustine's Abbey at Canterbury. The other fourteen were wrecked in a storm.

The Conqueror's son, William Rufus, began great works on the new Westminster Palace after 1087. He created the first Westminster Hall, traces of which yet remain. It was begun in 1097 and was ready for a Whitsun Feast in 1099.

*A scene from the Bayeux Tapestry showing King Edward on his throne in the Palace of Westminster.*

*The Bayeux Tapestry depicts the funeral procession carrying the body of King Edward to Westminster Abbey.*

The largest hall in Britain and probably in Europe, it was 240 feet long and sixty-seven feet six inches wide. The huge span was roofed by means of a row of posts - eleven on each side - leaving a central aisle about double the width of the side aisles. These posts and the corresponding buttresses between the windows were subject to a strange discrepancy - those on the west side were some four feet to the north of those on the east. It is possible that this was due to the fact that the Great Hall was erected around an existing building, making the measurement from side to side difficult. The Norman windows, fragments of which were discovered in the nineteenth century, ran along each side above where is now the Richard II cornice.

This vast hall became the ceremonial centre of the kingdom. Westminster and Winchester were the principal royal seats but because the Exchequer settled at Westminster, that became the capital. Henry II had a subsidiary treasury at Westminster but King John caused Westminster to absorb Winchester. The Courts of Common Pleas and Kings Bench followed, in or close to the hall.

Every department of Government eventually came to the Palace which had begun as a royal residence. Westminster remained the principal royal seat and judicial and administrative headquarters until Henry VIII moved the court to Whitehall, leaving Westminster to officialdom and eventually to Parliament.

Henry III extended and aggrandized the Westminster Palace. To him we owe the origins of the Painted Chamber which survived in one form or another until the Great Fire of 1834. Its name would have lived on in the New Palace had Prince Albert's Commission had their way.

The King's Great Chamber was a long, tall room in Westminster Palace which Henry III used as a combined audience and bedchamber. After a fire in 1262 the King commissioned three of the most talented artists of the period to redecorate the room with wall-paintings of battle scenes, biblical stories, symbolic figures and most significant of all, a painting of the coronation of Edward the Confessor on the wall above the King's bed. These were the magnificent paintings which gave the room its name. They were covered by whitewash and tapestries when Capon recorded the chamber in 1799 but his watercolours do show the flat ceiling ornamented with ribs and bosses, the precursor of A.W.N. Pugin's ceilings in the nineteenth century Palace. In 1819 the medieval wall-paintings were discovered by Edward Crocker. Recognizing their beauty he copied them, providing us with some idea of the work produced by the school of Westminster artists which flourished under Henry III.

Henry III spent considerable sums on an existing St. Stephen's Chapel founded possibly by King Stephen (1135 - 54). There was also a Chapel of St. John the Evangelist, the site and history of which is long forgotten.

*A Norman Arch in Westminster Hall, drawn by R. W. Billings in 1834.*

*The New St. Stephen's Chapel*

In April 1248 Henry III was present when his cousin, King Louis IX of France, consecrated his Sainte-Chapelle in Paris. Henry was determined to rival this work, though troubled times prevented his making a start.

Edward I made no substantial addition to the Palace, save alterations to existing buildings for the benefit of his first wife, Queen Eleanor of Castile. After her death in 1290, the King preferred York House where he resided with his second wife, Queen Margaret, daughter of Philip III of France, and her children. However, in 1292, he began rebuilding St. Stephen's Chapel.

Stephen of Knill was the Clerk of Works appointed to supervise the project which was undertaken "in honour of God, the Blessed Virgin Mary and the blessed Stephen." Curiously, the name of Knill was to be associated again with Westminster Palace when it was rebuilt by Barry and Pugin - Pugin's third wife was Jane Knill.

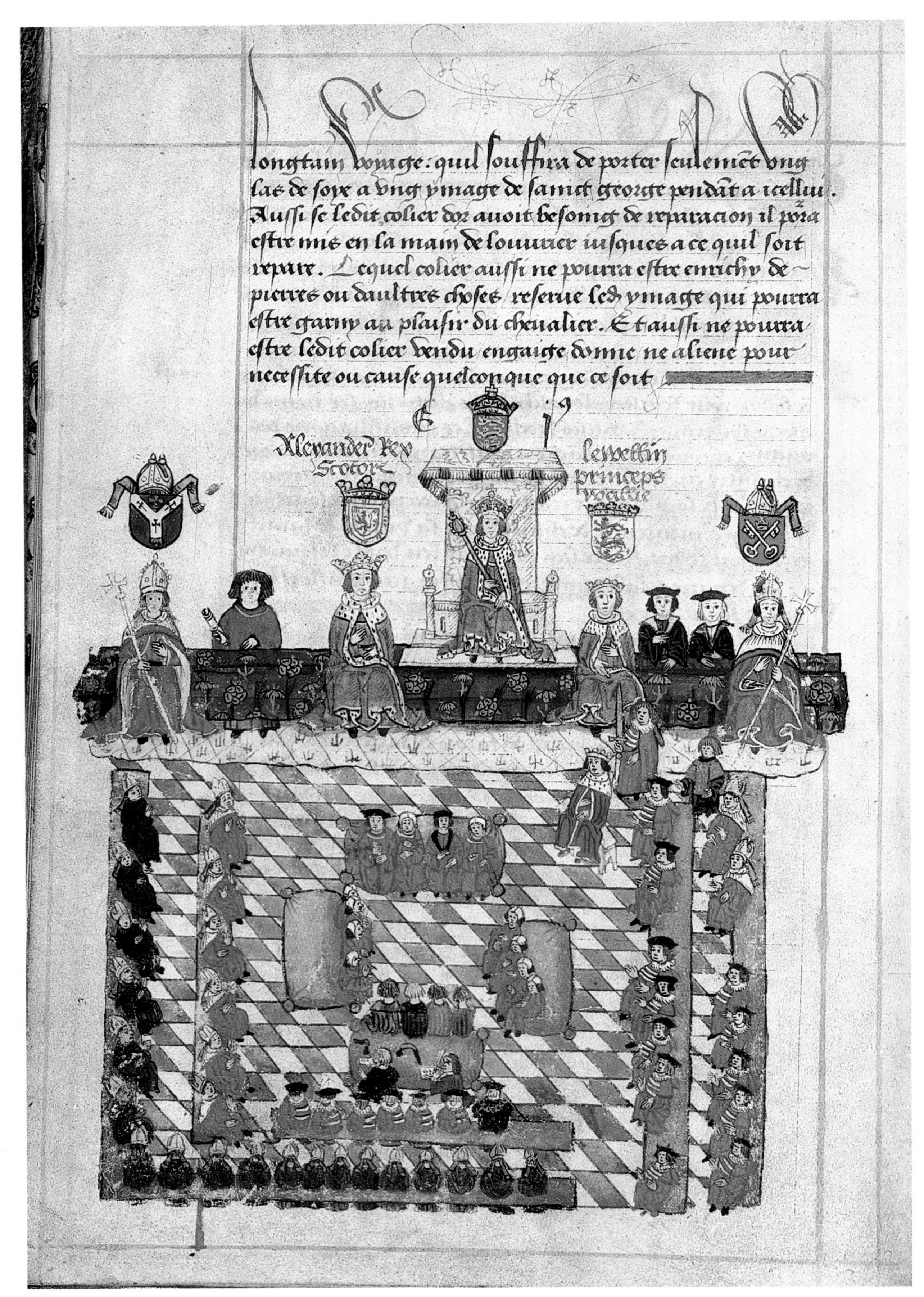
longtain voyage: quil souffrira de porter seulemēt vng
las de soye a vng ymage de sainct george pendāt a icellui.
Aussi se ledit colier dor auoit besoing de reparacion il pora
estre mis en la main de louurier iusques a ce quil soit
repare. Lequel colier aussi ne pourra estre enrichy de
pierres ou daultres choses reserue les ymage qui pourra
estre garny au plaisir du cheualier. Et aussi ne pourra
estre ledit colier vendu engaigie donne ne aliene pour
necessite ou cause quelconque que ce soit



*Parliament in the 1270s. from the Garter Book of Sir Thomas Wriothesley.*

A fire in 1298 caused severe damage at Westminster, thus Edward II inherited in 1307 a half ruined Palace. Apart from the Great Hall, only the Painted Chamber and the Exchequer were in reasonable repair. In early 1308 huge temporary buildings had to be erected for the coronation.

Towards the end of his reign Edward II prepared to undertake further work on St. Stephen's Chapel. Great quantities of wrought stone and timber were prepared but work was again halted before they could be used.

It is not easy to unravel the history of the building by the three Edwards, but surviving documents give certain salient facts. In 1321, under Edward II, the Caen stone arrived for the Chapel. The accounts after 1323 show considerable activity, including the purchase of shaped stone and timber both for the Chapel and a new gallery between it and the Painted Chamber. However, the winter of 1325-6 brought an interruption. It was not until 1331 that work resumed with a new King. Gradually the work proceeded with more Caen and Reigate stone and in 1345 the walls were sufficiently complete to allow the use of all the great store of worked timber which had lain waiting since 1326.

By 1348 Edward III was able to establish a College of Canons to serve the Chapel, now completed, though the interior was not yet furnished or ornamented. It took nearly another fifteen years to paint the walls and glaze the windows and to provide altar, stalls, screen and statuary. The altar was purchased in 1350 and made of Purbeck marble from Dorset. The Upper Chapel paving was of the same stone and marble benches were fitted around the walls. The total cost of the Chapel has been estimated at approaching £10,000 at contemporary prices.

The Star Chamber belied its romantic name, for it housed one of the most effective instruments of Tudor Government. The court originated in the middle of the fourteenth century on a site which it occupied until the time of the fire of 1834. The first reference to the Star Chamber occurs in 1366 and in 1367 it is referred to as "the Star Council Chamber near the Receipt." Even when rebuilt by Henry VI and later by Elizabeth I the traditional decoration of gilded stars was retained. Under the Tudor monarchy the Court of the Star Chamber was a court which no subject in the land could hope to outwit. The site of this awesome institution is still remembered in Star Chamber Court.

Edward III made one substantial addition to the Palace, the erection in 1365-7 of a clocktower in New Palace Yard opposite the north door of Westminster Hall. Henry Yevele was the architect for this beautifully proportioned structure. The bell in this tower was known as Edward of Westminster. It weighed four tons and could be heard in the City of London.

"It is recorded, that Ralph de Hingham, the Chief Justice of the Court of King's Bench was fined 800 marks for altering a record, from motives of compassion however, and that sum was laid out in the erection of a tower opposite to the gate to Westminster Hall." Afterwards a clock was placed in it, of which an old chronicle says, that "its intent was, by the clock striking continually, to remind the judges in the neighbouring Courts to administer true justice, calling thereby to mind the occasion and means of its building."

After the destruction of this tower, its site was marked by a sundial on a stone pediment in the upper part of a brick front of one of the houses which were erected on the spot; with the motto over the dial "*Discite justitiam, moniti.*" (Be warned and be mindful of Justice)[2]. The motto yet reminds from over a mirror in what is now the Prime Minister's Room.

In 1698, the belfry was given to the parishioners of St. Margaret's Westminster. They demolished the tower and the bell was sold to the Dean of St. Paul's for his new cathedral. The bell was damaged on its way to the City and has been recast twice.

The College of St. Stephen consisted of twelve Canons, the Dean and thirteen Vicars; all of whom had to be accommodated. To the north of the Chapel and to the east of the Great Hall they were given land on which to erect the buildings needed to serve the Chapel. It is from this provision that the name of the present Canon Row originated. Cloisters within the Palace were part of the scheme but the present two-storeyed cloisters were built by the last Dean of the College under Henry VIII. At the south-east corner of St. Stephen's Chapel was the Chapel of St. Mary de la Pewe or Our Lady of the Pew. Allegedly the scene of frequent miracles, it became a place of special devotion. Indulgences were granted to those who worshipped there, the sale of which produced a steady income.

The prodigious endowments which the College of St. Stephen received from successive monarchs and the munificence shown by Edward III in his benefactions to the Dean and brethren of the Royal Chapel of St. Stephen aroused the jealousy of the Abbots of Westminster. The matter eventually reached the Court of Rome where a decision was made in favour of the Abbot, only to be rejected by the College of St. Stephen. A compromise was agreed in 1394, the Chapels of St. Stephen, St. Mary Undercroft and Our Lady of the Pew were to be exempt from the jurisdiction of both the parish of St. Margaret and the Abbey so long as the Dean of St. Stephen's was willing to be instituted and installed by the Abbot of Westminster.

Writers on the history and architecture of the new St. Stephen's Chapel, in their quarrelling and contradicting of each other, could be likened to the protagonists in the Charles Barry/Augustus Welby Pugin family pamphleteering which began ten years after Barry's death and rumbled on even until our own time. There it was a question of who did what in the New Palace. In the case of the new St. Stephen's, it is the reality of the building at the point of its completion which excites the scholars. Their verbal onslaughts upon each other are reminiscent of a medieval

*The Sainte Chapelle in Paris, built for Louis IX, inspired the architecture of Saint Stephen's Chapel, Westminster.*

tournament. In this case alas there is no certain prize of a fair lady who will immediately confer her favours upon the winner.

At least two of the most picturesque and well-known nineteenth century reconstructions of St. Stephen's Chapel are wrong in one significant respect. It is clear from the earliest views of Westminster, by Anthonis van den Wyngaerde (*circa* 1550) and by Wenceslaus Hollar (1647) that the Chapel was of a great height, as high perhaps as the ridge of the roof of Westminster Hall. All the early drawings of the Chapel make it clear that there were two rows of great windows in five bays (although one Hollar engraving shows but four bays). Wyngaerde shows buttresses clear of the walls but Hollar does not emphasise this feature. These artists must have made their drawings looking across from the south bank of the Thames. It is therefore possible and certainly excusable that the finer points of detail eluded them. The Thames was a much wider river at this time, both sides having since been embanked.

The demolition of the clerestory of St. Stephen's Chapel and the lowering of the roof by Sir Christopher Wren in 1692 produced a truncated building which appears to have misled some nineteenth century antiquarians, but not Frederick Mackenzie. He was commissioned to compile the official record of the ruins of the Chapel after the fire of 1834 had cleared later excrescences from the medieval fabric. Even Mackenzie's fiercest critics conceded that he drew with masterly precision and that nothing escaped his attention. He did, however, confess to substituting

*New Palace Yard by W. Hollar (1647), showing the clock tower and conduit.*

*The Palace of Westminster and Westminster Abbey, from the panorama by Anthonis van den Wyngaerde, circa 1550.*

missing details with the best examples taken from other sources of Gothic architecture in the United Kingdom. His grounds were that St. Stephen's was the finest building of its kind and therefore contained elements of the finest designs of the age.

Mackenzie's synthesis of what he was able to measure and observe, together with the accounts for the materials used in the building of the Chapel, enabled him to produce a brilliant series of drawings which were published in 1844.[3] Considered alongside the watercolours of the wall-paintings in the Chapel, made before they disappeared forever either at the hand of James Wyatt or after the fire of 1834, it is possible to appreciate the rare beauty of St. Stephen's. The fire of 1834 revealed the great elaboration and depth and projection of the cornice.

Mackenzie found on the extreme edge remains of octagon shafts indicating that here was a curtain arcade behind which there was a narrow passageway running round just inside the external glazed windows. In the Middle Ages these galleries were used for processions.

Mackenzie's measured drawings show this clerestory gallery. This was described by some who examined the ruins as a rain gutter, which it certainly could not have been, being in entirely the wrong position, and where, if it had served that purpose, it would have produced grave problems for the roof, had such a roof existed at this point.

*The east and south elevations of Saint Stephen's Chapel, drawn by F. Mackenzie following his examination of the ruins after the fire of 1834.*

Evidence was found in the north-west turret of an ascending staircase connected with the gallery.

Mackenzie suggests that the design of the Chapel was changed during the long process of building and that perhaps the clerestory was an afterthought. He also cites, in support of the tall narrow shape of the new St. Stephen's, the dimensions of other chapels of similar style and finds that it accords with them in its proportions.

For the decoration of the interior the comptroller's rolls record "the placing of the pryntes on the marble columns there." Evidence following the fire proved that they were not confined to the columns but were used extensively all over the Chapel.

The stars which were placed in the panel heads of the spandrels and between the bosses in the cornice were gold on a blue ground. The angels in the panels and these stars were not visible immediately after the fire of 1834, but became faintly perceptible three or four months later, from the effect of the winter's rain in cleansing the surface; and one of the painted canopies on the splay of the piers (not before visible) then appeared perfectly distinct and fresh so as to admit of its being accurately drawn.

From the exact similarity of form of the lions, and of the fleurs-de-lys, and other flat painted and gilt ornaments found in the Chapel, there is reason to think that the "leaves of tin" were not only used for the purpose of forming stamps, or moulds, for the embossed ornaments, but were also cut and applied in the manner of modern stencilling.

All the hollow mouldings were bright blue, resembling ultra-marine or cobalt; all the ogees and other large convex mouldings, all the large flat mouldings, were red; and all the fillets and other small mouldings, also all the roses and foliated ornaments, mouldings of canopies, base mouldings, capitals, pinnacles, etc., were gold; and some of the deepest hollows had an embossed gilt fillet laid on the blue ground at the back of the hollow, probably to soften the harsh effects by the dark shadow with the blue alone. (A similar technique is used in the niches above the throne in the 1847 House of Lords. Here the blue background to the gilded figures is relieved by a gilded foliated ornament). All the panels throughout the Chapel not occupied by statues in relief, were filled with paintings.

The precise details of the new St. Stephen's Chapel will never be known here on earth but we are fortunate to have something rather better than the descriptions of temples found in the Holy Scriptures. We do not have to rely entirely on those who can dream dreams and see visions. We know what some of the saints and angels looked like and how the music sounded. For some, this will be enough to create an image more satisfying than can ever be captured on the printed page.

From the time of William II to Richard II no alterations are recorded. A fire in 1315 during a royal banquet does not seem to have caused serious damage. The hall survived coronations and carnivals but had become old-fashioned when compared with Henry III's reconstructed Painted Chamber and the glorious newly-finished St. Stephen's Chapel.

Richard of Bordeaux, surviving son of the Black Prince, son of Edward III, came to the throne on June 21, 1377 at the age of ten. Throughout his troubled reign he endeavoured to maintain his authority by means of a huge household of more than 10,000 persons. The coronation in the Abbey and festivities in the Westminster Hall were magnificent occasions. The King's marriage to Anne of Bohemia, daughter of the Emperor Charles IV, in 1382 led to the decision to rebuild (called the repair of the roof) Westminster Hall. The Queen's tragic death in 1394 did not prevent the pursuit of this great endeavour.

The Palace to which the great New Hall was to be the most splendid of additions "was at this time the scene of the utmost prodigality, as well as of licentiousness; and his household servitors were more numerous than were ever retained either before or since by an English King."

Richard's second marriage to Isabella, daughter of Charles VI of France, and the celebrations which followed exhausted the contents of the Exchequer despite a considerable vote of Parliament meeting at Westminster shortly after the Queen's coronation. The King then resorted to making the most affluent of his subjects put their seals on blank charters (cheques) which were afterwards filled up with whatsoever sums he felt proper to exact.

In the first Parliament of 1397 Sir Thomas Haxey moved that "the great and excessive charge of the King's household should be amended, and the multitude reduced of the bishops and the ladies with their servants who now lived in the King's house and at his cost." For this the King had him condemned to death, but the Bishops eventually secured his pardon.

At this time the King was certainly saddled with the responsibility and the expense of a vast establishment. Although it undoubtedly contained excesses, it embodied a substantial civil service which included the forerunner of the Ministry of Works with all the artists and craftsmen required to maintain Westminster and other Royal Palaces and projects.

King Richard was determined to have a hall (already one of the largest in Europe) in the style of his age. Gothic was to replace what appeared to be a clumsy Norman original. The pillars which obstructed the floor were to be removed.

Those responsible for the transformation of the hall were: the master mason or architect, Henry Yevele, and Hugh Herland, the master carpenter.

*Portrait of Richard II (1377-99), who initiated the rebuilding of Westminster Hall roof.*

Henry Yevele was a man of business as well as a master mason or architect–he and his wife were engaged in buying and selling property in London in the manner of twentieth century property developers. Yevele was appointed disposer of the King's works of masonry in the Palace of Westminster and the Tower of London in 1360 and he subsequently constructed the clock tower in New Palace Yard. He was also responsible for the design and construction of many fine tombs, such as Richard II's tomb in Westminster Abbey, which he was designing coincidentally with Westminster Hall.[4] Yevele was undoubtedly the greatest English architect of the Middle Ages, with the added good fortune of securing the patronage of Edward III and Richard II. Westminster Hall was one of the last but probably the best known of Yevele's buildings and part of its success lay in the skilful collaboration of the mason Yevele with the carpenter Herland. Yevele displayed true genius in designing his walls and windows to lead the eye up towards the great glory of the hall, Herland's roof.

The skill of Hugh Herland was exercised on many of the King's works - at the castles of Kenilworth, Rochester and Leeds as well as at Westminster Palace and at Winchester, which led to his employment by William of Wykeham at Winchester College and New College Oxford. In 1383 Herland conceded briefly to old age by officially retiring from his post as the King's master carpenter, only to be recalled to execute the roof of Westminster Hall.

"The repair of the roof" was the phrase used throughout the building accounts to refer to the work on Westminster Hall but this was an understatement, for the repairs amounted to a complete reconstruction. The Norman walls were raised and resurfaced, a great new cornice enriched with the King's badge of the white hart was created below the springing of the roof and heavy buttresses were added to the exterior of the west walls to withstand possible lateral force of the new roof. It has been calculated that a single hammer post measuring thirty-eight and a half inches by twenty-five inches in section, with a length of twenty-one feet six inches weighs three and a half tons and that the entire roof weighs 660 tons. All the buttresses on the east side of the hall have been removed but those on the west remain, restored by Pearson in 1883. Such is the subtlety of archbrace and hammerbeam that the weight is mostly resolved downwards with little outward thrust.

The oak for the roof came from many forests, it was fashioned near Farnham in Surrey then shipped up-river to Westminster from Chertsey. The carpenters who sawed the great timbers received sixpence a day for their labour; those who worked on the carving of the angels and the sheilds of royal arms were hired individually at various rates. The stone statues for the hall had been commissioned as long ago as 1385 from Thomas Canon of Corfe, who had contracted to carve thirteen statues of Kings, representing each monarch from Edward the Confessor to Richard II at a cost of £2 six shillings and eight pence a statue. When the new hall was ready six of these statues were set up in the appropriate niches, three on each side of the south window. The remaining seven statues were used to adorn the exterior of the royal entrance to the hall, along with two larger statues also carved by Canon. Sadly the niches on the exterior of the hall are now empty but inside six Kings remain in the niches rebuilt by Barry in the nineteenth century and another five stand in the window recesses.

Two of the masons contracted to construct the new cornice for Westminster Hall were Richard Washburn and John Swallow from Gloucestershire. Their indenture, written in Norman French survives. It is dated 18th March 1395 and it reveals that the cornice around Westminster Hall cost one shilling a foot and the twenty-six corbels twenty shillings each. The total cost of the 1394-1401 rebuilding was less than £10,000.[5]

Westminster Hall was used for the coronation banquet of Queen Isabella in January 1397 even though the roof was unfinished. At the

*Carving from the roof of Westminster Hall (1394-1401).*

deposition of King Richard two years later the hall was still incomplete. Richard's successor, Henry IV, immediately confirmed the appointments of those masons and carpenters still working on the building and the hall was completed in 1401. The impact of the new Westminster Hall was not confined to this country - its design and particularly its roof - were to be echoed throughout the world, from Batalha to Sydney.

The monastery of Batalha was founded by King Joao of Portugal in 1388 to commemorate the victory of Aljubarrota, a victory which he owed in part to British soldiers. Batalha was designed by Afonso Domingues but it contains elements of English Gothic architecture and this was due to the fact that Yevele had dispatched designs and masons to Portugal. William Beckford, who visited Batalha in 1794, found that the nave reminded him of Winchester and Amiens cathedrals. He admired "The grand western façade of the great church - grand indeed - a portal 450 feet in height, surmounted

*The indenture document of 18th March 1395 commissioning two masons from Gloucestershire to construct the cornice of Westminster Hall.*

by a window of perforated marble of nearly the same lofty dimensions, deep as a cavern, and enriched with canopies and imagery in a style that would have done honour to William of Wykeham, some of whose disciples or co-disciples in the train of the Founder's Consort, Philippa of Lancaster, had probably designed it... the nave, which reminded me of Winchester in form of arches and mouldings, and of Amiens in loftiness,...The Plantagenet cast of the whole chamber conveyed home to my bosom a feeling so interesting, so congenial, that I could hardly persuade myself to move away..."[6]

More recently, the Great Hall of Sydney University in New South Wales, Australia, built in 1859 by the architect Edmund Blacket provides an echo of Westminster on the other side of the globe. Westminster Hall was also an inspiration to the Gothic revival in England and in France through Viollet-le-Duc. Augustus Charles Pugin had little sympathy for the exterior of the building but the interior was another matter. "Excepting the north end, which being the principal front, was adorned with a rich porch, and a number of tabernacles, and statues, Westminster Hall presents but little external beauty. Its deep roof resembles some huge barn; but though its

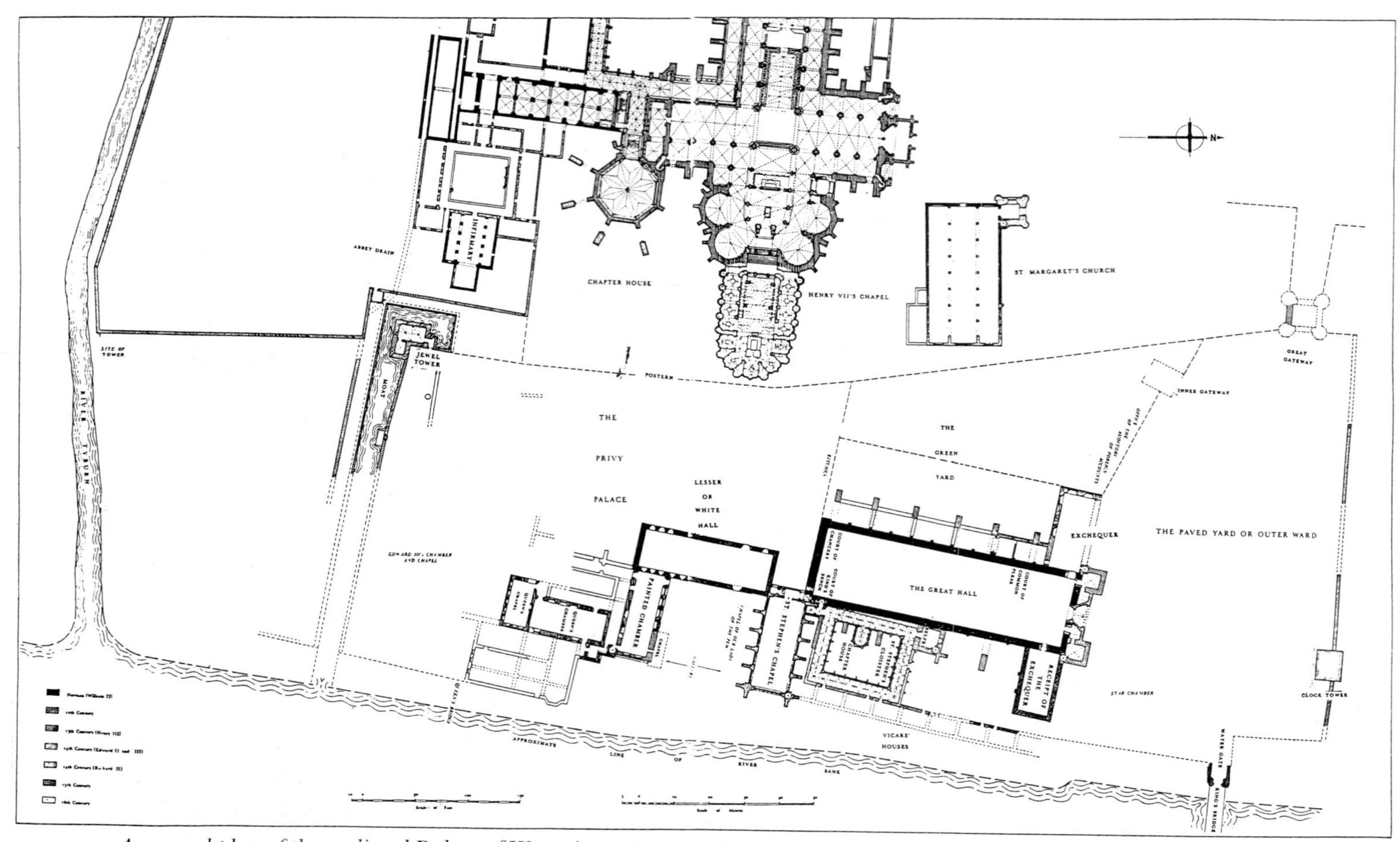


*A ground plan of the medieval Palace of Westminster (pre 1540).*

sides have been stripped of their lead covering, and mean looking slates substituted, it has yet an air of grandeur inseparable from such dimensions. The interior, however, makes ample amends for any external want of elegance. An extent equal to a cathedral church is presented in one view, unbroken by pillars, and the roof delights the scientific spectator by the intricate and skilful arrangements of its timbers, in which lightness, strength, and ornament are combined in the happiest manner."[7] Despite a disastrous fire of 1512 which left only Westminster Hall, St. Stephen's Chapel and the Exchequer undamaged, and Henry VIII's abandonment of the Palace for York House, he created within the enlarged Westminster Palace a tennis court (part of which survives encased in Barry's Treasury) a cockpit and bowling alley, for he was fond of these diversions. He is credited with playing tennis in Westminster Hall. Tennis balls were found embedded in the roof during a restoration of half a century ago. There is what is known as the Henry VIII wine cellar which would be under the present Ministry of Defence had it not been moved sideways and downwards in order to secure its preservation.

In the early years of his reign Henry VIII was a handsome, athletic youth, authoritative, attractive and boisterous. Westminster Palace provided a fitting background for banquets, masques, dances and tournaments. Lord Herbert of Cherbury states that "The King finding now all things safe both abroad and at home, took those liberties which became his youth; yet were not his exercises sportful alone, but had in them a mixture of Letters and Arms. Therefore though some relate that he used singing, dancing, playing on the Recorder, Flute and Virginals, making Verses, and the like: yet his more serious entertainments were study of History and School-Divinity, (in which he especially delighted,) Justs, Turneys, Barriers, and that not in an ordinary manner, but with the Two-handed Sword, and Battle-ax. These, again, were set forth with costly Pageants and Devices, and those so frequently, that it took up not only much time, but consumed a great part of the Treasury."[8]

The birth of a son to Queen Catherine of Aragon provoked extraordinary celebrations at Westminster. A temporary theatre was erected to accommodate a pageant featuring forest scenery, hills and dales, all ornamented with trees, turf, and flowers contrived from velvet, damask, silk and satin. In the forest was "a castell standing, made of gold, and before the castell gate sat a gentleman freshly apparelled making a garland of roses for the prise." Another sumptuous pageant featured an arbour of gold in the garden of pleasure–a spectacle which proved too tempting for the spectators, who tried to seize the gold ornaments and decorations from the costumes. Ironically, the infant Prince around whom the festivities centred, died nine days later.

The Palace was not always the scene of rejoicing. In stark contrast to the King's pageants was the King's justice. It left a yeoman named Newbolt hanging for two days on a gallows in the Palace as a punishment for the manslaughter of one of Lord Willoughby's servants. On another bizarre occasion known as Evil May Day 1517, four hundred men and eleven women were led into Westminster Hall with halters round their necks, having been guilty of rioting against foreign traders in the City. Due to the intervention of the Queen they were pardoned.

In later life Henry VIII became increasingly acquisitive. Following the fall from favour of Cardinal Archbishop Wolsey in 1529 the King promptly appropriated York House, Wolsey's palatial residence and the nucleus of Whitehall Palace. This was confirmed by an Act of Parliament. "Be it therefore enacted that all the said soil, ground, mansion, and buildings, together with the said park, etc., and also the soil of the said ancient Palace, shall be the King's whole Palace at Westminster, and henceforth, be reputed

*The Palace of Westminster in Henry VIII's reign. A conjectural reconstruction by H. W. Brewer in the nineteenth century.*

and called the King's Palace at Westminster, forever. And that the same Palace shall include all the street or way leading from Charing Cross to the Sanctuary Gate at Westminster, and also all the houses, buildings, lands, and tenements, on both sides of the said street, until Westminster Hall, from the Thames on the east part to the park wall on the west part, and enjoy all the right prerogatives, liberties, preeminences, jurisdictions, and privileges, as appertained to the King's ancient palace."[9]

With a characteristic gesture of supremacy Henry VIII thus acquired more land and extended York House, creating the new royal palace of Whitehall.

"From that period the Palace of Westminster, becoming less associated than before with the personal and domestic history of our Sovereigns, loses much of its interest; although many important affairs have been since transacted within its precincts."[10]

*The Gunpowder plotters, who were executed in January 1606.*

# II

## Royal Home of Parliament

It was a political act of Edward VI to which one boy King set his seal that gave the Commons their first permanent home. The Abbey had long been anxious to extinguish their rivals at nearby St. Stephen's. Persuading the King to give the Chapel to the Commons, the Abbey rid themselves of their tiresome ecclesiastical neighbour and their sometimes unruly secular remnants at a single stroke. This tragic architectural disaster was paralleled by the evolution of the British House of Commons into at times the most influential legislative Chamber in the world.

The Commons were housed in their Gothic Chapel, which remained unaltered but crumbling until Sir Christopher Wren transformed it into a Classical debating Chamber in the early eighteenth century. The House of Lords, meanwhile sat securely in their ancient chamber until 1801 when they moved to the Court of Requests. Westminster Hall still dominated the Palace despite appendages within and without. Nearby eighteenth century residences housed first the Speaker and the Clerk of the House of Commons and later there were a series of largely abortive projects for a New Parliament House. These progressed only as far as the provision of new Law Courts on the west side of Westminster Hall and some insubstantial but grandiose Parliamentary buildings principally serving the House of Lords.

### *The Chambers of the House of Commons*

The House of Commons, the House of Lords and possibly King James I narrowly escaped destruction by Guido Fawkes and his fellow conspirators on 5 November 1605. This is dryly recorded in the Journal of the House of

Commons for the following day. "This last night the Upper House of Parliament was searched by Sir Thomas Knevett; and one Johnson, Servant to Mr. Thomas Percye, was there apprehended; who had placed thirty-six Barrels of Gunpowder in the vault under the House, with a purpose to blow King and the whole company, when they should there assemble. Afterwards divers other Gentlemen were discovered to be of the Plot." Three days later Sir Edward Hext moved that Mr. Speaker "should make manifest the thankfulness of the House to God, for his safe Deliverance." It was not until the House re-assembled in January that the enormity of the Gunpowder Plot was revealed and deplored. Sir George Moore talked of "the late Conspiracy, the like whereof never came upon the Stage of the World," and the need to consider how to settle the safety of the King and prevent the danger of papistical practices.[1] Immediate revenge was taken by executing the offenders then displaying their heads on poles. The bells of St. Margaret's Church rang out in thanksgiving and a bill was read in the Commons to preserve the fifth day of November as a day of public thanksgiving for the deliverance of Parliament from such a dastardly popish plot.

For eleven years after 1629 the country was governed without a parliament at all and for the next eleven was to be governed without a monarch. The House of Lords was abolished soon after the execution of Charles I and a Commonwealth proclaimed. The Rump Parliament was still the official lawmaking body but in practice power lay with the Council of State and the army. Lord Protector Oliver Cromwell dissolved Parliament in 1655. The Great Seal of the Commonwealth shows that the Chamber was then a sombre place hung with tapestries and denuded of the royal coat of arms. The Members in their distinctive tall hats continued to occupy the old Chapel stalls and the Speaker's Chair also seems to have remained intact. The tradition of green upholstery in the House of Commons dates from this period, the ends of the seats being painted "green in oyle" and the benches covered in green serge.[2]

The Restoration of 1660 signalled a new lease of life for the House of Commons, as for the country generally. A new gallery of communication was constructed between the Commons and the Painted Chamber, the room which was used for conferences between the two Houses. (In the rebuilding of the Houses of Parliament after the fire of 1834 Barry provided a similar conference room called the Painted Chamber on some plans but the room was soon diverted to other purposes.) Both Houses were supplied with new clocks by Edward East in 1673, representing a considerable advance on the old glass sundial set in a window of the Commons Chamber.

The year 1678 was the year of the Popish Plot. Both Houses of Parliament were anxious to prevent a repetition of the events of 1605, so when suspicious sounds were heard in the vaults, an urgent investigation was ordered. Sir Christopher Wren, Surveyor General of the King's Works reported there could be no assurance of safety unless the vaults under the building were cleared and guards placed therein. The subterranean investigation begun in the interest of security was extended to the roofs of the Palace. It then developed into an architectural assessment of the state of the building.

Wren appeared before the Bar of the House of Lords on 2nd November to give an account of the "weakness and craziness of the roof of the House of Commons, of which there might be danger of falling in stormy weather, and likewise the roof of this House is bad." The Commons were informed of their danger and removed forthwith to the Court of Requests while the roof of their Chamber was shored up. In the next year, 1679, the stonework of the upper part of St. Stephen's Chapel was overhauled. The safety of the ancient roof was a source of continuing anxiety as it was again inspected by Wren five years later, and again in the summer of 1691, and in December of that year the Commons asked for a report on its condition. Wren told them that their ceiling was made of plaster of Paris and not of lime and hair as is the modern way. And so, for greater caution, it was fit there should be a new ceiling. He also gave account of his careful stewardship of the structure leading up to that time. He concluded that "notwithstanding though the roof were not now in danger, yet it is very old and the covering hath been much neglected in former times, neither can it be presumed to last many years longer, and therefore it seems most reasonable that erelong a new room be thought of where the important affairs of the nation may be transacted without suspicion of this thought or otherwise for the present, that the records be removed from above and a new ceiling be laid and some other repairs done as soon as an interval of sessions and the season of the year shall permit."[3] A Commons committee was appointed and on 9th January 1692 reported that they found "the walls and timber so much decayed that the building is in a dangerous condition and not capable of further repair." A humble address was sent to the King asking him to provide them with some other place in which to meet. His Majesty replied that he "doubted it would be difficult to find a convenient place on a suddaine," but he ordered the Surveyor General and Controller of his Works to wait upon the committee. Sir Christopher Wren and William Talman joined the committee. As a result, the upper part of the walls were taken down much lower and a new roof constructed. The fourteenth century clerestory and roof were removed and the new roof constructed at a lower level. The ceiling was lower still. There was therefore a new floor running right across the Gothic windows which were blocked up and sash windows put in their place. These were rectangular in the side walls, and the familiar range of three round-headed ones were put into the east wall.

The interior of the Chamber was wood panelled with galleries, supported by brackets alone, along the north and south walls. At the west

*The House of Commons painted by P. Tillemans, circa 1710.*

end, where the galleries returned in front of the lobby, were two columns flanking the entrance. Wren describes these as being of iron with capitals of iron by Jean Tijou. He is famous for his great screen and gates at Hampton Court. When the side galleries were widened in 1707 the wooden capitals were carved by Grinling Gibbons. So as not to obstruct the view of the proceedings in the House, slender iron columns were used as supports to the galleries, a device not generally used until at least fifty years later.

The transformation of the Commons Chamber, which Wren achieved by the end of 1692, was a source of satisfaction to the Members. The Treasury, however, were displeased because the cost had come to £4,500 which was £2,000 more than the estimate. To this we owe a detailed statement

*Queen Anne in the House of Lords by P. Tillemans (1708-14).*

of works from Wren. The side galleries and the greater part of the panelling of the House was new; all the seats had been given new backs, stairs and passages had been cut through the corner turrets of the Chapel to get to the galleries, some small extra work had been done at the request of the Speaker, a new and splendid clock had been provided, the two iron pillars by Tijou are mentioned, the gilding around the clock and the Speaker's Chair and the ironwork, the panelling to the lobby, the Smoking Room, the Serjeant's Room and conveniences made for the Clerks, the Housekeeper and Doorkeepers, and "a particular clossett made for Mr. Joddrell" (Paul Joddrell was appointed Clerk of the House in 1688). The damage done by taking down so much stonework and working in the gardens of the adjoining houses, particularly Sir John Cotton's, had proved more than expected. A more convenient and safe passage had, by the Queen's command, been made for the King from the landing place to the House of Lords with a pair of new stone piers and gates, four large oaken doors and doorcases, and the passage room made out of the toll house and decently fitted, several pavements and necessary drains made. Finally, the passage from Westminster Hall to the Parliament stairs had been made lighter. It would seem that the great Sir Christopher had delivered value for money indeed in 1692.

By 1707, a fresh problem was presented as the result of the Act of Union between England and Scotland. There were forty-five extra Scottish Members. Wren believed that by creating two rows of seats in each of the side galleries, where but one existed, and at a cost of £270, the problem might be solved. Although these changes provided the necessary accommodation, the subject of ventilation was by 1701 concerning a committee, assisted by Wren, and they considered methods of improvement. They tried openings in the ceiling through which they hoped the exhausted air would escape into the space above. This was not a complete success. In 1715 the Speaker invited a Fellow of the Royal Society, Dr. J.T. Desaguliers, an experimental physicist, to "propose a method to evaporate the unhealthful breathing in the House of Commons." Wren had constructed four square apertures, one at each corner of the ceiling. These gave into truncated pyramids in the room above. When the lids on the top of the pyramids were opened the foul air from below and the steam of the candles should have found its way into the room above. However, the air above being colder and denser, all that was achieved was a down-draught on to "those Members that sate under those Holes." Dr. Desaguliers constructed a pair of closets, one at each end of the room above. An iron duct from the top of each of the pyramids led to a jacket round a fire-grate in each of the closets. It was intended that the fire should be lit at noon, thus drawing up the air from the House below. Needless to say, Mrs. Smith, the Housekeeper, who had the use of rooms above the Commons, found the new apparatus a nuisance and did her best to defeat the operation of these machines. She neglected to light the fire at the appointed hour. The House got intolerably hot, and the cold air above resisted its escape, making conditions even more intolerable. Mrs. Smith was in due course called to order. Provided that she carried out her instructions to the letter, the House was kept cool. Desaguliers received a reward of one hundred guineas for his invention. Forty-six years later, Members were complaining of the great inconvenience from the heat of the House of Commons when it was full and from the cold when it was thin. The Office of Works installed new stoves below the House and larger vents were formed in the ceiling and a new louvre, with moveable shutters, was inserted in the roof. This became a prominent Westminster landmark. A year later, loose masonry at the north-east corner turret fell through the roof of the Speaker's withdrawing room below. In 1791 a committee of the House was set up to look again at the problem of heating and ventilation. Henry Holland's new ventilators in the roof, a patent air machine and "two new large pieces of foliage" (to conceal the vents) sufficed for a while.

The admission of the Irish Members in 1800 meant that the accommodation of the House must yet again be extended. James Wyatt, the most fashionable architect of the day, hit upon the idea of enlarging the area of the room by making the walls thinner. When the wall panelling was removed the medieval wall paintings of St. Stephen's Chapel were revealed "as fresh and vivid as if they could only boast a twelve months date." J.T. Smith and Richard Smirke (who was specially commissioned by the Society of Antiquaries) were able to make a record of the paintings before the walls were cut back. Having destroyed the finest medieval wall paintings in Westminster, Wyatt proceeded to introduce fake Gothic tracery in brick and plaster at the east end of the Commons Chamber in place of Wren's round-arched windows.

Following Wyatt's death, John Soane found himself in charge and was quick in revenge. Many defects remained unremedied and he hoped that Parliament would consider the restoration of St. Stephen's Chapel to its original splendour as a Chapel, and the construction of a new House of Lords and a new House of Commons on either side. Substantial repairs were carried out to the house of John Hatsell, who had been Clerk of the House since 1768 and who lived in his house in the Cotton Garden until 1820, though he had put his son-in-law, John Henry Ley, in charge of his duties since 1797. Repairs to their two houses, and to Hatsell's house when Ley moved into it, accounted for many hundreds of pounds in addition. It was Ley's reluctance to give up his residence that impeded further progress on Commons improvements, although the committee had recommended that a new residence be built for him between the north end of Westminster Hall and the river.

Early in the nineteenth century there was great pressure on

accommodation due to increase in Parliamentary business. Committee rooms were overwhelmed by the growth of business, Private Bills for paving and lighting, canals, docks and the turnpike roads. A Select Committee considered the matter in 1824. Of the ten committee rooms available, three were so exposed to the noise of the street as to be hardly usable; some committees could not find a room at all and had to sit in the body of the House.

In 1825 a Select Committee on committee rooms and printed papers heard evidence from Soane and others. Four Public and thirty Private Bill Committees had endeavoured to meet on the same day and nineteen were appointed to meet in the same room. The Chamber itself, and even the Court of Exchequer, had to be pressed into service; also the Long Gallery and Members' Waiting Room. Six rooms were too small for contentious business. The conclusion was that ten more rooms were needed urgently. The Library was an inadequate size and had shelving for the papers of less than two future sessions. In achieving their aim the committee and the House were thwarted by their immovable Clerk who held his position by letters patent from the Crown, and therefore could not be removed against his will. Temporary rooms were provided for committees and a further Select Committee in 1826 preferred Soane's thwarted proposals but accepted the inevitable and sanctioned a reduced plan. The Treasury gave directions on 14th July 1826 that the work be put in hand and completed by 1st February 1827. It was to have cost £10,560 by Soane's estimate. The Library so constructed was fifty-five feet by twenty-three feet and thirteen feet six inches high, on the first floor with an oriel at the east end, Gothic windows and a low vaulted ceiling. It earned high praise from Creevey who thought it the best and most agreeable room in London. The works were completed on time but they cost more than the estimate, due to the necessity to shore up the house of the obstructive Ley.

The Chamber of the House suffered no architectural change during this time, but warming and ventilation continued to receive a great deal of consideration. During the recess in 1816 the floor of the House was relaid and the fireplace in the Lobby was replaced with a stove. In 1818 a new staircase and two doors were created to enable Members to leave the galleries for divisions and in the following session, the Marquis de Chabannes was called in to provide a new system for heating and ventilating the House. He was authorized to start in March, the estimate was £1,100 and he was not to receive payment until the success of his method had been demonstrated. He reported on 21st April that all was ready but Members were not satisfied with the results especially as £1,678.4s.4p. had been spent. Twelve months later Chabannes claimed £256 for his ventilating machine, constructed by the Speaker's order, but finally settled for £200. In 1826 the Commons turned to Feetham, a manufacturer of stoves who was consulted about heating.

History does not relate whether any committee, reporting in October 1831, on "The possibility of making the House of Commons more commodious and less unwholesome" had taken evidence from Benjamin Wyatt, Robert Smirke, and Wyatville. They decided that there was no satisfactory way of enlarging the existing House and that a new one was necessary. A similar Select Committee in the 1833 session took the same view and its report had attached designs by George Allen, George Basevi, Edward Blore, Decimus Burton, John Deering, Francis Goodwin, James Savage, John Soane, Jeffry Wyatville, Adam Leigh and three M.P.s - J.W. Croker, Rigby Wason and Charles Hanbury (later Hanbury-Tracy), a name that was to figure large in the history of the rebuilding of the Palace after 1834. Joseph Hume, the Member famous for his attacks on public expenditure was most disappointed that the Treasury was not forthcoming with funds to meet his demand for improved accommodation.

*Chambers of The House of Lords*

Between the restoration of Charles II and 1801 when their Lordships moved to the former Court of Requests, the interior of the House of Lords

*John Soane's scheme of 1825 for the river front of the Palace of Westminster.*

was substantially unchanged. It was a simple room from which all traces of the medieval building which surrounded it were concealed. John Pine's engraving of 1742 shows a barrel-shaped ceiling with irregularly placed dormer windows providing light from above. The walls were covered with the Armada tapestries, between which sconces for candles provided illumination. There was a fireplace in the east wall and the throne with its canopy was situated at the south end.

This Chamber served well enough for debate but it was uncomfortably crowded on State occasions. A gallery was erected in 1704 to accommodate Queen Anne's numerous female attendants but this addition did not meet with universal approval and was removed five years later. A committee of 1735 recommended a gallery which could be put up on royal occasions; this was not carried out and the question of the Lord's gallery remained unresolved. In 1737 the Office of Works put up a gallery with four rows of seats, then three years later their Lordships ordered that it should be taken down.

In 1778 the House requested Sir William Chambers to construct a large gallery outside the walls of the House, looking down into it through a hole cut in the wall opposite the throne. The order was given but nothing happened during the summer recess. In December the House demanded of Chambers why he had done nothing. Following debate, it was decided not to proceed with this scheme. George III complained to James Wyatt at the lack of a gallery but the solution eventually found was not a structural one, but the removal of the House to the larger Court of Requests in 1801.

Although the interior of the Lords changed little, there was an episode in the reign of George I which is of particular interest. Wren's successor as Surveyor General, William Benson, had ambitions to rebuild the Houses of Parliament. He was not slow to make all of what he mistakenly thought was a golden opportunity. The ceiling of the lobby between the House and the Prince's Chamber collapsed during the winter of 1718-19, an accident which naturally prompted their Lordships to inquire as to the condition of the roof of the House itself. On 15th January 1719 their Lordships' committee directed the Officers of the Works to inspect the roof of the House and produce a report on the following day. On the 17th Lord Clarendon reported, on behalf of the committee, that the Officers of the Works were not yet ready with their report, but they had discovered that the roof of the Prince's Chamber was showing signs of strain under the weight of the documents that had been deposited there. A few days later the committee received a report signed by Colin Campbell (Deputy Surveyor), Benjamin Benson (Secretary to the Board of Works and brother of William) and Robert Barker (master carpenter). It was necessary, they thought, to erect a number of props and shores in the lobby and they listed the defects in the walls, the roof of the House, the Painted Chamber and other adjoining

*William Pitt the Younger addressing the House of Commons in 1793, by Carl Anton Hickel.*

buildings. A report of 22nd January stated that with much propping up all could be made safe temporarily. Benson and his colleagues appeared at the Bar of the House armed with pieces of rotten wood as evidence that the rafters were rotten. The Lords became both alarmed and suspicious. Authority was quickly given for the roof to be supported by props as soon as possible. Even so, the Officers of Works "would not guarantee the security of the roof for a minute" and William Benson, as Surveyor General, confirmed this opinion. The order was given for a temporary House of Lords. However, a number of Peers who had not been impressed by Benson insisted upon a second opinion. This report flatly contradicted much of what Benson had claimed. It also suggested that the work of propping up begun by Benson had actually injured the structure. There was nothing radically wrong with roof, walls or floor and "the props set up within their Lordships' House for the intended security of the roof could be of little or no use." Their Lordships then set up a new committee with the Lord Chamberlain, the Lord Steward, four Dukes, eight Bishops and forty-five other Peers to inquire into the matter and study the reports. Nine days later, they reported that they were satisfied that the House could, in a few days, be put in sufficient and secure repair for the present. The temporary repairs were ordered immediately on the understanding that there would be no need for obtrusive props and shores.

Notwithstanding this discreditable episode, substantial works of repair and refurbishment were carried out in succeeding years. In particular the old Court of Requests was given a new roof and completely remodelled within. It was given a stone paved floor, well supported from below; the decayed roof lights were abolished and a row of semi-circular windows high up in the walls on either side were incorporated in a great coved ceiling. The room was first used for an entertainment of the Knights of the Order of the Bath (recently revived) in October 1725.

An architect's report of 1789 stated that the House of Lords, the Prince's Chamber and the Painted Chamber, were buildings of great antiquity, and were in many parts defective and had been repaired or altered so often as to defy further repair. At this apparent impasse John Soane came on the scene. The commission to build the Bank of England had established his professional status. In 1790 he secured his first government appointment as Clerk of the Works at Whitehall, Westminster and St. James's. He had long dreamed of designing a senate house at Westminster but his introduction to the Palace was on a more modest scale - he was asked to improve the ventilation of the House of Lords, for which he received £500. In 1793 he was asked to supply plans to a number of other architects whom the Lords considered to be more eminent than Soane himself - Holland, Mylne, Samuel and James Wyatt, S. P. Cockerell, Brettingham, James Adam and George Dance. In the following year Soane himself was requested to consider improvements to the Lords' accommodation. At first Soane was tempted to submit a Gothic design for a new House of Lords, an idea he relinquished "chiefly in consideration of the unfitness of that manner of building for the purposes of public speaking, and the enormous expense and great delay that would have attended its execution." His final scheme was an imposing Classical structure with grand façades towards the river and the Abbey. The Painted Chamber was to be reinstated as nearly as possible in its original style, and St. Stephen's Chapel was to be stripped of its alterations and restored to its ancient magnificence as a Chapel for the use of both Houses of Parliament. The scheme would have cost £124,600 and taken five years to complete.

Soane's suggestions found favour with George III until the influence of James Wyatt came to bear. Wyatt was working for the King at Windsor Castle and while he remained alive, Soane was ousted. It was Wyatt who fitted up the Court of Requests for the Lords. He designed a new Royal Entrance to the Lords and remodelled the Speaker's House with adjoining offices to form a new river front to the Palace in a battlemented Gothic style. Wyatt's House of Lords, buildings in Old Palace Yard proved both unpopular and expensive. His aim was to Gothicise Old Palace Yard, an aim that was confounded by his use of brick and stucco battlements, cast iron window-frames and lath and plaster oriels, which created a flimsy effect. His contemporaries, whether politicians or architects were quick to criticize.

Wyatt's Gothic work is perhaps better known at Fonthill, which he designed for the sometime M. P. William Beckford. This fantasy in Wiltshire featured a 276 foot tower; it captured the imagination of Constable and Turner, and influenced the architecture of Eaton Hall and Toddington. These houses in their turn were to find an echo in the new Houses of Parliament by Barry and Pugin.

Coincidental with Wyatt's work on the Palace, the Westminster Improvements Commission cleared away many of the buildings which had obscured the major monuments. Westminster Hall, the Abbey and St. Margaret's Church could all now be seen to better effect. New and Old Palace Yard were cleared. All this at a cost of more than a quarter of a million pounds. Additionally, Parliament spent more than £14,000 on St. Margaret's between 1799 and 1813. Larger sums of public money were expended on the Abbey and Henry VII's Chapel was restored at a cost of more than £42,000. This work was well done using the best of stones and a competent mason, Gayfere, now commemorated in the nearby street named after him.

Between 1800 and 1812 works on the reconstruction of the Houses of Parliament and the Speaker's House totalled more than £180,000 on which Wyatt or his executors received five per cent. His death in a carriage accident whilst travelling in Wiltshire with his friend and patron, Christopher Codrington of Dodington on 4th September 1813, left the way clear for John Soane to reappear at Westminster. In 1814 he was appointed one of the three architects with personal responsibility for the public buildings in Whitehall, Westminster, Richmond Park, Kew Gardens and Hampton Court Palace. In 1816, Soane reported that Wyatt's alterations to the Court of Requests for the use of the House of Lords had been made chiefly with combustible materials. The Royal Entrance, constructed of wood, was covered only with oil cloth. When George III came to the throne in 1820, alterations and improvements to the Lords were carried out as a matter of urgency. A new throne was provided on new steps. In preparation for the King's divorce proceedings against Queen Caroline a temporary gallery was erected in the course of two weeks, Soane taking personal responsibility for the work. They were heartily approved of by the Peers who thought them highly ornamental.

In 1822 Soane embarked upon major works on the House of Lords which were carried out in stages. When the King gave his approval for Soane's designs for the new Law Courts in the Stone Building, Soane was also charged with improving the Royal Entrance to the Lords. He built a little carriage entrance in Gothic, but the Royal Staircase, the ante-room and the Royal Gallery were in his characteristic style, and grand indeed they were. Approaching £100,000 was spent on the Lords and its committee rooms between 1822 and 1828. However, by the end of the session that year, their Lordships were demanding better heating and ventilation of the Chamber. In September 1831 they asked to have back the temporary galleries of 1820. But in October they asked for them to be removed. At this point, Sir John Soane retired from his public appointments and was succeeded by Robert Smirke. Smirke, together with Soane and Nash, had been one of the three official architects attached to the Board of Works since 1813. He had a reputation for reliability rather than brilliance in design. In view of their earlier adventures with other architects, he did have a certain appeal to Parliament, at least before the Great Fire. He put up a new gallery across the lower end of the House of Lords and constructed additional benches where the central fireplace had been. Their Lordships still required further space and he built for them an enlarged library. The contractors on this occasion were Messrs. Grissell and Peto, names to become famous in the New Palace.

### *Projects for a New Parliament House*

Neither the House of Commons nor the House of Lords was entirely satisfied with its accommodation in makeshift buildings in and around the remains of the medieval Palace. The Lords Chamber was not large enough for ceremonial occasions. The Commons Chamber was almost intolerable when Members were present in strength. The "evaporation of their unhealthful breathings" defied solution.

In 1733 Sir Robert Walpole's government went so far as to instruct the Office of Works to submit plans for a completely new Parliament House. There had been some previous attempts to promote a new building, dating from the Inigo Jones/John Webb plan for Whitehall Palace (1647). It was largely due to the over-enthusiastic approach of Wren's successor, William Benson, dismissed for his part in the affair of the Lords' ceiling, that the matter lapsed. The initiative of 1733 came in the wake of concern about the future of the library collected by Sir Robert Cotton, who lived within the precincts of the Palace. Parliamentarians had come to enjoy the use of this great library, bequeathed to them by Sir Robert. The committee considering the library's future decided that they must consider the library in relation to any proposed new Parliament House.

In a debate of March 1733 Mr. Gibbon moved that "His Majesty might be addressed to build a new House" and this was agreed, the House promising to make good the expense. By the end of the month the King had accepted the proposal. The project began to excite the interest of architects including the theatrical Earl of Burlington. Nicholas Hawksmoor left forty-three designs for the Parliament House amongst his papers and soon William Kent, an architect more in tune with Burlington's ideas, entered the fray. The idea was kept alive, to be revived in 1739 when *Reed's Weekly Journal* reported that plans for a magnificent House of Lords and Commons had been laid before his Majesty and approved, and that it would cost £200,000. Meanwhile, a survey was to be taken of the Banqueting House and of Somerset House Palace to see which would be more convenient for Parliament until the new work was completed.

The first step was to survey the site, its possibilities, and the temporary accommodation of Parliament. The Board of Works produced a three phased rebuilding scheme which would have left the Lords and Commons undisturbed. This scheme estimated that a new House of Commons, Speaker's Apartments, Committee Rooms and other conveniences could be built on Crown land for £46,000, a new House of Lords with vestibule, conference room, portico and cupola for £75,000 and thirdly an arcade, the Court of Requests, passages and appendages for £39,000.

Several alternative arrangements were proposed for the Commons suggesting that the seating in the Chamber could be arranged in a circle, elliptically, in straight lines with curved ends, or else in the traditional monastic fashion. A circular arrangement would provide the maximum number of seats - 528 for a total of 513 Members at that time. It is by no means clear what was proposed for the House of Lords.

Plans for the proposed new House of Commons were discussed at a meeting between the Speaker, Arthur Onslow and the Board of Works.

*Old Palace Yard with James Wyatt's façade to the House of Lords (1808).*

This resulted in the approval of a plan for the Commons Chamber and adjoining accommodation but significantly Mr. Speaker excused himself from proffering his opinion as to the general plan and elevations. Arthur Onslow here displayed that sagacity which enabled three generations of his family to hold the Speakership; Onslows are still prominent at Westminster.

The general plan and elevation which Arthur Onslow viewed with apprehension would have entailed abandoning the central curved recess on the west front and the substitution of a straight façade to the Court of Requests. More fundamentally, this building was transposed eastwards, thus encroaching upon the Thames which would have been embanked as it later was. All plans were overtaken by international events - hostilities with Spain from 1739, followed by the war of Austrian Succession. Walpole, under whose administration the plans had been drawn up, left office in 1742. The Treaty of Aix-la-Chapelle was not achieved until 1748, the year in which the architect William Kent died. The financial constraints which accompanied the conclusion of the war prevented the government from pursuing the project for a new Parliament House. John Vardy presented Kent's plans to the Treasury together with a scaled down version of the same, in which a truncated façade served only to disguise the miscellaneous buildings behind it.

In the event nothing of Kent's great scheme for the two Houses was carried out, though Vardy and his assistant engrossed themselves in the painful process of creating a new building facing St. Margaret's Lane and flanking Westminster Hall, known as the New Stone Building. Its history is linked to that of the Courts of Justice at Westminster.

## *Westminster Hall*

Whilst Wyatt, Vardy and Soane altered the appearance of several of the buildings which made up the Palace of Westminster, Westminster Hall emerged comparatively unscathed by improvements. The hall continued to be the setting for major State occasions and trials, reflecting in microcosm major historical events from the Elizabethan *via media* to the trial of Charles I and the Revolution of 1698.

Cromwell was sworn into office as Lord Protector in the Chancery Court at Westminster. He was inaugurated in that title in Westminster Hall on 26th June 1657. There was an elevated platform at the south end of the hall. Under a prince-like canopy of State stood the Coronation Chair, which had been brought from Westminster Abbey. A table in front of it was covered with pink Genoa velvet with a gold fringe. On it were the Bible, Sword and Sceptre of the Commonwealth. Banks of seating were erected at each side for Members of Parliament and the Speaker, Sir Thomas Widdrington, had

*The deserted House of Lords during the passing of the Reform Bill in 1832.*

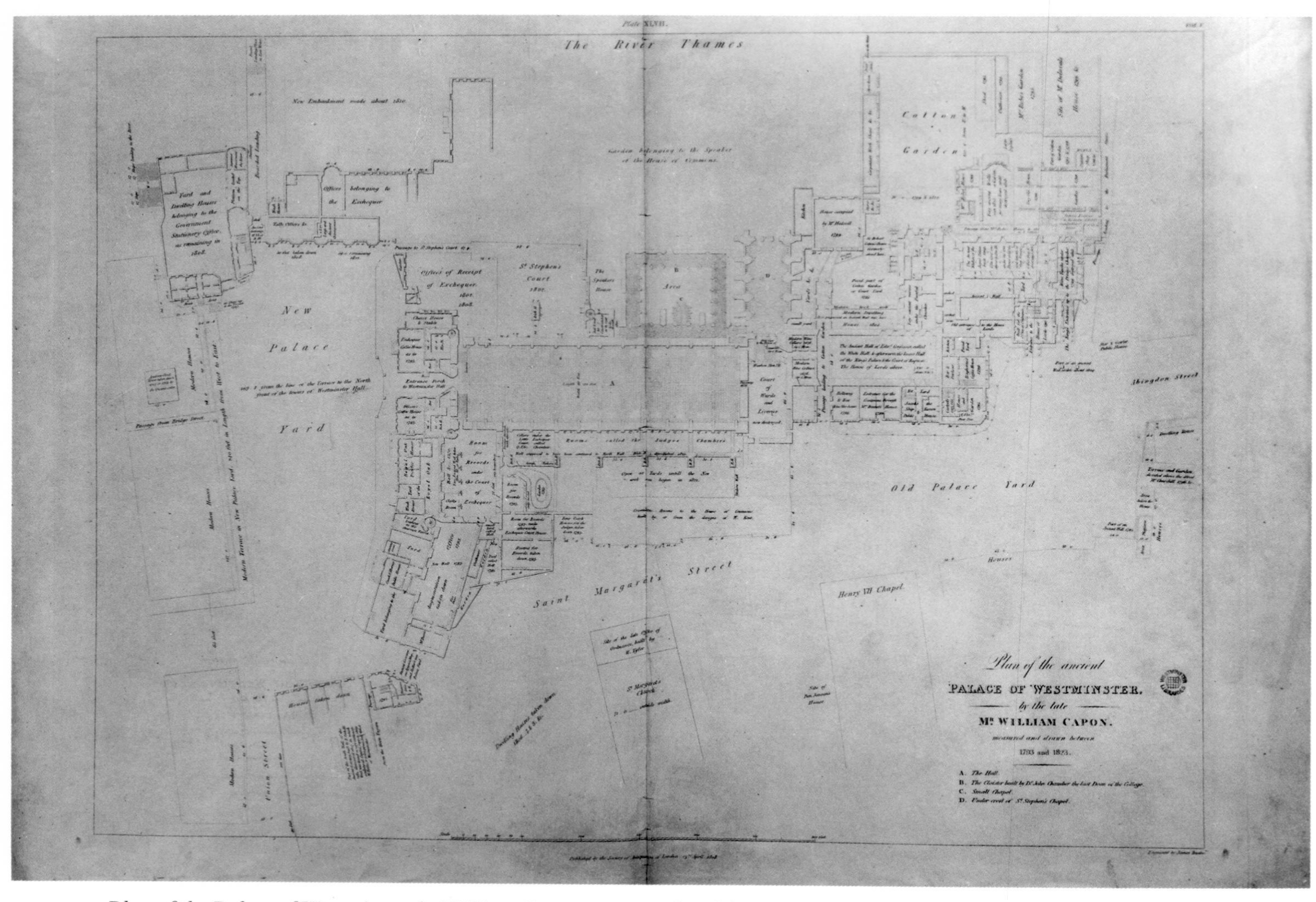


*Plan of the Palace of Westminster by William Capon, measured and drawn between 1793 and 1823.*

a chair beside the table. Cromwell entered the hall preceded by the Lord Mayor of London.[4] He died at Whitehall on 3rd September 1658. On the 26th he was buried privately in Henry VII's Chapel in Westminster Abbey.

Following the restoration of the monarchy, Cromwell's body was dug up and dragged to Tyburn and exposed upon the gallows. Both Houses of Parliament, on 8th December 1660, ordered that the carcasses of Oliver Cromwell, Henry Ireton, John Bradshaw, and Thomas Pride, whether buried in Westminster Abbey or elsewhere, be with all expedition, taken up, and drawn upon a hurdle to Tyburn, and there hanged up in their coffins for some time; and after that buried under the said gallows. The bodies were buried at Tyburn but the heads were cut off and set up upon poles at the south end of Westminster Hall where that of Cromwell remained for twenty years.

On 8th May 1661 at a meeting of Charles II's Pensionary Parliament, first summoned eighteen years before, it was ordered that the Solemn League and Covenant devised to strengthen the popular cause in 1643 be burnt by the common hangman in Cheapside on 22nd May. Six days afterwards, the Acts of the Trial of King Charles I, the Abolishing of the House of Peers, the Establishing of a Commonwealth, Renunciation of the Stuarts, and the Security of the Protector's person, were similarly destroyed in the middle of Westminster Hall, while the Courts of Law were there sitting.

The coronation banquets in Westminster Hall became successively more extravagant, particularly under the Hanoverian monarchy. At the coronation banquet of George III and Queen Caroline in 1761 the hall was illuminated by three thousand candles, miraculously lit simultaneously at the arrival of the King and Queen. The candle wax ruined the dresses of the ladies who sat beneath and the heat was so intense that many fainted. The last coronation banquet to be held in Westminster Hall followed the coronation of George IV in 1821.

*The Courts of Justice*

Originally the King's presence and the King's justice were indissolubly fused. It was not until the thirteenth century that the Courts of Justice evolved as independent courts in Westminster Hall - the Court of Common Pleas along the west wall near the entrance to the Exchequer, the Court of King's Bench against the south wall on the east side, the Court of Chancery against the south wall on the west side. Here they stood, apart from temporary dislocations for ceremonial occasions, from the fourteenth to the nineteenth century. This informal arrangement disguised the serious nature of the courts. The Lord Chancellor's great table of Purbeck marble gave dignity to the scene. Despite a revival of interest in this ancient piece of furniture on the part of Lord Hailsham of St. Marylebone, no trace of it has yet been found.

The enclosure occupied by the Court of Common Pleas, at the north end of the Hall was most inconveniently placed, being close to the north door of the Hall. A proposal to move this court into a back room of the Treasury was vetoed however by Lord Chief Justice Bridgemen on the gounds that to move the court would violate Magna Carta. By the eighteenth century it was commonly acknowledged that the Courts of Justice gave the impression of slovenliness. James Ralph commented "they should be more pompous and magnificent in order to enforce the respect which should ever attend on justice." The Board of Works failed to propose viable improvements to the existing arrangement, so in the time of Lord

*William Kent's unexecuted design for the Houses of Parliament (1733).*

Chancellor Hardwicke, William Kent was asked to present new designs. His version of a Gothic screen with ogee windows and octangular buttresses was built at the south end of Westminster Hall. There was a central passageway, for access to the House of Commons. Elegant enough to look upon, Kent's enclosure had no ceiling, so the lawyers were uncomfortably cool. Isaac Ware and William Robinson attempted to remedy the situation by doubling the height of the screen and building a ceiling over the court. The Chief Justice of Common Pleas, whose court was situated at the north end of the Hall, then persuaded the Board of Works to provide him with a new home, on the site of the Office of the Custos Brevium, outside the Hall and south of the Court of Exchequer. An enlarged doorway, adorned with an ogee arch in the style of Kent's screen led to both these courts.

The inadequate accommodation of the courts again came to the fore as part of the proposals for an entirely new Parliament House. A scheme for the removal of all the Judicial Courts had been proposed a year before the Court of Common Pleas was relocated and what became known as the New Stone Building was built between 1755 and 1770 on the site now called Cromwell Green.

The central part was built first for the records of the King's Bench, the Exchequer, Remembrances, Pipe, Augmentations, and Tally Offices, and the Auditors of the Imprests and the Usher and Clerks of the Exchequer.

Bit by bit the New Stone Building was constructed in Portland Stone. Purchase of property and building operations cost about £12,000. Sir Henry Cheere and other private occupants had to be bought out, and Alice's Coffee House agreed to surrender their lease in return for a new building of equivalent size. This was eventually fitted in the north east angle of Old Palace Yard. It took until 1760 to complete the central portion; the southern part was completed in 1769 when it was occupied not by one of the Courts of Justice but by the Board of Ordnance. Then when the Board of Ordnance moved across the road to a site east of St. Margaret's Church, in 1780, the Commons took possession of the accommodation, partly for committee rooms and partly as a residence for the Clerk Assistant to the House. It was not until 1793 that the Augmentations Office was finally moved. It took another thirty years before Soane completed the building first envisaged by William Kent in 1739.

We may note here that Henry Bankes, M.P., of Kingston Lacy in Dorset, who lived in Old Palace Yard, was a strenuous opponent of Soane's scheme for the reconstruction of the Law Courts to the west of Westminster Hall, and that he succeeded in so thwarting the scheme as to make several of the courts impossibly small.

A later member of his family employed Charles Barry to aggrandize Kingston Lacy where Marochetti was employed to provide bronzes on the great new marble staircase. Barry transformed a modest seventeenth century house into something resembling an Italian palace. Here the eccentric family lived on, later in complete seclusion, until the last resident Bankes left the whole estate to the National Trust who had to realise substantial assets from it virtually to rebuild the top-heavy structure.

It had been a combination of factors that launched the Government of 1820 to embark upon the new Law Courts west of the Hall. In 1817 an additional Chancery Judge had been appointed (the Vice Chancellor) and he needed a court. Restoration work in Westminster Hall was to include the clearance of excrescences in New Palace Yard and the restoration of the entrance front at the north end. George IV's coronation banquet had required the clearing of all the courts from within the Hall.

Against this background the imagination of Sir John Soane was brought to bear. He believed that he could adapt that part of the Stone Building which already existed; it was the return to New Palace Yard that caused great vexation, both to the architect and to Parliament. Soane first proposed to keep the Tudor Gothic elevation as far as a stair turret on the corner and to continue in that style to the completed Stone Building. However, he was overtaken by the restoration of the towers of Westminster Hall, with which he thought it inadvisable to compete. He proposed, therefore, a Palladian elevation to match the Stone Building. Three different designs were submitted.

The front as actually built was even grander than the designs. At this point Henry Bankes succeeded in defeating the government and a select committee was set up to examine the affair. As a result of their deliberations the new front was demolished despite Soane's attempts to Gothicise it. The alteration entailed the loss of a law library and rooms for barristers and judges, it added nearly £9,000 to the cost and produced an elevation to New Palace Yard that could hardly be called distinguished.

The new courts were fitted up during 1825, but in the years that followed a number of shifts and changes culminated in a move which was the direct cause of the Great Fire of 1834. A new bankruptcy court was to be fitted into the old Tally Office. It was the burning of the tallies in the stoves beneath the House of Lords which caused the Great Conflagration. Out of that arose, phoenix-like, the great New Palace which we see today.

In 1865 a Bill was passed to enable the removal of the Law Courts to the Strand. G. E. Street won the competition and his new Law Courts were completed in 1883. Soane's courts were then demolished and J. L. Pearson restored the west side of Westminster Hall. Here he created the Grand Committee Room and fitted eight other rooms between the restored flying buttresses.

*The Speaker's House*

It was not until 1794 that the Speaker had an official residence in the Palace. He previously had a drawing room close to the Commons and four

*William Kent's triumphal arch, erected in Westminster Hall for the coronation of King George II and Queen Caroline (1727).*

*In the eighteenth century Westminster Hall was lined with stall-holders. The Lord Chancellor occupied a dais at the south end.*

rooms in St. Stephen's Court. This did not constitute a proper residence but could be used as a *pied a terre*. Access to the Speaker's Chambers was from behind the Speaker's chair and there was also a private door to enable him to leave the building. This facility seems to have been abused by others for on 29th January 1674 the House made an order that the back door into the Speaker's Chamber be locked up every morning and the key laid and left on the table during the sitting of the House to prevent Members slipping out unobserved. Perhaps the ancestors of the modern Whips had something to do with this order.

The Clerk of the House of Commons was also to obtain an official residence, as the result of a petition to the Treasury from Jeremiah Dyson. He claimed that in addition to having charge of all books and papers belonging to the Commons he was obliged to be in constant personal attendance at or near the House. He was consequently given a three storeyed house with an attic in Cotton Garden, finished in March 1760 at an estimated cost of £3,159.

*The north front of Westminster Hall, by Michael "Angelo" Rooker (1770s).*

*The ceremony of presenting the sheriffs of London in the Court of Exchequer (1811).*

James Wyatt's "improvements" to the Palace of Westminster embraced the Speaker's House, its adjoining buildings and St. Stephen's Chapel, forming an irregular river front to the Palace. The work was carried out in the Gothic manner with the intention that this would "add extremely to the effect of the Speaker's House and give entirely the air of a grand old dwelling of which the House of Commons would appear to be the Chapel." Unfortunately the so-called Gothic composition was finished in plaster. The weakness of the architectural "improvements" made by Wyatt is attacked in the history of the Palace written by Brayley and Britton in 1836.

"However melancholy and deplorable the scene of ruin after the late destructive fire, it is scarcely less to be regretted than the wanton and reckless alterations formerly made by an architect, and by officers of government, in the Chapel and Cloister now under review. Whilst the latter was partly fitted up for the appendages of a kitchen, for servants' offices and the most menial purposes, the area was occupied by a large shed-like kitchen; part of the exquisite lower Oratory was converted into a scullery; and chimneys, sinks and closets were cut into, or patched up, against its florid windows and tracery. The upper Cloister was divided into numerous small apartments and offices and even the vast abutments of the Great Hall were cut into or hacked away, without the least regard either to the stability of the edifice or to its architectural character. The beautiful ornaments, paintings and minute sculpturings of the Chapel itself were ruthlessly defaced, or broken to pieces to give place to modern wainscotting, ceilings, windows, passages, stairs etc; whilst chimneys and fireplaces were worked into, or affixed to the buttresses and walls.

At the time of the fire, this house was spacious and replete with conveniences; and it is but justice to the late occupant to admit that he manifested great anxiety to preserve all the fine and beautiful parts of the cloister, crypt etc. which were left when he obtained possession from further injury and defacement."[5]

The age old problem of accommodating the two Houses, a solution to which had eluded generations of Parliamentarians and innumerable Select Committees and a legion of architects, was solved at last in 1834. The Clerk of the Works, one Richard Whibley, was instructed to destroy a huge pile of obsolete wooden tally-sticks used for tax collection prior to 1826. They stood in the way of yet another accommodation for the Law, a new Bankruptcy Court. Phipps, the Assistant Surveyor, consulted Whibley, who suggested burning the tallies in the Lords' furnaces. By six o'clock on 16th October the overheated flues had begun the Great Conflagration which swept away all of Wyatt's work and reduced both Chambers, the new Commons Library and much else to utter ruin. In *The Times* of 18th October it is observed that Mr. Hume's Motion for a new House is carried without a division.

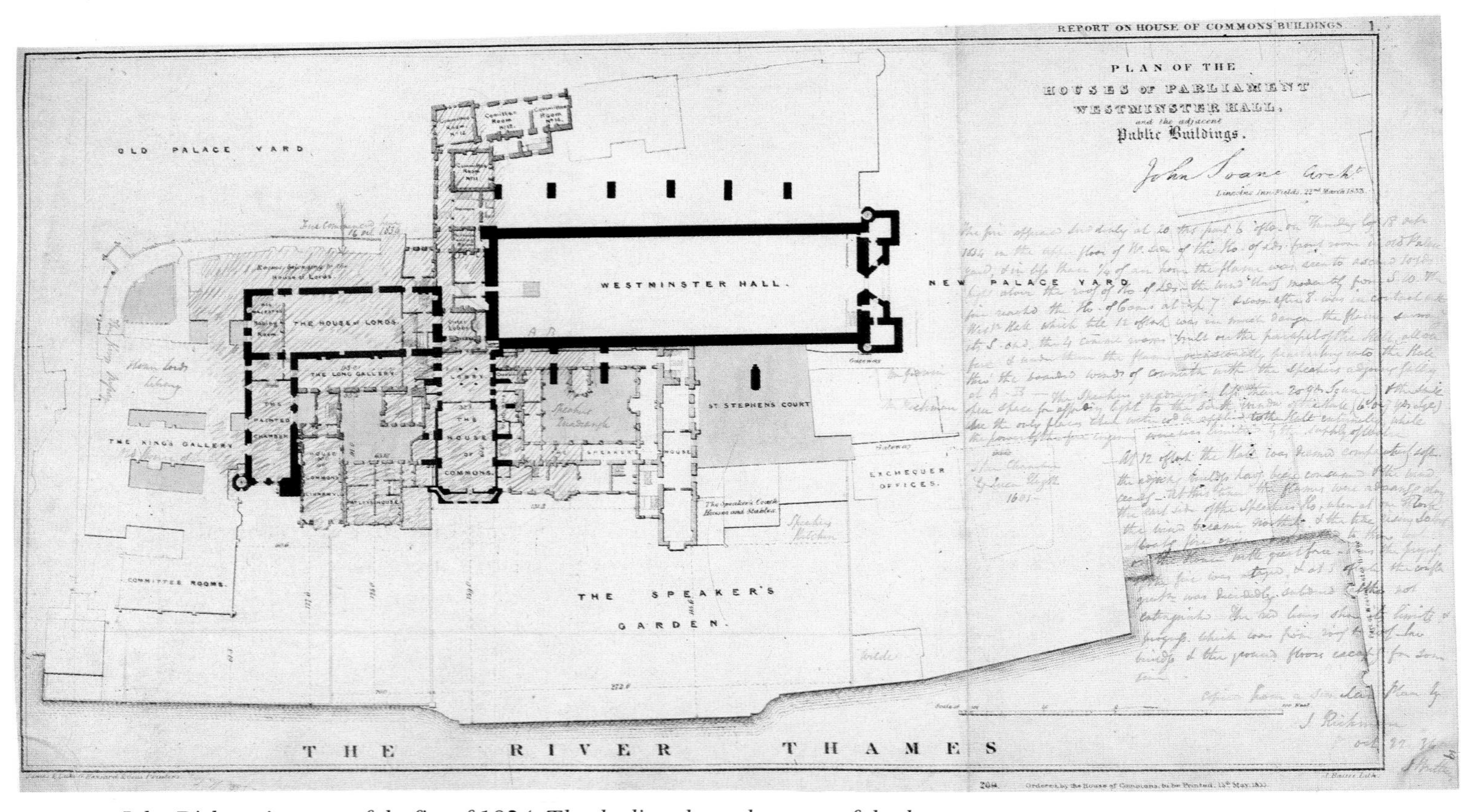


*John Rickman's report of the fire of 1834. The shading shows the extent of the damage.*

# III

## The Great Conflagration

"The fire appeared suddenly at twenty minutes past six o'clock on Thursday evening 16 October 1834 on the upper floor of the west side of the House of Lords front room in Old Palace Yard, and in less than quarter of an hour the flame was seen to ascend ten yards height above the roof of House of Lords. The wind blows moderately from south-west, the fire reached the House of Commons at approximately seven and soon after eight was in contact with Westminster Hall which till twelve o'clock was in much danger, the flames surrounding its south end. The four Committee Rooms built on the parapet of the Hall all on fire and under them the flames occasionally penetrating into the Hall through the boarded windows of connection with the Speaker's adjoining gallery at AB. The Speaker's quadrangle, less than twenty yards square, and the small open space affording light to the south window of the Hall six or seven yards square were the only places which water could be applied to the Hall externally while the power of the fire engines was limited by the supply of water. At twelve o'clock the Hall was deemed completely safe, the adjoining buildings having been consumed and the wind ceasing at this time the flames were advancing along the east side of the Speaker's House when at one o'clock the wind became northerly and the tide rising so that the afloating fire engines were enabled to throw water on the House with great force. Thus the progress of the fire was stayed and at three o'clock the conflagration was decidely subdued, although not extinguished. The dark lines show its limits and progress which was from roof to roof, low buildings and the ground floors escaped for some time. Copied from a similar plan by J. Rickman October 22, 1834."[1]

So wrote John Rickman, Second Clerk Assistant in the House of Commons, with the Great Conflagration fresh in his mind. Rickman was a considerable Westminster figure and character. He became Secretary to Mr. Speaker Abbott through their joint work and early interest in the census. Rickman's promotion to the Table of the House came in 1814. He was the means by which the stranglehold on the Clerk's Department exercised by John Hatsell and his deputy, John Ley, and Ley's two nephews was broken. Of the considerable relics which remain of Rickman's work with the pen, his view on Parliamentary Reform is of particular note. "Certain ruin to an old, shattered edifice, very unsafe for its inmates already."[2]

There were others who witnessed the demise of the old shattered edifice, very unsafe for its inmates as it perished on that night in October 1834.

### *Pugin*

Auguste Charles, Comte de Pugin (circa 1769 - 1832), fled to England from France to escape the Revolution. He was employed in the office of John Nash where he supplied the Gothic detail in which Nash was deficient and cordially disliked. A. C. Pugin collected many examples of Gothic detail and published several books on the style. He also collaborated with Rowlandson on the *Microcosm of London.*

*John Rickman (1771-1840), the Speaker's Secretary, painted by Samuel Lane.*

It is recorded that George IV sent Monsieur Vilmet his *chef de cuisine* to see Augustus Charles Pugin so that he might be instructed in the art of drawing and design, thus enabling him to deck the royal dinner table with taste and that the piles of food should be built up in artistic forms.

Augustus Pugin married Catherine Welby and their son, Augustus Welby Northmore Pugin, was born on 1st March 1812 at 39 Keppel Street, Russell Square, London. He was educated as a day boy at Christ's Hospital, "Whether in Latin, Greek, Mathematics or any other branch of education he would learn in twenty-four hours what it took other boys many weeks to acquire... As a mere child he was quick in all that he attempted and fluent in speech, expressing his opinions in the most dogmatic manner with volubility and vehemence."[3] The young Pugin soon displayed an interest in and talent for architectural drawing, particularly in the Gothic style. Some of these drawings appear in his father's published work. According to his mother, his major contribution to his father's books consisted of more than three parts of A. C. Pugin's *Paris* . Other early work, alas now lost, consisted of caricatures produced in his father's office. Each week he drew a wheel of fortune with the favourite pupil of the hour standing at the top. His interest in Gothic frequently led him to draw in Westminster Abbey.

His passion for architecture and for accuracy twice nearly cost him his life. Whilst excavating at Rochester he was all but buried alive and was lucky to survive a fall whilst measuring an inaccessible part of a building. The year 1827 found him designing Gothic furniture for Windsor Castle where a chance meeting with George Dayes brought him into the theatrical world. George Dayes worked on the stage scenery at Covent Garden Theatre and through him Pugin developed an interest in the stage, to the extent that he constructed a model theatre, inside his father's house. Pugin's work at Covent Garden over a period of some two years was mainly concerned with operatic scenery of a Gothic flavour, culminating in a splendid production of *Kenilworth* in 1831. He was also involved in designing for Rundell and Bridge the royal goldsmiths. At the end of 1829 he first met James Gillespie Graham, a Scottish architect, for whom he produced some drawings, including "all the interior decorations of a large mansion." It was also at this time that he began business on his own account in "the carving and joinering line" at 12 Hart Street, Covent Garden. This business did not prosper but fortunately he was rescued by his mother's family. Henceforward he was scrupulously careful in financial matters.

Perhaps the turning point in his life was the middle of 1831. He had developed a great love of sailing and the sea. He is quoted as saying that "there is nothing worth living for but Christian architecture and a boat." Some of his most inspired architectural creations were set on paper whilst sailing alone in the English Channel. An adventure in 1831, however, resulted in the wreck of his boat, *Elizabeth* near Leith. It was Gillespie

Graham who then provided a destitute genius with some money and the sound advice to concentrate in future on architecture. As a memento of this, Graham gave Pugin his own pocket compasses. Pugin used them throughout his life. They appear in J. R. Herbert's portrait now hanging at Westminster. Engraved upon them is "James Gillespie Graham, architect Edinburgh 1830."

In 1832 Pugin married Ann Garnet. She died in childbirth before the year was out. In this year Pugin's father also died. In 1833 Pugin married his second wife, Louisa Burton, and in this year his mother died. The Pugins moved to Ramsgate. He took a sketching holiday in Europe in 1834 and this became an annual event.

Thus as the fateful autumn of 1834 approached, Pugin had acquired by the age of twenty-two a wealth of experience, both of life and of architecture and of art. "Mr. Augustus W. Pugin was fundamentally instructed in all the elements and principles of Gothic architecture in the office of his father, who brought up a class of pupils in that class of art. Adopting the Roman Catholic Creed, and advocating all its dogmas, as well as canons, he has been caressed and patronized by the gentry and clergy of that religion, and thence employed to build and adorn several distinguished edifices." He had not met Charles Barry.[4]

The night of 16th October found Pugin in London where he witnessed the event which led to the greatest opportunity of his life and for which he will ever be remembered. Writing to E. J. Willson on 6th November, Pugin described in his characteristic manner the progress of the flames at Westminster. He does not shrink in his exultation at the sight of so much bad architecture perishing in so short a time. "You have doubtless seen the accounts of the late great conflagration at Westminster which I was fortunate enough to witness from almost the begining till the termination of all danger as the hall had been saved which is to me almost miraculous as it was surrounded by fire. There is nothing much to regret and much to rejoice in a vast quantity of Soane's mixtures and Wyatt's heresies (having) been effectually consigned to oblivion. Oh it was a glorious sight to see his composition mullions and cement pinnacles and battlements flying and cracking while his 2(s). 6(d). turrets were smoking like so many manufacturing chimnies till the heat shivered them into a thousand pieces. The old walls stood triumphantly midst the scene of ruin while brick walls and framed sashes, slate roofs etc. fell faster than a pack of cards. In fact the spread of the fire was truly astonishing from the time of the house of commons first taking fire till the flames rushed out of every aperture it could not have been more than five or six minutes and the effect of the fire behind the tracery was truly curious and awfully grand. What is most to be regretted is the painted chamber the curious paintings of which I believe are totally destroyed. I am afraid the rebuilding will be made a complete job of as that

*A. W. N. Pugin (1812-1852). by J. R. Herbert.*

execrable designer Smirke has already been giving his opinions which may be reasonably supposed to be a prelude to his selling his diabolical plans and detestable details. If so I can contain myself no longer but boldly to the attack will write a few remarks on his past work and if he does not writhe under the last his feeling must be harder than his cement as if I spare him I hope to sink myself. His career has gone on too long and this will be a capital opportunity to show up some of his infamous performances."[5]

Our next witness Charles Barry, was the fourth son of Walter Edward and Frances Barry. He had been born in Bridge Street, Westminster, on 23rd May 1795 in a house which eventually lay under the shadow of the clocktower of the New Palace at Westminster.

Charles Barry's father was a stationer who supplied the materials used at the Government Stationery Office. His mother died when he was but three years old to be replaced by a stepmother, Sara, who was left to care for the children on her husband's death in 1805. She had to run the business to support them. Of all the children, Charles, "even from his childhood, manifested artistic taste and capacity, and chose for himself, in spite all difficulties, a new path in life." He was "a warm-hearted and spirited boy, handsome and engaging in appearance not very studious, full of fun, and by no means averse to mischief. He was taught drawing by a most incompetent man, and his best practice was in caricatures, especially of his drawing master."[6] Charles first attended Wright's Academy in Lambeth, and later Christ's Hospital.

At the age of fifteen or sixteen Charles transformed his small attic bedroom into an hermitage, creating a rocky interior with openings looking out on to a sunny landscape. The construction and painting of the room was his own work and he was constantly drawing large scale figures on the walls. In 1812 when not yet seventeen he had a drawing of the interior of Westminster Hall accepted by the Royal Academy.

With his share from his father's will he resolved to embark upon an architectural tour of the continent. On the eve of his departure in June 1817 he became engaged to Sara Rowsell whose father, Samuel Rowsell, was also a stationer. Charles Barry's continental travels were usually made alone, with the exception of a tour of Greece and Turkey with Charles Eastlake. In Sicily and Italy he was accompanied by J. L. Wolfe before returning alone through France in August 1820.

"He was not then, nor did he ever become, an admirer of Italian Gothic. Many of the greatest buildings, particularly in Venice, were offensive by the multiplicity and prominence of their details. He was more attracted to the public prison at Venice than to the Ducal Palace."[7]

On his return to England, Barry had little money of his own to fall back upon while waiting for a first opportunity to prove himself a competent architect.

He had met in Egypt Mr. William Bankes of Kingston Hall (Kingston Lacy) whose home was one of the first houses upon which Barry was engaged to make massive alterations. In Rome Barry had met the Marquess of Lansdowne (for whom he worked at Bowood). Through him he met the Hollands and through the Holland House circle Barry was introduced to many noblemen of the Whig party. His first buildings of any consequence were two Commissioners' churches in the Gothic style at Prestwich and Campfield, Manchester, approved of at the time but in later years these two churches were a continual subject of laughter to his friend, Mr. Pugin, and to Barry himself. He used to retaliate by reference to Mr. Pugin's early work at Windsor Castle which certainly gave him full opportunity for retort. In the 1823 competition for new buildings at King's College, Cambridge, which were to be in the Grecian or Gothic style, Barry proposed a Greek building, for he had not yet mastered Gothic architecture. His son maintained that "Excepting Gothic as the style for church architecture, he would have preferred those forms of it, which secured uninterrupted space, and gave a perfect sense of unity in the congregation, even at the cost of sacrificing features beautiful in themselves, and perhaps of interfering with the 'dim religious light' of 'impressiveness and solemnity.' He differed widely from Mr. Pugin, on these points and warm discussions of principle arose in consequence."[8]

Barry was never so thoroughly attracted to the Holland House circle that he did not come back with constant relief and pleasure to the quiet of his own fireside where he could enjoy the society of his wife and children. He could draw up plans whilst in the midst of family activity, with music, as a background. His recreations included the London theatre and meetings of the Royal Institution.

Charles Barry designed his first clubhouse, the Travellers' in 1829 entirely in the Italian Renaissance style. He made alterations to the Royal College of Surgeons in 1833; Bowood alterations followed in 1833; Kingston Lacy alterations in 1835.

Barry's reaction to the fire, which he also witnessed, makes a fascinating complement to Pugin's account. "By happy chance on that same evening in 1834 Charles Barry was returning from Brighton on the coach, when a red glare on the London side of the horizon showed that a great fire had begun. Eager questions elicited the news, that the Houses of Parliament had caught fire, and that all attempts to stop the conflagration were unavailing. No sooner had the coach reached the office, than he hurried to the spot, and remained there all night. All London was out, absorbed in the grandeur and terror of the sight.

The destruction was so far complete, that preservation or restoration was out of the question; the erection of a new building was inevitable, on a scale, and with an opportunity, and the conception of designs for the future, mingled in Mr. Barry's mind, as in the minds of many other spectators, with those more obviously suggested by the spectacle itself."[9]

The fire left Westminster Hall comparatively unscathed. There was never any question but that the hall was to be restored and form a part of whatever replaced the Westminster ruins. St. Stephen's Chapel, on the other hand, was badly damaged.

This chapel, out of the medieval shell of which had been burnt all the later accretions, presented a picturesque problem. There were scholars who hankered after its restoration. An equal number were opposed to any attempt to recreate what they regarded as insufficient evidence. Meanwhile, the ruins stood in the way of new works. The cloisters, also sadly damaged, did not present quite so great an impediment to any grand new design.

It would have been possible to have grafted onto the surviving buildings at Westminster new Chambers for the two Houses of Parliament. There was also just a possibility that Parliament would abandon Westminster altogether, in favour of the Royal Palace nearing completion at the far end of St. James's Park. King William IV offered Buckingham Palace to Parliament but it was decided that the cost of conversion would be too great and that the site was unsuitable. Parliament's inclination to cling to precedent and to avoid violent change soon concentrated the mind upon Westminster.

The first consideration was to accommodate the two Houses for the new session beginning in January 1835. Herculean efforts by the Office of Woods and Works, under the direction of Robert Smirke, produced a temporary House of Commons within the walls of the old House of Lords, whilst the Lords were temporarily accommodated within the walls of what had been the Painted Chamber. These arrangements were by no means unsatisfactory and there were some who then said that a new building was unnecessary.

The Office of Woods and Works had asked Smirke to prepare a scheme for rebuilding the Houses of Parliament on "a moderate and suitable scale of magnitude" in November 1834, but Smirke's designs did not greatly improve upon the work of James Wyatt, which many had condemned. At this point public opinion took a hand. Smirke had not distinguished himself elsewhere and it was perhaps his mistake to award the principal contract for work on the temporary Houses to his brother-in-law.

The Press took a lively interest in the proposed rebuilding of the Palace of Westminster. *The Times* had called for a noble Parliamentary edifice before the ruins had had time to cool. *The Spectator* wanted comprehensive rebuilding on Reform principles. "The Palace of the Legislature, where the laws are propounded and settled, and the interests of the whole people are discussed, should include every accommodation that past experience and forethought of the prospect of future improvements may show to be

*The fire at the Palace of Westminster, 16th October 1834.*

required. It is a structure to endure for ages; and as such, should anticipate, as far as may be foreseen, future wants. The cost is not an object: money is not to be wasted but not to be spared."[10]

*The Westminster Review* wanted a building "of wondrous power, but composed of a multitude of parts adjusted to a thousand special functions, yet combining for the production of one grand general effect."[11]

There was a general demand for a public competition to discover who was capable of carrying out such a monumental and difficult task.

A former Member of Parliament, the Hon. Sir Edward Cust, wrote an open letter to Sir Robert Peel, the Prime Minister, in which he advocated that a Commission of unpaid amateurs should organize and judge a competition for designs, then superintend the erection of whatever building emerged.

The Government responded to the call. On 2nd March, 1835 it was ordered "that a Select Committee be appointed to consider and report upon such plan as may be most fitting and convenient, for the permanent accommodation of the Houses of Parliament." The committee included the

*The House of Lords in ruins; the Great Conflagration of 16th October 1834.*

Chancellor of the Exchequer, Lord John Russell, Lord Stanley, Mr. O'Connell, Mr. Hume, Mr. Ridley Colborne, Sir Robert Inglis, Mr. Tracy, and Lord Granville Somerset. They had before them the Report of the Office of Woods of October 17th, 1834:

"Report upon the damage done to the Buildings, Furniture, etc. of the Two Houses of Parliament, the Speaker's Official Residence, Official Residence of the Clerk of the House of Commons, and to the Courts of Law at Westminster Hall, (occasioned by the fire, on the 16th day of October 1834,) as far as at present the same can be ascertained.

House of Peers – The House, Robing Rooms, Committee Rooms, in the West Front, and the rooms of the resident officers, as far as the octagon Tower at the South end of the building, totally destroyed. The Painted Chamber totally destroyed; the north end of the Royal Gallery abutting on the Painted Chamber destroyed from the door leading into the Painted Chamber, as far as the first compartment of columns. The Library and the adjoining rooms, which are now undergoing alterations, as well as the

*Ruins of the Houses of Parliament as they appeared on the morning after the conflagration.*

Parliament Offices, and the Offices of the Lord Great Chamberlain, together with the Committee Rooms, Housekeeper's Apartments, etc., in this part of the building are saved.

House of Commons – The House, Libraries, Committee Rooms, Housekeeper's Apartments, etc., are totally destroyed excepting the Committee Rooms, Nos. 11, 12, 13, and 14, which are capable of being repaired.

The Official Residence of Mr. Ley, Clerk of the House. This building is totally destroyed.

The Official Residence of the Speaker. The State Dining Room under the House of Commons is much damaged, but capable of restoration. All the rooms from the oriel window to the south side of the House of Commons, are destroyed; the Levée Rooms, and other parts of the building, together with the Public Galleries, and part of the Cloisters, very much damaged.

The Courts of Law – These buildings will require some restoration.

Westminster Hall – No damage has been done to this building.

Furniture – The Furniture, Fittings, and Fixtures, to both the Houses of

Lords and Commons, with the Committee Rooms belonging thereto, are, with few exceptions, destroyed; the public furniture, at the Speaker's House, is in great part destroyed; the furniture generally of the Courts of Law has sustained considerable damage. The strictest inquiry is in progress as to the cause of this calamity, but here is not the slightest reason to suppose that it has arisen from any other than accidental causes."[12]

Three months later, on 3rd June 1835, the committee reported "that it is expedient that the design for the rebuilding of the Houses of Parliament be left open to general competition, and that the style of the building be either Gothic or Elizabethan."

The choice of style was a clear rejection of the Classical senate houses favoured by the advocates of Parliamentary reform.

The events which led to the momentous decision to embark on the great Gothic adventure at Westminster are many and various. Social and literary and architectural movements combined to create a mood which set the style and profoundly influenced the creation of the New Palace at Westminster.

Benjamin Disraeli described himself as a conservative to preserve all that is good in our constitution, a radical to remove all that is bad. It was on this platform that he stood at High Wycombe from 1832. It was as a Tory that he was finally elected one of the Members for Maidstone in 1837.

One of Disraeli's closest friends was the artist, Daniel Maclise. Maclise's early work includes "The Chivalric Vow of the Ladies and the Peacock" (now in the Palace of Westminster) and similar subjects of a chivalric or medieval feeling, some of them inspired by the writings of Sir Walter Scott. Through Maclise, Disraeli met Bulwer Lytton, a lesser writer than Scott but at Knebworth he created a wilder Gothic fantasy out of his ancestral home than did Sir Walter Scott at his Gothic Abbotsford.

Lytton's friend, Charles Tennyson d'Eyncourt was in the 1830s embarking on the medievalising of the ancestral seat at Bayons in Lincolnshire. Later he sat alongside Disraeli on House of Commons committees concerned with the New Palace. The text which accompanied Maclise's portrait of Disraeli in *Fraser's Magazine* said that "Benjamin's politics are rather preposterous; but he is young, and may improve."[13] Whereas Disraeli had come from nowhere, there were others with better political connections with whom he felt himself entirely in tune. Lord John Manners, George Smythe and Henry Baillie-Cochrane became known as the "Young England Group" shortly after they entered the House of Commons in 1841. John Manners and George Smythe had spent many years together at Eton and Cambridge where they had been preceded by Ambrose Phillips De Lisle and Kenelm Digby, author of *The Broad Stone of Honour* . Smythe wrote a sonnet to Manners at Cambridge.

*"Thou shoulds't have lived, dear friend, in those old days*
*When deeds of high and chivalrous enterprise*
*Were gendered by the sympathy of eyes*
*That smiled on Valour - or by roundelays*
*Sung by the palmer minstrel to their praise.*
*Then, surely, some provencal tale of old*
*That spoke of Zion and Crusade, had told*
*Thy knightly name, and thousand gentle ways."*

Manners in his turn dedicated a volume of verse, *England's Trust,* to Smythe. In it he deplores the decline of the power of church and monarch and seeks a return to the days in which "each knew his place - King, peasant, peer or priest, the greatest owed connexion with the least."

Disraeli's novels are full of characters and scenes drawn from this circle and their attitudes. In an early novel *The Young Duke* (1829) he pokes gentle fun at architectural adventures, but more of that later. In Disraeli's most famous novel, *Coningsby,* Lord John Manners figures as Lord Henry Sydney. The scene "Christmas at Genevieve" involves Eustace Lisle who is based on Ambrose Phillipps de Lisle (who was a close friend of Augustus Welby Pugin). St. Genevieve is described as a "pile of modern building in the finest style of Christian architecture; its great hall had a rich roof, gallery and screen."

"Gothic or Elizabethan"... It was against the background of all of the above that the decision on the style to be followed in the New Palace was made. It was not however made by young visionaries dreaming of the Middle Ages but by hard-headed and tight-fisted Parliamentarians with an eye to catching what they imagined to be the tide of public opinion.

"The opportunity occurred at a critical time in the progress of our architecture, when the long empire of classicism was being broken, and the claims of Gothic began to be recognised. There were all the energy and enterprise abroad, which belonged to a period of change. The whole artistic world was on the alert, and the public generally were eagerly desirous that the opportunity should be used to the utmost."[14]

The active Commissioners were headed by Charles Hanbury-Tracy, who had served on the committee which had set all in motion in Parliament and chosen the style. Because he was a Member of Parliament, he assumed the chairmanship. He was joined by Thomas Liddell, an amateur Gothic architect, Sir Edward Cust who had inspired the method for proceeding and George Vivian, who had written extensively on architectural matters in the public domain, but who was not wholly devoted to the Gothic style. Others were invited but declined to serve and some who wished to serve, were not invited. The Commissioners were attacked for their aristocratic background, particularly by Joseph Hume.

Charles Hanbury-Tracy was the third son of John Hanbury of Pontypool Park, Monmouth and Jane the daughter of Morgan Lewis of St. Pierre, a fine medieval house in the same county. He was educated at Rugby and Christ Church, Oxford. He married Henrietta the daughter and heiress of Henry the last Viscount Tracy of Rathcoole, to the family estate of Toddington in Gloucestershire.

Charles was already attracted to Gothic architecture through his mother's home, and more particularly, Christ Church, Oxford, the most magnificent college in the university, founded by Cardinal Wolsey. His marriage to the Tracy heiress linked him with ancestry going back to the Holy Roman Emperor Charlemagne. The Tracys could also claim their descendancy from Edward the Confessor and several saints. Charles

*Benjamin Disraeli (1804-81) as a young man, by Daniel Maclise.*

Hanbury-Tracy served as Member of Parliament for Tewkesbury from 1807-12. He then was out of the House for twenty years until his return in 1832.

It was thus that a man endowed with great riches and steeped in the traditions of the Middle Ages was able to embark upon a new and vast house at Toddington which combined all of his own ideals and which he personally designed and directed over a period of twenty years.

The grandest façades of the house contain "ornamented windows, with mullions, tracery and label mouldings; also string-courses, with bosses and heads; (a series of English monarchs from William the Conqueror to Henry VIII) panels, enriched parapets, pinnacles, turrets etc. whilst a square tower with crocketed pinnacles and a perforated embattled parapet, forms an apex to the whole. The walls and the dressings being all built with a fine stone of a warm tint, (Stanway stone) constitute a mass so picturesque and imposing from every point of view, that there has been no necessity for planting out, or concealing any part." The golden stone of the exterior has survived in crisp perfection for 150 years. "The stone of the cloister and staircases whiter in colour, finer in grain, and is worked to a clean, smooth, and beautiful surface."[15]

Whilst the exterior owes much to Christ Church and Magdalen at Oxford the interior takes elements from a number of Gloucestershire Gothic buildings and there is a roof based on Crosby Hall.

Both within and without the influence of this unique building upon the future New Palace at Westminster can everywhere be seen. To the spectator unaware of the chronology it would be possible to conclude that Toddington was an echo of the New Palace. In fact it is the solid and practical heir to the picturesque but insubstantial Gothic predecesors of an earlier age like Fonthill by James Wyatt (1794-1807) or the Eaton Hall of William Porden (1804-12).

At Bayons in Lincolnshire, Charles Tennyson D'Eyncourt, like Hanbury-Tracy, was his own architect.[16] His letters, many of them written whilst attending to his Parliamentary duties at Westminster, go into architectural detail to a rare degree.

Parallel to the arduous work of the Commissioners, the committee and architects at Westminster the new age of chivalry had taken a firm grip upon society. The coronation of George IV had been grand, costly and controversial. Lord Melbourne, Queen Victoria's first Prime Minister, had advised against a coronation banquet in Westminster Hall. There was thus no role for a Queen's Champion, Earl Marshal, Lord High Steward, or Lord High Constable at Westminster. In the House of Lords Lord Londonderry complained that "time-consecrated forms and ceremonies had been abandoned" and this implied an attack on the monarchy.

Some of those denied their moment of glory at Westminster combined

*Eustace Tennyson D'Eyncourt entertaining his tenants in the great hall, Bayons Manor (1842).*

with the Earl of Eglinton to provide a spectacle which was to outshine by far any official pageantry at the beginning of the new reign. Preparations centred round Samuel Pratt's armour showrooms in Lower Grosvenor Street, London. Here the architect, L.N. Cottingham, had created a Gothic setting for a rapidly expanding business. No Gothic castle was complete without armour and other trappings of the Middle Ages. Even Pugin designed and had made (for Lord Shrewsbury's Alton Towers) a larger – than – life armoured knight complete with tilting lance, seated on a horse also suitably armoured and all on a great Gothic heraldic base. Nearly 150 potential knights gathered at Pratt's showroom as a prelude to rehearsals for the tournament held in July at St. John's Wood. Approaching three thousand attended the dress rehearsal there prior to the tournament at Eglinton Castle planned for 28th August 1838.

*The tomb of Lord and Lady Sudeley, Saint Andrew's Church, Toddington, Gloucestershire.*

In the months that led up to the tournament, there were several references in Queen Victoria's diary to conversations with the Prime Minister, Lord Melbourne, in which fun is poked at Lord Eglinton and his friends. Later they took a particular delight in the deluge which washed out the first day of the tournament. Notwithstanding a wet start, the tournament took place to the delight of all who participated and the amusement of many who did not.

The Queen of Beauty at Eglinton was Lady Seymour, wife of the Lord Seymour who became First Commissioner of Works in 1851-2. He had charge of the works at the New Palace of Westminster just before Lord John Manners became First Commissioner.

Less than three years later, the Queen, by now married to Prince Albert, the epitome of chivalry, gave a costume ball at Buckingham Palace. The theme was that of the court of Edward III and Queen Philippa. The costumes worn by the royal couple on this occasion followed closely the details of the statues of Edward III and his Consort, later to be placed in the Central Lobby of the Palace.

The Commissioners having been announced in advance of the competition for the New Houses of Parliament there was of course the possibility that some architects might design with a view to pleasing one or more of them. Amateurs in any case have a habit of communing with professionals. Some of the Commissioners had personal links with architects who were likely to compete.

It took some little time before the conditions which the competitors had to satisfy were made available. At the end of July architects were invited to apply to the Office of Woods, although the plan of the site was not available until the end of August. Entries had to be in by the closing date of 1st November, which meant that some eight weeks only were available following receipt of the plan. The closing date was later extended to 1st December 1835.

The time available to the architects was absurdly short but those who had followed public events closely could have anticipated the competition by many months.

Pugin first worked for Barry in 1835 when he was already busy supervising the building of his own house to his own design. St. Marie's Grange still stands in a somewhat altered form. Pugin claimed that it was unique among contemporary buildings in that it was "complete in every part in the ancient style." It was a small house without hall or corridors, the floors being served by a single spiral staircase. It had been built on a steep slope adjoining the road and overlooking the river valley, with a distant view of Salisbury Cathedral. Entry was made at first floor level across a drawbridge. The single spiral staircase led on this floor into a parlour, through which one reached a library, beyond which was a chapel with an adjoining sacristry. Below this floor were the usual domestic offices and above it the bedrooms. Even Pugin's devoted second wife found the curious plan of the house too much of a strain when expecting her second child, so Pugin resolved to sell it. Substantial alterations had to be made before it was marketable and eventually sold in 1841.

The Commission for Birmingham Grammar School (1833-36) entailed a study of Gothic principles and details which served him (Barry) well in the architectural competition for the New Houses of Parliament, for which he was preparing.

"There was another reason which made him look back with pleasure to this work. It was in connection with it that he first made the acquaintance of Mr. Pugin, whose assistance he secured in making out some of the drawings for details. The acquaintance ripened into friendship, a friendship unclouded by a single misunderstanding, and closed only by the death of his gifted coadjutor."[17]

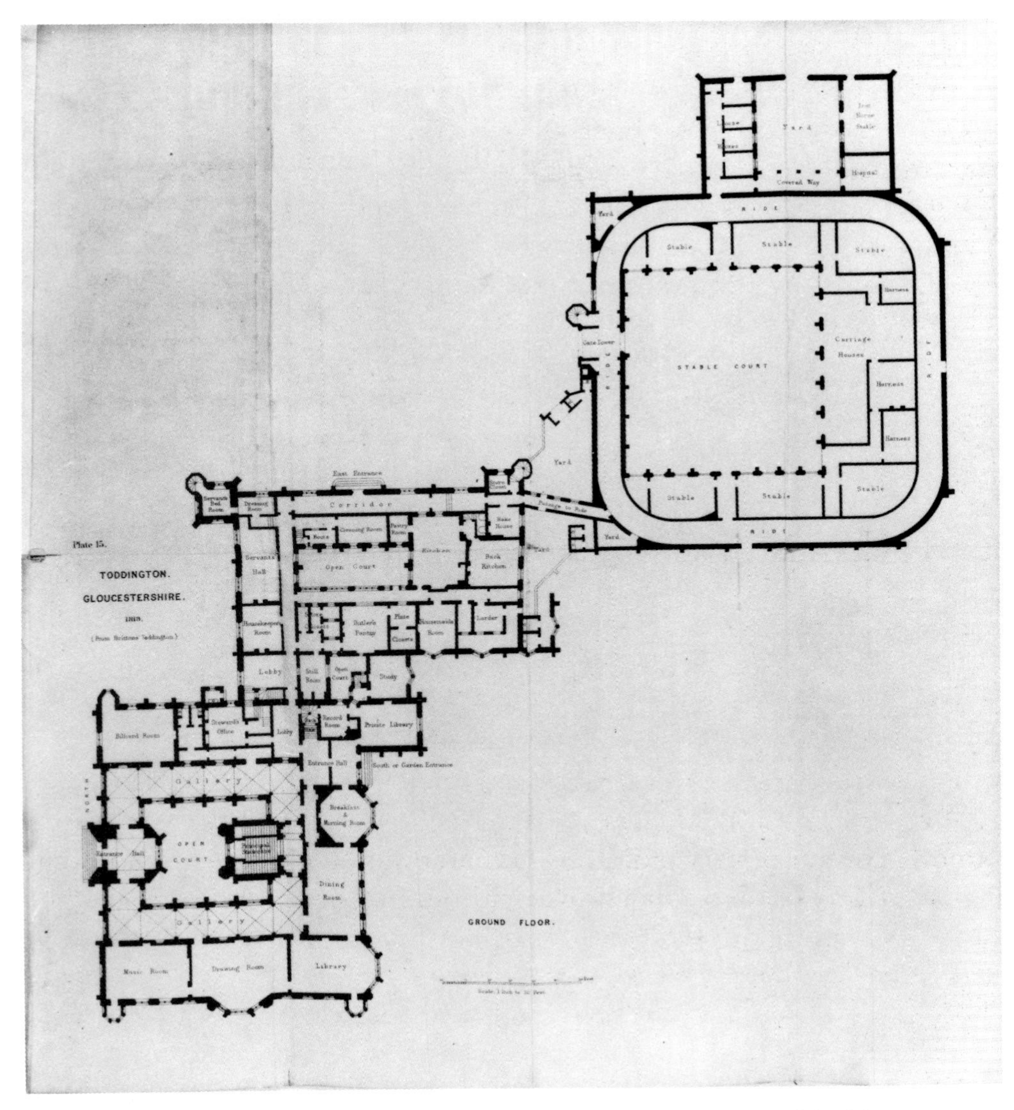


*The ground-plan of Toddington Manor, Gloucestershire, the home of Lord Sudeley.*

"The first aid which he received (at Westminster) from Mr. Pugin was under the pressure of shortness of time in making the original design. Working under Mr. Barry's own eye and direction, Mr. Pugin sketched for him in pencil a complete set of details, in a style perhaps bolder, less carefully proportioned and less purely English, than would have been adopted by himself.

Mr. Pugin would have recommended irregular and picturesque grouping of parts utterly at variance with the regularity and symmetry actually adopted.

After Mr. Barry's appointment as architect, he still received the same aid in preparing detailed drawings for the estimate, most of which however, by changes in design, were afterwards set aside.

*The garden front of Toddington Manor, Gloucestershire, sketched by R. Kitton.*

Every drawing passed under his eye in all cases for supervision, in very many for alteration. Mr. Pugin's originality and enthusiasm never interfered with this understanding; he would carry out vigorously and heartily what he himself could not altogether approve. His suggestions and criticisms, freely given and freely received, were invaluable; and his enthusiasm, even in its eccentricities, was inspiring and irresistable."[18]

The entries had to be identified only by a symbol, not by name. Some competitors disguised their identity more effectively than others. In advance of the judging many had shown their designs to their friends and it was early whispered abroad that Barry had produced a design of rare power and beauty.

There were ninety-seven entries each one to be examined and carefully considered by the Commissioners. Not surprisingly they asked for more time, managing to complete their work by 29th February 1836. They had been invited to select up to five designs. They recommended four only: those by Barry, Buckler, Hamilton and Railton.

Most significantly the Commissioners, whilst full of praise for Barry, stated that the chosen plan needed revision before execution and that the architect's drawings should be submitted from time to time to competent judges of their effect. This left the way open for the Commissioners or whoever succeeded them to influence the design.

"It is impossible to examine the minute drawings for this design and not feel confident in the author's skill in Gothic architecture." Nevertheless, they were determined to keep a close watch on the architect. "Lest from overconfidence, negligence or inattention to the execution of the work, we fail to obtain that result to which our just expectations have been raised. ... We are conscious that in the plan we have selected for your Majesty's approbation, the enriched appearance of the several elevations will naturally excite suspicion, that it cannot be carried into effect but at an enormous expense. In the absence of the detail of any portion of the work, we can form no perfect idea of the architect's intentions, but even with the minute drawings before us, we have sufficient evidence to lead us to the belief that, from the unbroken character and general uniformity of the different fronts, and external decorations being wholly unnecessary in any of the courts, no design worthy of the country, of equal magnitude, can offer greater facilities for economy in the execution."[19]

From the foregoing it will be seen that the Commissioners were careful to distance themselves from any debate that might ensue on the subject of the cost of executing Barry's designs. At the same time it is obvious that they were greatly beguiled by the drawings which Barry had obtained from Pugin and which, bending the rules of the competition, he had sent in to accompany his plans.

Having chosen Barry as the winner of the competition and with or without his help, having made many improvements, the Commissioners then had to justify their choice to the Parliamentary Committee on 10th March 1836. Hanbury-Tracy told them that certain guidelines had been laid down and the Commissioners had based their decision upon "The general disposition and convenience of the several entrances, and of the different communications of the interior; the situation of the different offices; the situation of the houses with respect to each other; the communications to them, private and public; the situation of the libraries, committee and refreshment rooms, and the various conveniences required." From the want of competent knowledge on the subject of artificial ventilation and acoustics they had made neither of them or the shape of the Houses a point for their consideration in determining the merit of any plan.

Hanbury-Tracy was closely questioned as to why Barry's plan was the best. He found this difficult to answer, remarking that it was "impossible for anyone to look at that of Mr. Barry, and not feel it is difficult to describe, the great superiority of it over every other that has been submitted to the

*The Queen of Beauty at the Eglinton Tournament.*

Commissioners." It had particular beauty as a Gothic building though it was a design simply and easily executed.

The Commissioners, led by Hanbury-Tracy, were subject to vigorous cross-examination by the committee; it was even suggested that there had been some kind of collusion between them. Hanbury-Tracy stated that he had never met Barry but had heard so much of the merits of his plan that when Barry's design passed before him in the wake of many others, he had a strong suspicion from the beauty of it, that it could be none other than Barry's. Certainly he had architectural attitudes which led him to favour the Barry design, though he had a high regard also for Buckler as an architectural draughtsman and historian. Had not Hanbury-Tracy's own house, Toddington, been a collection of elements from other buildings much as Buckler's entry for Westminster had been?

The fame of Toddington Manor impelled John Britton to visit the house. "It was said to possess much originality of design, with elaborate details, and many pecularities." Britton went on to point out the obligation which the public owed to Hanbury-Tracy, who was created Lord Sudeley in 1838.

*Queen Victoria and Prince Albert dressed as Edward III and Queen Philippa at her Majesty's Bal Costumé in 1842.*

"As one of the Committee to select from the competing designs for the new Houses of Parliament, His Lordship not only devoted much time and zealous attention, but manifested an intimate knowledge of the science and art of architecture. Whatever differences of opinion prevailed amongst professional architects and legislative critics, on that conflicting occasion, it may be safely predicted, that the designs by Mr. Barry, unanimously fixed on by the Committee, will hereafter be equally an honour to the architect, to England, and to the three distinguished gentlemen who, after choosing the enormous design, rendered many useful, if not important, hints to the artist."[20]

In the course of some one hundred and thirty questions from the committee, the Commissioners had to defend even the choice of style and whether it would produce a durable building. Commissioner Liddell made the prophetic pronouncement that "I am of the opinion that Gothic architecture suffers less by the ravages of time than Grecian, because any reduction in the sharpness of the mouldings destroys the character and symmetry of a Grecian building, which is not the case in Gothic, as most of our finest specimens in this country are in a ruinous state, that their beauty is unimpaired." Tracy attempted to rescue the situation by stating that all depended upon the durability of the materials used. Joseph Hume's persistent criticism of the plan of the building eventually caused Tracy to exclaim "There must be communications... unless you could leap across the courts." Hume was not shaken off by this remark, he was even suspicious at the improvements made to the winning design in relation to the two Houses and their approaches, implying that ideas had been borrowed from other entrants. "Dr. Reid's name figures ominously in the conversation you held with Dr. Reid, were you able to form some general conception of the principle on which he proposed to construct rooms, so as to render them fit for the transmission of sound?"

"I cannot say that I was; it was a subject I felt others more competent to decide upon than myself. Architecturally I did consult him, and heard for the first time, to my astonishment, that projecting galleries were disadvantageous to sound, and should be particularly avoided, but that receding ones were admissable."

"Supposing that principle of construction to be good, would there be any difficulty in modifying Mr. Barry's plan, so as to adapt it to Dr. Reid's principle of construction?"

"None at all. The object we had was to see that there was plenty of space, and to leave the question of the form of the Houses to those who understood better than ourselves the nature of acoustics."

Hume managed to generate a friendly argument between Liddell and Tracy on the definition of Elizabethan, but Cust came to the rescue. "We thought Elizabethan an improper term to designate a style which is found all over Europe before and after our Elizabeth's Reign; it is, in fact, a mixed style of architecture the original Roman or (if you please) Grecian, grafted upon the Gothic."

It transpiried that both Cust and Tracy had argued in committee that the cloisters and the remains of St. Stephen's Chapel and its crypt should be incorporated in any new building. This had not been made a condition of the competition and both said that Barry's preservation of them had not been a factor in his victory.

It was Hume, probing further on the subject of alterations which the Commissioners had made to Barry's plan, who discovered that "possibly we may be accused of presumption in saying so, but we thought we saw the way to make the alterations ourselves without consulting him." Sir Robert Peel, on discovering that plans other than Barry's provided satisfactory accommodation and convenience asked whether it would be possible "to select the most convenient of the plans, and apply the interior to Mr. Barry's elevation?"

"Impossible," answered Tracy who went on to assure Sir Robert that "Mr. Barry can make all the alteration requisite, and render his plan more perfect, I should say than any other; I have no doubt that his plan may be much improved. In my opinion the situation of the House of Lords should be removed more to the south, to get a greater space between the general central lobby and that of the House of Lords, to afford additional light and air to the basement, as well as alteration."

The Chairman made every one of the four Commissioners voice their approval of Barry's plan. Tracy in conclusion stated, "there is no such thing as perfection in architecture; Mr. Barry may go on improving this plan, and I do trust that if it is adopted it will be improved from time to time in parts not actually under hand until the building is completed."

Sir Robert Peel asked whether a model would be helpful but Tracy observed that nothing is more deceiving than a model to an experienced eye. It was then the turn of the Chancellor of the Exchequer to ask whether the Commissioners had formed any judgement with respect to the expense of Mr. Barry's plan. Tracy answered that "I see no reason for believing that the plan will cost more than £500,000. Considering the magnitude of the building, it is impossible to conceive a design equally magnificent, and at the same time less expensive than that proposed by Mr. Barry." This exchange led to Peel raising the subject of the kind of stone to be used and that "some public department of the Government should institute very minute inquiries as to the comparative advantage of taking particular kinds of stone, and as to the effect of a London atmosphere upon those classes of stone respectively."

The very last question was from Sir Robert Peel. "Would it not be much better to appoint some persons permanently to superintend it (the building) rather than to leave it merely to any department of Government?"

"I should say so. The Commissioners have given this as their opinion in their report." Thus spoke Tracy. His last words in his capacity as a Commissioner.

On the 22nd April 1836 Tracy had resumed his seat upon the Select Committee which proceeded on that day to examine Charles Barry, Esq.

It seems that further alterations had by then been made, even improving upon what the committee had had before them on the 10th March. Barry opened with the answer that "the principle alterations are the removal of the entire building from Westminster Bridge to an extent of 150 feet, instead of being, as in the original design, sixty feet; an extension of the riverfront, which has enabled me to enlarge the whole of the internal courts for the purposes of increased light and ventilation; a removal of the two Houses to a greater distance from each other, and certain modifications in the arrangements of the offices, residences, etc. The plan, in all other respects, remains much the same, except in being more square and parallel with Westminster Hall, in consequence of a late alteration in the line of embankment towards the river. The composition and character of the design remains nearly the same." On the subject of what became the Clock Tower, "You have altered the small tower, the last was infinitely more beautiful and more in character, was it not?"

"It is still in the same character in its detail as the rest of the building."

"Was your object in altering the smaller tower for the sake of reducing the expense, or from an idea of your own that it would improve the building?"

"Not for the purpose of economy, but to make it accord with the modified plan as well as to improve the external character of the design. In the original design the tower contained the Speaker's dining-room, which in the amended plan has been removed, so that so large a tower was unnecessary."

"Then, in your judgement, it improves the elevation of the building?"

"Yes, it is a great improvement."

"How long do you think it would take to complete the building?"

"I imagine about six years for the entire completion; it will be possible, however, to complete the Houses and committee rooms long before that period, perhaps in about two years." A long series of exchanges on cost, even of a cubic yard of concrete laid for 7s. 6p. culminated in a question. "You are well acquainted with the degree of ornament on Henry VII's Chapel; can you give the committee an idea as to how far the ornament on the face of your proposed building will be richer, or what comparison the ornaments will bear to those of Henry VII's Chapel?"

"The fact is there is no comparison between them; the front of Henry VII's Chapel is panelled all over; in the front of the proposed building it is not intended to panel the plain face of the walls."

"What kind of roofs do you mean to put on the building, and what estimate have you made of them?"

"I have made no separate estimate; but I can ascertain the amount if it be the wish of the committee. The covering is to be of slate."

Sir Robert Inglis, later to chair committees to which Barry was answerable asked, "In what period do you apprehend (the foundation being laid in the course of the present summer) the two Houses of Parliament would be fit for the reception of the Members?"

"In about two years."

Thomas Chawner, an architect in the Office of Woods and Forests was the next witness. "Are you in the practice of estimating buildings?"

"Occasionally."

*Sir Robert Peel (1788-1880), artist unknown.*

He assented to a gross amount of £724,984 but upon the understanding of material reductions in the ornamental parts of the original design, and that the interior in general would be finished in as plain a manner as is consistent for the relative apartments.

Henry Arthur Hunt was then called in. He was a surveyor with seven years experience in estimating buildings. He had knowledge of the prices involved at the Birmingham Grammar School for which Barry had been responsible and he had examined the quantities involved at the Carlton Club House. Both the Carlton Club and the Oxford and Cambridge Clubhouses were plain buildings in appearance, but very expensively constructed and finished. By taking their cost per cubic foot and adding fifty per cent he had arrived at the figure which had applied to the New Palace. Hume had the

*Barry's revised design for the north front of the New Houses of Parliament and (right) the south elevation. Signed and dated 21st April 1836.*

*Barry's west front of the New Houses of Parliament. Signed and dated 21st April 1836.*

last word with Barry on the subject of expenditure. "How long would it take a person to make a detailed specification and the working drawings, so as to enable a correct estimate to be formed of the whole building?"

"At least a twelve month." To which Mr. Hunt added that it would take at least four months for him to produce his report upon that evidence.[21]

### *Barry's Designs*

The design which won the competition was not that which was adopted by Parliament; very considerable alterations were made both in plan and in elevation. The plan of the winning "competition" design had the bulk of the building aligned with Westminster Hall and a St. Stephen's Chapel restored as St. Stephen's Hall. There was no octagonal Central Lobby and the two Houses were set either side of a central hall on the axis of the new St. Stephen's Hall.

The river front was aligned with the river. This left a series of courts, each one wedge-shaped, in descending size as they approached the north end of the site. There were two great towers. The State Entrance tower, later called the King's Tower, was eighty feet square and 178 feet high. The tower at the north end of the building, roughly on the site of where the Clock Tower was eventually erected, did not serve that purpose but, contained on the principal floor the Speaker's State Dining Room.

The adopted designs saw both towers heightened and the most northerly one evolving into a Clock Tower. The King's Tower was seventy-five feet square on the original plan. The dimensions here are those stated by Tracy and Hume in committee. Both towers eventually emerged with different dimensions. The Old Palace Yard elevation was realigned in relation to Westminster Hall. The two Chambers were placed further apart separated by an octagonal central hall and a pair of linking corridors and lobbies. The arched windows which appeared in the winning design and which were later abandoned for the main body of the east elevation, survive in the twin towers at either end of it.

The Commissioners, Parliament and the architect were all criticized for the changes made in the design and plan. Barry was attacked because some elements of his amended design echoed those who had lost to him in the competition. The Commissioners and Parliament were criticized because they allowed elaboration of the design which departed from the simplicity of the original. It also seemed that, having won the competition for a highly economical building, Barry was indulging in something far more extravagant. Hanbury-Tracy had estimated that the original entry could be constructed for a mere £500,000 and the cost per cubic foot was thought to be no more than one shilling.

*Thomas Hopper's design for New Palace Yard.*

A number of the losers banded together, and with Parliamentary allies, attempted to get the result of the competition overthrown. In this they failed, for the obvious reason that, had they objected to the method of proceedings, they should have done so in advance of their entry. By entering they had accepted the terms and conditions of the competition.

Some of the losers published their designs. One of the most picturesque entries, extensively illustrated, was that of Thomas Hopper. He was a versatile architect who could design in anything from the Norman to the Greek Revival style. He is famous for Penrhyn Castle (Norman), the Gothic Conversatory at Carlton House and Leigh Court in Somerset, built for the Miles family of bankers. His grand staircase with figures in medieval costumes disposed about it shows yet another architect attempting to embark at Westminster upon a great Gothic Adventure.

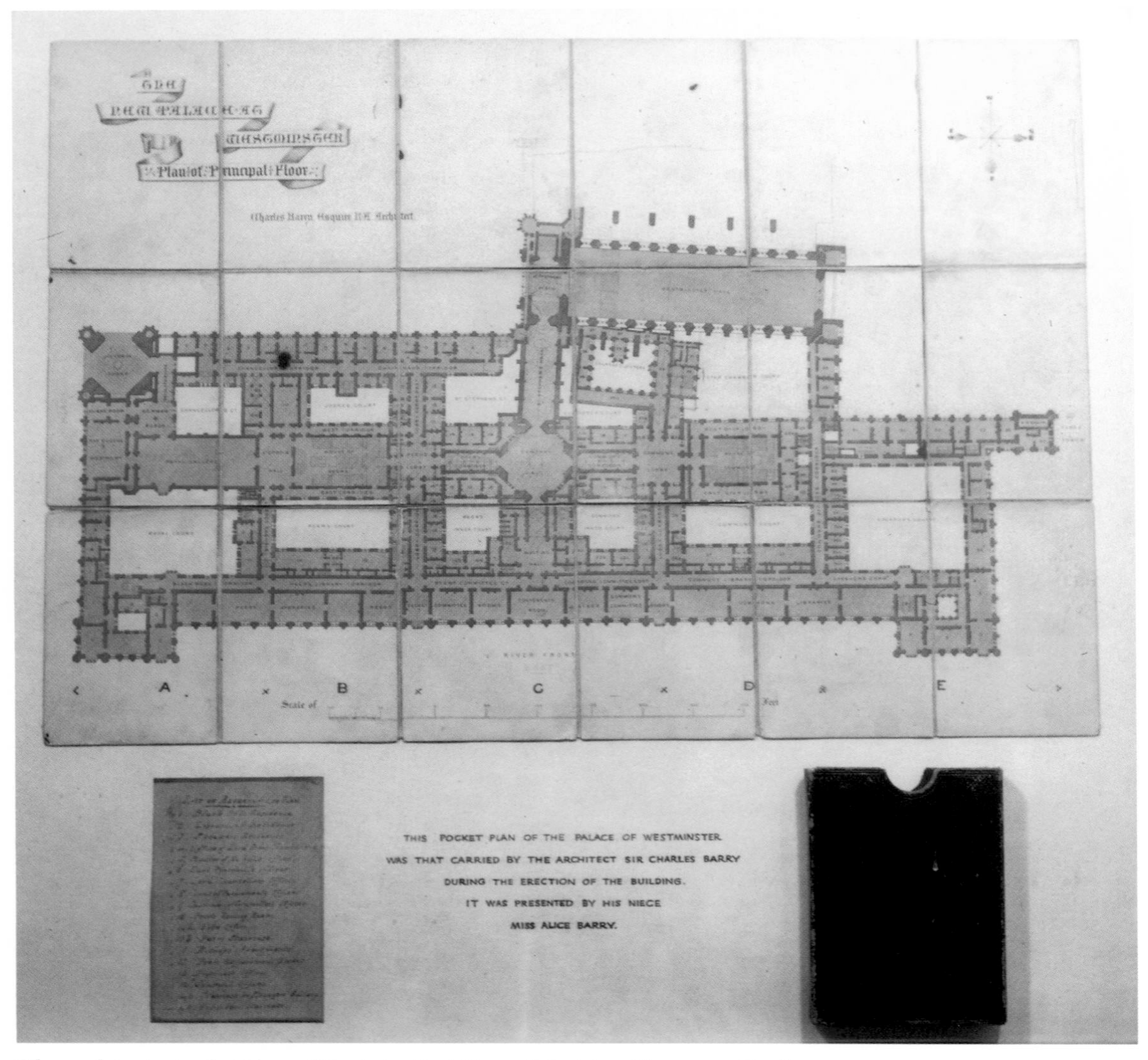


*The architect's pocket plan of the principal floor of the New Houses of Parliament.*

# IV

## Triumph in the Lords

Barry won the competition with a beautiful set of drawings supplied by Pugin which did not entirely tie up with his master plan.

The design which was adopted by Parliament was the result of changes made by Hanbury-Tracy's Commission and a committee which included Hanbury-Tracy as a member.

The published ground plan of the adopted design contains many interesting features, all of which were superseded. The focal point is a square Public Central Hall (56), from which leads off to the north at an awkward angle the Outer Public Lobby of the House of Commons (58), leading to the Inner Public Lobby of the House of Commons and staircases to the Galleries (33). This is rectangular with its longer side against the House of Commons, (28) which is square in outline. Beyond this is another rectangle forming the Commons Division Lobby (34). All of this awkward arrangement was before long altered.

The central spine of the building in the adopted plan was neither a straight line nor aligned parallel with the River Front. The inventive architect soon began to make improvements, some of which caused trouble with some people.

The adopted plan shows two sets of steps leading up from the Thames onto the Terrace, opposite the Terrace Entrance for Lords and Commons. These steps can be seen in some of the published views of the Palace but (perhaps in deference to the views of the Duke of Wellington upon matters of fortification and defence from attack from the rear) they never became a reality.

From the big Central Hall the Public Staircase to the Commons Committee Rooms on the floor above (59) ascended in two straight flights to the east. The Outer Public Lobby of the House of Lords (57), is shown square to the Public Central Hall and leads into a rectangular Public Lobby and Staircases to the Galleries of the House of Lords (10). Beyond this is the House of Lords, flanked by Peers' Private Corridors connected with the House (the precursor of the voting lobbies). At the throne end of the House is the King's Robing Room, with access to the House of Lords at each side of the throne (15). Beyond that is the King's Gallery (14) running east and west, to the south of which is the King's Staircase.(13) At ground level is the King's Entrance Hall or Vestibule. (12) This is reached from the lower part of the tower described as the King's State Entrance.

Amongst the many other features which were not executed in the form shown was the new front to the Law Courts. (61) It was the clear intention in the adopted design to face these buildings in a manner similar to that of the New Palace.

The key to the resolution of all the problems which flowed from the misalignment of Westminster Hall and St. Stephen's Chapel with the river was the introduction of an octagonal Central Hall which enabled subtle changes of direction to be cleverly disguised.

Whilst Barry was later applauded for many of the alterations which he made either on his own account or in response to suggestions from the innumerable committees which interested themselves in the emerging New Palace, he eventually fell foul of his longstanding supporter and admirer Charles Hanbury-Tracy. The drastic changes which Barry made to the Royal Entrance, its Staircase and Robing Room provoked criticism from Lord Sudeley and the Lords.

The next stage was the preparation of the estimates drawings upon which the cost of the undertaking could, it was hoped, be ascertained and without which a start on building operations could not be made.

Here too there was feverish activity and correspondence between Pugin and Barry. "He still received the same aid in preparing detailed drawings for the estimate, most of which however, by changes in design, were afterwards set aside."[1]

The Government quantity surveyors had by April 1837 arrived at a figure of £707,104 for the building as then proposed from which some £14,000 could be deducted for old materials recovered. This produced the beguiling figure of £693,104 which was approved by the Rebuilding Committee. To this had to be added the architect's fee, the cost of the embankment and the coffer dam required to build it, the cost of land purchased, the sum of £10,000 for ventilation and warming (which later events proved to be derisory) and £17,000 for furniture and fittings. This produced a grand total of £865,000 for which Parliamentary approval was never sought.

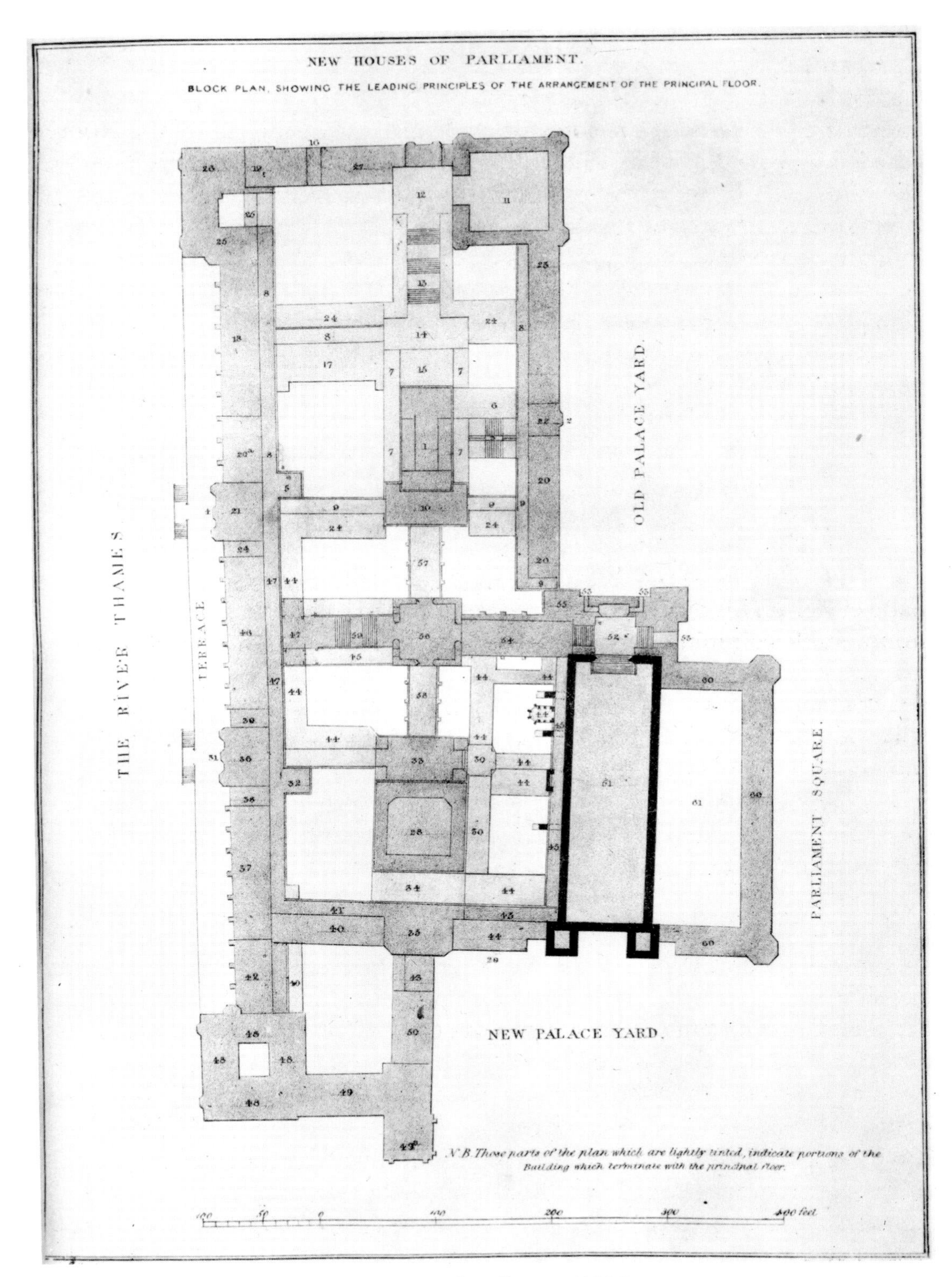


*Plan of the adopted design for the New Houses of Parliament (1836).*

By now Pugin had done enough for Barry to make substantial progress with the great undertaking. The collaboration was later to be resumed to marvellous effect. The first phase of Pugin's work on the New Palace earned him nearly £500, the sum that Barry received as a prize winner.

The estimates were based on an extrapolation of details designed by Pugin as they applied to the plan by Barry. Although virtually all the details were altered or refined in their execution they formed a vital stage in the translation of an imaginary Palace into eventual reality. They were a firm foundation of detail from which Barry could have completed the Palace, after a fashion. They must have given him a sense of security from which he could face the troubled years which lay ahead.

It was Sir Robert Peel who suggested that a Commission should be appointed to recommend a suitable stone for the great undertaking. This Commission, of which Barry was a member, spent many months of 1839 visiting buildings and exploring quarries. After a number of false moves it was to the quarry of the Duke of Leeds at Anston in Yorkshire that they directed their attention. It was only here that blocks of sufficient size could be obtained. Some idea of the requirements can be obtained from the size of the heavier battlements which measure five feet by two feet.

For the interior of the building great quantities of Caen stone were imported from France, although stone from Painswick in Gloucestershire had been the original choice. There are many places in the interior where a mixture of stone has been used, producing sharp constrasts of colour which do not relate to the architectural detail. This can be seen in some of the oriels of the River Front and in the Central Lobby.

Whilst the search for a suitable stone for the New Palace proceeded, domestic conditions were the concern of the Commons. The problems of lighting and ventilation in the Commons were not solved by "the carrying of Mr. Hume's Motion" on the night of 16th October 1834. The Temporary Chamber so swiftly created by the Office of Works was soon the subject of Select Committee activity, headed by the persistent Mr. Hume. Candlelight, the traditional form of illumination, was not to everyone's satisfaction. The Report of 7th August 1839 contains a diagram in which three different arrangements of candles of various lengths are explained.

There had been an experiment with gas lighting but the Committee of 1839 devoted most of its time to exploring the benefits and the most beneficial position of an oil lamp called the Bude Light. This apparatus, managed by one Goldsworthy Gurney, involved the introduction of oxygen into the centre of the flame of an oil lamp. It was capable of giving out a brilliant light but its operation was, in the opinion of some, not without hazard. In a statement read to the Committee by Sir Frederick Trench, M.P., on the practicability of applying the Bude Light to the present House of Commons he stated that, "the whole breadth of the horizontal part of the

*The adopted design for Old Palace Yard. A watercolour by J.P. Neale (1836).*

roof is ten feet, five feet of which are taken up with the lenses etc. Now, in the space of ten feet there are to be arranged eight lenses or lanterns, eight lanterns with eight burners each, eight vessels of oil, eight of these double-iron chimneys, with all the pipes to supply each of these eight lamps with oxygen. The Beams are strong, but the Panels are very slight and very combustible, and so is the lath and plaster intermediate roof; and with such an upward Current as we have, a spark would produce an instantaneous blaze not very easily extinguished.... The friends of the Bude Light say there is no Possibility of the Lantern falling, or Glass being broken, or Oil being spilled, or of a Messenger overcome by Azote or Sleep or Beer tumbling through a panel on the Head of the Chancellor of the Exchequer. But I say that such Accidents are not quite so impossible as suits their Argument; and, if they should occur, Woe to the heads that may be underneath them!"

On 8th July Sir Frederick had attempted to get a letter from Professor Brande inserted in the appendix to the Report of the committee. On this question the committee divided, Sir Frederick being the only vote for the ayes, there being four noes he was defeated. However, in an additional statement to the committee, Sir Frederick managed to quote Brande "in regard to the Bude light, I entertain a high opinion of its value as applicable to lighthouses; but I can not bring myself to believe that it can be conveniently and economically applied to the purpose of lighting the House of Commons, nor do I see the object of attempting its application to such a purpose. I think I would give a guess, but it would not be civil." So ends Sir Frederick's last word on the subject.

Although all this was concerned with the Temporary House of Commons erected under the superintendence of Sir Robert Smirke (with his brother-in-law as the contractor), Charles Barry made an appearance. He chose not to be drawn too deeply into the technical debate.

The Chairman's first question was "Have you attended the experiments made by Mr. Gurney in lighting the House with the Bude Light?"

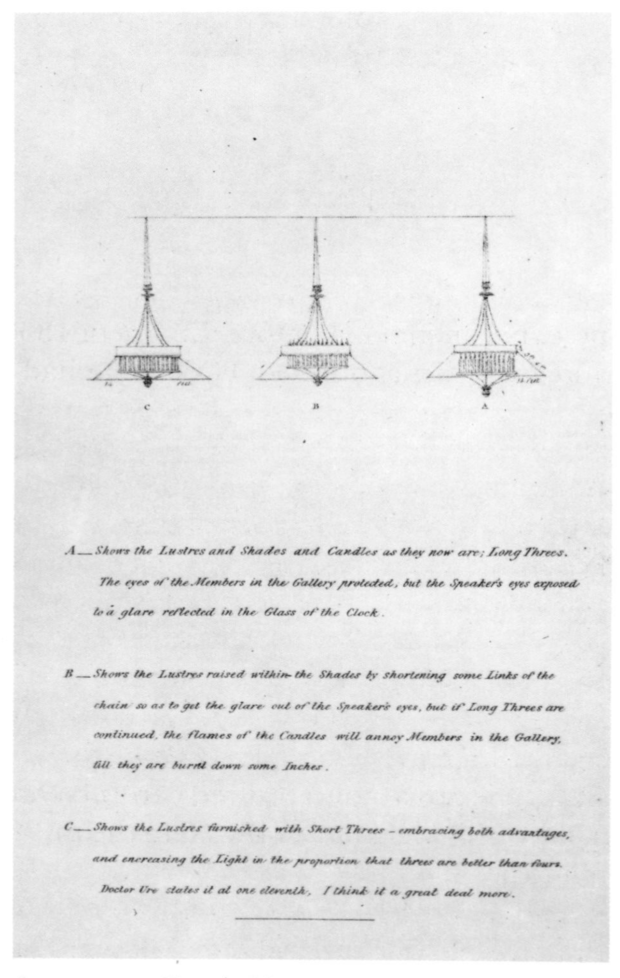


*Proposals for lighting the temporary House of Commons (1839).*

"Yes, I attended on one occasion for a very short time in the body of the House."

"Will you state your opinion of its practicability?"

"My opinion was, that the lights were not sufficiently beneath the ceiling, and the consequence was, that, as the ceiling is ribbed, nearly the whole of it was thrown into shade."

Chairman: "Would that unpleasant effect be removed by the roof being smooth and of a lighter colour?"

"Yes, that effect would partly be removed by such means; but it would not be desirable in point of taste that the ceiling should be plain and colourless." Barry then briefly explained with the aid of a drawing, that lights suspended from three feet six inches or more below the ceiling would have a better effect. In his own House of Commons Chamber, even after the modifications of its roof, the gas chandeliers, whilst they existed, hung a long way down from the roof and were not without their problems.

### *Ventilation and Heating*

The heating and ventilation of public buildings had been the source of much discussion and experiment long before the fire of 1834. It was a field in which enthusiasts and eccentrics abounded. Parliament had experience of both but this did not prevent some Members of both Houses being beguiled into a further adventure as a result of their visit to the British Association for the Advancement of Science, meeting in Edinburgh in the summer of 1834. They met there Dr. David Boswell Reid who impressed them with his experiments on ventilating and heating and acoustics. Blinded by science and carried along by Reid's self-confident enthusiasm they turned to him for advice on the Temporary Chamber. His upcast shaft system involving a huge chimney 125 feet high with a furnace at the bottom was designed to drag the impure air away from the ceiling of the House and up the shaft. The fresh air came in through the floor, having come down from roof level through another shaft. The apparatus required careful management. Compared with what the Members had endured in the pre-fire House, Reid's system was felt to be an improvement.

The Office of Works and Parliament might have done well to heed the evidence given by the irascible Doctor Reid together with that of Sir Robert Smirke to the Select Committee of the House of Commons on the Ventilation of the Houses of Parliament in 1835. They were taking evidence on this vital subject at the very moment that the competitors were preparing their entries. This had not prevented Reid from pressing upon them a design of his own for the new House of Commons Chamber. It was sealed off completely from natural ventilation and direct daylight. "The air is supposed to be admitted at a regulated temperature by the iron grating along the floor, and also at the back and lower part of every seat along its whole extent." There were eight benches on either side of the floor and a further four on either side could be revealed by "the curtains or moveable framework being pulled up between the pillars so as to render all or any part of the Gallery available when the House is very full."

The whole has something of the feel of the Train Shed at Temple Meads station in Bristol which was designed by Isambard Kingdom Brunel.

The answer given by Sir Robert Smirke on the 28th of August 1835 should have served as a sufficient warning to any who thought that the problem could ever be satisfactorily solved by such technology or theory as was then available.

Barry had to contend not only with the continuing interest of the two Houses but also their continuous presence in the remaining unburned parts of the Palace which occupied a substantial part of the building site.

He decided therefore to embark upon the River Front or east elevation first. Here a coffer dam was needed to restrain the Thames. Foundations had to be constructed for an embankment projecting substantially further into the river (particularly at the north end) than had any previous building at Westminster.

Although the dam was complete at the end of 1838 the contractors, John and Henry Lee, were found to be far from competent. By the autumn of 1839 the famous firm of Grissell and Peto had obtained a contract to build the shell of the River Front for the sum of £157,615. It was Thomas Grissell who managed the building contracting at Westminster. Morton Peto, his partner, was involved mainly in railway construction.[2]

Grissell had hoped to start work at the beginning of 1840. "The first stone of the superstructure of the New Palace of Westminster, being the angle of the plinth of the Speaker's House nearest the bridge was laid by the architect's wife without any public ceremony, and in presence of a few personal friends only, on the 27th of April 1840."[3] Probably not one person in a million when asked who laid the foundation stone at the New Palace of Westminster would answer that it was the architect's wife. It would be an interesting operation to stand on Westminster Bridge, ask a sample of the passing population this question, then record their answers.

The works on the River Front had been in progress for a year when Barry found himself involved with yet another formidable force determined to leave its mark upon the New Palace.

A committee of the House of Commons was appointed on 29th April 1841 "to take into consideration the promotion of the Fine Arts of this country in connection with the rebuilding of the Houses of Parliament."

The committee was unanimous that "so important and national a work as the erection of the new Houses of Parliament afforded an opportunity that ought not to be neglected of encouraging not only the higher, but every subordinate branch of Fine Art in the country." They recommended that a Royal Commission should be appointed to assist "whatever department of the Government might be charged with the execution of the plan best calculated to realise the objects of the Committee."

In the next Parliament Sir Robert Peel, by now Prime Minister, announced on the 30th September 1841 that a Royal Commission, presided

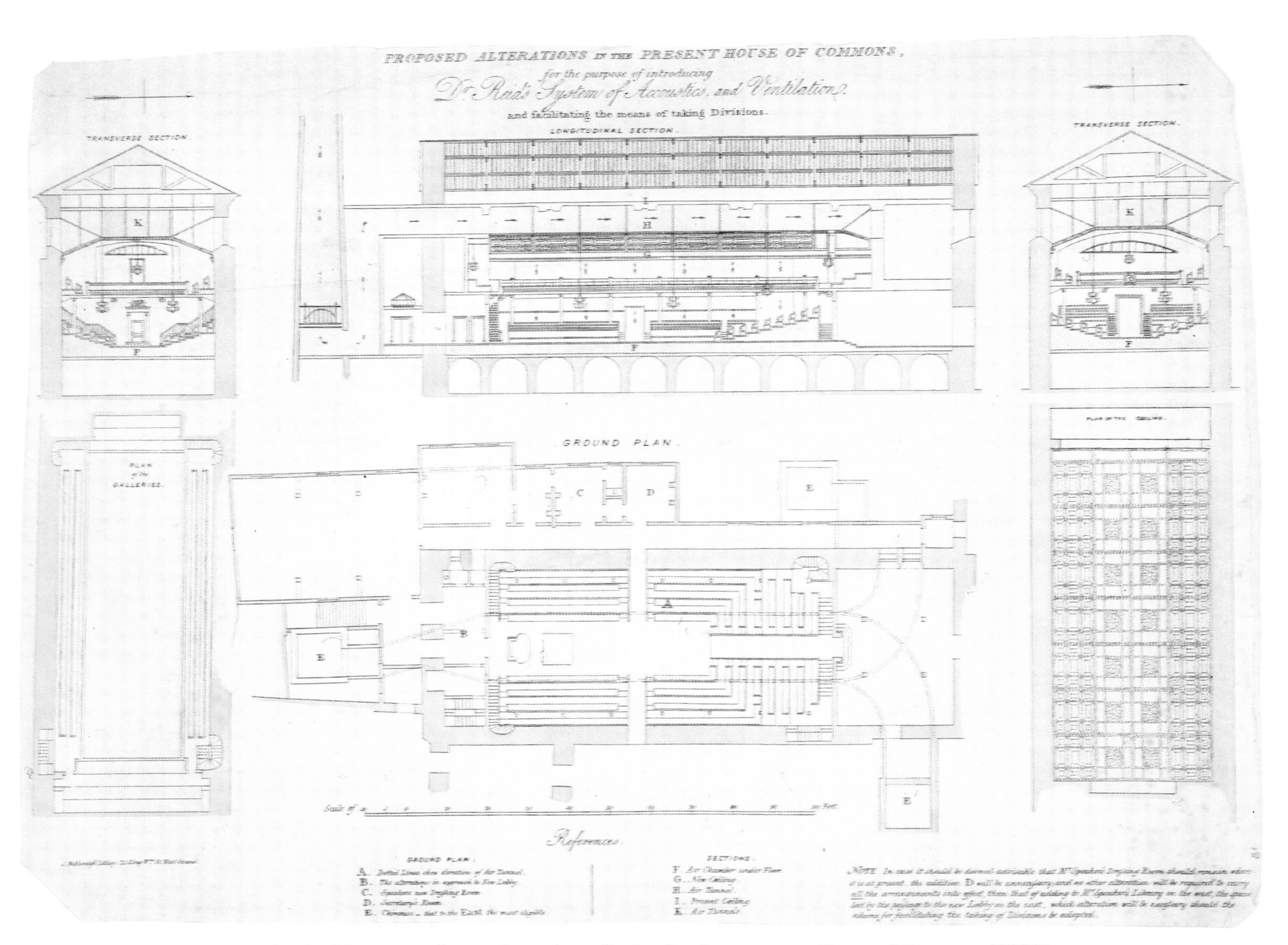


*Dr. Reid's system of acoustics and ventilation for the temporary House of Commons (1835).*

over by Prince Albert, was to continue the inquiries which the committee had commenced. Charles Barry was not invited to be a member of this Commission, yet as architect he was expected to respond to their every suggestion. Barry's Report of the 22nd February 1843 goes into great detail about the possibilities which he saw for the use of painting and other decoration, also the erection of sculpture both within and without the building. He also included suggestions for the completion of the Palace by building round New Palace Yard. He regarded the rebuilding, at a lower level, of Westminster Bridge as an essential complement to the low lying Palace and he made suggestions for the enlargement of Old Palace Yard and for the improvement of many buildings within sight of the New Palace.[4]

In its first Report of the 22nd April 1842 the Commission stated that should it be found practicable, the most desirable mode of decoration was that of fresco painting. Because that form of art had been too little practised in Britain they could not at once recommend its use. Moreover, it was uncertain whether paintings executed in that manner could be preserved from the hostile influences of climate, and equally uncertain whether artists existed in England competent to produce works "of large dimensions and in

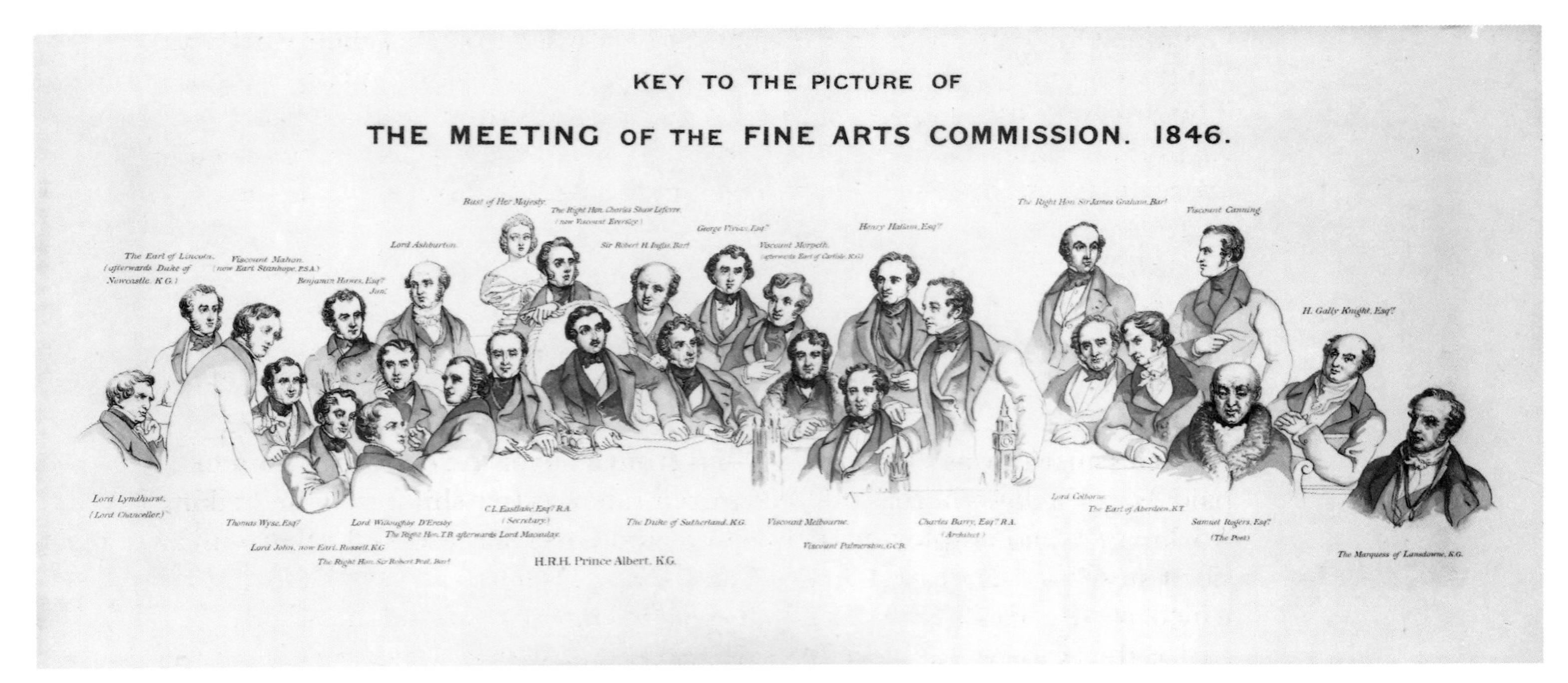


*The Fine Arts Commissioners.*

the grandest style." They recommended that a competition of large cartoons between ten and fifteen feet long in chalk or charcoal be held. The figures contained in the cartoons were to be life-size and the subjects were restricted to British history or the works of Spenser, Shakespeare, or Milton.

The cartoons were exhibited in Westminster Hall in 1843. Together with the advice of the Secretary to the Commission, Sir Charles Eastlake, and the expert knowledge of the "eminent German artist Cornelius" the success of the exhibition led the Commissioners to recommend the introduction of pictures in fresco on a large scale as the chief feature in the decoration of the New Palace.

Thus the Commission had addressed themselves to the question as to what was the most appropriate form of art to be employed within the Palace and had satisfied themselves on the technical aspects of the proposal. They had completed the work for which they were appointed.

The Commission however remained in office, first in an advisory and later almost in an executive capacity, although the Reports of the Commission were all couched in the language of recommendation to the Board of Works. The Report for 1847 gives a complete list of the subjects of the pictures which were intended to cover the wall spaces of the Palace, and of the statues which were proposed to be erected within it. Though subsequently somewhat modified from time to time, this list remained substantially unaltered during the remaining fifteen years of the Commission's existence. This is what they intended to do but their work was left unfinished. Later Reports indicate the progress that was made.[5]
The drawings upon which Grissell's contract were based produced yet further alteration and refinement. Even these drawings were not followed in every detail and the River Front developed a greater subtlety of parapet, turret and roof.

All did not go smoothly with Grissell's contract. His foreman, George Allen, had had trouble with the stone masons in Birmingham in an earlier year and these same masons were working at Westminster in 1841. He endeavoured to institute a spirit of competition between one worker and another. This did not please the union. A strike began in October 1841. Grissell's answer was to engage masons from all over the country whom he paid 3s. 6p. a day whereas the recognized rate was five shillings. The striking workman found employment elsewhere and Grissell presented Allen with a silver snuffbox. Engraved on the lid is a view of the River Front beneath which are the words *Charles Barry R.A. architect, T. Grissell, F.S.A. builder.* Inside the lid is engraved: *To Mr. George Allen: In acknowledgement of the zeal, integrity and judgement displayed in the execution of the Mason's Work, of the New Palace of Westminster. From Mr. Grissell.*

Charles Barry's office, always under his closest personal control, contained a number of able assistants. Two of his sons played a memorable

*A public exhibition of frescoes and sculpture in Westminster Hall.*

part in the great work at Westminster. His elder son Charles joined the office in 1840 at the age of seventeen. Six years later he began a diary which contains intimate glimpses of family life and official business.[6]

The younger Charles Barry's diary contains the names of many of the personalities involved in his father's highly organised office. Its arrangement was the precursor of the modern architect's practice where a number of partners are involved on most projects. In Barry's case he was in sole command, supported by chosen lieutenants to whom he alloted specific responsibilities. Young Charles performed the duties of confidential secretary combined with a growing personal architectural skill. Thomas Quarm, who figures largely in the diary, seems to have graduated from Clerk of the Works to Chief Superintendent at the building, a title which in his opinion meant that no one could do anything save through him. Young Charles is critical of Quarm, who must have had his limitations. He survived at the New Palace until the end of 1860. Edward, who commenced his professional life on the 5th October 1846, is Edward Middleton Barry, a younger brother of Charles, who succeeded his father at Westminster in 1860. E. M. Barry joined his father's office when young Charles left in 1847 to set up in partnership with Robert Richardson Banks who had served in the office as an assistant since before the Westminster competition. Alfred, the second son, entered the Church and wrote his father's biography.

Also of great assistance to Barry was Alfred Meeson, a skilled engineer employed by Barry from 1844. He also received an official salary. It must have been in an official capacity that he assumed Reid's responsibilities in the Lords because in evidence to the Select Committee he stated that Sir Charles Barry never had any responsibility for the ventilation.

It was in mid 1844 that Charles Barry, pressed to prepare for the completion of the Lords Chamber and much else, once more sought the aid of Augustus Welby Pugin.

Pugin's immediate response to Barry's approach contained these words. "I am sure I can never do you real service except in absolute detail; you should fully make up your mind as to every arrangement and then turn the small work over to me. It is next to impossible for me to design any abstract portion of a great whole in the same spirit as you have conceived the rest, and I know it is only a waste of time in me to attempt it... I can do you far more service by adapting the best examples and getting them carried out in execution than by making a lot of drawings which could never be worked from. Remember, I never made a drawing which was of any real use to you yet, and it is a dreadful loss of time to me, incessantly occupied as I am with Church work, to attempt it; as I said before, I can do you no good except in actual detail, and in that more by ferreting out the fine things that exist than by composing new ones..." There is reference here to the many drawings made for the estimates which although of value for the purpose were never worked from.[7]

By the autumn Barry urgently needing assistance, suggests a congenial meeting at Brighton.

"Dear Pugin, I am in a regular fix respecting the working drawings for the fittings and decorations of the House of Lords, which it is of vital importance to me should now be finished with the utmost possible dispatch. Although I have now made up my mind as to the principles, and, generally, as to the details of the design for them, including a new design for the throne, which is at last perfectly satisfactory to me, I am unfortunately unable to get the general drawings into such a definite shape, as is requisite for preparing the working details, owing to a lameness in one of my legs, which has laid me on my back, either in bed or on the sofa, for the last ten days, and is, I fear, likely to keep me in the same position for some days, or, perhaps, weeks to come, at this place, where I have been advised to take up my quarters for the advantage of change, sea air, bathing, etc., etc. Now, as I know of no one who can render me such valuable and efficient assistance, or can so thoroughly relieve me of my present troubles of mind in respect of these said drawings as yourself, I am induced to write to you in the hope that you may be both able and willing to pass two or three days, or even a week, with me for the purpose of making out the drawings in question, and of enabling me to consult you generally, and enter into some permanent arrangement that will be satisfactory to you, as to occasional assistance for the future in the completion of the great work, as well as for the discharge of my obligations to you for what you have already done. I feel quite sure, that, if we were here together quietly, for a few days, we should be able to make out definitively every portion of the design of the House of Lords' fittings, etc, in general drawings, so that you might be able to supply me with the details subsequently, from time to time, according to your leisure and convenience. I earnestly hope you will give me a line, by return of post, expressive of your consent to fall into the arrangement which I have proposed, and to name a time when I may expect to have the pleasure of seeing you. I have all the requisite drawings with me, together with a good supply of drawing-paper, tackle, etc. It would really do me good, both in body as well as in mind, to have you with me; therefore, pray do not disappoint me if you can in any way help it."[8]

By the end of 1844 Pugin was back in harness at Westminster with a new status which made it clear that he was no hidden hand hired to provide the Gothic detail in which Barry was deficient. Pugin's new position at Westminster was as an employee of the Government. As Superintendent of the Works of Wood Carving at the New Palace his responsibilities also covered stained glass, tiles, and metalwork.

The position carried a salary of £200 a year. In addition Pugin would be free to receive a commission on works undertaken by firms in which he had an interest. There are a number of entries in his diaries giving details of

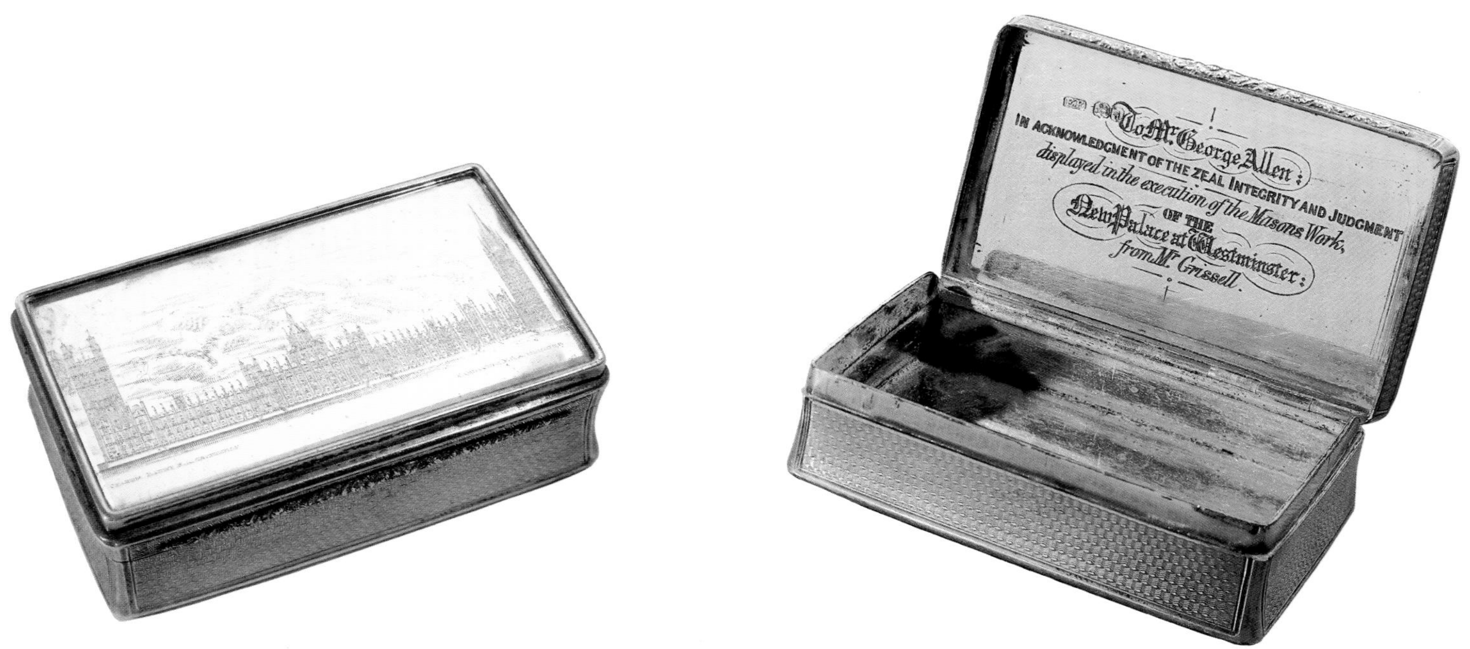


*The snuff-box presented by T. Grissell, building contractor, to his foreman G. Allen.*

payments in this respect and several of £50 or more from Barry himself.

Unlike Barry he would not have to appear before innumerable committees but he would, like Barry, have to contend with the Royal Commissioners on the Fine Arts. This involved, in one important instance, the employment of a firm for whom he had little regard and with whom he and Barry had nothing but trouble.

Prince Albert's Commission interested themselves in woodcarving, metalwork and ornamental pavements in addition to stained glass. They held competitions and sought to have the best entrants employed at Westminster. In the event none of the artists or craftsmen were prepared to work under supervision in the Government workshops at Thames Bank, Barry was right to insist on having control over this kind of work at the Palace. In almost every instance where the architect failed to gain control, the works are ill-suited to their surroundings.

Pugin eventually secured approval for the employment of Hardman's for all the decorative interior metalwork and eventually for the stained glass, Mintons for the tiles and Frederick Crace and Son for all the gilding and painting. Barry had to contend with pressure and criticism from many Parliamentary and Government sources. Although he found appearances before committees and Ministers exhausting and at times frustrating his performance was usually both masterly and effective. There was one occasion however when their Lordships cross-examined him at length about changes which he had made (apparently) without authorization. In the session of 1844 a Select Committee held five sessions with Barry and in these they were led by Lord Sudeley who had been so potent a force in the choice and guidance of Charles Barry a decade ago.

He had been alerted by the publication in *The Illustrated London News* in September 1843 of a plan of the principal floor "now definitely decided on for completion. The original bears the signature of the architect; and we are assured that no deviation shall be made from this arrangement."[9]

This plan revealed a further realignment of the bulk of the building, producing regularly shaped courts throughout. An octagonal Central Hall cunningly disguised the fact that St. Stephen's Hall was not square to it. All the Grand Staircases had been dispensed with. The Royal Approach was now from within the base of the Victoria Tower, by the arch on the north side leading to a landing from which an uninterrupted flight of some twenty-five steps reached a vaulted Lobby with a central pillar. This led either into the Victoria Gallery or into the Guard Room which connected with the Robing Room. The Grand Royal Approach had been sacrificed but the Victoria Gallery created instead. The other Grand Staircase leading from the Central Hall up to the Committee Rooms was replaced by a more discreet affair, leading out of the Lower Waiting Hall and involving three changes of direction before it emerged into the Upper Waiting Hall or Poet's Hall. The House of Commons Chamber and its Division Lobbies bore no resemblance to the adopted design. Each House had between it and the Central Hall a House Lobby (in which four pillars are shown), and the connecting corridors first introduced in the adopted design. In the 1843 plan there is still a stepped entrance in Old Palace Yard into St. Stephen's Porch. The regular Gothic refronting of the Law Courts is not shown on this plan.

In his substantial private publication, which runs to nineteen pages of text and four plans, Sudeley questions the wisdom of Barry's "unauthorized" modifications both on grounds of convenience and of taste. He asks who "allowed him to alter at his pleasure the original designs, without first submitting the substituted plan to some competent authority to judge of their fitness and propriety?" He seems here to be hankering after the continued existence of the Commission of which he was Chairman. In his preface he explains why his observations relate only to the Lords' end of the Palace - "he has not had sufficient leisure to consider satisfactorily the rest of the arrangements."[10]

Mindful perhaps of his original claim that the New Palace could be constructed for perhaps half a million pounds, Sudeley points out that an additional two acres have been included (they were in the adopted plan) and despite this, the grand approaches have been sacrificed. However in his observations, specifications of the accommodations required in the principal floor by each House were delivered to the committee. On investigation, they

*Portrait of Lord Sudeley by Sir Martin Archer Smee, circa 1840.*

appeared so enormous, that it was suggested that the ground lying between Parliament Place and Little Abingdon Street should be purchased if necessary. Barry did not use this additional space in his competition entry but by the time his design was adopted it had been included. Sudeley makes play of the fact that the original adopted design had been approved by the Sovereign. "Imagine for the moment the surprise of the Sovereign on reaching the State Apartments at the Palace; instead of the spacious Staircase, the Grand Hall, the Robing Room adjoining the Throne, all of which he had been led to expect, to find the staircase reduced in width from thirty-four feet to fourteen, with twenty-five steps without a quarter space, the Hall vanished and the Robing-room removed 150 feet from the throne and, on expressing his surprise, to be told 'Your Majesty is quite wrong in supposing there has been any alteration from the original plan, which is precisely the same; these are mere modifications and alterations of details!'"[11]

Grand ceremonial staircases, as Barry well knew, took up a great deal of space. In Thomas Hopper's rejected design and in that unique echo of Westminster, the Parliament Building in Budapest, a staircase of monumental proportions is a major feature but of no great use to the legislators who have to work within the building.

Originally it had been intended that the Royal carriages should enter the base of the Great Tower at the west side and proceeding round the central pillar, allow their passengers to alight at the eastern arch leading up the King's Staircase. Sudeley makes great complaint that "now (1843) the carriages, having set down their passengers at the north side within the tower will have to proceed through a long dark tunnel some 165 feet long, unlit and hardly wide enough for the state carriage."

This aspect of the State Opening of Parliament is not one which is witnessed by great crowds. Subsequent events proved that Barry's revised arrangements are satisfactory. On the occasion of the first State Opening by King Edward VII the coronation coach was used and found its way safely through the tunnel.

Sudeley's remedy was the revival of the Commissioners, but they would not have been in direct communication with the architect. They would remain answerable to the Woods and Forests who would refer to the Commissioners for advice on any alterations which the architect proposed. This procedure he maintained would have protected the Office, and the Commissioners would have been prevented from making idle objections.

The result of all his labours was the creation of the Prince's Chamber between the Victoria (Royal) Gallery and the Peers' Chamber. Without the Prince's Chamber life in their Lordship's House would have been somewhat bleak, with only the Victoria Gallery in which to converse when not at work in the Chamber. The Prince's Chamber is a useful and congenial meeting place, the very centre of activity when their Lordships are sitting. The Royal Gallery is a useful overflow but of such vast dimensions as to be hardly a congenial place for the conduct of business.

Lord Sudeley concludes with the strongest plea "that the proposal for inclosing entirely New Palace Yard should not be proceeded with. Doubtless the intended elevations would do credit to the Architect who designed them; but, however imposing they may be, they can be no compensation for the loss of the open space; besides which, their grandeur and effect would be lost, unless seen at a proper distance, which can only be secured by removing the greater part of Parliament Street. Far too little attention is ever paid to situation by those who build. Beautiful perspective drawings are given from situations from which the work, when completed, can never be seen. Hence many of the disappointments and mortifications which too frequently attend those who meddle with brick and mortar."

As a result of Sudeley's broadside and intense committee activity in the Lords, involving no less than five sessions with Barry, the Prince's Chamber was created. The new arrangement by which the Sovereign passed from the Robing Room in the south front through the Victoria Gallery and the Prince's Chamber to the House of Lords in the Robes of State and wearing the Imperial Crown found particular favour with the influential Sir Robert Peel. It is an arrangement which has enabled more persons to witness the State Opening of Parliament than any other plan by Barry. Sudeley's 700 feet long processional route would have been used only occasionally and would have involved the sacrifice of the whole of the principal floor of the west front and much else besides.

Barry's encounter with the Lords aroused the interest of the Commons who immediately (May 1844) set up a committee chaired by Lord Lincoln, the First Commissioner of Woods and Works. Four sessions with Barry exonerated him as far as they were concerned. Whilst recognising the need to press on with the works they were anxious lest premature occupation of unfinished rooms should lead to an unsatisfactory final result. Committee rooms in the east (River Front), were brought into use in 1846 although they were in an unfinished condition. Lord Lincoln's attitude was that the architect should not be interfered with, but should proceed with the job as best he could, within the financial constraints placed upon him.

The Lords returned to the field. Between May and August 1844 they cross-examined Grissell, the contractor, Dr. Reid and Lord Lincoln. Nothing of great significance emerged from the meetings though their examination of Dr. Reid might have been more useful had they discovered that his demands for space for his system would wipe out all the space beneath the two Houses which Barry had intended to use as arcades for carriages in waiting, the nineteenth century equivalent of parking space. Barry, of course had not intended that the Westminster carriage horses should become in any

*Queen Victoria returning from the House of Lords after the opening of Parliament, by Joseph Nash.*

way involved with his original system of heating and ventilation. They would, however have been an added hazard to the later modification.[12]

In the public debate which followed the Parliamentary activity, Barry found considerable support. *The Illustrated London News* called him "the only directing mind in the whole business." *The Times* on the whole supported Barry. They had little good to say about Reid - "Aerial Guy Fawkes" as he was dubbed.

The Lords eventually realised that their Chamber was unlikely to be completed so long as Reid had any responsibility for its services. They

*The entrance to the House of Lords as proposed by Thomas Hopper.*

eventually came to the conclusion that he was the only "impediment to the preparation of the New House of Lords, for the commencement of the session of 1847." That was the end of Reid in the Lords.

In the Commons where the Doctor had some support, the First Commissioner, Lincoln, was induced to agree to arbitration by three experts, Michael Faraday, Robert Stephenson and Andrew Graham. The result was inconclusive and Reid continued to have responsibility for the Commons.

On the 16th January 1840, Barry had received a letter informing him that the Office of Woods and Forests had placed "the ventilation of the Houses of Parliament in charge of Dr. Reid, I am, on behalf of the Board, to desire that Dr. Reid may receive from you, from time to time, as the architect of the building, such assistance as he may require in regard to the plans which have been prepared under your inspection for his use, and that generally, in order to second as much as possible the objects which have induced the Government to select Dr. Reid for the superintendence of this important service, you will, in all matters of detail connected with the structure and arrangement of the new buildings, afford him every requisite facility and assistance in carrying it into effect."

The committee then set off with Barry on a tour of the New Palace. They wanted to know which parts of the structure Dr. Reid had required for his purposes as distinguished from those "which he has since added to his requisition." Barry replied that without plans and a mass of documentation he could not specify but he told them that the solidity of the building had been much affected by Reid's requirement. "Here has been a foundation cut through, which is 15 feet in width, to get those holes" (showing the

*The river front of the Hungarian Parliament building (1909).*

*A photograph taken by Sir Benjamin Stone M.P. of the coronation coach of King Edward VII.*

same). Lord Palmerston, pointing to certain round holes in the room asked whether they were for ventilation.

At the next session on the 10th of March David Boswell Reid, Esq., M.D. was examined. "Will you state to this Committee at what period you were first communicated with by Her Majesty's Government in respect to an improved system of warming and ventilating the New Houses of Parliament?"

"I was sent for in 1835, after a letter addressed to me by Lord Sudeley, then Mr. Hanbury Tracy, who, in that letter, made inquiries in respect to what he had heard in reference to my classroom at Edinburgh, connected with sound and ventilation."

Reid had replied in general terms and this had resulted in an official summons. "A kind of summons to attend the Committee on acoustics and

*The New Houses of Parliament under construction in June 1842.*

ventilation of the House of Commons in 1835." Reid's first official appointment "authorising you to take measures for the introduction of your improved system of ventilation and warming of the New Palace had come in January 1840." But previously to that there were letters, which, though not officially recorded, were in fact those in which the real business was transacted. Reid stated that the first of such letters was addressed by Mr. Barry to the Earl of Bessborough, then Lord Duncannon, "in which my name was mentioned in connection with the warming, lighting and ventilation of the New Houses."[13] This letter was the very one in which Barry had advised against employing Reid. Reid's official letter of appointment from the Office of Woods dated 24th January 1840, when interpreted by any reasonable man, set out with some clarity how the ventilator must work with the architect.

Reid's reply accepting the appointment although mostly concerned with his domestic arrangements contains the words "I hereby agree to undertake the duties therein specified according to the terms proposed"... Reid's replies to a further hundred questions returned again and again to his complaint about not having adequate plans and drawings. When asked how he had responded with drawings to match those of the architect he invariably slid away from this issue.

There had been a proposal to store Parliamentary records in the roof and Reid made much of the potential dangers from fire. "The records being under the roof exposed to 121 degrees temperature in the sun, and being largely surrounded by ventilating flues"... Reid admitted that the central ventilating tower had been his idea.

Reid claimed that the architect had been responsible for all flues built into walls and that he had required none. The committee survived a session of 125 questions to Reid. The pace quickened and two days later he was recalled. This time he waxed eloquent on the virtues of metal. It appeared that his proposals for a New House of Commons in 1836 had indeed contained "metallic pendants and metallic cornices, this metallic apparatus being introduced where wood is generally employed." Metallic bookcases were favoured for the Library. The committee then buried itself in intricate technicality with Reid calling in aid his experience at Buckingham Palace. It transpired that some sixteen persons were likely to be required to work Reid's system which was to ventilate 767 different places within the Palace. Returning to the subject of fireproofing Reid repeated his metallic theory. "Now my notion of the things is, that there should be nothing but metallic ceilings, metallic roofs, metallic floors, metallic tables, metallic chairs; and that in a permanent building, such as the Houses of Parliament, there are means for increasing, to a vast extent, by cement and metal, that which would be the available method of preventing the destruction of all kinds of important documents, as well as furniture. In the ceilings of the House of Peers there are twenty-five tons of wood."

Reid claimed that if the wood burned, the brick and iron fireproof floors would fall apart and all would be consumed. His remedy was that everything that could be made of iron should be. "Do you think that tables and chairs should be made of iron?"

"Most certainly; everything that can be so constructed should be of cement, or a non-combustible material in a true fireproof building."

Lord Palmerston, who had previously indulged in some probing questions, was now inspired to ask Reid whether he knew that in Scotland "people clean a chimney by setting the soot on fire?" Reid said this was all right if the chimney was properly constructed. This question was merely a warm-up for a body blow. "What is the largest building to which you are aware that any systematic arrangement for ventilation in conformity with your principle has hitherto been applied?"

"There is none where it is completed so largely as the Houses of Parliament. There is a building to which it is now being applied in Liverpool"... (St. George's Hall).

"Are you not aware that this plan for ventilating St. George's Hall at Liverpool has failed, or has been abandoned?"

"It is impossible; it could never have failed, because it has never been built."

On the subject of the Lords Chamber Reid complained that Barry had not supplied him with details of the finishings and furnishings. It is perhaps Reid's answer to question 1005 which resulted in his exclusion from the Lords. "What impeded your progress, therefore, was the remainder of the details of the finishings?"

"Not alone; it was that, in so far as was dependent on an adjustment between Mr. Barry and me. His last words are, as far as I recollect, 'You have not detailed the places for your fountains.' Then I say, in regard to that, 'How can I detail everything? I must know what you will permit. Will you meet me on the subject? Will you give it here or there; or how much will you give here, and how much there?' He may give me one side for a fountain of air, and it may be useless for the quantity of restricted air; he may give me another side, but it may not suit me."

"Then you did not, in answer to that requirement of Mr. Barry, send to him any detailed plans of the air fountains you propose to construct?"

"I have not done so; there have been so many things to attend to, it is impossible to overtake everything."[14]

The foregoing extracts from the proceedings of the Select Committees of the two Houses are but a small part of what Barry had to endure as he struggled to complete first the Lords and later the Commons. The diary of his son Charles provides an intimate picture of the effect that so much often wasted effort had upon the architect.[6]

On the 26th of March Pugin had set out for Boulogne and by the day of the first sitting of their Lordships in the Chamber (which owed so much to his genius) he was happily immersed in the Middle Ages at Carcassonne. He proceeded thence to Rome where he dined with Prince Doria on the 28th and had an audience with the Pope on May 1st. From Florence, Pugin went to Venice for a fortnight of intense heat. The next month he was back in medieval France but fell very ill with fever at Troys. At Reims he was better, returning to Ramsgate on the 16th of June and thence to London.

On his first full day in London he and Charles Barry showed Mr. and Mrs. March Phillipps round the Houses of Parliament.

Alfred Barry, the younger son of Sir Charles, echoed his brother's description of the House of Lords and defined Pugin's part in its decoration. "In the gorgeous decorations of the House not a little was due to the work and the influence of Mr. Pugin, which added a stimulus hardly needed, to the architect's own love of enrichment. The carved and metalwork and generally the purely ornamental details, were designed by Mr. Pugin, under Mr. Barry's direction, and subject to his frequent alterations; the painted windows were not only designed by Mr. Pugin but carried out under his superintendence, the architect only stipulating for a sufficient amount of white glass to produce the jewelled effect he admired in many ancient windows. ...The ceiling was a subject of much consideration; Mr. Barry wished to produce as much as possible the effect of solid gold, the enrichment of colour being purely subsidiary. His notion always was that decoration, if begun, should be thoroughly carried out, and that only by failure in this respect, and by partiality of decoration, was the effect of tawdriness produced.

The House of Lords he considered as not a mere place of business, not even a mere House of Lords at all, but as the Chamber in which the sovereign, surrounded by the Court summoned to the Royal presence the three estates of the realm. He thought, therefore, that it should partake of royal magnificence, and lavished upon it all the treasures of decoration."[15]

Pugin himself defined his responsibilities in a letter to *The Builder*, 6th September 1845, headed "Decorations of the New House of Lords."

"I think it incumbent on me, in justice to Mr. Barry, to state that I am engaged by him and by him alone, with the approval of the Government, to assist in preparing working drawings and models for all his designs of all the woodcarvings and other details of the internal decorations, and to procure models and drawings of the best examples of ancient decorative art of the proper kind, wherever they are to be found, as specimens for the guidance of the workmen in respect of the taste and feeling to be imitated, to engage with artists and the most skilfull workmen that can be procured in every branch of decorative art, and to superintend personally the practical execution of the works upon the most economical terms, compatible with the nature of it and its most perfect performance. I do not do anything whatever on my own responsibility, all models and working drawings being prepared for Mr. Barry's designs, and submitted to him for his approval or alteration, previous to their being carried into effect. My occupation is simply to assist in carrying out practically Mr. Barry's own designs and views in all respects."

Late in 1846 Pugin, exhausted by this task at Westminster, suffered from an eye disease and for the next five years his health was precarious. The effect of anxiety and overwork on an unstable and intensely creative temperament proved fatal and in September 1852 Pugin died, aged forty.

The triumphant opening of the House of Lords in 1847 was accompanied by much achievement elsewhere. We are fortunate to have eloquent, contemporary descriptions, accurate in their architectural details and filled with all the enthusiasm with which an admiring public viewed the emerging New Palace.

*A water colour showing the proposed central tower of the Palace. The painting was presented to Tsar Nicholas I by Barry.*

Queen Victoria's own version of her visit to the new Lords Chamber shows that Her Majesty missed none of the finer architectural points or Parliamentary nuances. The First Commissioner of Works had the honour of dining at Buckingham Palace that evening. But it was Lord Spencer who sat next to the Queen. Queen Victoria's Journal for 14th April 1847 reads:

"Another cold day. The children's coughs and colds much better. Again went to the riding school. At twelve we went to see the new House of Lords, which is unfortunately to be opened without the House of Commons, as the Lords are so impatient to get into it. The building is indeed magnificent, in Gothic style, very elaborate and gorgeous. Perhaps there is a little too much brass and gold in the decorations, but the whole effect is very dignified and fine. The throne is very handsome and the proportions of the Chamber or Hall splendid. A Gallery runs round it, into which we went and there is also a Reporter's Gallery. Over this there is a very fine fresco by Dyce, representing the Baptism of Ethelbert by St. Augustine. There are still five more frescoes to come, as well as statues in bronze of the Magna Charta Barons. The lobby is very pretty, with tessalated pavement and stained glass windows, as well as the Royal Ante Chamber, into which we first entered... We took a short walk in the afternoon, and it was bitterly cold. We played etc. The Duchess of Sutherland, Lord and Lady Spencer and Lord Morpeth dined. Lord Spencer sat next to me."[16]

Barry's friend, John Wolfe, maintained that Barry himself was disappointed in the the House of Lords. "Barry intended that the House of Lords should be as beautiful as art could make it. It was to be the centre of attraction – the gem of the Palace. But after all the thought, labour and cost bestowed upon it, B was disappointed. Its effect as a fine hall was ruined by the gallery. B looked upon all galleries with the horror of an Ecclesiologist – but here was a monstrosity that would disfigure a meeting house. B would walk up his House with pleasure – but the return was a trial."[17]

*The River Front*

"The most important façade yet complete is that towards the river or the east front, it is in all 940 feet in length, of which the projecting portions in wings at the extremities are each 120 feet in length, leaving between them a fine paved terrace overlooking the water 700 feet long and 33 feet wide. This façade may be said to consist of five portions, the centre which has three stories above the ground floor, and the north and south curtains which each have two stories only above that level, while the wing towers (the beautiful design of which is best seen from the river) are the most lofty portions. The portion of this front which is between the wing towers is composed of bays, separated by hexagonal buttresses, richly panelled the entire height of the building, terminated in hexagonal open worked pinnacles, carrying gilt vanes. The carved decorations have as is the case throughout the building, historical significance; the rich band of carving between the windows of the principal and one-pair floors is composed of a succession of the Royal Arms of England in each reign, from William I to our present Sovereign. These arms have their appropriate supporters under each dynasty, except in those which precede the time of Richard II, when there were no heraldic supporters to the royal coat, and this want is supplied by human figures, expressing in some way the leading events which mark the various reigns, as for instance, the figure supporting the arms of Rufus bears a model of Westminster Hall, as being founded by him. The supporters to that of Edward III are figures of St. George and the Dragon, the order instituted by him - the heirs in like manner. The bank below the principal floor window has inscriptions bearing the date of each Sovereign's accession and decease - while the panels on each side of the coat of arms have sceptres and labels with appropriate badges and inscriptions. In the parapet of each bay is a niche with the figure of an angel bearing a shield. The carved panels to the oriel windows, of which there are six in this front have the coat of arms of the present Sovereign, which also appears ending the series, indicating that the building was erected in her reign. The wing towers are most harmoniously grouped together, and rise considerably above the rest of the roofs; at each angle are rich octagonal stone pinnacles, while the towers themselves are surmounted with steep roofs, with elaborately perforated ornaments in iron at the angles and tops, reminding one of the steep picturesque roofs of some of the chateaux and belfry towers on the Continent, especially in the Low Countries.

Three horizontal banks of decorative carving (exclusive of the quatrefoil frieze under the cornice of the Towers) are carried immediately below the cills of the windows on each storey above the Ground Floor. The first bank below the first or Principal Floor windows contains, in Tudor characters, the royal initial letters and appropriate mottoes of the three kingdoms, corresponding to the several devices carved upon the coats of arms and shields in the bank above, viz. - *Victoria Regina feliciter regnans - Dieu et mon droit - Nemo me inpune lacesset - Quis separabit,* etc.

The second bank running through the oriel windows contains the arms of Her present Majesty (Queen Victoria), flanked by panels containing shields, with the letters "V. R.", and surmounted by a helmet and lion crest. The remainder of this band between the Towers contains crowns over shields, bearing the crosses and emblematic flowers, and in the panels on either side the sword and sceptre crossed by ribands with mottoes, and entwined by stems of foliage, flowers etc., appropriate to the three kingdoms.

The third band above the oriels and windows of the Second Floor consists of a series of panels containing crowns and badges, with the mottoes and shields, bearing the devices assumed by the various Sovereigns since the Conquest.

On either side of the upper windows of the Towers are ranged shields, with the rose, shamrock, and thistle; and above, on small pedestals, in niches formed out of the parapet, are placed the supporters of the Royal Arms,

*The south wing towers of the New Houses of Parliament, J. Johnson (1849).*

holding shields, with the letters "V. R." entwined by a cord and tassels. Similar niches in the parapet of the bays between the Towers contain angels, with shields bearing the royal monogram.

The pinnacle in the centre of the front of each of the Towers above the parapet is recessed, so as to form a niche, with projecting canopy, and contains a statue of Queen Victoria, as the Sovereign in whose reign the present Palace is being erected.

The south flank of the Towers is divided into two bays by a square projecting buttress running up the entire height, and crowned by a pinnacle; in which are ranged, in six niches, with canopies, statues of the Patron Saints of the United Kingdom, together with St. Peter and St. Paul, as the representatives of the two metropolitan churches."[18]

*Construction Methods*

"But an architect's work is not purely artistic. The construction both of the New Palace itself and of the scaffolding used in its erection, taxed heavily scientific knowledge and ingenuity. In fact, the whole timber or framed scaffolding, with travellers, by which a stone, perhaps elaborately carved, could be raised from the ground, and placed in its proper position, had seldom, if ever, before been employed on so large a scale. The constructional difficulties introduced by the need of preservation of old buildings, and of piecemeal occupation of the new ones, were great."[19]

To the words of Alfred Barry should be added the words of Charles Barry Junior. His paper, read to the R.I.B.A. on June 15, 1857 contains detailed drawings of the ingenious contrivances by which the three great towers were built.[20] On the subject of the scaffolding he is less explicit "although much anxious thought and contrivance have been required, the result has perhaps been a mere pencil drawing, or a verbal direction, illustrated at the moment with a piece of chalk on the nearest wall." One feature however was common to whatever scaffold was in use. The tramways on the scaffolding and the hoists which they carried enabled blocks of stone, in many cases weighing four or five tons, to be raised and transported and accurately placed in position without damage or danger. This meant that an elaborately carved piece, the product of many skilled hours of work on the ground, could be lowered into its final resting place with every expectation that no further finishing would be required. Such was the ingenuity of the scaffold and its machinery that even the internal decorative masonry could be placed in position as easily as that of the exterior.

The internal masonry of the Central Hall as far as the springing of the vault was erected in similar manner. Young Barry was unable to produce details of the centering upon which the octagonal stone vaulting had been erected but he remembered that it contained several novel and peculiar arrangements. Fortunately we have young Charles's personal description of the work on the Central Tower as it proceeded upward from the vault. "It will be seen that the central lantern is supported upon a cone starting from the springing of the vaulting; a powerful chain bond is here introduced, by means of which the resolution of the entire weight of the stone lantern on to the base of this cone is effected, which of course adds to the security of the groining itself. The cone, which was constructed of brickwork and afterwards cased with the stone tabling, was itself a work of some difficulty. The arrangements of the elaborate system of ventilation introduced into the building by Dr. Reid, which had reference to the central tower as the point of ultimate extraction of all the smoke and vitiated air, required that very large orifices of communication with the surrounding roofs should be maintained through the base of the lantern, as well as into the lantern itself. It was therefore necessary to perforate the brick cone by large arched openings; the consequence was that the portions between them had to be built isolated from each other up to the spring of these openings, and were therefore obviously overhanging walls. As a second system of centring would have been very expensive, it was determined to attempt to build the cone by means of a trammel, only working round a centre pivot in such a manner that the inner surface or interior should be kept true all round. Ties of chain bond of iron were introduced at the points shown, to prevent all chance of the work afterwards spreading outwards at the foot when subjected to pressure; and the whole was successfully and rapidly accomplished. The leaning portions, which looked very insecure to the unpractised eye, were duly connected by arches turned through the whole thickness of the wall, and connected with iron struts, as shown; the system of the trammel answered perfectly, and the brick cone or base for the stone lantern was completed (without the accidents confidently predicted by many) and, perfectly true in form and plan, was ready to receive the further works about the latter end of 1841."

When it came to the Clock Tower, Barry Junior explained, "the principal peculiarity of the scaffolding used in this and in the Victoria Tower is, that it rose with the building; being, if I may so express it, self-raising and self-adjusting. The other great peculiarity of all the tower scaffolds consisted in the employment of steam power to hoist, the steam-engine being placed at the top, and close to its work, instead of at the bottom, where it would generally be fixed. In the erection of the Clock Tower the stone and other materials were raised inside from the ground to the summit, so that, there being no appearance externally of a scaffold or other contrivances, the tower seemed to grow, as it were, by some inherent vital power. From the plan it will be seen that there is in the interior a shaft, intended to be eventually occupied by the staircase and a lift-machine: advantage was taken of this shaft to raise all the materials by the machinery."[20]

Barry explained the mechanics of the scaffolding of the Clock Tower in detail and claimed that it cost about £700. "It raised about 30,000 cubic feet of stone, about 300 rods of brickwork, besides many tons of iron and other matters. It did all this so quickly and continuously, that there was no excuse for the workmen, either below or above, wasting time; while its manifest economy and precision of working need no further illustration.

At the Victoria Tower much the same principle of arrangement, as far as regards the position of the steam engine and the rising frame work of the whole, was made use of through the much larger dimensions of the structure caused some important differences. The internal diameter of the tower is fifty-one feet, and over to over of the turrets, seventy feet. In the first place, a strong trussed frame, over the whole area of the tower on plan, had to be constructed to carry all the machinery, and sufficiently stiff to bear being raised at once by the screw power without any racking or straining, and consequent disturbance in the position of the apparatus upon it."

It was a source of satisfaction that no accident happened during the erection of the scaffolding, in spite of a hurricane.

"One very severe trial was experienced when the former tower was raised to the height of nearly 200 feet. The workmen, on leaving work, had omitted their usual custom of lashing one of the radiating travellers, to prevent the wind by any chance moving them. A hurricane arose during the night and lasted the following day, and a violent gust acting upon the radiating arms moved them round on the circular rail, and blew them together with terrific violence, as may be supposed, when it is mentioned that they were fifty feet in length. The report of the blow as heard at a great distance, and those engaged on the work fully anticipated that the framing must have been shattered; but when they ventured up to examine, as soon as the wind abated, it was most satisfactory to find that no trace of damage was to be seen, the whole arrangement having proved amply stiff and strong to resist the concussion."

Charles Barry concluded his paper with a reference to his father's zest. "Into all these difficulties Mr. Barry himself fully entered. He felt a positive pleasure in the expedience by which they were to be met; and in the invention of such expedience he was full of resources, and bold even to the verge of rashness."[20]

### *The House of Lords*

"Without doubt the interior of the House of Lords is the finest specimen of Gothic civil architecture in Europe; its arrangements and decorations being perfect. Entering from the Peers' Lobby, the effect of the House is magnificent; the length and loftiness of the apartment, its finely proportioned windows, with the gilded and canopied niches between them; the Throne, glowing with gold and colours; the richly carved panelling which lines the walls; the roof, most elaborately painted; its massy beams and sculptured ornaments, and pendants richly gilded; all unite in forming a scene of Royal magnificence.

The House of Lords is ninety feet in length, forty in breadth, and of the same height. In plan, the House is divided into three parts; the northern and southern being each considerably smaller than the centre, which constitutes the body or floor of the House, wherein are the Woolsack, Clerks' Table etc.; on either side the seats for the Peers, in rows. The southern end is the part of the House in which the Throne is placed, and is also for the accommodation of distinguished foreigners, and others. The northern has the Bar for its boundary and is for the service of the House of Commons, when summoned to the Upper House to attend Her Majesty or the Royal Commissioners; and where, also, counsel stand during judicial investigations. The House is lighted by twelve lofty windows, six on each side, filled with stained glass, representing the Kings and Queens - both Consort and Regnant - of the United Kingdom, standing under canopies of elaborate design. At both ends of the apartment are three archways, corresponding in size and mouldings with the windows; and on the surface of the wall, within the arches, are spaces for the frescoes. Those over the Throne are 'The Baptism of St Ethelbert' painted by Mr Dyce; 'Edward the Third conferring the Order of the Garter on the Black Prince' and the 'Committal of Prince Henry by Judge Gascoigne' by Mr. Cope; the three at the back of Strangers' Gallery are 'The Spirit of Religion' by Mr. Horsley, 'The Spirit of Chivalry' and 'The Spirit of Justice' by Mr. Maclise.

The archways at the northern end of the House are very deeply recessed, affording space for the Strangers' Gallery. Between the windows, the arches at the ends and in the corners of the House are niches, richly canopied; the pedestals within which are supported by demi-angels holding shields, charged with the armorial bearings of the Barons who wrested Magna Carta from King John, and whose effigies, in all eighteen, will be placed in the niches.[21]

The ceiling is flat, and is divided into eighteen large compartments; these are each again divided, by smaller beams, into four, having in their centres lozenge-formed compartments, deeply moulded. Different devices and symbols, carved, fill the lozenges, and all of them are gilded. Amongst the devices, and immediately over the Throne, is the Royal monogram, crowned, and interlaced by a cord, the convolutions of which are so arranged as to form loops at the corners; whilst similarly crowned and decorated, the monograms of the Prince of Wales and Prince Albert fill the lozenges over their respective seats. The cognizances of the White Hart, of Richard the Second; the Sun, of the House of York; the Crown, in a bush,

*The House of Lords lit by wall lights, by Joseph Nash (1851).*

of Henry VII; the Falcon, the Dragon, and the Greyhound, are in some of the lozenges; whilst the Lion passant of England, the Lion rampant of Scotland, and the Harp of Ireland, fill others. Sceptres and orbs, emblems of regal power, with crowns; the scales indicative of justice; mitres and croziers, symbols of religion; and blunted swords of mercy add their hieroglyphic interest: while crowns and coronets, and the ostrich plume of the Prince of Wales, form enrichments more readily understood, and equally appropriate. These devices are encircled by borders, in admirable intricacy; and all of them are most elaborate in workmanship. In the vacant corners, between the lozenges and the mouldings of the beams, the ceiling is painted of a deep blue, and surrounded by a redu border, on which are small yellow quatrefoils. Within the borders are circles, Royally crowned; and from them proceed sprays of roses, parallel to the sides of the lozenges. The circles contain various devices and shields: amongst the former are the rose of England, the pomegranate of Castile, the portcullis of Beaufort, the lily of France, and the lion of England; and in the latter are the fanciful armorial bearings of those counties which ages since composed the Saxon Heptarchy. Where the lozenges are filled with the mitre, the circles are gules, and charged with a cross; and issuing from the circle are rays, instead of sprigs of roses.[18]

These panels were painted on canvas applied to the woodwork above. Some of them were changed by having other devices pasted over the top of the first version. The vast majority were rescued from the decaying woodwork and refixed to new panels in the great restoration of 1983.[22]

"The whole are gilded, and enriched by colour. The ceiling is, as may be inferred, most striking in its appearance; the massive tie beams, apparently of solid gold, rich as they are with that precious metal, and the minute carving which fills up the lozenge-formed compartments, aided by the colours of the devices, painted on the surface of the ceiling produce a most imposing and gorgeous effect."

Under the windows the walls of the House are covered with oak panelling, of a varied pattern. In alternate panels are beautifully carved pillars, crowned with a small bust of one of the Kings of England. The pillars in the southern division of the House have pedestals affixed to them, on which are lions, serjeant, holding shields emblazoned with the arms of England. Above the panels, between each bust, runs the inscription, *God save the Queen*, in open-worked letters of the Tudor character. A canopy springs from this, the surface of which is gilded, and decorated with the armorial bearings of the various Lord Chancellors of England, from Adam, Bishop of St David's, in 1377, to the present Chancellor, Lord Cottenham."[18]

The series was continued until all the spaces were filled. Then the series continued in the corridor leading from the Prince's Chamber to the top of the Peers' staircase. "These escutcheons present a remarkably rich and

*The interior of the House of Lords in 1847.*

unique decoration; and the variety of colours so displayed is very striking. The arms of the various Sovereigns under whom the Chancellors have held office, are also similarly painted.

At the northern end of the House, the episcopal arms fill the spaces of the canopy. The front of the cove, or canopy, is moulded, and at every space corresponding to the pillars of the panelling is a small carved pendant; above it is a lion's head in strong relief, and thence spring the standards to the brass railing of the Gallery. This railing is of simple but exquisite design. The standards are partly twisted, and between each runs a rail, supported by segments of arches." This gallery railing was the subject of much alteration in the course of its design. It was also the cause of a reprimand signed by two Ministers.

"The centre of the southern end of the House is occupied by the Throne, and on either side of it, below the Gallery, is a doorway leading into the Victoria Lobby (Prince's Chamber).

The Throne is elevated on steps, the central portion having three, and the sides two steps, covered with a carpet of richest velvet pile. The ground colour of the carpet is a bright scarlet, and the pattern on it consists of roses and lions, alternately. A gold-coloured fringe borders the carpet." (The present version of this carpet has lost much of the sharpness of the original design.)

"The canopy to the Throne is divided into three compartments; the central one, much loftier than the others, is for her Majesty; that on the right hand (as if seated on the throne) for the Prince of Wales, and that on the left for Prince Albert (i.e. the King's or Queen's Consort). The back of the central compartment is panelled in the most exquisite manner. The three lowest tiers have lions passant of England, carved and gilded, on a red ground; and above them is a wide panel, arched and enriched with quatrefoiling, are the Royal Arms of England, surrounded by the Garter, with its supporters, helmet and crest, and an elaborate mantling, forming a rich and varied background. The motto *Dieu et mon Droit* is on a horizontal band of a deep blue tint. Above the brattishing is a series of five panels, with ogee arches. The crests of England, Scotland, Ireland and Wales, richly carved and gilded, fill the panels. The ceiling is flat, divided into many small squares. In the centre is the monogram V. R. surrounded by a border beautifully designed and carved. The flat surfaces of the ceiling are enriched by stars painted on them. As before mentioned, the overhanging canopy of the central division projects considerably before the sides, and is supported by spandrils rising from octagonal pillars, having small roses and fleur-de-lis wrought in trellis-work, with the most delicate execution, upon their several sides. The capital of these pillars are peculiarly beautiful, having a coronal form, with floreated enrichment. The spandrils are enriched with quatrefoil tracery, and in their angles are representations of St George and the Dragon, beautifully executed."

*A detail of the ceiling in the House of Lords.*

"The panelling at the sides, on either hand of the Chair of State, consists of two rows of open-worked arches, with elaborate tracery, and above them other panels filled with floreated enrichments of the most exuberant fancy.

Her Majesty's State Chair is particularly splendid in its enrichments; in general outline it is similar to the chair in which the Sovereigns of England have been wont to sit at their coronations, but in detail it differs widely from its plain prototype. The legs of the Chair, resting upon four lions couchant, have pinnacled buttresses on each side, those at the back being, of course, considerably higher than the front ones. The arms are boldly moulded, and in the sunken panels beneath them are lions passant. On moulded capitals, above the pinnacles to the back legs, a lion and unicorn are seated holding scrolls. The back of the Chair is gabled, of lofty pitch; and within it, in a circle, is a quatrefoiled ornament, of eight points, having, in the centre, the monogram V. R. entwined by a cord. A broad border surrounds the square part of the back of the Chair, on which are, alternately, large and brilliant egg-shaped pieces of rock crystal, and lions with quatrefoils enamelled. The addition of crystals as enrichments to the Throne is a peculiarly happy idea; the effect, the sparkling brilliancy they impart, being peculiarly striking. Within this border are the Royal Arms of England, worked in embroidery on velvet.

The State Chairs for the Prince of Wales and Prince Albert, are exactly alike in form and general details, the only variations being in the embroidery on the velvet backs; and in the monograms. The backs are circular-headed. The velvet backs are most magnificent specimens of embroidery, and in design command unqualified praise, ornament and appropriateness being so happily blended."[18]

This was the original scheme. The large chair or throne is the one which is normally kept in the Chamber. An additional very slightly smaller chair or throne was made by King Edward VII's order for Queen Alexandra and this is brought in by The Lord Great Chamberlain when required at the State Opening of Parliament. The Prince of Wales's Chair has had the embroidery altered to a Prince's coronet. The original made for Prince Albert left the Palace but was recently retrieved by the National Heritage Memorial Fund. It would be possible to restore the matching pair of chairs to their original design and to install them in the Chamber thus recreating the original scheme. There are nineteenth century views of the Lords in session in which the single throne and the pair of chairs are displayed without covers. At the present time it is customary to have the throne covered unless a Royal Commission is taking place.

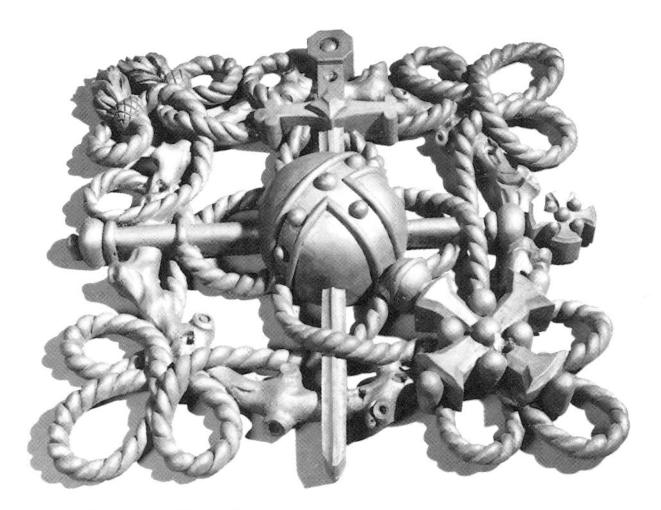

*A detail of the ceiling in the House of Lords.*

"The panelling is alike in both compartments, the lowest row containing fanciful bands, with rich foliage interwoven: the second and third series quatrefoils; and the fourth richly traceried ogee arches. Within the quatrefoils P. W. and P. A., respectively, are carved and gilded, relieved by a deep blue background. The arches in the upper row have shields of arms helmeted and crested with Royal crowns. Tall arched panels display the armorial bearings of the Prince, in gold and colours, surrounded by the Garter, and having crowns above them. On blue labels, under the arms, are the respective mottoes, *Ich Dien* and *Treu und Fest*, in slightly raised letters. The arched coves are each divided into four panels by enriched ribs, the two central panels containing shields helmeted and mantled, in which, in the Prince of Wales's Canopy, are the armorial ensigns of the Principality, and the Royal Arms of England; and in Prince Albert's are the escutcheons of Saxe Coburg Gotha and England; the two outer panels have lions and unicorns sitting, and holding banners displayed, on which are the triple ostrich feathers on an azure ground, and a red cross on a white ground, respectively."

The evolution of this, the central feature of the grandest room in the New Palace was a long, complicated story. Undoubtedly much of the detail and the quality of the workmanship is due to the influence of Pugin but the final version of the composition is undoubtedly Barry's. Many early drawings, including one by Pugin executed in about 1842 when he was neither at work on the estimates drawings nor re-employed in an official capacity in charge of the woodcarving had a distinctly ecclesiastical flavour. Pugin continually hankered after a truly Gothic outline for the whole composition often embodying an ogee arched centrepiece. One of Pugin's last attempts at an ecclesiastical approach amounted to a Gothic version of Soane's work in the old House of Lords for George IV. Pugin won the day over the design of the two chairs which flank the original throne. The whole complex history has been brilliantly unravelled by Alexandra Wedgwood in "The Throne in the House of Lords and Its Setting."[23]

"In the centre at the northern end of the House is the Reporters' Gallery. The Strangers' Gallery is above the Reporters'; and, as before mentioned, is placed in the recesses of the great arches.

The Reporters' Gallery is most convenient, both in its arrangement and ease of access, the comfort of the gentlemen of the Press having been well studied.

From the floor of the House, the appearance of this Gallery is eminently beautiful. It projects several feet from the wall, and is supported by five arches, three in the front, and one at each end; the central arch in the front being of wider span then the others; the compartments over the centre door having within them the coat armour of the Saxon, Norman, Plantagenet, Tudor, Stuart and Hanoverian houses painted on shields; whilst in the

*A coffer from a ceiling bay in the House of Lords.*

*The throne and chairs of State for the Prince of Wales and Prince Albert.*

compartments over the side door are the arms of the Archiepiscopal sees, and some of the Bishoprics, in continuation of the series of Episcopal arms, emblazoned at this end of the room.

The Bar is about nine feet wide and three deep; and each corner of the Bar is a post, having on its outer faces the monogram, V. R. within quatrefoiled circles. The angles of the posts are ornamented by moulding. The two inner posts of the Bar are crowned with small figures of the lion and unicorn holding shields; and the two outer are embattled. Affixed to the wall, on the right hand of the Bar, is the enclosed and elevated seat of the Usher of the Black Rod: it is panelled and decorated in corresponding style with the extreme ends of the Peers' seats, which have panels of extremely intricate treillage of vine, oak, rose and thistle patterns, beautifully sculptured and pierced, let into them. That on the left for Peers' eldest sons, who have the privilege of standing on the steps of the Throne. The extreme ends of the seats rise in steps, corresponding to the steps on which the seats are elevated, and at their corners are badges of some of the Royal Houses of England: the white hart, dragon, greyhound etc.

On each side of the House are two doors, one near either end, leading into corridors (lobbies). The doors are panelled, with open-worked arches in the upper portion, glazed with plate glass.

The corridors are very handsomely panelled, and ceiled with oak, extending the whole length of the House. Their appearance is singularly rich and effective, the warm colour of the panelling harmonising thoroughly with the stained glass and the rich blue of the carpet; the windows are square-headed, divided by mullions, and traceried. The glass is richly diapered; and the motto *Dieu et mon Droit*, in labels running diagonally, is many times repeated. In recesses opposite to the windows are seats cushioned and covered with red leather. In recesses, also, are branches for gas, and opposite the doors leading from the House, globe lights hang from the ceiling.

Two magnificent Candelabra of brass rise from the posts at the end of the Peers' seats. They are about twelve feet and a half high, and consist of a shaft, ornamented with a leaf pattern, and supported at the sides by short pillars, crowned with fleurs de lis; at about eight feet from the ground, the shaft has eight flying buttresses projecting from it; and from them, in curves, spring out branches, with sockets for lights. Above this series of lights, four others, of lesser dimensions, add to the general richness, and the whole is crowned by a single light, rising from the centre. The workmanship of these Candelabra is most elaborate, and worthy of their exquisite design."

The pair of candelabra on the Bar are shown in early views of the Lords Chamber. Their present whereabouts are unknown.

"There are two other beautiful specimens of Candelabra, of great richness of design, one on either side, a little in advance of the Throne." (An early view of the Lords shows a pair of table candelabra of similar design.)

"The seats for the Peers are covered with red morocco, and are extremely comfortable. There are four rows, each disposed in three ranges, so as to allow of free passage up the alleys between them.

The carpet is of deep blue, ornamented with roses in gold colour."[24] There has been a recent attempt to recreate this carpet. The colour used is not really a deep blue. It is questionable whether the "roses in gold colour" are of an appropriate size and spacing. No fragment of the original carpet having come to light, the 1980s design was based on a fragment of "Pugin" carpet found on a hassock in the church adjoining Leighton Hall (a house decorated by Crace in the Pugin manner). A Brussels weave carpet was worked up from this design. It is somewhat harsh and unyielding and fits ill up the steps in the Peers' Chamber. It might be considered appropriate to try a pile carpet of the correct colour and of a more authentic design at the next replacement. The view of the Duke of Wellington, speaking in the

Lords for the last time, shows the kind of carpet which probably existed and the two Nash views although not identical are both helpful.

The two earlier horizontal Nash views are of particular interest. The area shows the brackets round the walls arranged in pairs beneath each of the statues; they contained the Faraday gas burners. The other horizontal view shows the gas burners suspended from the ceiling which caused such havoc to the woodwork from the heat given out by them.

*Members of the House of Commons at the Bar of the House of Lords (1847).*

Contemporary with the opening, without ceremony, of the Peers' Chamber, the Prince's Chamber, Peers' Lobby, Libraries and Refreshment Rooms were first brought into use though some lacked their final embellishments. The Prince's Chamber never received the new Armada Tapestries and the Peers' Dining Room is as yet unadorned by the planned series of paintings. Landseer's "Monarch of the Glen" produced for this room never found its way into the Palace.

### *The Peers' Lobby*

"This is the principal entrance to the House of Lords, and the decorations, both architectural and pictorial, are most magnificent. In form it is square, each side being divided into one wide central and two smaller compartments.

The wide central compartments, on either side, have lofty arches, or doorways, of similar proportions and arrangement. The doorways on the east and west sides correspond with each other in detail, having quatrefoils in the spandrils, with the rose and portcullis in their centres. Above each arch is a series of six panels, separated by small buttresses with pinnacles: within them are painted the arms of the six different Royal lines who have swayed the English sceptre - the Saxon, Norman, Plantagenet, Tudor, Stuart and Hanoverian - each surmounted by a Royal Crown. Below each arch, and forming, as it were, a base to it, is a small panel, quatrefoiled, and bearing in its centre a shield, on which the initials of S.N.P.T.S.H. are painted, to correspond with the armorial bearings above them. The north doorway opens into the long corridor leading to the House of Commons; whilst the eastern and western open into corridors connected with the Libraries, and other rooms. The doors are of oak, the hinges and locks being of brass.

At each corner of the Lobby is a magnificent standard of brass, for gas lights. It consists of a shaft about twelve feet high, rising from a plinth, of Parian cement, to represent black marble; from each corner of which rises a small circular pillar, to support the shaft, crowned with a lion's head. Every part of the pillars and shaft is elaborately worked out in lozenges and hexagons with quatrefoils. The shaft is surmounted by a wrought coronal for the gas jets. The standards are gilded, relieved by gilt bronze." (These have long vanished from the Peers' Lobby. The remains of one was still in the basement within living memory).

"The East, West, and North Entrances, have recessed doorways, with arches of lower pitch, to correspond in general character with the South Door, but of much plainer design. Each recessed doorway is divided into three parts - a central and two narrow compartments. In the central one is the doorway; above it the wall is formed into three quatrefoil panels, having within them shields containing the arms of England, Scotland, and Ireland, royally crowned, and with blue labels, on which are Anglia, Scotia, and Hibernia alternately. The doors are of oak, richly panelled, and having plate-glass. Over the East and West Doors are clocks, the dials of which are beautifully enamelled in white, gold and blue. On either hand, in the thickness of the wall, are small doorways, leading to the galleries, and into small rooms."

The lower parts of the walls of the Peers' Lobby flanking each of the four doorways are presently mostly filled with unsightly frosted glass. Many Noble Lords have expressed the hope that this blemish could be remedied by installing appropriate stained glass.

"The South Door, opening into the House of Lords, corresponds, in its general form, with those on the other side of the Lobby, having six panels over it, embellished, like them, with the Royal armorial bearings; but in the details of the archway itself, the utmost magnificence is displayed. The arch is deeply moulded, whilst, at intervals, are Tudor roses, very boldly sculptured in alto relief, royally crowned. Recessed about four feet is another arch, but not of so lofty a pitch as the external one, and, within the mouldings of this, oak-leaves, gilded, are introduced. The space over the arch is divided into five compartments, the central one quatrefoiled, and bearing in its centre a shield of the Royal Arms of England, surmounted by a crown, and having the motto "*Dieu et mon Droit*" on a blue label; whilst, in the panels on either side, likewise quatrefoiled, are the lion and unicorn, each bearing a small banner: roses and thistles fill up the other panels, whilst shamrocks form a cresting round the arch; and as all parts are coloured and gilded, the effect is magnificent."

The massive brass gates under the south door are splendid specimens of intricate workmanship by Hardman; in weight one ton and a half. They are a finer and more truly Gothic achievement in metalwork than the gates of Henry VII's Chapel in Westminster Abbey from which they are derived. The tomb and gates of the Chapel have a strong Renaissance flavour. In the brass gates to the House of Lords Pugin has purified the style.

"The Encaustic Tiled Pavement is the finest specimen of the present day, the richness of the colours are particularly striking; these were manufactured by the firm of Minton, in Staffordshire. The marble margins of the floor, with that of the centre, is the produce of Derbyshire. The texture of these marbles is equal, in all respects, to the finest jasper: surrounding the centre is a very fine enamel, inlaid with brass, by Hardman. The stained glass windows represent the arms of the early families of the Aristocracy of England."

The fine enamelled brass star in the centre of the floor has worn away, not due to the passage of Pėers over it, but due to the millions of visitors who have come to admire the work.

*Lord Chancellor Campbell in the Peers' Lobby (1861), by R. Dudley.*

*The Peers' Libraries*

"This magnificent suite of rooms has been arranged with the utmost attention to the comforts and convenience of its occupants, every portion is complete and harmonious, and even every article of furniture in the rooms has been designed and manufactured in strict accordance with the architecture, indeed, we could quite fancy ourselves in one of those artistic and lordly apartments of olden time, once to be found in the old mansions of Henry's and Elizabeth's time, such as Nash or Cattermole delight to paint, but few of which known now remain in their pristine state. The walls are completely lined with bookshelves in dark oak, while, above the shelves is a frieze, the panels of which have the armorial bearings of the Chief Justices of England, arranged according to date. The ceiling is covered with paneling, harmoniously and elaborately painted, while the recessed windows giving a fine view of the Thames, are most inviting places for quiet study."

*The Peers' Refreshment Rooms*

"These refreshment rooms are situated on the north side of the Bishops' Corridor, leading from the Victoria Hall to the Peers' Libraries. The extreme length is 102 feet, width nineteen feet, and height fifteen feet. These are conveniently arranged, the one as a Dining Room the other as a Tea Room, the double screen in the centre, dividing and yet connecting these rooms, and which is so great an ornament to them, forms a waiting room for the attendants and gives access to the Kitchens, which are immediately under it. By means of a staircase connecting them and also by an hydraulic lift for raising and returning dishes, the utmost convenience and dispatch is ensured. The decorations of the ceiling are extremely simple, but in perfect harmony with the rooms, the panels being filled with a neat design, enriched with pomegranates, pines, and other fruit. At present the sides of the rooms have a crimson and gold paper, of elegant design; but it is proposed that the spaces will, at a future period, be decorated with paintings."

*The Victoria Lobby (Prince's Chamber)*

"It is impossible to conceive a more Regal apartment than is the Victoria Lobby, every detail being in such exquisite taste, and so gorgeously enriched by colour and gold; and in addition to its splendour, there is the prevailing feeling that the embellishments are all art, no hackneyed design or copied enrichment being introduced: all are new and beautiful. Indeed, we doubt whether even King Louis (Ludwig) of Bavaria, that art-loving monarch, ever imagined a more perfect specimen of art-decoration than this room will present, when all the architect's intentions are carried out. Even now, there is not a single decoration, or piece of furniture, which does not bear the stamp of genius and consummate taste; and when the pictorial beauties are added to its architecture, no room in Europe will exceed it in magnificence and appropriateness."[24]

*The Visit of Her Majesty*

"The fittings of the House, save a few minor points, were finished by Tuesday evening; and by Wednesday, at noon, the superb edifice was prepared for the inspection of her Majesty. Mr. Barry had received notice of the Royal visit, as had likewise Sir Augustus Clifford, the Gentleman Usher of the Black Rod; and Mr. Pulman, the Yeoman Usher, who likewise holds the office of Norroy King-at-Arms. At twelve o'clock, three of the Royal carriages arrived at the Queen's entrance, and her Majesty alighted, with her Ladies in Waiting, together with the Lord Chamberlain, the Lord Steward, &c. Prince Albert accompanied the Queen; and, it was evident to all present that her Majesty was hardly prepared for the graceful, chaste, and subdued magnificence of Mr. Barry's *chef-d'oeuvre*. The Queen inspected every portion of the House, and, says *The Times*, 'took up her station for a few minutes in almost every point of observation from which the House could be viewed, and from each successive Inspection appeared to derive unalloyed satisfaction; no term of praise seemed too strong to bestow upon the architect who designed and the artists who executed this superb portion of the edifice. The best proof of the interest and pleasure which it afforded to the Queen was to have been traced in the evident delight with which she traversed all the completed portions of the building. Over the throne there is a small private box - we know not how otherwise to describe it - in which, during the deliberations of the House, two or three ladies might ensconce themselves. Her Majesty very leisurely examined it, and for some time placed herself within it. This private view taken by the Queen lasted from twelve o'clock till about a quarter past one; when she departed in the same unpretending manner in which she arrived, without any state or ceremony.'

"The persons present were strictly limited to the attendants of the Court, to half a dozen officials connected with the House of Peers, to the architect, Mr. Barry, and to Mr. Grissell, of the house of Peto and Grissell,

*The Peers' refreshment room in 1854.*

who are the principal contractors for the works. Mr. Barry, as might be expected, attended her Majesty over every part of the building, and appeared to receive from the Queen every mark of the most gracious condescension."

*The Opening of the House*

"On Thursday, the magnificent Chamber in the new Palace of Westminster, appropriated as the place of meeting for the upper branch of the Legislature, was occupied for the first time by their Lordships. The

House assembled at half-past four o'clock; and, on our admission after prayers, we found a considerable number of Peers already present. The Lord Chancellor had taken his seat on the woolsack, and was in conversation with several noble Lords; while groups were standing here and there, surveying the noble apartment, and conversing with each other on the effect of its general appearance. Nearly a quarter of an hour elapsed before any business was attempted; all present being engrossed in the contemplation of the truly gorgeous spectacle which had opened before them.

Before five o'clock the number of members in attendance had become much greater than usual. The Duke of Wellington entered the House exactly at that hour, dressed in full military uniform, but wearing a close cloak above, and took his seat on the cross benches, nearly in the same relative position to the Woolsack as that ordinarily occupied by him in the old House. Lord Brougham arrived at about the same time as the noble Duke; and soon after, the Marquis of Lansdowne, Earl Grey, and other members of the Government took their seats on the Treasury Bench. Lord John Russell was for a short time in the body of the House, and, afterwards, also in the alley for Members of the House of Commons. The Episcopal Bench was much better filled than usual; and the steps of the Throne (which was uncovered) were crowded with the sons of Peers and distinguished strangers, while in the galleries allotted to the Members of the House of Commons a considerable body of gentlemen from that House were seated. The Strangers' Gallery had also its quota of visitors; and, as a matter of course, the gallery, set apart for the accommodation of reporters, was filled with the representatives of the press. It is not our part here to describe the appearance of the new House; but we may be permitted to say that but one feeling of admiration pervaded all who had the privilege of being present on this interesting occasion. There was, however, one drawback, and that a serious one: it became obvious, in the course of the proceedings, that the Chamber is but ill-fitted for the purposes of public speaking. There is not only difficulty of hearing, but there must be great difficulty in long sustaining the voice at an audible pitch.

Prayers were read by the Bishop of St. Asaph. Shortly after the Lord Chancellor had taken his seat on the Woolsack Lord Campbell rose for the purpose of addressing the House. His Lordship, however, was, by an accident, deprived of the honour of being the first person to bring forward any business in the new House, for, before he could commence his address, the Usher of the Black Rod announced a message from the House of Commons, whereupon Mr. Greene and other Members were called in and brought up several bills. This was the first public business transacted in the new House of Lords."[25]

*Old Westminster, by G. F. Robson (1808).*

# V

## Tribulation in the Commons:

## Hang the Architect

The opening of the new House of Lords with royal and general approval marked a high point in the building of the New Palace and the reputation of its architect. The Commons, by contrast, was a source of criticism and tribulation.

### *The 1848 Debate*

In the early years Barry had been unable to spend all the money voted by Parliament. It was unfortunate that the years which followed the opening of the Lords coincided with a period of industrial depression, Government weakness and Parliamentary moves to contain public expenditure. At the very moment when Barry needed extra money, to pay for works in progress and to meet new demands for additional accommodation he found his vote cut from £150,000 in 1847 to £100,000 in 1848. This resulted in the postponement of works which the new First Commissioner, Lord Morpeth, described as ornamental. This in turn resulted in the loss of craftsmen who had grown skilled in the Westminster work. Rumbles of dissatisfaction in the Commons culminated in the debate of the 2nd March 1848 in which Sir Robert Inglis moved for a "Select Committee on the New Palace and upon the present state of Westminster Bridge." He claimed to have the support and agreement of the Government.

"The additional expenses incurred in the erection of the New Houses of Parliament, and the delay that had taken place, had been greatly exaggerated in the House. When hon. Gentlemen complained that the buildings were now to cost £1,400,000, and that even after that there would be some yet undiscovered expenses which could not be calculated on until the bills should actually have come in, they should recollect that a large amount of expense had been incurred by the prosecution of works which formed no part of the original estimate." Such were, for instance, the river wall, the expenses of the architect and the surveyor, and others. He was surprised that such an outcry against the expenses incurred by works that gave so much employment should be raised by hon. Gentlemen who prided themselves upon being political economists and who should remember that not only a vast number of workmen obtained employment, but that about twenty-five per cent of the outlay was returned to the Exchequer in the shape of duties. As to the blame that had been cast upon Mr. Barry, he had never been a blind idolizer of that eminent gentleman; but he had never for one moment doubted his skill and extraordinary talent as an architect He only doubted whether there had been a sufficient check upon the alterations in the design, and upon the consequent expenditure.

The First Commissioner, Viscount Morpeth, accepted that the Government was responsible for the control of the expenditure and that the resources of his Department were inadequate. It was the Chancellor of the Exchequer who was really responsible. In defence of the building and its architect he produced a letter from W. H.Playfair, an architect celebrated for his Greek Revival buildings in Edinburgh. Playfair stated "I have examined the Houses of Parliament inside out; time and money could not have been better employed. I think Mr. Barry's genius is beyond the age he lives in; and depend upon it he will be immortal." There he might have left it. However, the House of Lords had to be defended, on the grounds that it was a place "wherein the Sovereign met the assembled estates of the land, the representatives of foreign powers, and the beautiful and the fair of our country, it should be worthy of the nation in point of splendour and decoration." Then he sank to the differences between Mr. Barry and Dr. Reid on the subject of ventilation. He believed that it was "his duty to prevent Parliament being trifled with, he had insisted upon Dr. Reid making specific drawings of the plans which he required to be carried into effect to complete his system of ventilation. These drawings had been furnished, and Mr. Barry, who professed his readiness to carry them into execution, was now engaged in making the necessary arrangements for giving effect to Dr. Reid's designs." Morpeth then found himself in difficulties over the frescoes. He ended by stating that the Government was not prepared to agree to a Commission "in its present shape."

Sir Benjamin Hall attacked the committee proposed by Inglis. "The

Government would screen themselves behind the decision of that committee because it had been arranged with their concurrence." Those who were proposed as members ought not to serve but appear as witnesses before a powerful Commission.

The Earl of Lincoln, First Commissioner in the previous administration, believed that his successor must accept responsibility for expenditure. However, he believed it might be desirable for some functionary to be appointed who should have the superintendence of the New Houses of Parliament. Lincoln was against "an amateur Commission of noblemen and gentlemen."

Inglis wound up the debate by pressing his motion for the committee. It had Government backing and he intended to insist on claiming a division. The Chancellor of the Exchequer, who had been criticized for being absent early in the debate, now attempted to rescue the Government. Although he thought the appointment of a dilletante Commission would only lead to expense he was prepared to recommend a Commission with adequate powers which would be a purely controlling body not allowed to recommend increased expenditure. He was inclined to think that the Government had better take upon themselves the appointment of such a Commission. Morpeth would now recommend such a course. In doing so Morpeth "thought the members of it ought to be very few indeed."

In the event a Commission of three under the Chairmanship of Sir John Fox Burgoyne, Inspector-General of Fortifications, with Thomas Greene M.P. (who had served the House with distinction as Chairman of Ways and Means) and Lord De Grey, President of the Institute of British Architects, a distinguished amateur of architecture, was appointed. They came too late into the field to have any real effect. They did for a time keep the heat off the Government but by the end of 1851 they recommended their own dismissal.

The existence of the Commission did not prevent the two Houses setting up committees of their own. The Commons on the 18th June 1850 created the Select Committee on the New House of Commons with Thomas Greene as Chairman. This powerful body, which contained the Chancellor of the Exchequer, Sir Robert Peel, Sir Benjamin Hall, Mr. Disraeli and Sir Robert Inglis amongst others, was busily at work making expensive improvements to Barry's Chamber at the very same moment that the luckless Commission (of which Greene was the leading member) was labouring to contain expenditure and secure the completion of the New Palace.

In the case of the Lords, the old House was completely gutted leaving only the bare walls and ceiling so that there was no going back. The Commons, in contrast, remained in the familiar and reasonably comfortable surroundings of the Temporary Chamber, from which they made

*View of the New Palace of Westminster from Lambeth Palace.*

experimental and critical visits to the splendid new room upon which Barry and Pugin had lavished so much care and skill. This resembled in feeling the more colourful Chamber of their Lordships of which many Members of the Commons were critical and some, no doubt, jealous. With its high, flat ceiling and graceful traceried windows, below which a narrow gallery ran along the sides, it could hardly have been a greater contrast in shape and in feeling to the Temporary Chamber.

The summer of 1850 was hot and there was nothing of particular importance to concern the House on the occasional Wednesday mornings when they debated in the new Chamber. No very serious effort was made to come to terms with the new surroundings. As the summer dragged on, no very definite conclusions were reached. The debate in the Temporary Chamber on the 2nd August was conducted against this background.

### *The Debate of August 2nd, 1850: the new House of Commons*

The Commons debate on August 2nd, 1850 was concerned with the proposed alterations to the Commons Chamber, estimated at £9,400. This sum was to provide for a new ceiling in which the sides sloped down to the transoms of the windows. The galleries were to be enlarged and alterations made to the lobbies.

The Select Committee had heard evidence from several eminent gentlemen but the results had not been conclusive. It was on the subject of acoustics in the new Chamber that the controversy still raged. Colonel Sibthorp, who had already achieved a public reputation for his attacks upon the concept of the Great Exhibition to be held in 1851, was early into the debate. There were too many steps. "Members were in danger of breaking their necks even before dinner, and what might be the case afterwards he could not say. The New Palace at Westminster was not a house built for business. As he had said before, he thought the building was more fitted for a harem than the purpose for which it was intended."

The Chancellor of the Exchequer, Charles Wood, later 1st Viscount Halifax, reporting upon the deliberations of the committee found himself "quite unable to give any positive assurance on ... the subject of acoustics." Doctor Reid, Mr. Scott Russell, Professor Wheatstone, and Professor Faraday were examined... but he did not think the committee gained much knowledge from their evidence. The committee had felt that they were unable to come to any conclusion without trying experiments upon this subject and they determined to try the experiment of a boarded roof in the New House of Commons, which hon. Gentlemen had seen on Wednesday, and which cost little more than £100. During the sitting on that day several members of the committee endeavoured to ascertain the opinions of

Members as to whether they were able to hear adequately or not. He believed that of some twenty or twenty-two Gentlemen he had asked, ten were of one opinion, and twelve of the other. The Chancellor spread out a plan on the table of the House. On it he indicated that the screens on either end of the Chamber were to be moved some two feet backwards. Two Members suggested that drapery hung around the House would improve the acoustics, just as it had in the Whitehall Chapel (the Banqueting House). Sir Benjamin Hall stated that out of the 656 Members of the House there were not perhaps three hundred who attended constantly, and if there was accommodation on the floor for 320, and for 150 more elsewhere, it would be sufficient.[1]

Mr. Bernal Osborne maintained that "the new House would be unable to contain the Members, and that they would not be able to hear in it. The only thing the House was fit for was to hold the Exhibition of 1851. He did not wish to make any attack on Mr. Barry, because he thought that the gentleman had acted quite right, since the Government and the House were so undecided, to indulge his own taste, and to make them pay for it." He cross-examined the Chancellor on the subject of Barry's remuneration. He believed that Mr. Barry had a just claim for far more than the £25,000 originally agreed.

On the House seating Thomas Greene believed that "if they made it large enough to hold all the Members, it would be found utterly unfit for the transaction of business." He believed that there would be room for 446 Members in the new House, that was allowing them only twenty inches for each seat. (This proved to be too small a space and it was enlarged, thus reducing the numbers.)

Mr. Alderman Humphrey said, "the present House was so small that it held out an encouragement to vice; because Members who could not find room in the House went into the Smoking-Room, where they would not go if they could find room in the House, and some went into the Library. They might see numbers in the Library, where they sat and slept."

The Chancellor of the Exchequer agreed "that Mr. Barry was entitled to a much larger remuneration than the £25,000 which he was to be paid under the original estimate; but what the precise sum might be had not yet been settled."

Mr. Bright urged that more accommodation should be available to strangers because "they came and understood the forms in which the business of the House was conducted, many of them most admirable forms; they had created in them a strong interest in public affairs, which was communicated to their families, and to the circles in which they moved; and he thought the more they could bring the actions and the opinions of that House into harmony with the intelligent portion of the public out of doors, the better."

*The Staircase, Members' Entrance, by E. N. Holmes (1865).*

*The Library of the House of Commons in 1854.*

Sir D. Norreys - "Mr. Barry had had the uncontrolled expenditure of the largest sum of money that any one architect had ever had before. Well, were not the committee ashamed of the result?"

From the plans in the hands of Members, he believed that hon. Members would find themselves, after the recess, in a more inconvenient House even than the New House was at present. For example, if a Member were in the Gallery of the New House and wished to vote with the Ayes, the door being locked according to custom, when the question was put the Member would find himself in the lobby with the Noes.

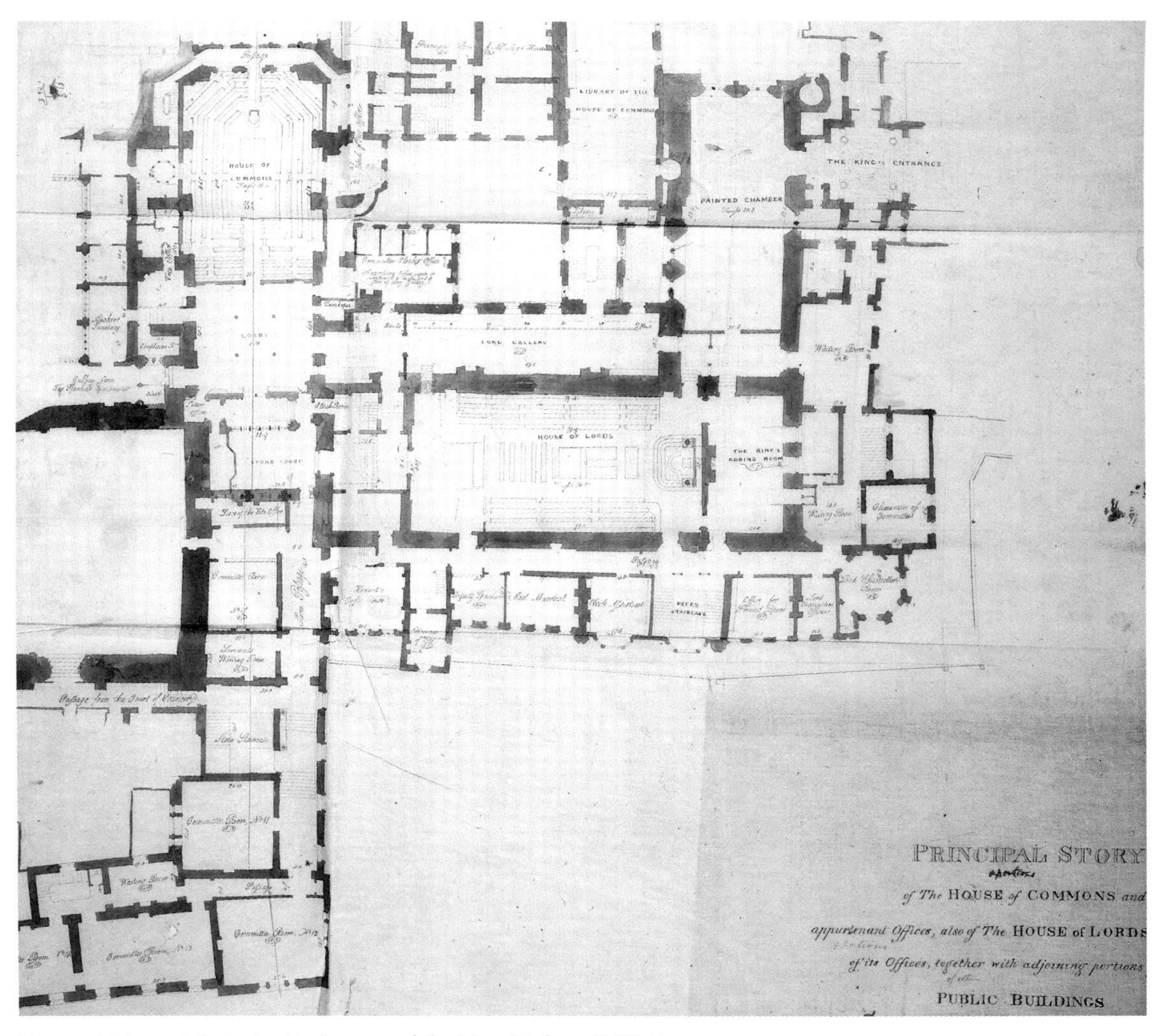


*Ground Plan of the principal storey of the New Palace (1853).*

In a notable intervention Benjamin Disraeli (who had been silent in committee) concentrated on responsibility. He would recommend the Government to reflect seriously on the fact that no profession had ever yet succeeded in this country till it had furnished what was called "an example."

"For instance, you hanged Admiral Byng, and the Navy increased in efficiency till we won Trafalgar. The disgrace of Whitelock was followed by the victory of Waterloo. We had decapitated Archibishop Laud, and had thenceforward secured the responsibility of the bishops. That principle we had never yet applied to architects; and when a member of that profession was called to execute a very simple task and utterly failed after a large expenditure of public money, it really became the Government to consider the case, and they might rest assured that if once they contemplated the possibility of hanging an architect, they would put a stop to such blunders in the future."

Parallel with the debates upon expenditure ran the long controversy on the subject of the architect's remuneration. At the outset Barry had been far more interested in securing the great commission than in procuring adequate remuneration for himself. No entirely satisfactory formula has ever yet been devised. If the architect is paid a percentage of the cost for the works carried out, then it is in his interests that his client spends as much as possible. An economical architect actually receives less than one who gets away with extravagance. There were many in Parliament, some no doubt who had had experience of the cost of building houses themselves, who seized on this awkward principle. It was perhaps because of this that in 1838 Barry had been offered a fixed sum - £25,000 based upon what was then believed to be the total cost of the works to be undertaken. By the beginning of 1848 Barry had received nearly the whole of the £25,000. As the result of the remarks of the Chancellor of the Exchequer in the debate of August 2nd, 1850, Barry received a further £10,000 between that year and 1852 though at no time was the principle of a percentage on outlay conceded. When Government and Parliament grew increasingly concerned at the rising expenditure to which they found themselves committed, they became less inclined to be generous to Barry but expected him to pay for the services of extra staff required to exercise a tighter control. Eventually the Treasury conceded that Barry should receive three percent on the cost of the works and that he should not have to pay for the cost of measuring the completed work. Barry stood out for five percent, which had become the recognised fee in what we should call today the "private sector." - But the best that the Treasury were prepared to offer by 1856 was three per cent plus an extra one percent for measuring. He had by 1854 received £40,000 in all. Barry entered into public controversy, even writing to *The Times* in 1856 and asking for arbitration. As his friend, John Wolfe noted, Barry was "always

*Benjamin Disraeli, Earl of Beaconsfield (1804-1881), by Robert Fowler.*

pertinacious in claiming the uttermost farthing of what he considered due to him."[2] He also at this time produced a calculation that the £25,000 originally agreed came to four percent of his original estimate of £626,500. Based on this he was entitled, he claimed, to four percent on the whole outlay plus one percent for measuring. The Treasury response was to threaten to withdraw any offer unless Barry was prepared to agree to their latest proposals; Barry acquiesced under protest. The R.I.B.A. passed resolutions in his favour, the Lords Commissioners of the Treasury replied to them by hanging their case on Barry's agreement of 1838. That could have been the end of the matter, However, further difficulties of detail arose resulting in a further formal protest by Barry. By now the Board of Works were employing as their surveyor H. A. Hunt, who had previously worked for Barry. Ironically, it was left to him to produce the Board's rebuttal of his former employer's claim.

The relationship between Charles Barry and the Parliamentary Committees at Westminster, continually demanding to know how long the work would take and how much it would cost to complete the New Palace had a perfect parallel in Disraeli's Sir Carte Blanche. In his novel *The Young Duke* (1831), the character of Sir Carte owes much to both Barry and George Basevi, Disraeli's architect uncle by marriage.[3]

*The Lobby of the House of Commons in 1872-3, by H. Barraud.*

*St. Stephen's Hall, by Vacher and Son (1859).*

Disraelian architectural fantasy was by 1852 matched by the reality of Barry's new home for the House of Commons. Contemporary descriptions of the Chamber and its surroundings provide a vivid picture of the rich and complex detail only slightly less elaborate than that created for their Lordships.

*The House of Commons*

"The plan of the New Palace shows the master mind of its architect which has given so large an amount of accommodation for the various requirements of the Government, has made ample provision for the personal comfort of many of its officers and of the members of the legislature, and has also produced an arrangement of the parts of the building convenient and symmetrical: thus the Peers' Corridor, the Peers' Lobby and the House of Peers are extended to the South of the Central Hall and the Commons' Corridor, the Commons' Lobby and the House of Commons occupy the corresponding situation and extent to the North of it; the space from the Speaker's Chair to the Throne forming, when the doors to the two Houses are open, a magnificent vista from north to south of nearly five hundred feet in length; in which richly moulded and elaborately carved archways and groining of stone, with their subdued tones and grey shadows, are alternately combined with the spacious and more brilliantly lighted Central Hall, Lobbies, and Chambers; possessing not merely the beauty of strictly architectural proportion and detail, but a series of thoroughly artistic and picturesque effects, unsurpassed in any other building devoted to civil purposes.

The size of the House is as small as is permissible with the business transacted within it, particular regard having been had to the necessity of hearing, in all parts of the House, speeches delivered from any portion of

*The Opposition benches, photographed in June 1897.*

the lower part of it; a peculiarity which is not required to the same degree in any other apartment, perhaps in the world; and it may be worthy of notice that a committee sanctioned the arrangement of the plan before it was carried into effect.

The chief entrance to the House is at the South end from the Commons' Lobby (where the doorkeepers are stationed during the sitting of the House to prevent ingress of persons who are not Members) through a vestibule, on the right and left of which are the South entrances to the Division Lobbies, which are separated from it by oak screens of tracery work, glazed.

Passing from the vestibule through the inner doorway, which has handsomely glazed oak doors, the House is entered below the Bar, twenty feet in advance of it, and is shown in the view, which is taken on the right hand of the entrance, from the seats for Peers.

The Chair of the Speaker is at the North end of the House opposite the Bar; in front of the Speaker is the table at which the Clerks sit, and on the lower end of it the mace rests during the sitting of the House: when the House is sitting in committee, however, the mace is lowered.

The seats for the Members are ranged in five tiers, one above the other, along the sides, and are returned at the Bar end; a gangway separating those on the sides into two nearly equal portions. The benches are commodious, and have cushioned seats and backs, which are covered with green morocco; the small brass plates on the oak rail of the back are for the cards of the Members, who having taken a seat, retain it during the sitting of the House. The bench on the right of the Speaker is occupied by the Ministry, and that on the left by the leading Members of the Opposition.

A seat at the side of the Bar and facing the Speaker is provided for the Serjeant-at-Arms, and is always occupied either by him or his deputy during the sittings of the House. Below the Bar on both sides of the entrance, seats are provided for Peers and their elder sons. An entrance at the North end of the House, behind the Speaker's Chair, communicates with the Division Lobbies as at the South end; beyond this are retiring rooms for the Ministers who may desire to consult together during the debates; and for the Members of the Opposition for the same purpose.

The Division Lobbies extend along both sides and at the ends of the House to the vestibules, where the main entrances to them are, but there are also two other entrances on each side from the back tiers of seats in the House. The West Lobby is for those who say 'Aye' to a question put from the chair, and the East Lobby for those who say 'No'. There are three large oriel windows in each of the Division Lobbies, which add greatly to the space, and to the appearance both internally and externally.

Over the Division Lobbies are corridors divided into separate rooms and communicating with the galleries of the House; into these rooms the

*The Speaker's Chair, House of Commons.*

Members can retire, either to refer to documents, or for interviews; and a staircase at each end communicates with the corridor below.

The Ladies' Gallery is situated at this end, above where the reporters sit, but without the House; the Gallery being separated from it by a stone screen of rich tracery work, in which the open portions are filled with brass trellis. For the first time in the history of Parliament a place has been appropriated for the use of ladies, who if one may judge by the attendance of the fair sex, fully appreciate the privilege.

*The Ladies' Gallery, House of Commons (1870).*

Over the Division Lobbies are corridors divided into separate rooms and communicating with the galleries of the House; into these rooms the Members can retire, either to refer to documents, or for interviews; and a staircase at each end communicates with the corridor below.

The general aspect of the House of Commons and its adjacent parts is quiet and grave; the prevailing tone being given by the oak fittings with which they are lined in every part: this, however, in the House is enriched in some measure, by the decorated panels of the ceiling, the royal arms in succession which enliven the front of the galleries, and by the richly coloured glazing of the windows.

The windows of the lobbies are filled with stained glass in quarries, with occasional richer decoration; and they are of a similar character to those in the House.

The corridor at the North end of the House leads to the residence of the Speaker, and at the West end it communicates with the residence of the Librarian of the House of Commons, and that of the Clerk of the House, which are on the West side of the New Palace Yard; and also with the residence of the Serjeant-at-Arms on the North front.

*A water colour showing the proposed central tower of the Palace. The painting was presented to Tsar Nicholas I by Barry.*

*Gladstone introducing the Irish Land Bill, House of Commons (1881), by F. Sargent (1882).*

Although the House of Commons is more simple in its ornamentation than the House of Lords, and has less of colouring and gilding, there is a large amount of exquisite detail in it, which is not inferior either in design or workmanship to that in the nobler chamber of the Peers."[4]

The alterations made to Barry's House of Commons Chamber did not solve the problems of ventilation and lighting. The Select Committee set up in March 1852 included Lord John Manners, Thomas Greene and Viscount Palmerston. Ten days previously it had been ordered by the House that Mr. Goldsworthy Gurney be authorised to inspect the arrangements for the warming, ventilating and lighting for the New House of Commons and to report thereupon. Gurney was pursuing his inquiries at the same time that the Select Committee was cross-examining Dr. Reid and collecting other evidence.

Reid complained that he did not have access to the plans of the building, that he had no control over the drains, and that the gas lighting created air currents which interfered with the fresh air which he sought to introduce. There are several references to the high Central Tower such as is shown on the two perspectives which Barry gave to the Tsar. When Mr. Baillie

*Ceiling panel in the Members' Dining Room, House of Commons, restored in 1986.*

*Painted ceiling panels in the House of Lords.*

Cochrane asked Reid whether he was aware "that in all the public buildings in Paris, and on the Continent generally, there is no such thing as an elaborate system of ventilation attempted to be carried out?" Reid quoted his experiences in France at the Chamber of Peers in 1843. At the Tuileries the King of France had taken him to the top of the *salon des marechaux* where he had experienced the effects of 3,700 lamps and candles and the respiration of 5,000 people. The effects of this had led to the desire of introducing plans such as were seen here and in Her Majesty's yacht, "The Victoria and Albert."

"Are you not aware, generally speaking, they have never adopted any of these elaborate systems of ventilation on the Continent?"

"I am not aware of it; fifteen years ago I made for the Emperor of Russia a set of drawings, for plans to be introduced at a school at the great

*Star Chamber Court by E. N. Holmes (1865).*

works at Alexandroski... Instead of carrying all these products away to a great height, from which they may be discharged for ever, they may now loiter as they are seen to loiter at times, around the different courts." Here Reid was complaining that chimneys from various parts of the building not being carried up the Central Tower, discharged in places where their smoke was picked up by the air intakes.

On the subject of the lack of communication between the ventilator and the architect, Lord Palmerston took up the questioning.

"What do you mean by the system of communication?"

"I mean communication with the architect as to the works... Either the architect must design a system of ventilation that will suit his taste..."

Not only was there a lack of communication between ventilator and architect, it appeared that rival gangs of workmen sometimes encountered each other in surprising places.

"There is one important point which I should wish to mention, and that is, that I have no proper control over the workmen, who execute various works at the House of Commons from time to time, and who have done so since the opening of the House. For instance, sometimes the men working in my flues will encounter others who have penetrated them from the gas flues. At one time we found the vitiated air flue connected with the fresh air flues. At other times we have found openings knocked in the wall and the flues rearranged in connection with the gas operations, and all this during the sitting of the Houses, without any intimation being given to me."

"When Sir Charles Barry was appointed to this building he did not receive it as an ordinary building; but Parliament and the Government had previously said, 'Architects in general do not study acoustics and ventilation to the extent we desire: let us have an investigation upon the subject.' The architect then comes into my confidence for nine successive years; sees everything I have at Edinburgh; sees everything I have at London, obtains the result of those years of experience, and now he says, 'I will not show you the additions and alterations I have made in your own flues.'"

"When you required access to any particular place, or permission to do any particular thing, in order to assist you in making your report, to whom did you make application?"

"I applied to The Speaker, and he referred me to Lord John Manners."

"Lord John Manners has referred you back again to the House?"

"He does so practically; he gives me certain facilities; but as regards general questions, he considers them under the House of Commons since the resolutions were passed."

External forces were also at work. Foul air could arise from the surrounding area, from a bone meal works, a gas works, the polluted river or even from St. Margaret's Churchyard.

Gurney found the atmosphere of the House to be dessicated, oppressive and subject to constant disturbance from initial and retrograde currents passing in all directions, as if at random, and apparently without control. He also found that from the same want of proper control, offensive vapours and effluvia (emanating from contaminated sources) were drawn into the House.

Although he believed that most of the evils could be corrected by a simple arrangement, it was difficult to demonstrate on paper. Furthermore, on former occasions an unfair advantage had been taken of statements which he had made and parts of his plan had been adopted without consulting him.

He called in aid his recommendation which had satisfactorily ventilated the Chamber of Deputies in Paris and also in the Courts of Exchequer and Common Pleas at Westminster Hall. He believed that if the House were to be placed under the control of the Office of Works for a short time, he could, with their assistance, remove all the material evils.

The committee reported that "In consideration of the urgency of the case, they have since the commencement of their sittings, sat four days every week and have made a personal inspection of the Works connected with the Ventilation of the entire building.

*The back of the south wing towers and ventilating shaft, by J. Johnson (1849).*

*The west front of the New Houses of Parliament in 1854.*

They regret to state that they are not at present in a condition to suggest any specific alterations either in the Ventilation or Lighting, calculated permanently to remedy the defects complained of. They, however, recommend that during the recess, Dr. Reid should be allowed to effect the alterations described in his Report, under the supervision, and subject to the approbation of the First Commissioner of Works, and two members of the committee, Mr. Stephenson and Mr. Locke.

The evidence received up to the present moment being incomplete, the committee do not think it desirable to Report it to the House; but when Parliament reassembles, they will resume their labours."[5]

As a result of the foregoing Reid left the scene with Goldsworthy Gurney hovering in the background. Both Houses were for a time handled by the engineer, Alfred Meeson, whom Barry had employed, but he was placed under the control of the Office of Works. He made a number of alterations.

Barry's trusted contractor, Grissell, eventually fell foul of the Office of Works. Lord Seymour was unwilling to let Grissell proceed with the restoration of the cloisters and the building of the Members' Entrance to the House of Commons. Grissell in the event did not compete. The winner, John Jay, was soon complaining that his contract No. 11 of June 1852 needed to be revised on the grounds that materials and labour had much risen in price. He had quoted at a rate which was some thirty percent lower than Grissell had asked for the previous contract. When in the middle of 1856 the twelfth contract was on offer, Jay won with the lowest tender but his prices showed a huge increase on craftsmen's rates of but four years previously. Jay survived as the main contractor through the completion of the two great towers and the completion of the west front of the House of Lords to Old Palace Yard, the last part of the exterior to be completed.

Lord Seymour's successor, Sir William Molesworth, goaded by Parliamentary pressure, endeavoured to discover the sum that was required for the completion of the New Palace. He also tried to control the annual expenditure. Barry was asked to ensure that Jay, the contractor, rendered his account every two months and that other creditors should present their bills quarterly. Barry himself was expected to give details on coloured plans of where he proposed to spend the money which Parliament had voted. In response to Sir William's question, about the cost of completing the great work, it appeared that approaching £300,000 would be needed to pay for works that had already been approved. Much of this sum was to be devoted to 281 rooms alloted to various functionaries for residential purposes This huge allocation of funds and accommodation for the benefit of those who served the Members of the two Houses gave Barry ample excuse to revive his dream of completing the New Palace. The enclosure of New Palace Yard and a continuation on the site of the Law Courts to St. Stephen's Entrance would require a sum similar to the foregoing. The two together came to nearly £600,000. This sum added to that already required produced a total of £2,166,846. Barry believed that all might be completed by the end of 1859.

Unfortunately a number of factors gave Parliament the excuse to run away from so adventurous a proposition. New Government Offices were required for many public departments ill housed about Westminster and Whitehall. Although the Law Courts at Westminster were far from satisfactory, the time had not come for their removal to the Strand. Ministerial responsibility passed in July 1855 from Molesworth to the formidable Sir Benjamin Hall. With the Crimean War on the Government's hands and the formidable Sir Benjamin at the Office of Works this was not the moment for a generous approach to expenditure at the New Palace.

Barry and Hall were soon locked in controversy if not in conflict. Hall's employment of Hunt, who had previously been Barry's trusted servant, did not help Barry's cause. It was even suggested that all work should cease till accounts could be rendered. Although Hall did not go as far as that, he asked that accounts be rendered for all works that had been completed. He also required a list of works in progress and an estimate of their probable

*Lord Lincoln M.P. (1811-64), later 5th Duke of Newcastle. Portrait by F. R. Say (1848).*

*Sir William Molesworth, Bt, M.P., First Commissioner of Works 1852-5.*

THE RIGHT HON. SIR BENJAMIN HALL, M.P. FOR MARYLEBONE.

THE LATE LORD MOUNT-TEMPLE.

AUSTIN HENRY LAYARD, LL.D., DISCOVERER OF THE NIMROUD SCULPTURES.

MR. ACTON SMEE AYRTON, M.P. FOR THE TOWER HAMLETS.
FROM A PHOTOGRAPH BY MAYALL.

*The First Commissioners of Works at the New Palace.*
*Top: Sir Benjamin Hall (1855-8), William Cowper later Lord Mount-Temple (1860-5); below: A. H. Layard (1868-9), A. S. Ayrton (1869-73).*

cost. All the works needed for completion but not yet begun were to be the subject of drawings and specifications upon which estimates could be made, before any could be proceeded with. There was a firm instruction that no works of any kind were to be ordered which could not be met out of the remainder of the current year's vote.

Following this stern admonition from the formidable Sir Benjamin, Sir Charles fell suddenly and seriously ill. After a ten week absence Barry rose from his sick bed just in time for the Government's resignation and the end of Sir Benjamin Hall as First Commissioner. Barry's last letter to him contained the breathtaking statement, that before receiving Sir Benjamin's last commanding letter, he had given orders for all the works required to complete the entire New Palace. He was quite unable to stop any part of the works without a costly action for breach of contract.

Little more than five years after the death of Pugin the New Palace lost another of those to whom it owed its creation. The first Baron Sudeley of Toddington left £5,000 in his will for the erection of a tomb. The scale of the monument created by John Graham Lough in the manner of the fourteenth century was such that the eighteenth century church had to be rebuilt on a larger scale.

When Palmerston returned to office his new First Commissioner, Henry Fitzroy, did not survive for long. He optimistically assured the Commons that nothing new had been begun or was even contemplated. His death just before Christmas meant that it fell to his successor, William Cowper, Palmerston's step-son and heir, a gentle art lover, to preside over a period in which at least superficially the New Palace was completed.

By the spring of 1860 Mr. Speaker had moved into his splendid house and the two great towers were completed with the Great Clock chiming and striking in one of them. Both Houses had grown used to their new Chambers and those essential adjuncts of Parliamentary life, Smoking Rooms and Refreshment Rooms were functioning. Two floors of Committee Rooms looking out upon the river were in regular use. The Libraries of both Houses were complete, the residences provided at such great cost were occupied. A good start had been made upon the works of fresco and statuary inaugurated by Prince Albert.

### *The Speaker's House*

The Speaker of the House of Commons is also allowed a residence in the Palace of Westminster, his laborious functions requiring his almost constant presence in the House of Commons.

*Henry John, 3rd Viscount Palmerston (1784-1865), painted outside the north entrance of Westminster Hall by H. Barraud (1865).*

Mr. Speaker Addington had from 1795 a residence to the north- east of the House of Commons. It embraced part of the cloister and its State Dining Room occupied that part of the Crypt Chapel which was not used as a coal cellar.

James Wyatt carried out extensive works of reconstruction costing £70,000 between 1802 and 1808. Mr. Speaker Addington had an eye for history and did his best to ensure that the improvements did no further damage to the historic structures into which they were woven. His lasting memorial, in the great office which he occupied for twelve years, was the beginning of a collection of portraits of former Speakers. The descendants of many of them generously presented originals or copies. Sir John Cust by Reynolds and Charles Cornwall by Gainsborough are notable examples. Since the time of Addington every Speaker has had his portrait painted. Some of them were posthumous portraits, rendered necessary by the Speaker's death in office. In recent times Mr. Speaker has been painted shortly after assuming his arduous responsibilities, in order to ensure his preservation for posterity within the State Apartments.

Mr. Speaker Manners-Sutton was Speaker at the time of the Great Conflagration. His official furnishings perished and his private property sustained, he claimed, damage to the tune of some £6,000. At a Select Committee examination Manners-Sutton explained that he was uninsured because his policy had run out at a time when he was asked, unexpectedly, to continue in office. Precedents were quoted against him and the committee made no recommendation. Although their Report was reprinted for the benefit of further consideration nothing ever came of his claim. He did receive however, the traditional pension and was created Viscount Canterbury. Some furnishings of a grand nature, which he had taken over from his predecessor and which had been rescued, he offered to the Government for the future Speaker's residence. Initially his offer was accepted but when it was decided to demolish the remains of Wyatt's house and build something quite new as part of, but technically separate from the New Palace, the Lords of the Treasury went back on their agreement. Recently two items connected with Manners-Sutton have reappeared. A silver soup tureen bearing his arms has been added to the collection of official plate at the disposal of Mr. Speaker. A fine George I walnut secretaire cabinet found its way to Portugal. It was presented by Dr. Antonio Medeiros de Almeida, brought home to England by Christie's and restored by John Partridge. It now has an honoured place outside the Cabinet Room of 10 Downing Street.

The Speaker's House in the New Palace was always intended to occupy the North Wing Towers and part of the North Front. For the first hundred years the most northerly of the suite of libraries on the principal floor belonged to Mr. Speaker. On its surrender to the House of Commons the old Serjeant-at-Arms' Drawing Room was incorporated in Speaker's House. This room lay unused and unloved for twenty years until it became the State Bedroom.

The new Speaker's House enjoyed substantial ground floor kitchens and servants' quarters. The State Apartments were on the principal floor, the Private Apartments on the first floor and above, where many awkardly-placed servants rooms were accessible only by a single steep staircase.

Shaw Lefevre, who succeeded Manners-Sutton, did not reside in the remains of the old Speaker's House. It served a last historic purpose. There the Commissioners deliberated upon the designs for the New Palace. Mr. Speaker Denison first occupied the new Speaker's House in 1858. His arms are carved in stone above the porch in Speaker's Court and two

*Doors to State Dining Room, the Speaker's Apartments.*

*Sir Edward Coke, Speaker of the House of Commons 1592-3. Portrait by Hieronimo Custodis.*

*Sir John Trevor, Speaker 1685-95, by J. Clostermann.*

*Robert Harley, 1st Earl of Oxford, Speaker 1701-5. Copy c. 1804 after J. Richardson.*

*Sir John Cust, Bart, Speaker 1761-70, by John Rising after Reynolds.*

*Charles Abbot, 1st Baron Colchester, Speaker 1802-17. Portrait by Sir Thomas Lawrence.*

*Charles Manners Sutton M.P., Speaker 1817-34, by H. W. Pickersgill.*

*George Thomas, 1st Viscount Tonypandy, Speaker 1976-83, by George J. D. Bruce.*

*The present Speaker of the House of Commons, the Rt, Hon. Bernard Weatherill M.P., painted by Norman Blamey (1984).*

splendid Welsh dragons in the glass flanking the front door allude to his Welsh connections. This Entrance Tower is the dominant feature in the largest and otherwise the plainest of the internal courts of the Palace. The outer hall leads through to the Grand Staircase. The brasswork is particularly fine. Medieval details abound in what is essentially a Classical concept. Half way up the staircase the visitor is confronted by a massive fireplace rich in Puginian detail. Originally, tiled floors and stairs complemented bare stone walls. The stairs are now carpeted and the walls have been painted.

The State Apartments on the principal floor look down upon the Terrace, the Thames and Westminster Bridge. They surround a fan-vaulted corridor, or cloister, surrounding a central well. Mr. Speaker now uses as a business-room or library what was the Small Drawing Room overlooking the Terrace. The Crimson Drawing Room adjoining is still used as one of the official reception rooms. This leads to the "corner room" which was the Private Dining Room opening into the State Dining Room, beyond which is the State Bedroom.

The State Apartments were created after Pugin's death but his influence is everywhere to be seen. There are subtle differences here from the purest Pugin masterpiece in the Palace - the House of Lords Chamber. Some idea of the impact of these splendid rooms upon those who first enjoyed them can be experienced, without the colour, in Sir Benjamin Stone's photographs. These were taken before there was a conscious effort to obliterate the original in order to create lighter, paler interiors much favoured by Lewis Harcourt in 1907. With the exception of the State Dining Room all the decorated ceilings had their painted panels covered over with cardboard painted in pastel shades. It was in the time of Mr. Speaker Thomas (Viscount Tonypandy) that one of these pieces of cardboard worked loose enough for his curiosity to be aroused. With his enthusiastic approval, all was torn off to reveal the original painted decorations, untouched since the day they were put there. The ceiling in Mr. Speaker's Library could just be seen in one of Sir Benjamin's photographs. The fireplaces in Sir Benjamin's photographs looked quite different from the cream coloured rough cast which confronted Mr. Speaker Thomas. When this was removed the original grey marble was exposed, together with some of the brass enrichments. Other fine pieces of brass-work had long languished in the metal store in the basement. These turned out to be the enrichments of the spandrels of all the marble fireplaces. Much of the magnificent brass-work of the fire grates and the tiled surrounds had either been painted black or covered over with sheets of asbestos. All was removed to reveal the original in pristine condition.

By happy coincidence the recovery of the State Bed made for the Speaker's House in 1858 coincided with the foregoing discoveries.

Mr. Speaker Thomas at once agreed that it should be installed in the most westerly of the State Rooms which has now become the State Bedroom.

The State Dining Room has suffered least of all at the hands of changing fashion. In one respect it has been enhanced by the completion of the series of State portraits for which the walls were designed. The ceiling remains unharmed though the lighting has been altered. The sideboard which ran the length of the west wall has been cut through in two places to

*Left: Stained glass window in the west wall of the porch, Speaker's House.*

*Right: Stained glass window south of the entrance door to Speaker's House.*

provide doorways to the State Bedroom beyond. The set of Gothic chairs – one with a spire added to give it an added importance – proved to be uncomfortable and impractical. They were banished to the adjoining cloister. Four of these were lent by a Speaker to a Bishop. They never returned to Speaker's House but found their way into the antique trade. Two were sold to rival but friendly collectors of Pugin furniture and their whereabouts are therefore unknown. Of the other two, one was reserved for a Museum until the Palace discovered its existence. That chair, together with the fourth, were purchased for the Palace. Such, in the past, has been the fate of some of the historic contents. Losses there may have been but there

*The State Dining Room, Speaker's House.*

have also been gains. The cloister now contains a pair of fine walnut display cases in the manner of Pugin. These contain his personal china from his home in Ramsgate.

All of the original furnishings of the Speaker's House were the subject of a specification and tender put out to open competition in August 1858. Messrs. Holland & Son of 23 Mount Street, Grosvenor Square, contracted on 26th August 1858 to supply all for £5,381 13s. 10p. This was conditional on their supplying everything to the satisfaction of the First Commissioner by the 18th January 1859. The conditions included "if the entire completion is delayed beyond that day the contractor is to forfeit the sum of £50 per day for every day until the contract is completed." Hollands delivered all, on time, to the satisfaction of the First Commissioner. The twenty-five page specification covered everything from twelve Windsor chairs for the servants' hall to a spectacular Arabian Bed (the State Bed). Of the forty-one drawings which accompanied the specification some have survived. Some of these can be related to actual pieces still in the State Apartments.

Although all was complete in January 1859 there was the inevitable seepage of furniture from the Speaker's Apartments either by accident or design, and by the 1980s many pieces had disappeared from the Palace altogether or had been distributed elsewhere within it. The State Bed had been removed from the Palace into store and eventually accidentally sold by the Ministry of Works. The purchasers were unaware of its significance. Its existence and whereabouts were discovered following the publication of an old photograph at the time of the opening of the Pugin Room. It was due to the initiative of the National Heritage Memorial Fund that the bed was purchased and restored (with the advice of the Victoria and Albert Museum), returned to the Palace and given its new and honoured place in the State Bedroom. The bed owes its existence to the tradition that the Sovereign should sleep in the Palace of Westminster on the night preceding the coronation. No Sovereign has slept at Westminster before a coronation since the creation of the present State Bed.

Complementary to the bed are the pair of *prie-Dieu* chairs which had also left the Palace but have now been returned. The substantial wardrobe was reassembled from what appeared to be a miscellaneous pile of woodwork in a store. The dressing table, for which a drawing exists, had served as a desk but had been banished to an attic. Much of the rest of the Holland furniture had been distributed around the Palace. Some skillful negotiation with the new "owners" was required to secure its return to its rightful place.

The restoration of the State Apartments in the 1980s has proceeded slowly with the benefit of expert advice. It is a delicate balance to achieve authenticity and yet avoid the oppressive heaviness which the obliterators of 1907 were seeking to remove.

The State Apartments are used for official purposes and not as part of the residence. Mr. Speaker enjoys modest accommodation on the floor above. Here some long overdue improvements have created interiors worthy of the Palace and congenial to domestic life. That much of the furniture is that which Pugin designed for his own home seems appropriate. He was deeply sensitive to correctness in style and design, but was above all a family man who delighted in children and grandchildren. Such has been the flavour of life in Speaker's House in the time of Mr. Speaker Weatherill.

### *The Clock Tower*

"The Clock Tower stands at the north-east corner of New Palace Yard, marking in a conspicuous manner the northern extremity of the building and balancing in some measure, yet entirely differing from, the grand Victoria Tower at the southern end of it. The general design of the Tower, is appropriate in its outline and is elegant in its proportion and details; one principal feature in its composition being of course the Clock.

The plan of the Tower is square; the angles are marked by flat pilaster projections forming two sides of a square, these two faces being entered by the sides of a similar square placed diagonally. The faces thus formed are narrow and panelled. This arrangement is continued from the level of the cornice of the main building to the corbelling under the clock dials. At the lower part of the Tower the flat projections are strengthened by square buttresses in two stages, the upper one being panelled. The walls of the Tower, from the level of the cills of the principal floor windows to the corbelling under the dials, are divided into seven narrow compartments by slender buttresses placed diagonally; four of these compartments are pierced and form narrow windows in couples, of which there are five tiers in the height of the Tower; between them are bands of panelling across the Tower, which give a richness to the whole.

The present situation of the Tower, attached as it is to the building on one side only, is very unsatisfactory in an architectural point of view; and it is to be hoped that the original intention of the architect will be carried into effect, by the enclosure of New Palace Yard with buildings of the same character as those on the other side of it; the Tower, now almost detached from the Palace, would then obtain its proper relative position as forming an important part of a very beautiful composition.

The slender diagonal buttresses, which have been described as separating the compartments of the wall, terminate in moulded corbels, which project as far as the face of the piers at the angles of the Tower, and support a cornice, decorated with ribbons and roses, with a winged animal at each angle: the face of the clock storey projects beyond that of the wall below.

The second tier of corbels supports the square projecting mass of stonework within which the clock dials are placed, the most prominent feature of the stonework of the tower: over this is the upper and main cornice, decorated with large shields,, bearing the cross of St George, and at its angles are winged animals larger than those on the lower cornice, but of similar design.

Over the cornice is the parapet of pierced tracery; it surrounds the bell chamber and forms a gallery: the parapet has finials bearing orbs, one over each of the buttresses below.

There is a dial on each side of the tower, twenty-two feet six inches diameter, clear of the stone circle. The circle is comprised within a square,

*Charles Barry's preliminary studies for the Clock Tower.*

*Charles Barry's sketch for the clock face, coloured blue.*

which fills the space between the angle piers and projects beyond them: the angles of the square have octagonal shafts; they are carried above the parapet and are terminated by an imperial crown of stone.

The spandrils formed by the angles of the square by which the circle is bounded, are richly decorated with tracery and with heraldic supporters of the present and past sovereigns.

*Domine salvam fac reginam nostram Victoriam primam* is carved below" (on the north side the last part of the "m" is missing because there is not room for it).

"At each angle of the arcade is a flying buttress, which springs from an octagonal pinnacle at the angle of the parapet.

On the stone arcade forming the bell chamber stands the beautiful lantern spire, the seating of which is formed by a broad sole plate which is bolted down to the stonework; strong cast iron stancheons upon this plate support the iron head piece which forms both the gutter and the cornice of the lower roof, and likewise the foot plate of the lantern.

At the foot of the spire is a large moulded cornice of iron with foliage in the cove, and upon the face and at each angle of it are large shields, enriched with badges and heraldic devices, as the rose, shamrock, thistle, fleur-de-lis, portcullis, leek etc. On this cornice is a very rich brattishing of metal work, with finials at the angles of the roof.

The height of this part of the roof, from the top of the stone arcade to the top of the cornice is about twenty-six feet.

The front of this cornice is decorated with light tracery canopies which spring from the rolls of the roof, above which is a light iron railing of beautiful design, of iron and copper.

The lantern is of iron, and has its sides somewhat smaller than the top of the lower stage of the roof; it has on each side five openings with tracery in the upper part, having ogee crocketted heads; the mullions are moulded, and have square buttresses; the angles of the lantern are of corresponding design to the open compartments, but are narrower, and a light flying buttress stands over the angle of the roof below."[6]

### *The Ayrton Light*

The controversial and sometimes inhuman Acton Smee Ayrton has left for himself one memorial - the Ayrton Light, known also as the Speaker's Lantern, at the top of the Clock Tower shines forth when either House is sitting. (Similarly, the Union flag flies from the Victoria Tower when either House is sitting). Members of the public have been perplexed on occasions when their Lordships have been working long hours to complete business left behind by the Commons who have risen for a recess.

On 24th April 1945 Mr. Speaker informed the Commons that following a lapse of five years seven months and twenty-three days he proposed to relight the Lantern.

"I pray that, with God's blessing, this light will shine henceforth, not only as an outward and visible sign that the Parliament of a free people is assembled in free debate, but also, that it may shine as a beacon of sure hope in a sadly torn and distracted world."

The hands first designed by Barry in cast iron were too heavy for the clock to drive. The gun-metal hour hands which replaced them are far more elaborate than the sheet copper minute hands which the clock now carries.

"Between the inside of the tower wall and dial is the lighting chamber, five feet two inches in breadth from the glass to the face of the wall, which is finished white; and against it are fixed rows of gas burners, forty in number, a small jet being provided behind each of them, which may be lighted and kept burning during daylight. By this arrangement the two systems of burners are alternately lighted, one to burn by day, the other by night; and the supply can be regulated at the foot of the tower, so that the labour of ascending to the lighting-chamber every evening and morning is rendered unnecessary.

An archway is formed in each of the angle piers between the lighting-chambers, connecting them together."

The first Great Bell for the New Palace was born out of acrimony. Either Denison's metal recipe or the work of the bell-founders, Warners, must have been at fault. It arrived in great style being dragged across Westminster Bridge on a wagon pulled by sixteen horses. Hung on a temporary frame in New Palace Yard and subjected to blows from Denison's heavy clapper, the bell cracked. The bell was then broken up and cast by a different founders, Mears of Whitechapel.

The new bell, cast by Mears of Whitechapel on 10th April 1858, arrived back at Westminster on 28th May and reached the top of the Clock Tower in October of that year. Experimental tolling of the bell in November revealed a weakness in the framework. This having been rectified, by the next year Members were complaining of being deafened by the great bell and there was a row because the hands proved too heavy; then the bell cracked. It appeared that there were holes in the metal and that they had been plugged with cement. Denison attacked the bell-founders and they sued him for libel. For three years the hour was struck on the fourth quarter bell, Big Ben remaining silent. The Astronomer Royal recommended that the bell be given a quarter of a turn, the weight of the hammer was reduced from 6 1/2 cwt. to 4 cwt., and a platform was placed under the bell to safeguard the lower portion of the tower. In this condition it has marked the hours and occasionally the passing of Kings and Queens (and Sir Winston Churchill) to the present time.

## THE CLOCK (NEW PALACE, WESTMINSTER).

RETURN to an Order of the Honourable The House of Commons, dated 31 March 1859;—*for*,

A RETURN "stating the COST of the CLOCK in the CLOCK TOWER of the NEW PALACE at *Westminster*, and of all the Expenses connected therewith, up to the present period; an ESTIMATE of the AMOUNT further required; and a STATEMENT of the probable Time of its being completed."

| | £. | s. | d. |
|---|---|---|---|
| 1. Cost of Clock, Dials, Illuminating, &c. - - - | 8,279 | 13 | 8 |
| Bells - - - - - - - - - - - | 5,966 | 13 | 3 |
| Expenses connected with the Clock and Bells - - | 6,061 | 10 | 8 |
| £. | 20,307 | 17 | 7 |

2. Estimate of the further Amount required - - - £. 1,750 – –

3. Probable Time of Completion:

EXTRACT from Report of *E. B. Denison*, Esq., 11 April 1859.

"As to the time of completion, I can only say that the clock is now in the room, ready to be fixed as soon as the place is clear of bricklayers and plasterers, which I understand it will be in a few days. If so, I am assured that the clock will be going, and showing the time on all the dials, before the new Parliament meets. The bellchamber, however, is still in such a state that I should not rely on any promise which might be given as to the time when the clock will be able to strike the hours and quarters, but it ought not to be long after the going part is at work."

Office of Works, &c.
18 March 1859.

JOHN MANNERS,
First Commissioner of Her Majesty's
Works and Public Buildings.

258.

*The cost of the clock for the Clock Tower (1859).*

Charles Barry asked Benjamin Lewis Vulliamy in March 1844 on what terms he would prepare a specification for the Westminster clock, the Clock Tower then being in the course of construction. Vulliamy did not seize the initiative and Edward John Dent, more than eighteen months later, asked to be allowed to compete for the clock. He was armed with a testimonial from G. B. Airy, the Astronomer Royal. The First Commissioner (Lord Canning) asked Airy for his advice on how to obtain "the very best which the science and skill of the country can supply." Dent was recommended by Airy; Vulliamy or Whitehurst of Derby were alternatives. Although Vulliamy, the Royal Clockmaker, refused to enter into what he regarded as an undignified competition, he sent in a design of his own.

A design by Vulliamy for a clock was discovered in 1983 in a dusty cupboard in Barry's old office at Westminster. It was deposited in the Record Office. Airy described Vulliamy's entry as a village clock of very superior character. Barry's diary for 28th November 1845 records "Mr. Vulliamy here with drawings of clock."

Dent offered to make the clock for £1,600 in September 1846. This was a cut price in order to secure a prized commission. By the middle of 1847 he had been allowed to compete for the other clocks in the interior of the Palace which Vulliamy had been supplying.

It was in May 1848 that Edmund Beckett Denison wrote to the First Commissioner recommending Dent. Denison was a difficult man but an undoubted expert on clocks and also on bells. The new First Commissioner Seymour consulted Airy, who suggested that Denison should help him design the clock which they both hoped that Dent would make. The clock was duly made by Mr. E. Dent from the design of Mr. Edmund Beckett Denison, Q.C. Dent was given the contract though it was discovered that the clockroom was not large enough to accommodate the design, which was then modified. Dent then died. The contract did not pass automatically to his stepson and it was not until the middle of 1854 that Frederick (Ripon) Dent proceeded to finish the clock.

The firm of Dent continued to look after the great clock which they had built for the next hundred years. D.P. Buckney, Chairman and Managing Director and the great-grandson of the original Mr. Dent, was present on the occasion of the clock's centenary on 3rd June 1959.

However, it was not long after this great event that Dents ceased to be responsible for the clock owing to their inability to cope with that kind of timepiece. The job was given to Thwaites & Reed, successors to Aynsworth Thwaites, who had built the clock which yet serves Horseguards. At the time that they took over the care of Big Ben they were still in Clerkenwell where the firm was founded. In the summer of 1976 the shaft of the airbrake of the quarter chime broke. The weight descended to the bottom of the shaft spinning the mechanism with such violence that parts of it were thrown out

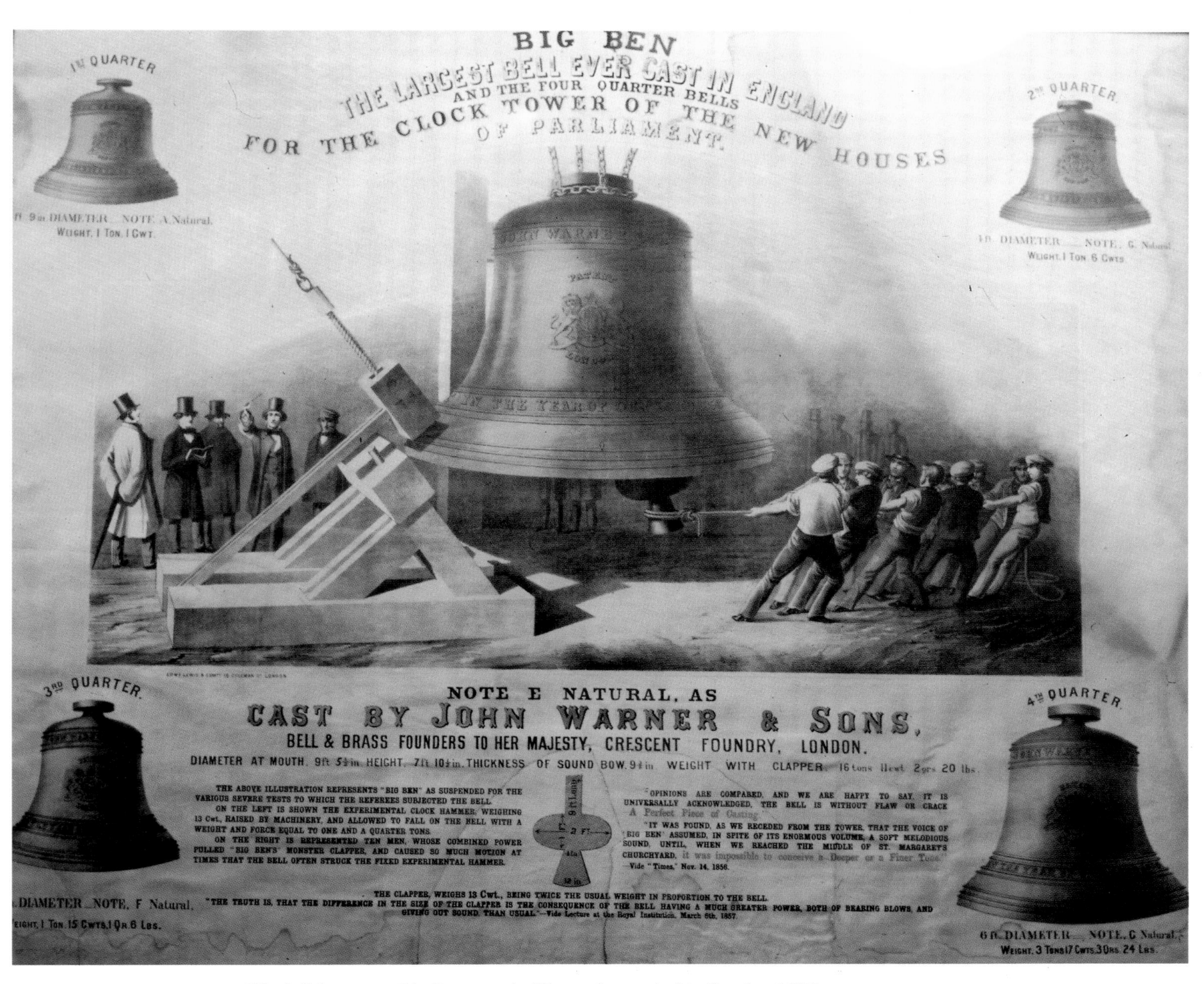


*The bell known as Big Ben, cast by Warner's, cracked in October 1857.*

of the clock frame and even embedded in the ceiling above. Despite this great catastrophe the broken clock frame was jacked back into alignment and the clock continued to mark the hours and even the hour bell was brought back into commission.

Many months of research and skilled work brought all back into working order in time for Her Majesty the Queen's Jubilee visit. The restored quarter chimes rang out for the first time at the moment that Her Majesty entered the hall. The Resident Engineer, Mr. John Darwin, had supervised the work but suffered a heart attack a few days previously. The sound of the chimes, which he heard from his hospital bed, began a steady recovery which resulted in his returning to work shortly afterwards.

"The clock frame is fifteen feet six inches long, and four feet seven inches wide. It is fixed upon iron plates, which cover the two stone walls before described as forming the top of the north and south walls of the great central shaft. The going part of the clock does not occupy more than two feet of this width, the front bushes of the wheels being carried on a separate frame-bar lying on two cross pieces bolted to the front and back girders. There are two great beams which go across the room from east to west above the clock to carry the motion work, and upon these beams is fixed a double-barrelled crab, the ropes from which descend through the space between the front of the going part and the great frame, and down the weight-shaft. The back of the clock-frame is two feet five inches from the West wall of the room, that is the east wall of the ventilating shaft, which runs all the way up the tower from the basement to the level of the bell-chamber floor. The pendulum cock is of cast iron, built into the wall. The pendulum chamber is made of cast iron and serves to protect the pendulum from wind; it is within the weight shaft, on the East side of it, and there is a ladder and trapdoor to descend into it. The floor over the weight shaft, and of course under the clock, is an iron grating lying upon beams.

There is communication by electric telegraph from the clock to the Royal Observatory at Greenwich, and contact between the clock and telegraph is made once every hour, so that the Astronomer Royal can ascertain the rate of the clock by day or by night. The time is reported at present twice a day, namely, at 11.40 a.m. and 12.40 p.m."[7]

The Palace Guide of 1856 states that "the Clock Works have been placed under the able superintendence of the astronomer-royal, Professor Airy, and will, it is expected be very remarkable for their excellency and the different indications of time, day of month and year, etc., that they will be made to show, and it having been proposed to set the time daily by electric communication with the Greenwich Observatory, the time shown by this clock will be of course the standard time for London." No details as to how the day and month were to be shown have yet come to light.

"The thickness of the Great Bell at the thinnest part is three inches. The weights of the hammers do not include the levers and tails which to the Great Bell weigh 782lbs. The hammer of the Great Bell has thirteen inches of oblique lift, or a little more than nine inches of vertical lift. The fall given to the hammers of the quarter bells is varied from seven inches to the smallest bell, to nine inches to the largest one. The weight of the clapper to the large bell is about 8cwt.

The following inscription is cast in raised letters round the bow of the large bell: *This bell, weighing 13 tons 10 cwt 3 quarters 15 lbs, was cast by George Mears, of Whitechapel, for the clock of the Houses of Parliament, under the direction of Edmund Beckett Denison, Q.C., in the twenty-first year of the reign of Queen Victoria, and in the year of our Lord MDCCCLVIII.*"[8]

Stoppages of the clock have been few. Frozen snow is an obvious hazard and a huge number of starlings settling on the hands stopped the clock on 12th August 1949. On one occasion a workman painting the clock-room sat on one of the driving shafts, unaware of its purpose.

The Clock Tower at Westminster has become the symbol of a nation and one of the most familiar landmarks in the world. It was not until the last moment that its outline was decided. As the Tower crept upward there were countless schemes for its completion. Pugin had designed a clock tower for Scarisbrick Hall, which looked much like an outdoor grandfather clock. Barry had spent much time in Venice and would have remembered Saint Mark's *campanile*. Pugin too had been to Venice. A synthesis of designs remembered contrived to produce the graceful outline with which the world has become familiar. The unique feature of the projecting clock stage has been copied with more or less success many times. The subtlety of Westminster is that the clock stage does not project very far beyond the body of the tower, though it overhangs the recessed panelled sides of the tower as they rise to meet it. In many echos of Westminster this feature has been much overdone, resulting in a top heavy appearance.

The Great Clock at Westminster, its bell, and the tower in which it resides is undoubtedly the most celebrated timepiece devised by modern man, but it is not the largest as regards the clockwork. In the Palace of Mafra in Portugal there is a musical clock whose winding handle embodies a lifesize cupid and whose machinery would fill the clock-room at Westminster many times over. The last music that it played was the national anthem which welcomed the King of Portugal as he approached his giant palace visible for many miles across a great open landscape. With the departure of that monarchy the largest clock in the world has been largely silent for many years.

### *The Victoria Tower*

"This Tower, which is the grandest feature of the Houses of Parliament and the largest and highest square tower in the world, serves two distinct purposes; the lower portion of it being the Royal Entrance to the Palace, whilst the upper part forms a magnificent repository wherein are to be preserved the muniments of the legislature of the nation.

The foundations of the Tower were formed by a double row of close piling, secured from spreading, and completely surrounding the site; the earth within this enclosed space was then removed, and concrete thrown in to a depth of ten feet, seven inches, and upon this, two courses of stone landings six inches thick were laid. From this level to the ground line the foundations are of brickwork, the area of the Tower being vaulted with brick nearly up to the same height, and forming a basement storey beneath it. The Tower rises majestically to the height of 331 feet, measuring to the top of the large metal crowns upon the angle turrets, the surface of the walls being nearly vertical; and the horizontal measurement across to the outside of the turrets is about seventy seven feet.

The Tower is square on plan, with an octagonal turret at each angle the whole height, and is attached, the height of the lower storey, to the building on the North and East sides; the West side facing Abingdon Street, and the South side being within the South enclosure.

The lower storey is essentially different in its treatment from the upper storeys, and, together with the tier of niches over it, has been already described. Above this niche band, the four sides of the Tower are uniform in design, except in the sculptures; the space between the turrets is divided

*River front view by E. Walker of the New Palace. The Clock Tower is incomplete.*

vertically into three principal compartments, occupying the same breadth as the great archways, and two smaller ones between these and the turrets; these compartments are marked by small square buttresses, of which there are, therefore, four on each side, running up to the parapet. The angles of the turrets are similarly marked by small buttresses placed diagonally, running up to the parapet of the gallery surrounding the upper lantern. All these buttresses are panelled throughout, and the monotony of their details and great height is dissipated by the moulded strings breaking round them: the entire surface of the walls is panelled, giving a beautiful diapered appearance to them.

The size of the Tower, measuring from the external face of the walls, is sixty three feet six inches square; the jambs of the great arches on the West and South sides measure thirteen feet six inches from the outer face to the inner one, the interior jambs being repeated on the North and East side; the area of the groining of the lower storey is, therefore, thirty six feet six inches square. The piers of this storey are built nearly solid to the level of the top of the groin. The interior of each turret forms a cylindrical shaft, eight feet diameter, from the basement floor to the top; the one at the South-east angle being the staircase from the ground to the top of the Tower, communicating with the void over the groin, with the roof, and the turret above; that at the North-east angle being used as a shaft for ventilating purposes, and the South-west shaft serving to supply fresh air to the interior of the building.

There are altogether eleven floors in the Tower, including the sorting room and the two in the roof; one of these being the base of the roof, a foot above the string course under the parapet, and the uppermost halfway up the roof. The other eight are each divided into eight rooms, in the manner above described; those at the angles of the Tower measure nineteen feet square, and those between them twelve feet nine inches by fifteen feet nine inches, the central octagonal staircase being nineteen feet in diameter.

The doors into these rooms are arranged one on each side of the staircase, and above these, in each of the eight floors, are other doors, from a gallery round the staircase, to galleries in the rooms, affording easy access to the upper tier of cases, which is like the lower one. These galleries are fixed to some of the rooms only, but the same arrangement will be carried out in the others as additional accommodation may be required. The floor of the galleries is of slate upon iron bearers; suspension rods at once giving support to the ends of them, and to the railing surrounding the galleries.

The central staircase is a very striking feature, on account of its spiral form, its lightness, and peculiar construction; the steps and landings being of iron trellis-work, with suspension rods at intervals to support them. The well-hole of the spiral is six feet diameter, and the steps are three feet long; the extreme diameter of the spiral is therefore twelve feet, and it reaches

*The Royal Entrance, Victoria Tower, by J. Johnson (1849).*

from the floor of the sorting room to the upper floor in the roof, a height of about 190 feet.

The walls form in plan an octagon of about nineteen feet diameter; the beams supporting the floors of the rooms are projected beyond these walls, and support the curb and landing surrounding the spiral staircase at each of the floors. These landings are paved with stone.

The enormous flagstaff is of wrought iron; it stands on two cross-beams at the level of the roof, in a socket, and passes through the above-named shaft, and additional support is given to it by strong gibs placed under one of its horizontal ribs and driven through the shaft. It is 120 feet high to the top of the crown at its summit, two feet diameter from its base as high as the top

*The Victoria Tower for Abingdon Street in 1859.*

of the shaft supporting it, above that point it gradually tapers to the top, where it is nine inches diameter. The crown is three feet six inches diameter and five feet six inches high, of copper, gilded.

Having now completed this description of the Tower, there remains to add only, that without a visit to its interior and to its summit, no adequate conception can be formed of its vast size. The view from the flat of the roof will amply repay the labour of the weary ascent up more than 500 steps, even when the atmosphere is only partially clear; but in fine weather it is truly magnificent: for in addition to the crowded metropolis, the buildings and localities in the vicinity, amongst which are the Abbey with its Cloisters and the School, and the old building known as the Jewel Tower of Edward the Third; farther off northward, Whitehall, the Mall and Charing Cross; eastward, Lambeth Palace and Church, and in the distance down the river, Somerset House and St Paul's Cathedral, are seen from here almost at a glance, and being intimately associated with the history of the nation, the scene cannot fail to bring to mind reminiscences of more or less interest to every Englishman; then the parks, the trees studded here and there amongst the buildings, the river, busy with the traffic which glides over its surface, and the surrounding country stretching to the horizon, add charms of nature to the whole.

From here, the building extending over nearly eight acres, can be seen to the greatest advantage, and nowhere else can the disposition of its numerous parts be so readily distinguished and comprehended and its magnitude be so thoroughly appreciated."[9]

It was thus in the knowledge that even if there had been some who had made Barry's life at Westminster arduous and frustrating, there were many many more, including the new Minister, who were delighted with the New Palace and everything that it represented.

On the 12 May 1860 Sir Charles and Lady Barry spent the afternoon at the Crystal Palace, which had been rebuilt with splendid gardens at Sydenham. Sir Charles seemed "very calm and cheerful, speaking of the natural dispersion of their children, and of the end of life, in which they should be thrown upon each other, as at its beginning. The evening had been spent as usual, and at the regular time, about 11 o'clock, he had retired to his dressing-room, there he was seized with difficulty of breathing and pain; and, before any of his children could be summoned, almost before it was known that there was imminent danger, all was over... It was a cause of thankfulness for his sake that it came so painlessly, and that, though his children, to their great grief, were absent, his wife was with him to the end.

It had been intended by his family that his funeral should be private, conducted in accordance with the privacy and simplicity of his life. but almost immediately the chief members of his profession expressed a wish that his body should be laid in Westminster Abbey."[10]

On the 22nd May 1860 Sir Charles Barry was buried in the nave of Westminster Abbey. The pallbearers included Sir Charles Eastlake, President of the Royal Academy, the Rt. Hon. William Cowper, M.P., Chief Commissioner of Works, Sir Edward Cust, A. J. Beresford Hope, C. R. Cockerell, President of the Royal Institute of British Architects. Sir Charles's five sons led the procession which took a quarter of an hour to file into the Abbey. The congregation included Lord John Manners, Sir Joseph Paxton, Sir Morton Peto, the artists J. R. Herbert, Sir Edwin

*Portrait of Sir Charles Barry by H. W. Pickersgill.*

Landseer, Daniel Maclise, David Roberts, the sculptor Richard Westmacott, and the architects George Gilbert Scott, Matthew Digby Wyatt, Benjamin Ferrey, Decimus Burton, David Mocatta and Anthony Salvin. Five hundred workmen from the New Palace walked at the head of the procession from Vauxhall, gave up a half a days pay, and asked leave to attend.

The service included "I know that my Redeemer Liveth" the aria from Handel's *Messiah* upon which the chimes of the Great Clock are said to be based. The anthem was "His body is buried in peace but his name liveth forever more."

All day the Union flag hung at half mast on the top of the Victoria Tower, yet to be crowned with its spectacular ironwork and flagstaff. This, the last work upon which Sir Charles had been engaged, formed the subject, together with a plan of the Palace, of the magnificent brass which was placed over the grave. Many of the details on this brass follow closely the designs of Augustus Welby Pugin.

*E. M. Barry's colonnade, New Palace Yard (1864).*

# VI

## The Building Stands a Great Fact

"The time is not yet come for a full and complete history of the whole subject of the New Palace at Westminster; but when the many difficulties which have environed the work are borne in mind, as well as the numerous masters under whom it has proceeded, it must, I think, be admitted that the architect has some right to expect that the criticism on his production, however severe it may be, should at least partake of a discriminating character. It is not for me to enter here upon questions of taste, which it would be most unbecoming on my part to discuss. The building stands a great fact, and will be calmly judged eventually on its merits and defects by posterity, whose verdict it is worse than useless to attempt to forestall, and who will probably remember that is was nearly, if not quite, the first attempt on a large scale to revive Gothic architecture as applied to civil public purposes - that it was erected in less than twenty years, and by a single architect."

Thus spoke Edward Middleton Barry, the third son of Sir Charles at the Royal Institute of British Architects on February 1st 1858.

The Prime Minister Lord Palmerston had been unable to witness the burial of Sir Charles Barry in Westminster Abbey due to a prior engagement on Epsom Downs (his horse was unplaced in the Derby). His wise and cultivated step-son and heir, William Cowper, First Commissioner of Works, turned at once to young Edward Barry for assistance. He charged him with carrying to completion all that his father had left unfinished at Westminster.

E. M. Barry's work at the New Palace is, on the whole, heavier in style than that of his father in collaboration with Pugin.

New Palace Yard, where Sir Charles had long advocated an enclosure by further building, is where E. M. Barry's work is most prominent. The grand design was abandoned in 1864, resulting in a shortage of accommodation within the Palace which is never likely to be remedied. Edward had somehow to tidy up what was to have been an internal courtyard. The unfinished base of the Clock Tower was decorated in sympathy with the other sides. The somewhat bare lowest storey of the west front was covered with a massively constructed colonnade built against it. Here, Portland stone was employed on the grounds that it was more durable. The architect indulged his taste for rich effect by combining a red sandstone with the Portland stone in the vaulting but the two reacted upon each other. All the red had to be cut out in the 1950s. Much of the carved detail is of the highest quality and some of the mythical animal sculpture is as good as any surviving from the Middle Ages.

The Portland stone pillars and railings on the remaining sides of New Palace Yard date from this time. They were meant to be of a light character but are amongst the most massive and elaborate work that Hardman's ever produced. Their continuance, in a refined form, to St. Stephen's Entrance in the south and to the river in the east was planned towards the end of the 1980s.

The younger Barry's greatest achievement in the interior is the restoration of the Crypt Chapel, properly known as the Chapel of Saint Mary Undercroft. First Commissioner Cowper strongly supported the work but he had to overcome critics of two kinds in the House of Commons. The anti-ecclesiastics combined with the anti-art lobby but another more powerful argument prevailed. The restored Chapel brought joy to all the multitude of men of all conditions who visited it whatever their faith or political philosophy. So it has been ever since. The Chapel is not an outpost of any of the Churches. It is widely used by Parliamentarians and their families for baptisms, marriages and memorial services and is a regular place of worship for all whose lives revolve round the Palace of Westminster.

E.M. Barry took great pains to reproduce the original decoration in his massive restoration (made necessary by the damage caused by the fire). He re-captured the atmosphere of the original and added the Baptistry with its spectacular font. The altar rails and pulpit contain some of the finest metalwork in the New Palace.

Progress towards the completion of the royal processional route had been slow but steady. The description of 1865 omits the painted decoration in the vault at the foot of the staircase and the mosaic which is so prominent a feature in the vaulting over the landing outside the Robing Room. The inclusion of a detailed account of the royal ceremonial centred on this area was no doubt intended as a distraction from its somewhat unfinished state.

*E. M. Barry (1830-80), who succeeded his father as architect of the New Houses of Parliament in 1860.*

*E. M. Barry's archway in New Palace Yard; the statues are by H. Armstead.*

"The Royal Entrance, of which a view has been given, is on the South side of the Royal Staircase, and opens on the spacious landing at the foot of it: a smaller entrance from the West front in Old Palace Yard opens on the same landing directly opposite the staircase, and is designed as the Peers' Entrance to this part of the building. The doors of the Royal Entrance are of elaborate design; they are panelled with tracery, and the margins externally are enriched with a continuous band of delicately wrought quarterfoils, the interior being fitted with locks of superior workmanship.

The Royal Staircase may be described as a flight of stairs nearly fifteen feet wide, consisting of twenty six steps, ascending between two parallel walls after the manner of the grand staircase in the Vatican. The steps are of Aberdeen grey granite, polished, eight feet nine inches long in one stone, five and one half inches rise, and sixteen inches on the treads; the ends are of rich marbles forming a border of two colours on each side; the risers are sunk, and have red marble inserted in the panels.

The walls are of stone, and the roof has a pointed vault of the same material, the whole length of the flight and following its inclination; the walls and vault are divided into three compartments in the length, by slender columns and moulded ribs; the space between them is decorated with panelling, the design being continued across the vaulting.

The upper landing of the staircase is enlarged to form an ante-hall, which is named the Norman Porch. In plan it is a square, the side of which is rather more than double the width of the staircase; it is vaulted with lierne groining in four compartments, springing from clustered wall shafts and a clustered shaft in the centre of the hall; against the bases of these shafts under the angles of the groining are placed stone pedestals, which are intended to support bronze statues of the Norman kings: four similar pedestals decorate the lower landing against the Royal Entrance, which is groined with a vault of the same design as the vaults in the Norman Porch. The two groins seen in the view are pierced with circular eyes for light, and from the centres of all these vaults brass chandeliers of elegant design are suspended.

The staircase is lighted on the North side from the State Office Court, by narrow windows, one being formed in each panel of the wall. These windows are glazed with flowered quarries enriched at intervals with royal badges having mottos between them: the two windows in the Norman Porch are on the same side, are larger, and have rich tracery in the heads. The glass in the centre light of the first window presents a full length portrait of Edward the Confessor, that in the centre light of the second window represents Her Majesty (Queen Victoria) seated in a chair of state, the side lights of both windows being enriched with heraldic banners and supporters: the window of the lower landing is larger and equally beautiful in the design of the stone-work and the glazing.

The landings at the foot of the Royal Staircase and the floor of the Norman Porch are paved with marbles of various colours arranged in bold design; the large pattern of which is rather injurious to the effect of the staircase. The decorative painting of this part is yet unfinished.

*Painting on the west wall of the Crypt Chapel, executed by Crace.*

*The baptismal font in the Crypt Chapel, designed by E. M. Barry in the 1860s.*

The doorway at the top of the staircase leads into the Royal Gallery. Over this doorway and also over the doorways leading to the Queen's Robing Room and Guard Room are carved elaborate tracery and heraldic ornaments.

Over the entrance from the Victoria Tower to the Staircase, the royal arms, motto and monograms are sculptured.

When Her Majesty opens or prorogues Parliament, the staircase is lined on the sides, by the yeomen of the guard in their quaint dresses, holding halberds (relics of the Tudor age); whilst the gentlemen-at-arms occupy the Norman Porch; and for a short time previously to the arrival of the Sovereign, the lower landing is thronged with the Officers of State who are apparelled in their gorgeous dresses, some of which are of antique design, and who on the arrival of the state carriage under the Victoria Tower advance to meet the Queen; the Royal procession then moves up the staircase to the Robing Room to which Her Majesty retires previously to going into the House. By means of a telegraphic wire which has been laid from the angle of the lower landing of the staircase to St James's Park, a signal is made the instant Her Majesty steps on to the pavement, so that the guns in the Park are fired simultaneously. On these occasions the Palace is seen to the greatest advantage as a work of art."[1]

*The Robing Room*

This was one of the last rooms to be completed under the management of E. M. Barry. It is fifty four feet long, thirty seven wide and twenty five feet high to the magnificent ceiling which owes its inspiration to Wolsey's closet at Hampton Court. The cove of the ceiling was originally intended to contain a series of paintings chosen by Prince Albert's Commission. Below is a frieze of sixty-four coats of arms relating to the Arthurian Legend. The wall panels were the subject of a contract with William Dyce who was commissioned to paint a series of frescoes illustrating chivalry in relation to King Arthur. He completed "Generosity", "Religion", and "Courtesy" by 1852. "Mercy" was finished in 1854 but "Hospitality" was not completed until 1865. Dyce did not live to paint "Fidelity" or "Courage" either side of the the Cloth of Estate but two fine portraits by Winterhalter of Queen Victoria and the Prince Consort now symbolize fidelity and courage. The Chair of State stands on a simple dias beneath a fine panel of needlework incorporating the royal arms. This was worked by the Royal School of Needlework in 1856. Set in the panelling of this room is a series of carvings by H. Armstead, depicting events in the Arthurian Legend. Opposite the Chair of State is a magnificent fireplace made of marbles from the British Isles. The metalwork of the fire-grate with the flanking figures of St. George

*Stained glass window at the foot of the Royal Staircase.*

and St. Michael is some of the grandest in the Palace. The floor has an inlaid border of heraldic devices in a not particularly Gothic style. The glass in the windows is unusual both in technique and in style. The subtle trailing Tudor rose pattern is worked upon large pieces of glass set in the bronze window frames and not in lead as so often found elsewhere. Apart from the Chair of State there was no other furniture specially made for this room. Their Lordships have often expressed the hope that suitable furnishings could be found, all in keeping with their surroundings.

Following the destruction of the House of Commons Chamber in 1941 the Lords immediately and generously offered their own Chamber to the Commons and had the Robing Room fitted up as a Temporary Chamber. The only record of this event and the only view of the Peers sitting in this Temporary Chamber was drawn by Brian de Grineau. The original drawing was presented to the House of Lords in memory of Samuel, 6th Viscount Hood in 1982.

The Lords returned to their own Chamber in 1950. It was on the 29th May (the day that Charles II was restored to the throne).

Dyce's frescoes in the Robing Room are sombre affairs compared with his magnificent work at Osborne, supervised at almost every stage by the Prince Consort himself. There he covered great areas of wall with naked sea-nymphs presenting the crown of Neptune to Britannia. The colours there are as fresh as the day they were painted. At Westminster the frescoes have given nothing but trouble.

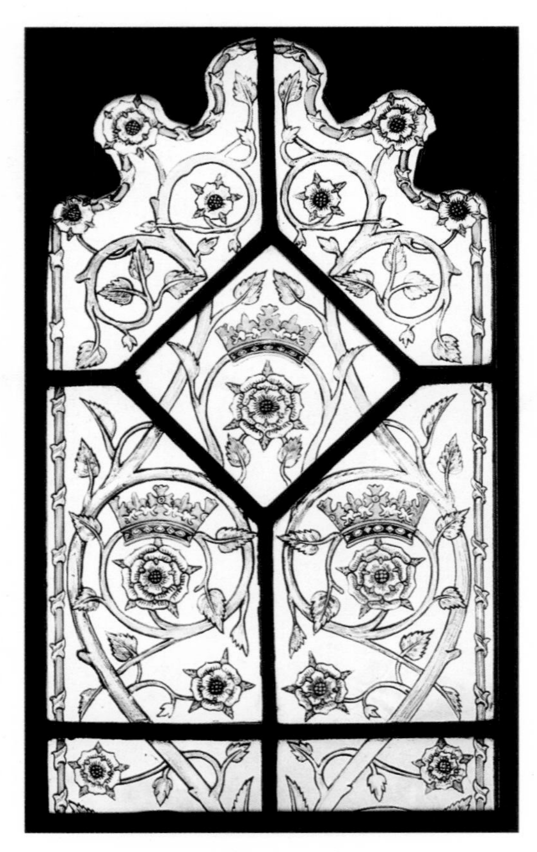

*Detail of the stained glass in the Robing Room.*

In the time of Sir Charles Barry the Royal Gallery had taken its final shape and form but was far from finished as regards its decoration. The description of 1865 gives a detailed account of what had been achieved under E.M. Barry and what was further intended.

*The Royal Gallery*

"This apartment, which is very fine both in its size and proportions, is 110 feet six inches long from north to south, forty four feet six inches wide, and forty five feet high. It is situated between the Queen's Robing Room on

*The fireplace in the Robing Room.*

the south and the Prince's Chamber on the north; and forms the approach to the House of Peers from the Royal Staircase. On State occasions when the Queen opens Parliament, Her Majesty passes in procession with the Great Officers of State through this Gallery into the House of Peers, and for the accommodation of the public, temporary benches are then fixed along the sides.

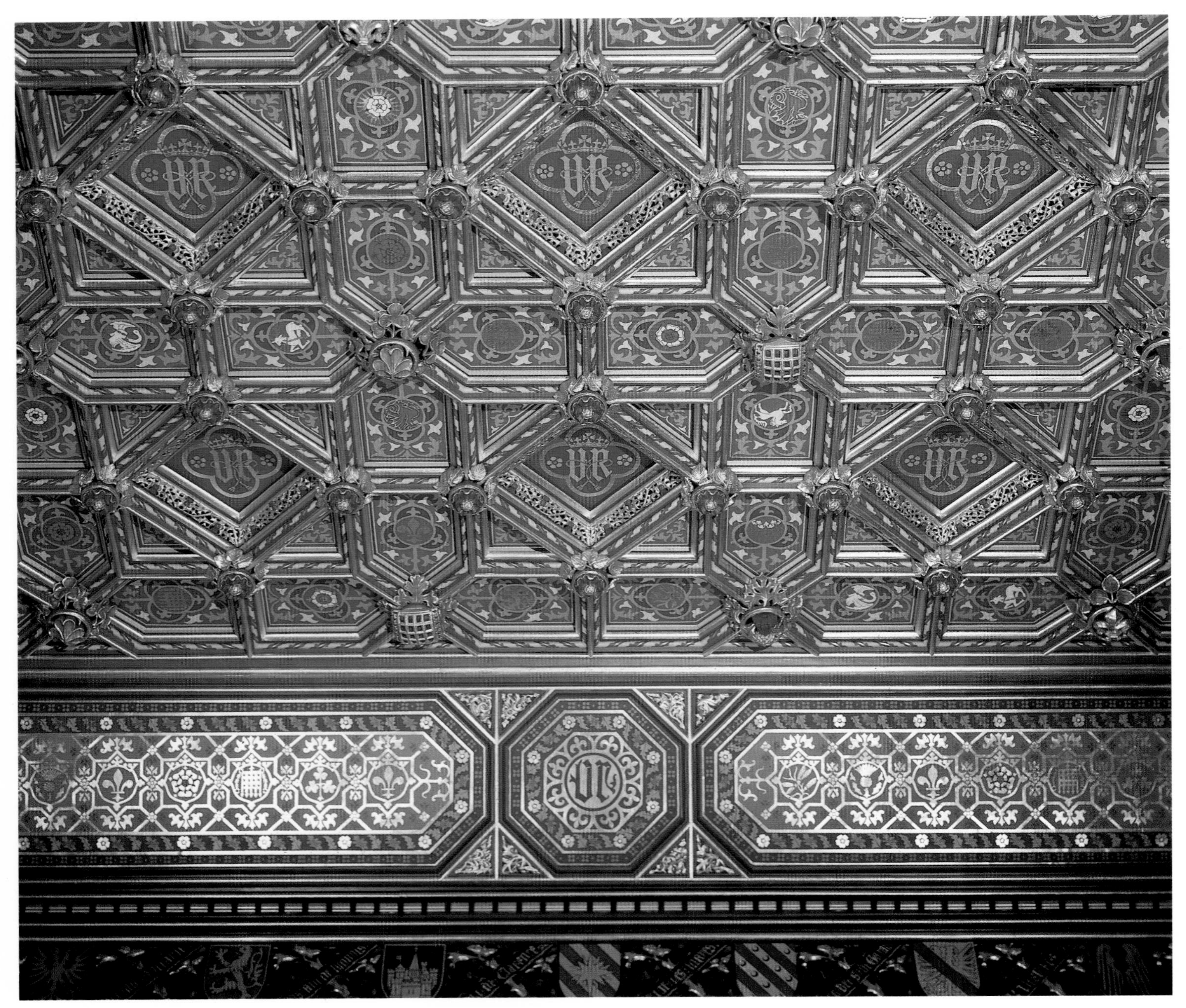

*Part of the Robing Room ceiling with the monogram VR in the central lozenges.*

The ceiling is very bold in its details and is richly decorated with colours and gilding; the ribs, which separate its main compartments are curved at the ends and are formed into large spandrils in which are carved the Royal supporters, rest upon corbelled shafts between the windows. Each of the smaller compartments of the ceiling is ornamented with a centre containing the rose *en soleil* carved and richly gilded; lions and roses in colours and gilding filling the surrounding panels.

The walls under the windows are formed into compartments for paintings, the subjects of which will be a series of remarkable events, relating to the naval and military history of the country, and the Fine Arts Commissioners have entrusted the execution of them to Mr Maclise, R.A. The two in the centre of the length of the Gallery are very large, being forty five feet six inches long and twelve feet one inch high. Upon that on the east side is represented the interview between Wellington and Blücher after the Battle of Waterloo; the largest work of this artist and altogether a grand production, thoroughly masterly in design and carefully worked out in all its details. Our limits prevent the introduction of anything like an adequate description of this important work of art; yet we must give a sketch of it. Its arrangement may be described as consisting of five principal divisions; the central group represents the Duke, tired, with a grave and thoughtful countenance, mounted on his horse, Copenhagen, and Blücher, also mounted, who, as he is leaving in pursuit of the enemy, turns to grasp the hand of the iron duke: on one side of this centre are the English staff, and on the other the Prussian; Gneisenau, with white plumes in his hat, Bulow and Ziethen, are amongst the latter; amongst the former, Sir Hussey Vivian (Lord Vivian) in a Hussar's dress, mounted on a white horse, will engage the attention of every one; for, besides being a principal light in the composition and richly coloured, the figures of both the horse and his rider are exquisitely painted and very carefully finished; the leopard skin is nature, and so is the horse and so are many of the horses in these groups of equine life, which are so skilfully arranged both in form and colouring, and contain so much of nature, that they command the admiration of every spectator. On each side of these are two minor groups, which constitute the remainder of the composition; numbers of wounded, dying, and dead men fill up the sides and foreground of the picture. On the right side a Highlander and a Fusilier carry off the body of 'young Howard', and near the centre three of the Life Guards, who are sitting on the ground wounded, brandish their sabres and cheer, though evidently with pain. Here are life and death in close embrace; suffering humanity displaying a great variety of muscular contortion; the wounded and the dead in postures as various as the figures, scattered throughout; whilst the dying and dead horses, implements of destruction, shot, shell, swords, broken musical instruments, and helmets, shakos and banners, are seen in every direction. The drawing of all these, in fact of every part, is marvellous."[2]

This picture was finished in January 1862, having occupied the artist about a year and nine months in its execution, after the cartoon was approved.[3]

"The subject of the companion picture on the west wall of the Gallery is the Death of Nelson the scene represented is the quarter-deck of the Victory; the hero having just received his death wound is stretched along, being partially supported by Captain Hardy, one of the group, who with anxious countenances are surrounding him.

The length of the compartment on which this picture is painted is the same as that of the quarter-deck of the Victory.[4]

The process adopted in the execution of these paintings is that of stereo-chrome or water-glass, the solution being applied to the painting after it is finished.

The lower part of the walls is lined with a richly panelled dado of wainscot, and a bench with stuffed crimson morocco cushions is fixed against it.

It is proposed to place upon the pedestals twelve marble statues of British Monarchs, from James I to William IV, comprehending the Sovereigns of the Houses of Stuart and Brunswick."[5]

Under Cowper, later Lord Mount Temple, E. M. Barry had achieved much. Lord John Manners' third and last term as First Commissioner followed. Austen Henry Layard was the new First Commissioner on Gladstone's becoming Prime Minister in 1868. He was as sympathetic as his predecessor, indeed he regarded himself as Minister for the Fine Arts.

The Central Hall, unfinished at Sir Charles's death, was the subject of much frustration. Although structurally complete with its spectacular vaulted ceiling, it presented a somewhat uneven and gloomy picture. The four great spaces prepared for art were filled with a shabby wallpaper. The unevenly coloured stonework (due to alterations because the statues had not fitted their niches) was covered with "a brown encaustic composition" to disguise the deficiencies. The tiled floor had been successfully executed. Barry resolved now to tie the existing elements together and complete the Hall in as cheerful and colourful a manner as he could devise. He wanted to substitute banded marble columns for the dirty stone and mosaics seemed to him to be preferable to frescoes. Layard and Barry obtained the services of the great Salviati of Venice. The decoration of the panels between the ribs of the vault was carried out during the course of a summer recess to the delight of some Parliamentarians and the fury of others. One only of the four planned mosaics, Poynter's "St. George", was completed before the sympathetic Layard had been re-shuffled away by Gladstone as Ambassador in Madrid. His replacement, Acton Smee Ayrton, was a fanatic. He deemed it his duty to lay about the Palace with an axe, to cut away any extravagant expenditure on anything whatsoever. In his anxiety to avoid further

*The Central Hall or Great Octagon in 1852.*

*The meeting of Wellington and Blücher after Waterloo painted by Daniel Maclise (1862).*

*The Death of Nelson painted by Daniel Maclise (1865).*

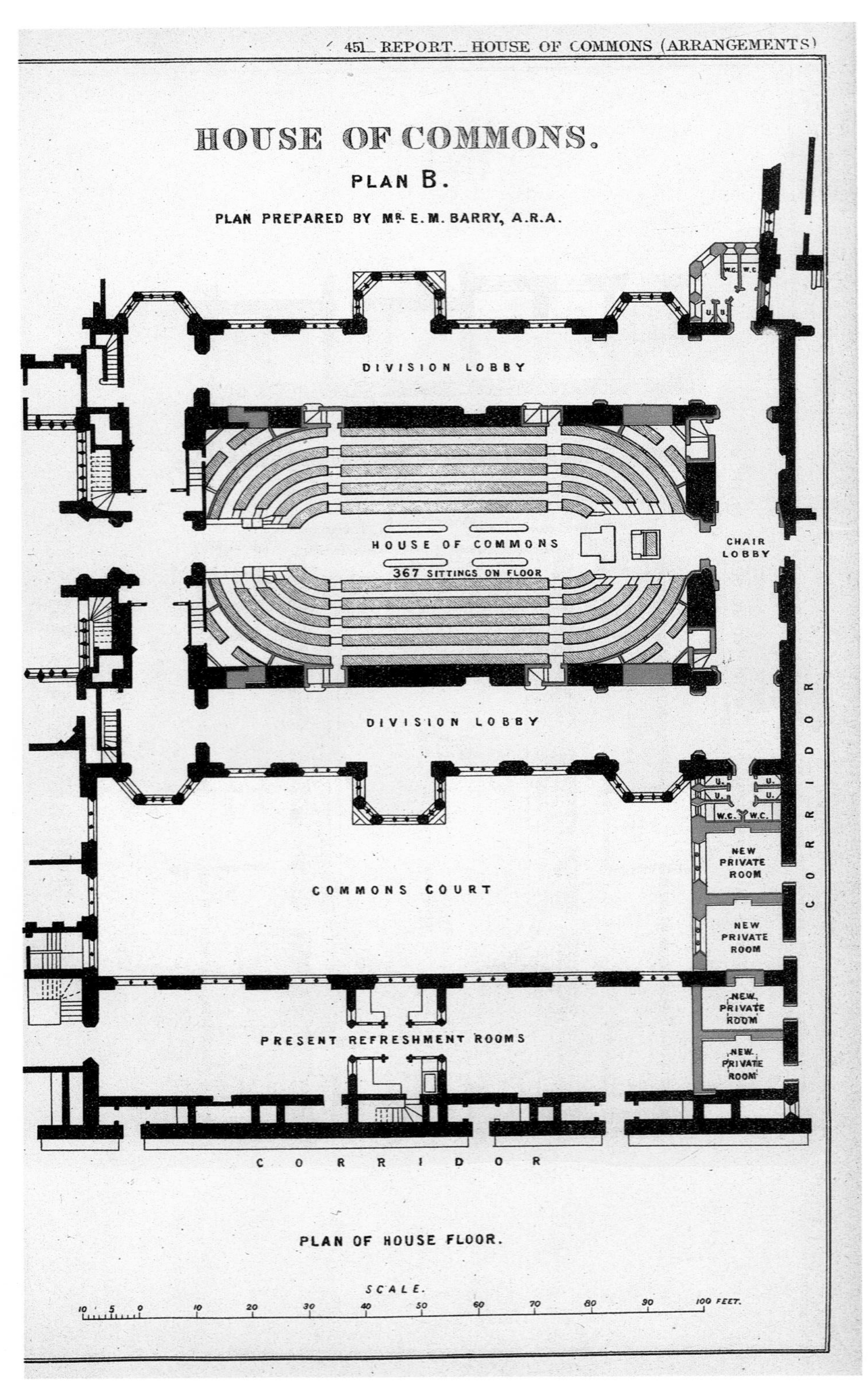


*E. M. Barry's plan to provide 367 seats in the House of Commons (1867).*

expenditure on doubtful frescoes or mosaics (which he regarded as mere copies of earlier work) he fell for the proposition of Henry Cole. The walls of the Palace could be decorated with "durable mural paintings produced by fictile vetrification by the newly discovered process." Thus the Palace of Westminster might have come to resemble a vast public convenience, similar to the shiniest and most garish interiors of a part of the Victoria and Albert Museum.

E. M. Barry, in addition to drawing up the various options within the existing walls, produced a proposal for an entirely new Chamber built in Commons Court and embracing the Refreshment Rooms to the east. This produced about 458 seats on the floor arranged almost in the shape of an octagon. This proposal, he claimed, had the advantage that a new Chamber could be constructed whilst the old was still in operation. The abandoned Chamber could be restored and converted to a new Commons' Lobby reserved exclusively for Members.

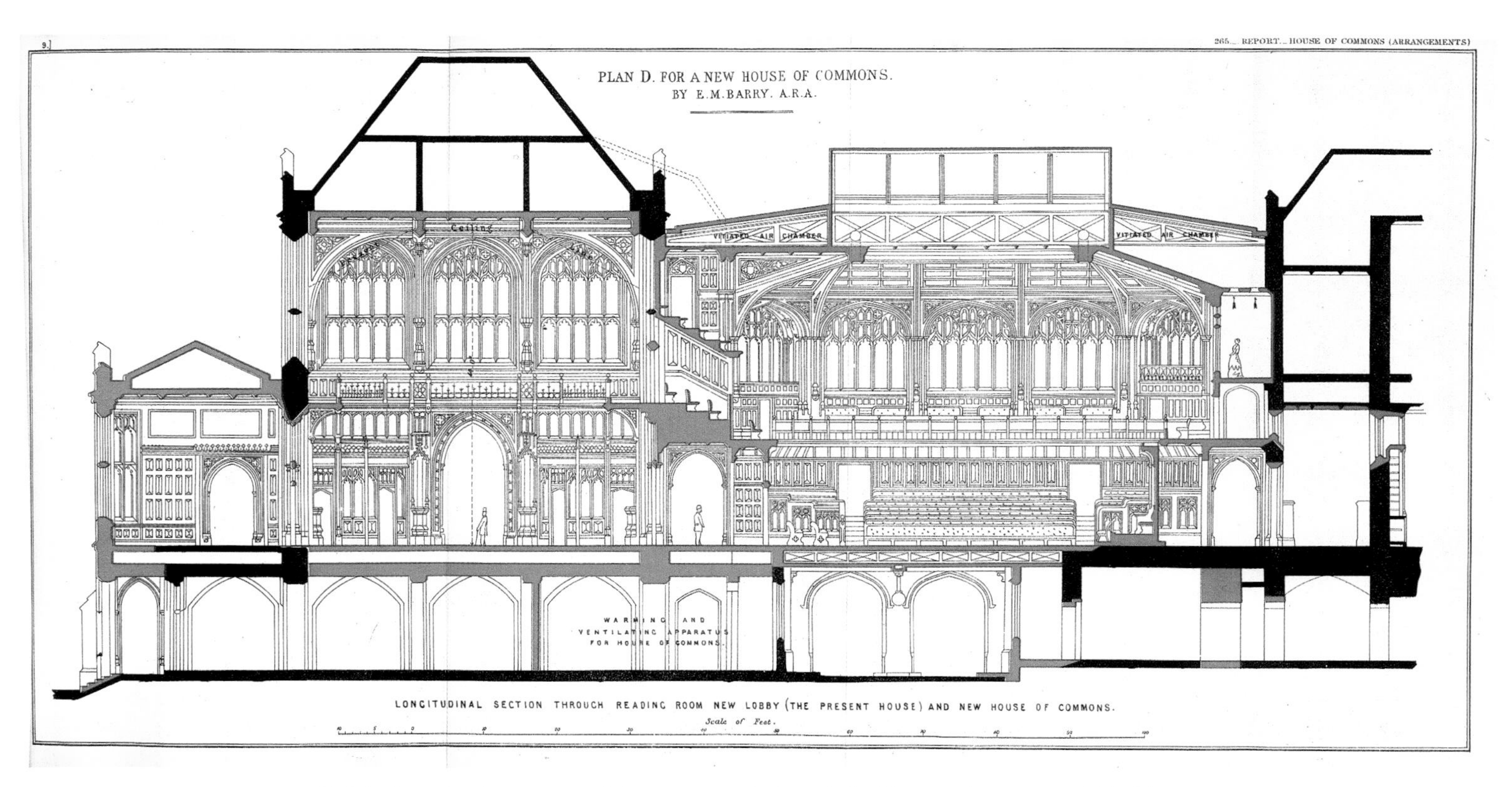


*E. M. Barry's plan to extend the accommodation of the House of Commons (1867).*

The succeeding committee reported on 12th May 1868. The session of 1867 had been an abnormal one due to "debates on the subject of Parliamentary reform" (this was the Irish question). Despite the special circumstances of that year the committee believed "that there are substantial grounds for the complaints that were then made, and that the present House of Commons is defective in the necessary extent of accommodation."

The committee then gave its consideration to E. M. Barry's masterly solution. Far from destroying the present House, it was neither "pulled down nor injured, but on the contrary restored to the much more beautiful shape it possessed in the year 1850, according to the designs of the late Sir Charles Barry, before it was subjected to any alteration. The effect would be that the ceiling would be raised, the height of the windows greatly increased, and the true architectural proportions restored. It would then become a Lobby exclusively for Members. A new Chamber could be constructed before the abandonment of the old by taking in the whole of Commons Court and the adjoining Dining Rooms (the tea room)."

The Report includes a long memorandum from E. M. Barry, which states that "the present House for 430 Members, is sixty eight feet by forty four feet and forty four feet high containing 120,000 cubic feet of space. The latter however, has no solid floor. The floor is little more than a large iron grating, thoroughly pervious to sound. The effect of this condition can hardly be otherwise than acoustically unsatisfactory, adding as it does to the size of the House so that the voice of a Member speaking, fills under unfavourable circumstances, not only the House itself, but also the chambers beneath it." This meant that the voices of the Members filled a space of 154,500 cubic feet.

The cubic capacity of the proposed new House was to be less than the foregoing. The floor was to be of solid wood, the ventilation was to be through the back of the seats and not through the dirty matting on the floor. The ceiling was to have sloping sides and a glazed central portion through which natural day-light would filter. The windows on either side would be capable of being opened and would add greatly to the cheerfulness of the House, according to E. M. Barry. After dark, gas burners above the glass ceiling would provide light. A number of other improvements would have flowed from this substantial change.

The cost of the Headlam proposals for a new Chamber and related works was estimated at £120,000. Previous experience led some Members to fear that something near half a million was a more realistic figure. The claim by the First Commissioner Layard that "one of the finest things in Europe" would be created did not help Members preoccupied with economy. Gladstone told the House that the problem would probably go away. There the matter was left despite occasional attempts at revival.

A fault common to all the proposals, (both recommended and not recommended), was that a substantial number of seats on the floor could not readily be seen by Mr. Speaker, who must have command of the House (in more senses than one).

In the next session Headlam's committee turned its mind to the construction of a new Dining Room. This too was on too great a scale for immediate acceptance. It was proposed to convert the little used Conference Room (Painted Chamber) and adjoining Commons Committee Rooms into dining rooms, shared by both the Houses. In the event the Lords declined to associate themselves with the Commons (despite several attempts to effect a marriage of refreshment departments they have remained separate to this day). The new First Commissioner, Ayrton, did make progress for the Commons but it was not until the early years of the twentieth century that the Conference Room was truncated to the north and its entire south wall removed to bring in the room next door. This is probably the most savage alteration made to the interior of the Palace but it would be possible to reinstate the room as much of the material and all the evidence is available.

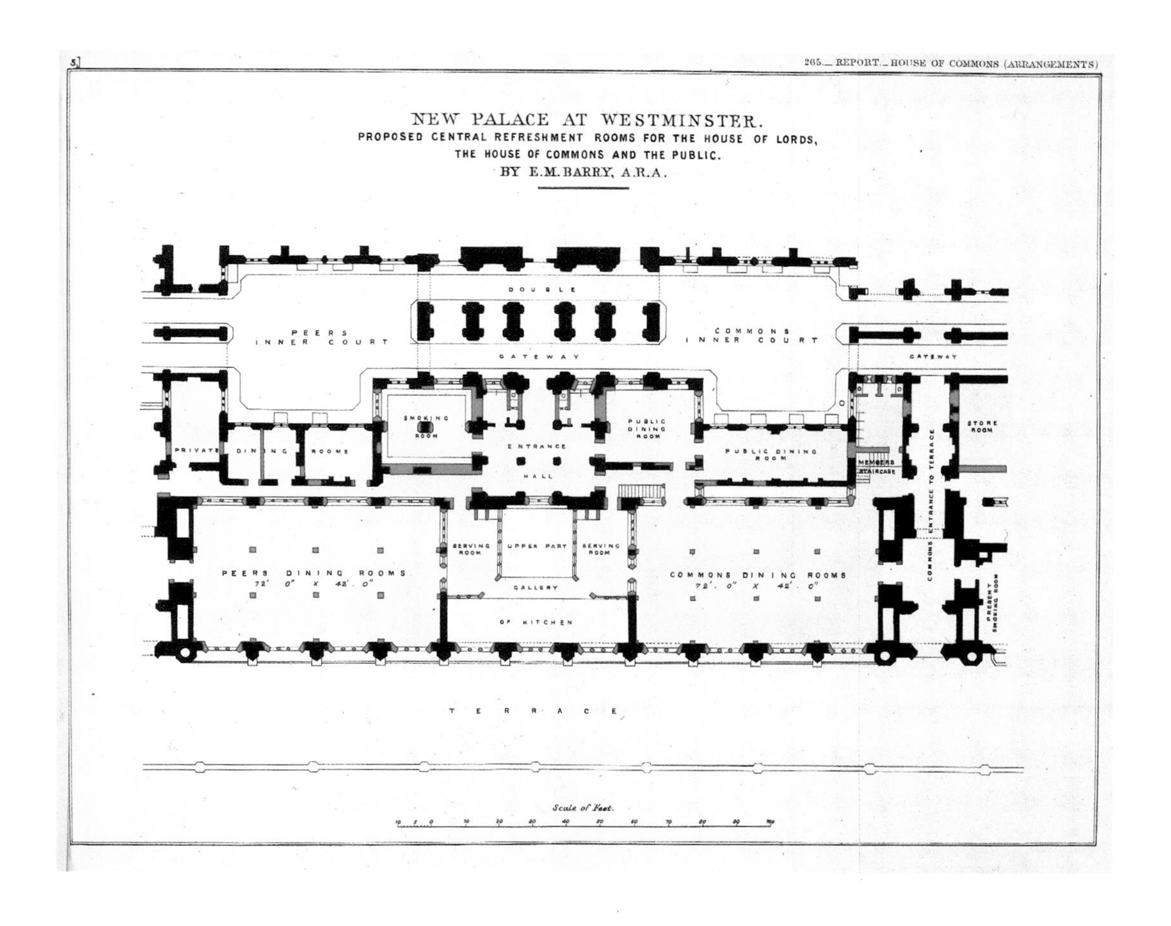


*E. M. Barry's proposed central refreshment rooms for the Lords, the Commons and the public (1867).*

The Lords in contrast were seeking a smaller Chamber. They were inclined to find that their grand surroundings were uncongenial when transacting ordinary business. Certainly on occasions when it was necessary for very few Peers to take part the small number in the large Chamber did feel a certain sense of isolation.

Edward Barry, remembering his bold suggestion for enlarging the Commons, here turned it on its head, suggesting that the Peers' Chamber be left untouched and that the far smaller Peers' Robing Room (Moses Room) be converted for ordinary business at the cost of a mere £40,000. No agreement could be reached and no structural alterations took place at this time.

By now Edward Barry had contrived to complete, or leave in a reasonable state of completion, the whole of the interior. He had even managed to remove the ill-fitting marble figures originally made for the Royal Gallery and had them set up in Westminster Hall. Here they looked sufficiently miscast to be offered to the City of London for the Guildhall, whence they gravitated to the Old Bailey. In the gilded niches in the Royal Gallery twelve gilded statues of Kings and Queens by J. Birnie Phillip had taken their places beside Maclise's "Waterloo" and "Trafalgar". The Norman Kings for the Royal Staircase had however not materialised. Art was experiencing a cooler climate under the eye of Acton Smee Ayrton. With the Prince Consort dead nine years, Sir Charles Barry for ten and Pugin for eighteen, Ayrton decided to strike. In January 1870 he had the Assistant Secretary in his Department inform Edward Barry, in a letter, that as from the end of the financial year on the 31st March the New Palace at Westminster would be entirely in the charge of the officers of the Department. Edward Barry was commanded to hand over all the contract plans and drawings and all other papers necessary for affording the complete knowledge of the building, and of the works carried on in connection therewith.

The manner in which Ayrton had proceeded was greeted with outrage both within and without Parliament. His insensitive approach had logic on its side. Public works must be the responsibility of a public Department. This did not prevent a Department from hiring the services of an architect or even from entering into a contract of employment with one. The Minister is answerable to Parliament, has to accept responsibility and therefore has to be in control. To the insulting way in which the principle was asserted was added the injury of the demand for possession of the drawings. Ayrton was advised by the Law Officers that everything required for a complete working knowledge was Crown property. In the face of this and a judgement in the Court of Exchequer (where it was decided that the drawings of a building belong to the employer of the architect), Edward Barry had no option but to offer everything to the First Commissioner. Barry was allowed to keep drawings which had been made by Sir Charles and himself with a particular view to their publication although he offered to sell those to the Government. Everything else was put into a Committee Room. Departmental officials picked out 1,648 drawings but returned 2,072 to Edward Barry.

Despite their treatment by Government and Parliament the Barry family subsequently have been more than generous with all that they have inherited and which relates to the New Palace. There have been gifts of diaries and drawings to learned institutions and ever an open-handed attitude to scholars seeking to unravel the history of the great monument to their family name. Edward Middleton Barry has left his mark upon the New Palace as did his father and Augustus Welby Pugin. He was the author of a number of distinguished public works, narrowly failing to secure the commissions for the new Law Courts and the rebuilding of the National Gallery, which he did extend. His rooms there were restored in 1986.

The end of the Barry family connection coincided with the end of the major works of construction at the New Palace, though there were some changes made to the interior and some attempts at disastrous tinkering with major features.

### *The Restoration of Westminster Hall*

The New Law Courts in the Strand, the work of G. E. Street, were designed to replace Soane's overcrowded Courts which adjoined Westminster Hall.

The demolition of the Law Courts at Westminster revealed the great buttresses on the west side of Westminster Hall in which interesting traces of Norman work could be seen.

With the abandonment of Sir Charles Barry's grand design for buildings for Parliament along the east side of St. Margaret's Street, J. L. Pearson was commissioned to restore and repair the west side of Westminster Hall and to address himself also to the north entrance front.

Great pains were taken to achieve an agreeable authenticity. Every shred of reliable evidence was worked up into a number of alternatives some of which were tried out in full size mock-up on the site. The version that was finally agreed was executed only in part. Pearson's proposal for heightening the towers which flanked the north entrance of the hall was not carried out.

What was achieved was a return to dignity of the west side of the hall, indeed by the time the work was finished in 1888 it looked a great deal grander than at any time in its previous history. A green was created between the hall and where had been St. Margaret Street but now is Parliament Square. The substantial difference in levels is visually counteracted by this arrangement, there being but a low wall between the pavement and the twenty foot drop to the green. The imposition of an ugly statue of Cromwell standing on a plinth of poor Classical design adorned by a single and feeble lion has not enhanced the scene but the potted palm trees which once surrounded it have long gone.

Pearson's interiors have a certain interest. His Gothic of the 1880s using oiled teak woodwork against white stone walls survives only in the Grand Committee Room, which has a roof like a medieval hall. All the other interiors perished either in the 1939 - 45 World War or as a result of a terrorist attack in 1974. However out of the ruins of the second devastation was created the Jubilee Room in 1977 in the manner of some of Pugin's richest interiors. The remainder of the space which Pearson created cleverly between the buttresses of the hall is presently divided up in a somewhat temporary fashion which does not preclude its reorganization as an adjunct to Westminster Hall and a route by which visitors to the Palace could learn something of its history before proceeding through its historic interiors.

*Report on the Sanitary Arrangements*

The manner of Edward Middleton Barry's departure and the assumption of control of the New Palace by the Office of Works did not promise well for its future management. Nor did Reid's dismissal, Meeson's efforts during the interregnum or Goldsworthy Gurney's unfounded confidence in an easy solution. The subject of heating and ventilation was as much a problem as it had ever been. By the 1880s Select Committees were at work again.

On the 23rd July it was ordered that a committee appointed to inquire into the ventilation of the House should have power to inquire as to the noxious smells which occasionally pervaded the House, and into the cause of the same.

The Chairman for these deliberations was W. H. Smith, M.P. the bookseller. He later became First Lord of the Admiralty and the model for that character in Gilbert and Sullivan's "HMS Pinafore".

The committee cross-examined Sir Joseph William Bazalgette, Director of Metropolitan Sewage, and architect of the Sewage Disposal for the whole of the metropolis, a world famous figure in his special field.

They questioned the Director of Operations in Westminster District. They cast their net far and wide. They endeavoured to discover whence the smells came.

The commiteee concluded that there was nothing wrong with the drainage arrangements of the Palace and that it was not the metropolitan sewers that offended but those under the control of the Westminster District

*The Grand Committee Room, Westminster Hall, designed J. L. Pearson (1888).*

Board of Works. Additionally, the activities of local manufacturers, particularly Doultons of Lambeth, came under scrutiny.

On the evidence of Mr. Alfred Evans Fletcher F.C.S. it appeared that the quantity of coal burnt at Doultons was about 500 tons per week. Those 500 tons of coal, taking the sulphur at one per cent, would throw off fifteen tons of strong sulphuric acid.

It is not difficult to see how the original stonework of the New Palace came to suffer from the London atmosphere.

There were also rubbish dumps not far from the Palace which could have been the source of trouble.

In January 1885 an Inspector, Major Tulloch, was sent from the Local Government Board "to inquire into the conditions of the sewers and drains in connection with the Houses of Parliament and those in the vicinity and to report to Her Majesty's Commission of Public Works and Buildings." Major Tulloch found that a main sewer of brick, five feet six inches high by three feet wide ran the entire length of the Palace and past the east of the Clock Tower, where it joined the metropolitan low level sewer.

The works, although beautifully executed, were deficient in design. There was not enough fall from the end of the Parliamentary sewer into the metropolitan. Accumulations of sewage beneath the Palace commonly built up and were festering there for many days at a time. A ventilation system involving a constantly-burning fire in the base of the Clock Tower was wholly ineffective because although it endeavoured to draw the gases up from the sewer, there was no inlet and thus no air current produced.

Tulloch stated "that all the arrangements were open to objection. They are not only complicated, but their action is, if anything, to prevent there ever being a free outlet for the sewerage from the Houses of Parliament...The sanitary arrangements for the Houses of Parliament should be altogether independent of the weather and of the state of the London sewers." In short, the Parliamentary sewer was far too big and accumulated great quantities of gas which were bound to cause great offence and distress. The remedy was to construct at the highest level within the brick tunnel a much smaller tube of iron which would carry away all the sewerage separately from the vast quantities of storm water which arose from the eight acres of iron roof.

However, the Palace authorities hit back. Their brick sewer of magnificent proportions had the great advantage that it could be regularly inspected. It was possible to walk along it without undue discomfort. They persuaded the Select Committee of 1886 that "the air of the Palace of Westminster is subject to contamination by sewer gas emanating from the low-level of sewer of the main drainage of the metropolis, with which the system of drainage of the Palace is in direct connection." The committee did however advocate a complete reconstruction of the main drain passing under the Houses of Parliament, and "an entire alteration of the means of discharging sewerage from the Palace in the main low level sewer...for the safety of the Members of the legislature and of the officers residing within the precincts of the Palace."

Their most important recommendation was that the drainage of the Palace be pumped into the metropolitan system by means of Shone's pneumatic ejectors, and that the main sewer passing under the Houses of Parliament be reconstructed on the most approved modern principles all at the cost of £8,000. In the appendix to the Report of 1886 there is a sketch of the ingenious machinery which makes all clear. It is signed by Major Tulloch.

In their second Report of 31st May 1886 "The Committee find that the architect of the building did not hand over to Her Majesty's Office of Works and Public Buildings any complete plan of the basement showing the position of the drains; nor have the officers of that Board, under whose direction the drainage of the building is placed, ascertained since then with precision the course of many of the drains leading from the closets... The Committee have next to call the attention of the House to a reprehensible practice which has been uniformly carried on, and one which they are of the opinion is a primary cause of the smell which has been so much complained of. This consists of allowing the waste steam from the warming apparatus, and the high-pressure steam and boiling water from the boilers to pass directly into the sewers.

To remedy this, the Committee have pleasure in calling attention to a scheme which has been prepared by the intelligent and zealous Resident Engineer of the Houses, where by this source of danger may be avoided, so that the steam would be condensed."[6]

The kitchen dustbins next received comment, and the smells of cooking, and especially the foul smells arising from boiling vegetables.

On the subject of ventilating the Chamber of the House, the committee suggested that although the use of the heated upcast shafts in the Clock Tower and in the Victoria Tower had produced satisfactory results for many years under the superintendence of Dr. Percy F.R.S., mechanical means were now available and that air pumps might well be brought into play with advantage.

A small matter of lack of sufficient fresh air under the Opposition Benches and in the No Division Lobby could be remedied by opening a window, and they recommended that "this change should be effected at once."

On the subject of drainage, in the course of which a shadow had been cast upon the sewers under the control of the Local Government Board but not those under the direction of the great Sir Joseph Bazalgette, the committee earnestly desired to point out to the House that "as sanitary engineering has now become a distinct speciality it is, in their opinion, absolutely essential, that looking to the magnitude and importance of the works they have recommended, and without throwing any imputation on the officers of Her Majesty's Board of Works, the designing and superintendence of the works in question should be entrusted to an independent expert of the highest professional standing, under whose personal direction the alterations suggested should be carried into effect."

This last veiled attack on the competence of the public servants involved was presumably meant to be off-set by the kind references to the intelligence and zeal of the Resident Engineer.

The Report concluded that "they were unanimously of the opinion that the health of the Members of Parliament and of the officers who reside within the precincts of the Palace of Westminster, is seriously imperilled by the defective drainage and sanitary arrangements which now exist in the building."

Alterations to the House of Commons kitchen were proposed. Improvement of the Dining Rooms and a new Smoking Room on the principal floor were recommended. The Press Gallery also received consideration but here they had been partly stymied by the attitude of the Clerk of the House of Commons. "Upon the general subject of finding additional accommodation for Members, your committee had the advantage of taking the evidence of Sir Reginald Palgrave. Your committee think that, under the existing pressure of Parliamentary business, it is desirable that the Clerk of the House of Commons shall be resident within the building and that office accommodation should be provided for the Clerk Assistant. Your committee do not consider that necessity exists for recommending any change at the present time, but they are of the opinion that, on the occasion of the next appointment to the Clerkship of the House of Commons, the question of taking the house now occupied by the Clerk, for the purpose of giving additional accommodation to Members and to the Press should receive attention."

Thus that scholarly late nineteenth century figure, who had perhaps had time to select a verse or two for the Poetry Anthology which bears the distinguished family name, in the occasional lulls which punctuate even the most arduous of public duties, lived on in his magnificent home in the Palace. Early in the twentieth century both the Clerk and the Librarian (who lurked in sumptious accommodation next door) were provided for elsewhere. The drawing room of the Clerk of the House, with its beautiful stained glass window containing the arms of Sir Denis LeMarchant, together with a tiny lobby outside and one small adjoining closet, has provided ample accommodation for every Prime Minister since A. J. Balfour.

The early years of this century saw great activity by the Select Committee of the House of Commons (ventilation). Innumerable permutations of velocity and direction of the air were tried. Attention was also lavished upon the washing, cooling, and heating apparatus. This was against the background of the much altered ventilation system which owed its ancestry to Dr. Reid.

By 1906 and four hundred pages of evidence later, the experts produced some interesting conclusions - some 62 per cent of bacteria sucked in from the inlet on the Terrace close to the river were removed by the washing screen, 83 per cent of the dust in the outside air was removed by a cotton wool filter but then the air had to pass through the matting on the floor of the Chamber where it picked up all the debris carried in on the feet of Members and visitors. In 1906 particles of horse dung were among the substances there identified though they were not thought to be a great health hazard. An adjustment to the Terrace air intake had resulted in the air in Refreshment Room D being pumped into the debating Chamber. As regards quantities of air, the intake fan was found to be not sufficiently powerful but the extract fan was too powerful, resulting in unfiltered air

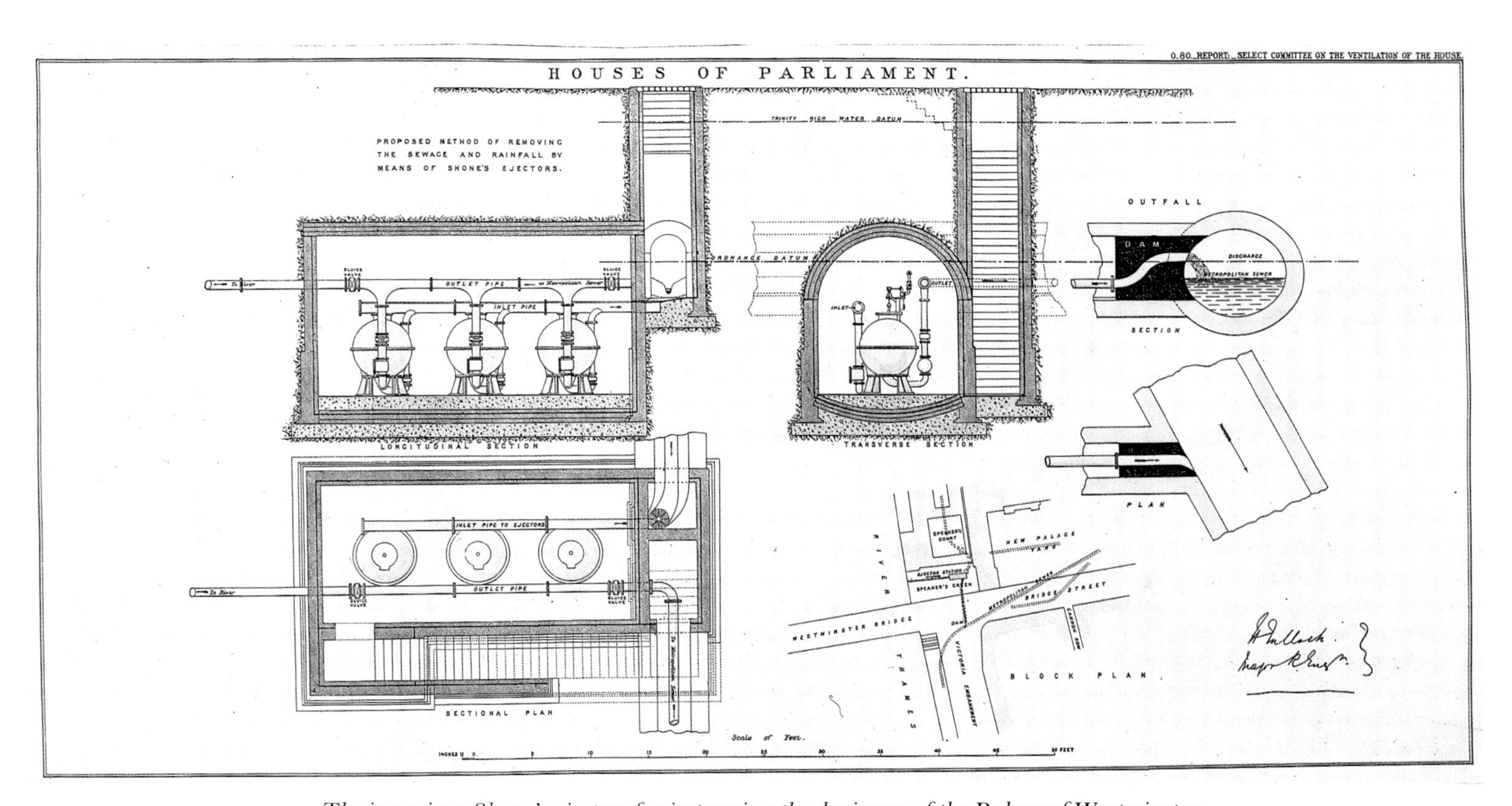


*The ingenious Shone's ejectors for improving the drainage of the Palace of Westminster.*

being drawn into the Chamber from the atmosphere outside the building. An influenza epidemic amongst Members of Parliament led to the placing of prepared plates in various parts of the Chamber upon some of which cultures of bacteria were grown. It was concluded that good ventilation in the Chamber, although it spread the bacteria further, diluted them and their powers of survival were in these circumstances limited. At least this applied to certain types of bacteria, though not to others.

The introduction of a vacuum cleaner in 1904 resulted in some forty-five pounds of dust being extracted from the debating Chamber in the first six weeks. And some forty-nine pounds was removed weekly from Libraries, Ministers' Rooms and corridors. During the Whitsun recess of 1906 more than a hundred-weight of dust was removed from the ceilings of the Division Lobbies.

We are fortunate that due to the devoted enthusiasm of a dedicated and skillful amateur photographer who was also a Member of Parliament, Benjamin Stone, it is possible to look into many of the interiors and study them as they were before twentieth century "improvements" had obscured the original intention of those who had created them.

The twentieth century had hardly begun before meddlesome hands were at work upon the Westminster inheritance. The nineteenth century interiors suffered from two defects. The decorations so skillfully planned by the Barrys and by Pugin and their craftsmen had become shabby, but worst of all they were unfashionable. The furniture was in a muddle and many of the fixtures and fittings brought in for gas lighting had either been mauled by conversion to electricity or cast aside.

Buried in the evidence embodied in the Report of the Select Committee of the House of Lords on the Palace of Westminster 10th July 1907 is the key to what was happening to the interior decoration of the New Palace. The committee was set up to discover what had happened to the plans left behind by the Fine Arts Commission after Prince Albert's death. The result is to be found in Chapter VII.

Several powerful witnesses unburdened themselves upon the state of the interiors and how they might be improved.

The first was R. Norman Shaw R.A. (the architect for New Scotland Yard now known as Norman Shaw North and occupied by the House of Commons). Nothing for which Shaw is famous remotely resembles the Palace of Westminster. Nothing in his philosophy in any way accords with what Barry and Pugin and the Fine Arts Commission set out to create.

"It appears to me that if anything is wanted in this building, it is repose and blank walls... I would have no sort of elaboration, because the building to my mind does not call for elaboration. It seems to me to be quite elaborate enough. If we could get it simpler and more restful, I should be more happy."

Here perhaps was the beginning of the move which led to the obliteration of much of the original decoration, the spread of cream paint and brown linoleum with which the Palace was all too well provided by the early 1960s.

The Chairman then turned to the subject of expansion. If the building had a fault, it was that it did not provide sufficiently for expansion. As a result many of the spaces which were meant to be devoted to art, were now devoted to utility. He then went on to inveigh against fine features or sites for pictures which were defaced with the ubiquitous telephone boxes or tables loaded with "Black bottles and sandwiches."

Shaw suggested that all the impedimenta should be shifted away from the fine features. There were such things as lifts after all. He then advocated adding a floor to the centre of the River Front, although it was only a hasty suggestion. He was against tampering with the courts because it would interfere with the light. What he described as the back buildings might, on the other hand, be heightened.

Lord Carlisle, however, in asking Shaw whether the building was really a worthy and admirable specimen of architecture, received the response "My opinion of the building is the very highest. I have known it intimately - more intimately fifty years ago even than I do now - and I have never wavered in my admiration for it. It is a most interesting building, and it was a perfectly marvellous building, considering when it was done and all the circumstances attaching to it. I have had the greatest possible enthusiasm for the building for the last fifty years, and I am not going to change my opinion now in my extreme old age."

Lord Carlisle ventured perhaps that people were not liable to appreciate the qualities of the building at the present time. Shaw: "No doubt that is so, but you must remember that people generally are profoundly ignorant and know nothing about it, and that applies, not only to the ordinary man - the man in the street, as he is called - but it goes a long way beyond him, it applies sometimes to people who are trained, though in their cases it becomes prejudice."

However, in commenting on the room in which they were meeting, Shaw said, "I must say I think this is a very ugly room. If you were to refer to what I was talking about just now, simplicity and restfulness, do you not think it would be much pleasanter if the panels on this wall were all obliterated and we had a plain wall? That is to say, if all that woodwork were taken bodily away, and we had a plain colour, or something of that kind, or a good patterned paper, treating it as one great wall."

"But these panels were meant for pictures were they not? Do you think that it was seriously meant to put pictures in this room?"

"Yes, I think so, certainly. I should be very sorry to be the painter," Shaw replied.

Lord Carlisle then went on to deal with the Dining Room, which had been treated by removing the varnish from the wood and by whitening the ceiling. "That is the direction that you would recommend is it not?"

"That is in the direction of simplicity and restfulness - I have no doubt that you would find that room more restful than this."

"You think a great deal could be done in that way?"

"A very great deal could be done in that way," Shaw agreed.

Shaw later supported tinting of the marble statues and said he found a dead white statue against a stone wall rather repellant. "I was looking at Westminster Hall as I came up just now. I believe in Westminster Hall, for instance, a panel of some simple material would go a long way towards making that more comfortable...sixpenny curtain material."

On the subject of tapestry, Shaw felt that it would be a very risky thing to embark upon. He did not condemn Barry's scheme for the completion of the Palace from the Clock Tower to St. Stephen's Entrance, but because it was a House of Lords Committee he pointed out that the accommodation provided would be for wall paintings. Shaw was cautious.

"The painter must be content to follow the architect?"

"To be in harmony with the framework."

Before he left the Committee, Shaw retreated from what he realised was a "rash suggestion" and a "very daring proceeding" i.e. the upper storey on the River Front.

As regards St. Stephen's Hall, Shaw favoured no paintings at all but in reply to Lord Plymouth, he had to admit that "in the later Gothic work they covered the whole thing with colour from floor to ceiling."

"We have tried it but seldom with success. The French have tried it very extensively and it is hideous and dreadful. It was so at Salisbury. At Salisbury the Chapter House is fully coloured. They found on the top of the capital little pieces of colour like pennies that had dropped down and made a little pool at the top of the capital. It was brillant vermilion and bright blue, but when we tried to treat it with brilliant vermilion and bright blue, the result is not very satisfactory." Shaw was in favour of toning (tinting) the statues in the St. Stephen's Hall to reduce "that extreme cutting white which is what I dislike very much."

The areas of stonework surrounding the House of Commons Chamber had been painted. "Do you know at all why the paint was originally put on the stone there?"

"I should expect it was because it began to get very dirty."

The next witness was Giles Gilbert Scott, architect of Liverpool Cathedral. His view of the interior was that "It is very much overdone. It struck me that there was far too much decoration, if you call it decoration. There is a lack of repose and a lack of concentration; there is not restraint." In the Royal Gallery "I should do away with a lot of the gilding;

*The Cloisters of the House of Commons, later the Members' Cloakrooms, photographed by Sir Benjamin Stone (1897).*

and the varnish on the oakwork strikes me as being out of character with Gothic work. I should have more white wall surfaces...there is far too much decoration at present, and that before anything is done there should be a good deal of simplifying in the way of getting rid of the gilding and the varnish and the various decorations that at present exist...There is much to be undone before anything is done."

Scott's attention was then directed to the Peers' Chamber "Would you tell us how you would set to work on the House of Lords itself, for example?"

"That is a room that I did not look at very long. That is the most gilded of all? Yes, I should do away with most of the gilding and varnishing and substitute simpler glass. I should have less colour - I should have white glass with coats of arms and so forth, which is more suitable for domestic work than figure subjects."

"I suppose you would extend the remark that you made as regards the glass in the House of Lords to the rest of the building?"

"Certainly," Scott continued, "there is one thing which I have just remembered. The tiled flooring throughout the building seems to me to produce a very cheap and, to my mind, shoddy effect. I think a far finer effect would be produced with marble, say black and white marble in large squares, or something of that kind."

Scott was in favour of some rich hangings in Westminster Hall. He was strongly in favour of tinting statues. (Scott had been present throughout the whole of the evidence given by Norman Shaw).

The last witness was the Rt. Hon. Lewis Harcourt, M.P., First Commissioner of Works, the son of the Harcourt whose statue had received so much attention. He was in favour of tinting it, indeed, had authorised the work.

There was much talk about who was really in charge of the Palace. It appeared that the Lord Great Chamberlain had the power of veto in the House of Lords but Lewis Harcourt as First Commissioner felt free to carry out works at the House of Commons end of the Palace, but that he would be slow to initiate activity by his Department in the Lords. "With regard to the works carried on in the Palace, is there any consistent permanent scheme on which any works are carried forward, or are they merely undertaken from time to time as occasion may arise?"

"I should say that they were undertaken from time to time as necessity arose for alterations, either for convenience or for decoration, but principally for convenience."

"The scheme, then, of decoration, as finally recommended by the Fine Arts Commission, is not looked to as a thing to be carried on? I think it has been abandoned for many years owing to pressure of finance."

*The Central Hall looking towards the Commons' Lobby, photographed by Sir Benjamin Stone in 1897.*

*The Drawing Room of the Speaker's House in 1897.*

"If I understand you aright, there is no conscious intention of filling up that scheme?"

"No."

Harcourt agreed that a fresh look could be taken in view of the lapse of nearly half a century. He favoured an advisory committee not necessarily limited to the two Houses, to be of assistance to the Minister.

Their Lordships had their eye upon tapestries at Hampton Court but Harcourt pointed out that they belonged to the Sovereign and that he could not help them. Harcourt was cross-examined on some suggestions that Norman Shaw had sent in, but they all seemed to be impracticable.

One of Shaw's suggestions had been to build in Commons Court, adjacent to the Lower Waiting Hall and in the process destroying the fireplace in order to create an access door.

Harcourt admitted to having painted the panels in many corridor ceilings white and to have thought about lowering the statues in the Members' Lobby. (This has been done in the case of Churchill and Attlee and the two vacant plinths opposite).

Harcourt admitted - "My object in tinting my father's statue was to educate public opinion up to the waxing; whether it has been successful yet or not I do not know. I have had some criticism of the waxing."

Harcourt referred to the removal of the original decorations and the painting out of the ceilings. "I may say that what I have done has been done on my own responsibility and tentatively in order to test the opinion of people as to the desirability of the work. I did one Dining Room at the House of Commons, leaving the other one which opens out of it as it was before so that people should be able to compare the two. If and when it was necessary to redecorate this room, my own opinion as to the simple thing to do, would be to remove the varnish from the oak, and possibly to paint the flock paper if it was good enough."

Harcourt confirmed that he had taken money for continuing the cleaning of the stonework and this included the Central Lobby.

Commenting on Norman Shaw's optimistic forecast that "It would be easy to get some fifty or sixty additional rooms at a very moderate cost - probably far more," Harcourt said that "It was a very interesting statement, both as to the number of rooms and as to the moderation of the cost. I think that if Mr. Norman Shaw knew what our structural alterations in this Gothic building cost when I have to make quite small ones, he would perhaps omit the adjective in that sentence."[7]

Lewis Harcourt is commemorated in the name of the Dining Room which he created for the House of Commons on the ground floor immediately to the south of what was once called the Peers' Terrace Entrance. It was formerly a House of Lords Committee Room. His father's statue which once stood in the Members' Lobby was much damaged in the Second World War but skillfully restored and replaced in the Lower Waiting Hall.

Despite the adjustments proposed and carried out, conditions in the Commons remained far from satisfactory.

The problems of the House of Commons were not the only concern of the Government. Amongst the archives of the Lighting and Ventilation Department of the Houses of Parliament is a Report of the Departmental Committee on humidity and ventilation in cotton weaving sheds. It was made to the Rt. Hon. Winston Leonard Spencer Churchill, M.P., Her Majesty's Principal Secretary of State for the Home Department. It is dated January 1911, Manchester. Cottonweavers, like Members of Parliament, were toiling in a hot, moist atmosphere and needed to be dried and cooled for the good of their health and performance.

*The Baptism of King Ethelbert, painted by William Dyce (1846).*

# VII

## Palace of the Arts

The committee of 1841 were unanimous "that so important and national a work as the erection of the New Houses of Parliament afforded an opportunity which ought not to be neglected of encouraging not only the higher, but every subordinate branch of Fine Art in the country."

Sir Robert Peel's inspired choice of H.R.H. Prince Albert to head the Commission ensured that, whilst the Prince Consort lived, original, even adventurous works of art would find a place in the New Palace.

The decision to revive the technique of fresco at Westminster produced the most prominent of the Commission's achievements in the New Palace. The decision was taken only after the examination of many expert witnesses and a public competition. The fruits of this were exhibited in Westminster Hall in 1843. At this time artists were also invited to send in models for sculpture, specimens of carved work in wood, specimens of stained glass, arabesque drawings, and ornamental metalwork and pavements.

The artists to whom the Commission awarded prizes were not all employed in the Palace and some artists who had not exhibited were subsequently commissioned to work at Westminster.

### *Paintings*

The six great frescoes in the Chamber of the House of Lords were the first to be recommended by the Commission and sanctioned by the Lords of the Treasury.

The Lords of the Treasury were following in the footsteps of none other than King Ludwig of Bavaria. With the help of Peter von Cornelius this art was revived for a royal patron who was besotted with Wagner and the builder of the most fantastic of folly palaces in all Europe.

William Dyce's fresco "The Baptism of Ethelbert" over the throne at the south end of the Chamber was in position for the first sitting of their Lordships. Either side of it Charles West Cope's "Edward III Conferring the Order of the Garter on the Black Prince" appeared in 1848 and the same artist painted "Prince Henry Acknowledging the Authority of Chief Justice Gasgoyne" (1849). At the north end of the Chamber J. C. Horsley's "The Spirit of Religion" dates from 1847. It is flanked by Daniel Maclise's "The Spirit of Justice" of 1849 and "The Spirit of Chivalry" by the same, artist (1847). Sadly all of these works soon became the subject of decay and discolouration. The history of the repainting of some and the restoration of others ran on into the twentieth century and even today they are the subject of a constant vigil. Dyce remained loyal to the traditional method of fresco, that of painting on fresh, wet plaster; others used fresco-secco. Watercolour was applied to dried plaster and sprayed with liquid silica; it was easier for the artist but the colours seldom endured.

In the Robing Room William Dyce was commissioned to paint a series of seven knightly virtues from the Arthurian legend. Dyce laboured under immense difficulties. Only in the summer was the climate right for his technique. The subject involved many figures dressed in the earliest form of armour, chain mail. This occupied the artist for many laborious hours. Dyce had many other calls upon his time, some of them more congenial, such as the religious frescoes in William Butterfield's Church of All Saints, Margaret Street. Work for the Prince Consort at Osborne and elsewhere could not be neglected for King Arthur at Westminster.

Dyce completed "Religion" in 1851, "Courtesy" and "Generosity" in 1852, "Mercy" in 1854 and left "Hospitality" unfinished at his death in 1864. Charles West Cope completed the work by 1866. "Courage" and "Fidelity" were intended to fill the two vacant spaces either side of the Chair of State at the east end.

Two commissions which were completed by the artist to whom they were assigned fill the Peers Corridor and the Commons Corridor, either side of the Central Hall. For the Peers, Charles West Cope was chosen to paint a series of four pairs of paintings representing parallel events in the development of the British Constitution. He painted a version in oil of a Puritan family leaving for New England, anachronistically represented at the departure of "The Mayflower". This version was superseded by a version in fresco followed by three others in that medium. His last four were painted in the waterglass method.

*Prince Henry acknowledging the authority of Chief Justice Gascoyne, painted by C. W. Cope (1849).*

*The Spirit of Justice, painted by Daniel Maclise (1849).*

*The Spirit of Chivalry, painted by Daniel Maclise (1847).*

*Edward III conferring the Order of the Garter on the Black Prince, painted by C. W. Cope (1848).*

E. M. Ward, in the Commons' Corridor, also switched from fresco to waterglass. His series continues the theme begun by Cope. Both these series exist in a recognisable condition and they have been made famous by their reproduction in history books. The paintings were executed on panels of plaster with a space behind designed to prevent damp from penetrating the surface from the exterior.

In the Poet's Hall (Upper Waiting Hall) it was originally intended to place eight statues of poets. The plinths never received the poets but they now support eight of the original statues from the exterior of the building. The eight wall panels were decorated with scenes taken from eight British poems.

Charles West Cope painted "Griselda's First Trial of Patience" from Chaucer and "The Death of Lara" from Byron. G. F. Watts produced "St. George Overcoming the Dragon" from Spenser, J. R. Herbert "Lear Disinheriting Cordelia" from Shakespeare, J. C. Horsley "Satan Touched by Ithuriel's Spear" from Milton, John Tenniel "St. Cecilia" from Dryden. Edward Armitage produced both "The Personification of Thames" from Pope and "The Death of Marmion" from Scott.

There was a space of some inches at the back of these plaster panels and in it the damp collected. There had been no provision made to ventilate the space, nor was ever any effort made to do so, with the result that the paint surface was soon affected.

The different artists employed their own individual techniques. Tenniel produced a result looking more like an oil painting on plaster than any of the others and it has survived more or less intact. Less than twenty years after their execution the other frescoes had become a source of Parliamentary ribaldry. A committee which included John Ruskin and Gambier Parry produced no helpful conclusion. Charles West Cope treated the series with paraffin wax in 1868. By the end of the century Professor A.H. Church was reporting that only "St. Cecilia" by Tenniel was worth preserving. For the next eighty years five of the frescoes were covered up, though looked at occasionally by various committees. In 1984 a cautious programme of restoration was begun and it is slowly proceeding; some parts of some paintings are missing. Purists will argue that they should not be replaced. Parliament may well decide otherwise, requiring value for money in wall decoration in view of the cost involved.

The scheme which the Commissioners proposed for the Peers' Robing Room (now called The Moses Room) was to symbolize "The Idea of Justice on Earth and its development in Law and Judgement viz. Moses Bringing Down the Tables of the Law to the Israelites"; "The Fall of Man, his Condemnation to Labour"; "The Judgement of Solomon"; "The Visit of the Queen of Sheba"; "The Building of the Temple"; "The Judgement of Daniel"; "Daniel in the Lion's Den"; "The Vision of Daniel".

*Hospitality* by William Dyce (unfinished at his death in 1864), completed by C. W. Cope (1864-6). The admission of Sir Tristram to the Fellowship of the Round Table.

*Generosity* by William Dyce (1852). King Arthur unhorsed by Sir Bors and spared by Sir Launcelot.

J. R. Herbert undertook to paint the whole room for £9,000. He began "Moses and the Tables of the Law" in fresco in 1858. Later he had the work obliterated and began again in waterglass. It took him until 1864 to complete this one picture. Herbert was paid £5,000 for "Moses" and produced no more paintings on the walls though his "Judgement of Daniel" in oil on canvas was hanging in the room by 1880.

The Commissioners had approached Daniel Maclise in 1854 with a view to his painting in fresco "The Marriage of Strongbow and Eva" in the Painted Chamber (Conference Room) in the centre of the River Front. For some reason Maclise felt that the light there was not good enough. Maclise was again approached in 1857 with a view to his painting a series of frescoes for St. Stephen's Hall but he preferred the Royal Gallery.

The original scheme was for eighteen paintings. "Boadicea Inciting her Army," "Alfred in the Camp of the Danes," "Brian Baroimhe overcoming the Danes at the Bridge of Clontarff," "Edith finding the dead Body of Harold," "Richard Cœur de Lion coming in sight of the Holy City," "Eleanor saving the Life of Her Husband, afterwards Edward I, by sucking the Poison from a wound in his Arm," "Bruce, during a retreat before the English, protecting a Woman borne on a Litter, and checking the Pursuers," "Philippa interceding for the Lives of the Citizens of Calais," "Edward the Black Prince entering London by the side of King John of France," "The Marriage of Henry V at Troyes with the Princess Katharine of France," "Elizabeth at Tilbury," "Blake at Tunis," "Marlborough at Blenheim," "Death of Wolfe," "Death of Abercrombie," "Lord Cornwallis receiving the Sons of Tippoo as hostages," "Trafalgar: The Death of Nelson," "Waterloo: The Meeting of Wellington and Blücher." Maclise agreed to fill the smaller spaces at a cost of £1,000 each but the two large compartments were each to earn him £3,500. He exhibited a cartoon for "Wellington and Blücher" at the Royal Academy in 1859. It was greatly admired by his fellow Academicians who presented him with a gold crayon holder as a mark of their admiration and respect.

Maclise found by August 1859 that there were insuperable difficulties. If true fresco was to be employed then small parts only could be worked at a time because of the great number of figures and their different uniforms. The dim religious light produced by the stained glass, together with the colours thrown upon the walls when sunlight filtered through the windows all seemed too much of a hindrance. Maclise sought to resign the commission.

The personal intervention of the Prince Consort persuaded Maclise to switch to the waterglass technique and to begin the great work. Prince Albert undertook to have the stained glass removed from the windows but in one form or another it has survived until the present time. By March 1862 "The Meeting of Wellington and Blücher" was ready for unveiling. "The Death

*Courtesy by William Dyce (1852). Sir Tristram harping to La Beale Isoud.*

*Mercy by William Dyce (1854). Sir Gawain swears to be merciful and never to be against ladies.*

of Nelson" was eventually finished in 1865.[1] Although Maclise had prepared three advance designs, for the remaining sixteen smaller paintings originally commissioned, no further progress was made by Maclise.

The scheme for the Painted Chamber was based on the theme of the "Acquisition of the countries, colonies, and important places constituting the British Empire." The subjects chosen were: "The Marriage of Strongbow and Eva, daughter of Dermot, King of Leinster," "Edward I presenting his Infant Son to the Welsh as their Prince," "James VI of Scotland receiving the news of the Death of Queen Elizabeth or Setting out for England as James I," "Lord Clive in the Battle of Plassy," "Penn's Treaty with the American Indians," "The Colonization of Australia," "The Treaty of Nankin," "Incidents illustrating the Voyages to the North and South Poles," "Incidents relating to the acquisition of Mauritius and the Cape of Good Hope," "Sir George Rooke planting the Standard of England on Gibraltar: and Surrender of Malta."

*Religion by William Dyce (1851). The vision of Sir Galahad and his Company.*

"In the Peers' and Commons' Refreshment Rooms the decorations will consist of views of places of chief importance in the United Kingdom, views of the most remarkable places in India and the colonial possessions of the Throne, and also subjects connected with rural scenery, such as the Harvest, the Chase etc."[2] There were other schemes for which subjects were chosen but artists were never commissioned.

Parallel with the adventures into fresco were the fruits of another competition to discover suitable artists and subjects for oil paintings to be hung in the Palace. One of the oil paintings which received a premium of £500 was "Alfred Inciting the Saxons to Prevent the Landing of the Danes, Encountering them at Sea" by G. F. Watts. This was purchased for £200 and has remained in the Palace. Pickersgill's "Burial of Harold at Waltham Abbey" also received a premium of £500 and was purchased for £400. "The Battle off Cape St. Vincent" by Knell, was purchased for £200 and "Richard

Cœur de Lion forgiving Bertram de Gourdon" by Cross was bought for £500. The whereabouts of this last is presently unknown.

One of the most interesting and successful schemes is the series of sixteenth century portraits in the Prince's Chamber. The twenty-eight subjects, all relating to the Tudor monarchy, were executed by Richard Burchett with the assistance of pupils at the Royal School of Art, South Kensington. The paintings are executed in oil on panel with embossed and gilt enrichment in the background. They were painted between the years of 1854 and 1860. An alternative version of the painting of Henry VII, discovered in a derelict room in the Clock Tower, now hangs in the Peers' Dining Room. The sketches for these paintings, recently purchased, now hang in the west front corridor.

The likenesses are all derived from historical sources where such exist. All the paintings have survived the passage of time unfaded and are as colourful as they must have been at the opening of the new House of Lords. They are well sited in the Prince's Chamber and are among the most admired paintings in the Palace.

These then were the achievements of Prince Albert's Commission in the field of painting. Their plans had been ambitious, the results uneven and much remained to be done. On the 14th December 1861 the Chairman died.

The Commission was dissolved on the grounds that its work was almost done (provided that its plans were carried out) and that no other Chairman could possibly replace the Prince Consort. He had been, from the start, the inspiration and guide of the great work.

The Report of the Select Commmittee of the House of Lords, 10th July 1907, sums up the sad state of affairs nearly half a century later. "How unfounded was the assumption on the faith of which this step (the dissolution of the Commission) was taken was very shortly shown. A few commissions already given were executed, a few of the plans already announced were for the next two or three years continued, but the regular and even progress of the past had ceased, and only occasional efforts were from time to time made to add to the works already completed. Amongst these the chief have been the statues in the Central Hall (Central Lobby) and the mosaic decoration of its vaulting."

The Select Committee saw that one of their first duties was "to ascertain how far the programme of the Fine Arts Commission, as shown in its Report for 1847 and subsequent resolutions, had as yet been carried out, and in what respects it still remained unfulfilled." They then related the sad catalogue of hopes unfulfilled.[3]

*The Royal Staircase.* Here there were seventeen pedestals all still vacant, not one having as yet received the statue which was meant to be placed upon it. "It will, the committee think, be granted that, the pedestals being there, they should not be allowed to remain permanently useless and empty. But

*King Alfred inciting the Saxons by G. F. Watts.*

on the other hand, it cannot be said that the supply of statues for them is an immediate necessity, or by any means one of the first objects to be considered in connnection with the completion of the decorative work of the Palace." There is a kind of Parkinson's Law about such spaces. In due course the pedestals were supplied with a highly incongruous and uneven collection of glistening white marble busts, in the Classical style, whereas the original intention had been saintly Gothic renderings of the Norman Kings.

*The King's Robing Room.* Here the committee drew attention to the fact that Dyce had left two blank spaces on either side of the throne when he left his series of frescoes of the legend of King Arthur unfinished. The committee recommended filling the spaces with paintings "in harmony with those already executed by Mr. Dyce." Nothing has ever been done about this but two fine oil portraits of the Prince Consort and Queen Victoria now fill the spaces.

*The Royal Gallery.* Here nineteen large pictures of scenes from English history had been proposed. Daniel Maclise had produced his "Death of Nelson" and the "Meeting of Wellington and Blücher at Waterloo," together with cartoons and sketches for a third, representing Queen Elizabeth at Tilbury Fort. These still existed in 1907 but owing to misunderstandings arising with respect to the painter's remuneration the (latter) picture was never completed.

Seventeen panels remain unfilled. It may be questionned whether the apartment would not gain in dignity by such a modification of the original scheme as would provide for a greater amount of plain wall space than was originally contemplated by the Fine Arts Commission.

*The Prince's Chamber.* Here the committee drew attention to the upper parts of the walls where there were to have been tapestries reproducing those in the House of Lords destroyed by the fire of 1834. They had represented the defeat of the Spanish Armada. The committee did not come out strongly in favour of this solution but felt that the room should not be left in its present half-finished condition. It may be that the painted version of one of the Armada tapestries which now hangs in Committee Room number fourteen was intended as a trial for this scheme of the Commission.

The committee were pleased that the House of Lords, the House of Lords' Lobby and the Peers' Corridor, had all been completed in strict accord with the intentions of the Commission. What is now the Moses Room contained the great fresco of "Moses and the Israelites" by Herbert and an oil painting of "The Judgement of Daniel" by the same artist.
The committee recommended that the decoration in that room should be completed, there being five further compartments to fill, including one whole wall.

*The Central Hall (Central Lobby).* Here four sitting statues of the greatest English statesmen were intended and four mosaics of St. George,

St. Andrew, St. Patrick and St. David were intended for the spaces above the four doorways (the two mosaics of St. George and St. David had been completed but St. Andrew and St. Patrick were still wanting). Admirable colour designs for the figures of the two Saints had been completed by Albert Moore in 1866 and were in the possession of the Government. It had been suggested that the wall between St. Stephen's Hall and the Central Lobby should be pierced and filled with open tracery. The committee felt that the standing statues on pedestals "go far to destroy the repose and dignity which the hall would otherwise possess, and their heroic size dwarfs its proportions, while the contrast between their size and that of the numerous and comparatively diminutive stone statues of Kings and Saints (actually Kings and Queens) in their immediate vicinity offends the eye."

*St. Stephen's Hall.* Here the twelve statues recommended had been put in place and the windows were filled with stained glass approved by the Commission. The twelve panels or compartments intended for pictures were still covered with paper "which gives a somewhat mean appearance to an otherwise noble gallery."

In the evidence taken by the committee there had been support for the original scheme of the Fine Arts Commission for scenes representing Parliamentary history. Others, however, had recommended "sculpture or inlaid marble decoration in colour" and some had urged that "the panels should be filled with tinted bas reliefs in gesso."

*St. Stephen's Porch.* A pair of statues had been recommended representing Marlborough and Nelson. The committee regretted that this, the last of the Commissioners' proposals, had not been carried out.

*Corridor from Central Hall to Lower Waiting Hall.* Six paintings had been proposed. The light here was good and this the committee believed "is one of the places to be first attended to in any attempt to complete the decoration of the Palace." Other areas in the Lords had either been completed according to the Commissioners' plans or their walls were covered with bookcases, thus preventing further action.

*The Dining Rooms (the Peers' Dining Rooms).* There were twenty-six panels here, all of which had been intended to be filled with pictures but none had materialised. "For one of these panels, Sir Edwin Landseer's well-known picture 'Monarch of the Glen' was painted, and he was also commissioned to paint three other panels. The sketches for these are believed still to exist, but the commission to the painter was subsequently cancelled. The light in these rooms is good, and the committee have no hesitiation in saying that in their opinion the intentions of the Fine Arts Commission should here be given full effect, and that the work of decoration as contemplated by them should be proceeded with, however gradually, until it reaches completion." By 1987, that is one hundred and forty years later, nothing has been achieved of the original intention for the walls of these rooms.

*The Upper Stairs Lobby, formerly known as the Poets' Hall (Upper Waiting Hall).* "This lobby was decorated by frescoes representing scenes from the works of eight British poets, Chaucer, Spencer, Shakespeare, Milton, Dryden, Pope, Scott and Byron. With one exception all these frescoes have entirely or mainly perished. The one exception is 'St. Cecilia', an illustration of Dryden's poem. This is not well seen, for a telephone box of huge dimensions and portentious ugliness has been placed immediately in front of it. One of the damaged frescoes, that representing Lear and Cordelia, might in Professor Church's opinion possibly be repaired, but the remaining six are absolutely destroyed. There are eight pedestals for statues in this lobby which are, however, unfilled."

The committee concluded that of one hundred and sixty-one panels which were intended to be filled with paintings, fifty-seven had been so filled and one hundred and forty remained blank. Rather less than half of the statues intended had been provided. Twenty-three were now present but twenty-seven had yet to come. Although there were great opportunities, amounting to many hundreds of square feet in corridors and Committee Rooms, it was to the more public apartments that attention should first be given.

The committee focused their attention on Westminster Hall - even if it was not strictly within their terms of reference. Here they drew attention to the evidence given by Sir Charles Barry before the House of Commons Committee of 1841. "Strong representations were made by him as to the desirableness of placing paintings or hangings on its walls, and that from various slight indications it is clear that the Fine Arts Commission did not consider Westminster Hall to be excluded from their sphere of action.

The statues which are now in the Hall were not originally intended to be placed there, but were found to be unsuited to their first destined site in the Royal Gallery. They are equally out of place where they now are. Their appearance is incongruous and as a series they are incomplete. Their removal would, the committee consider, be of a distinct advantage."

The 1907 committee, which took extensive evidence, believed that mural painting had reached such a stage in the United Kingdom that it was technically possible to complete the scheme contemplated by the Fine Arts Commission.

They were, however, doubtful whether artistic completion of the decoration of the Palace could be achieved without an advisory committee or council acting with the First Commissioner of Works, who is the Minister responsible to Parliament.

The committee clearly had little faith in the ability of the Minister acting alone. "Left wholly to himself, the First Commissioner, unless he happens to take a strong personal interest in the work, is exposed to many temptations to allow all decorative operations to languish. In any case, the mere pressure of other business and other interests may lead him to be indifferent to the subject and negligent of its claims, whilst a desire to present economical estimates may cause him, as has many of his predecessors, to abstain from proposing any outlay upon work of mere decoration. Or, again, if he be a man who not only has no knowledge of art, but actually despises and dislikes it - as has been the case in at least one instance, - not only will any future decorative work be brought to a standstill, but works of artistic beauty already completed may be removed or destroyed, sacrified to what he may deem the claims of comfort or convenience. The great improvements in the decoration of the Palace recently carried out by the present First Commissioner consist mainly in the removal of defacements made in the past either through want of proper advice or ignorance.

The committee wish to see an annual sum of £4,000 at the disposal of the Advisory Committee, that being the sum available to the Fine Arts Commission between 1850 and 1861. They were prepared also to countenance the use of funds from private sources." As a result of this suggestion, a number of commissions were executed under private patronage.

*The Poets' Hall.*

In an appendix to the Report is the date and cost of many of the works of art which did find their way into the Palace as a result of the activities of the Fine Arts Commission. Included are the seven statues of monarchs which were placed in Westminster Hall but later removed.[4]

Also included in the Report of 1907 is a plan of the Palace which shows those rooms appropriated to the service of the House of Lords and the approaches thereto. It shows that the Lords then had on the principal floor of the River Front the four library rooms, what is now the Peers' Guest Room and what is now the Pugin Room, the last two of which intercommunicated.

The Lords Committee of 1907 gave fresh impetus to the programme of historical paintings. Regrettably it came too late into the field to make use of the talents of the best of the Pre-Raphaelites. However the challenge was taken up by private patrons both in St. Stephen's Hall and the East Corridor. The challenge had been thrown down by a committee of noble Lords and it was picked up by a group of noble patrons. Every one of the paintings in St. Stephen's Hall and the East Corridor was paid for by a Peer of the realm.

"The choice of the subjects was made by the present writer, (Sir Henry Newbolt) in consultation with Lord Peel (the First Commissioner of Works), Lord Crawford (the Chairman of the Fine Arts Commission), and the Speaker - the initiator and sympathetic director of the whole scheme. The final list was only settled after long and careful deliberation, and after Sir D.Y. Cameron and the painters had contributed their views. It would evidently have been impossible to represent in eight pictures the varied and multitudinous scenes of a thousand years of national history. Moreover, it was felt that the later part of this long record was no very happy subject for the art of today. It was undesirable to revive smouldering embers of the party conflicts and personal feelings of the last two hundred years. It followed that only such scenes could be chosen as would be of the highest and most far-reaching significance, and that the period they were to cover must be the eight centuries which begin with King Alfred and end with Queen Anne."[5]

The eight paintings, described in Newbolt's words are as follows: "King Alfred's long-ships, newly built for the defence of the realm, attack vessels of the Danish invaders storm-beaten in Swanage Bay," (877). By Colin Gill. Donor - The Duke of Devonshire. The Second Picture - "King Richard the First, afterwards called Cœur de Lion, leaves England with an expeditionary force, to join the Crusade in Palestine for the recovery of Jerusalem from the Saracens," (December 11, 1189). By Glyn Philpot, R. A. Donor - The Viscount Devonport. The Third Picture - "King John, confronted by his Barons assembled in force at Runnymede, gives unwilling consent to Magna Carta, the foundation of justice and individual freedom in

England," (1215). By Charles Sims, R.A. Donor - The Viscount Burnham. The Fourth Picture - "The English people, in spite of prosecutions for heresy, persist in gathering secretly to read aloud Wycliffe's English Bible." By George Clausen, R. A. Donor - The Duke of Portland. The Fifth Picture - "Sir Thomas More, as Speaker of the Commons, in spite of Cardinal Wolsey's imperious demand refuses to grant King Henry the Eighth a subsidy without due debate by the House," (1523). By Vivian Forbes. Donor - The Viscount Fitzalan. The Sixth Picture - "Queen Elizabeth, the Faerie Queen of her Knights and Merchant Venturers, commissions Sir Walter Raleigh to sail for America and discover new countries," (1584). By A. K. Lawrence. Donor - The Earl of Derby. The Seventh Picture - "Sir Thomas Roe, Envoy from King James the First of England to the Moghul Emperor, succeeds by his mingled courtesy and firmness at the Court of Ajmir in laying the foundation of British influence in India," (1614). By W. Rothenstein. Donor - The Duke of Bedford. The Eighth Picture - "The English and Scottish Commissioners present to Queen Anne at St. James's Palace the Articles of Agreement for the Parliamentary Union of the two countries," (1707), By W.T. Monnington. Donor - The Viscount Younger of Leckie."

*The Duke of Suffolk and the Marchioness of Dorset by R. Burchett (1854-60), in the Prince's Chamber.*

The Fine Arts Commission had thought that the Central Corridor (East Corridor) might with advantage be adorned with pictures exhibiting in strong contrast the extremes which are separated by the interval between the introduction of Christianity and the Revolution. Six subjects were selected, in three of which Britain appears sunk in ignorance, heathen superstition, and slavery. In the other three she is instructing the savage, abolishing barbarous rites, and liberating the slave, viz. "The Phoenicians in Cornwall," "A Druidical Sacrifice," "Anglo-Saxon Captives exposed for Sale in the Market Place of Rome," "Cook in Otaheite," "English Authorities stopping the Sacrifice of a Suttee" and "The Emancipation of Negro Slaves."

In the East Corridor the six paintings are as follows:

1. "Plucking the red and White Roses in Old Temple Gardens," by Henry J. Payne. Presented by William, 7th Earl Beauchamp.

2. "John Cabot and His Sons Receive the Charter from Henry VII to Sail in Search of New Lands (1496)," by Denis Eden. Presented by William, Lord Winterstoke.

3. "Erasmus and Thomas More Visit the Children of Henry VII at Greenwich (1499)," by Frank Cadogan Cowper, A.R.A. Presented by George, 9th Earl of Carlisle.

4. "Henry VIII and Katherine of Aragon Before the Papal Legates at Blackfriars (1529)," by Frank Salisbury. Presented by Arthur, Lord Stanmore.

5. "Latimer Preaching Before Edward VI at Paul's Cross (1548)," by Ernest Board. Presented by Sydney, Lord Wandsworth.

6. "Entry of Queen Mary I with Princess Elizabeth into London (1553),". by Byam Shaw. Presented by James, Lord Airedale.

The East Corridor group followed closely on the heels of the 1906 Select Committee. They were painted on canvas fixed onto wooden panels and were all in position by 1910.

The St. Stephen's Hall series were completed by 1927. Two previous gifts of paintings had been hung in St. Stephen's Hall for a time. They were "The Flight of the Five Members" by Seymour Lucas and "Hollys and Valentine Holding the Speaker in His Chair" by Andrew Gow. These two were moved to the Committee Rooms. A study in oils for the Gow painting was purchased for Speaker's House in the time of Mr. Speaker Thomas.

There was one great project, more ambitious than any of its recent predecessors, which might have left its mark upon the Palace. The First Earl of Iveagh, in conjunction with the then Lord Great Chamberlain, the Marquis of Lincolnshire, conceived the idea of completing the decorations in the Royal Gallery. Paintings were to cover all the remaining wall space as a War memorial to the Peers and their kin who made the great sacrifice in the War of 1914-18. Frank Brangwyn was commissioned. He set to work on

*Portraits in the Prince's Chamber; King James IV and Queen Margaret of Scotland.*

condition that he could complete all the sixteen panels before anything was exhibited. For four years he laboured. His two patrons died. A growing impatience persuaded Brangwyn to allow the exhibition of the six panels that he had completed. The Royal Fine Arts Commission damned them as unsuitable for the Royal Gallery. The whole of that scheme was rejected. The rejected scheme had involved decorative and structural alterations to the Royal Gallery. One huge panel covered the whole of an end wall and involved the removal of a substantial part of the pilasters which divided it. It was entitled "The Call to Arms and the Departure to the Front."

Undaunted, Brangwyn laboured on for another seven years under the patronage of Lord Iveagh's trustees. His new scheme was first conceived as an heraldic display but this gave way to a series of British Empire panels representative of the fruits of the earth and the peoples who produced them. These too were deemed unsuitable. Exhibited at the Ideal Home Exhibition in 1933, they found a permanent place in the Guildhall at Swansea.

There was one other remarkable wall painting also presented by a noble Lord, Montague, first Lord Swaythling. It is Solomon J. Solomon's "The Commons Petitioning Queen Elizabeth to Marry." Her Majesty's refusal, "With this ring I was wedded to the Realm" is inscribed below the picture. Many of the figures were modelled on statesmen of the early twentieth century.

### *Mosaic*

In the Central Hall Edward Poynter's "Saint George" was the only mosaic completed before Acton Smee Ayrton put a stop to the work. Even "Saint George" did not meet with universal approval but at least it lies flat on the wall. Poynter's design for Saint David was carried out in 1898 but it was not until 1922-24 that "Saint Andrew" and "Saint Patrick" were completed to the designs of Robert Anning-Bell R.A. The same artist designed two further huge mosaics which were erected in St. Stephen's Hall. "Saint Stephen, the Proto-martyr" and "Edward III Commands the Rebuilding of St. Stephen's Chapel."

With the exception of the "Saint George" the method of execution of the mosaics is such that they look like coarse tapestries when illuminated. They cannot be considered one of the the great successes which flowed from the Reports of the Fine Arts Commission.

### *Sculpture*

The architectural sculpture both within and without the Palace is of exceptional quality and is everywhere an ornament to the building. It was all planned and executed under the eye of Charles Barry. Many of the other sculptures disposed about the interior are not particularly happy with their surroundings though they all have historic interest and importance. They represent but a fraction of what might have been, had the Commissioners lived to see all their schemes reach fruition. The Third Report of the Commissioners refers to Barry's Report of 1843. In various positions, both integrated and free standing, some 670 monuments could be accommodated.

With more precision, in their Fourth Report, the Commissioners were of the opinion that "six insulated marble statues might be conveniently placed in St. Stephen's Porch, and sixteen such statues in St. Stephen's Hall; and they recommended that the statues of Nelson and Marlborough be at once executed for St. Stephen's Porch, and the statues of Selden, Hampden, Lord Falkland, Lord Clarendon, Lord Somers, Sir Robert Walpole, Lord Chatham, Lord Mansfield, Burke, Pitt, Fox and Grattan, be placed in St. Stephen's Hall."

It also appeared that they had drawn up two lists. On one of these they had been unanimous and on another they had agreed by a majority to the names of sixty-three worthy subjects of Great Britain and fifty-eight others. They were firm in their resolve that eighteen niches in the House of Lords should be filled with that number of the principal Barons who had signed Magna Carta.

*Paintings in St. Stephen's Hall, circa 1927.*
*Left: King Alfred's Long Ships attack Danish invaders, by Colin Gill.*
*Right: King Richard I leaves to join the Crusade, by Glyn Philpot.*

*Paintings in St. Stephen's Hall, circa 1927.*

*Top: King John confronted by his Barons, by C. Sims. The English people accept Wyeliffe's Bible, by George Clausen.*

*Below: Sir Thomas More as Speaker, by V. Forbes. Queen Elizabeth I and Sir Walter Raleigh, by A. K. Lawrence.*

*Top: Sir Thomas Roe, envoy of King James I to the Moghul Emperor, by W. Rothenstein.*
*Below: The English and Scottish Commissioners with Queen Anne (1707), by W. T. Monnington.*

The St. Stephen's Hall scheme was carried out, but nothing ever came of the Nelson and Marlborough for St. Stephen's Porch. In the Royal Gallery Charles Barry assented to the commissioning of marble statues of monarchs. Those which arrived there turned out to be out of scale and were deposited to languish in Westminster Hall. Thence they were consigned to the Guildhall and eventually to the Central Criminal Court of the Old Bailey. Edward Middleton Barry commissioned the series (by Birnie Philip) now in the Royal Gallery.

The four monumental standing statesmen in the Central Lobby were apparently not quite what the Commission had intended; seated statesmen were originally thought to produce a feeling of greater dignity and repose.

A scheme which was considered, because a committee document recently discovered shows it in some detail, was the extensive embellishment of Westminster Hall. A plan shows the positions for no less than fifty-four statues interspersed with large wall paintings or frescoes with an additional

*The entry of Queen Mary with Princess Elizabeth into London, by Byam Shaw. East Corridor (1910).*

*Henry VIII and Queen Katherine before the Papal Legates at Blackfriars, by Frank Salisbury. East Corridor (1910).*

set of windows on either side of the roof to light the new display.[6] Nothing ever came of this scheme. In the 1970s the Central Office of Information were keen to install large panels displaying the History of Parliament upon the walls of the Hall. Expert advice was sought but no existing artistic means could be found that could fulfil this requirement. Had the Morris tapestry workshop at Merton Abbey been still in existence with Burne-Jones as a designer, something worthy of the Hall might have been possible.

The tradition of commemorative sculpture lived on after the demise of the Fine Arts Commission. A lifesize bronze of the Earl of Chatham stands just east of the Prince's Chamber and there is a bust of the 5th Earl Spencer at the top of the Peers' Staircase. A collection of busts of noble Prime Ministers has been placed on the plinths of the Norman staircase. A fine marble of the 14th Earl of Home is the latest addition.

In the Commons, statues of former Prime Ministers and some others have gradually accumulated in the Members' Lobby. Asquith and Balfour have been more recently joined by Lloyd George and Churchill. Earl Attlee is the latest arrival. Joseph Chamberlain also adorns one of the plinths. No fixed policy has been laid down. The emergence of a new statue has been the result of spontaneous interest, culminating in the setting up of an *ad hoc* committee.

Although Gladstone, larger than life, adorns the Central Lobby there was formerly no Disraeli. Recently his statue by Count Glieshen (1883) has been placed where the Committee Corridor crosses the Upper Waiting Hall. This unique position was decided upon for two reasons. Disraeli clearly deserved commemoration. Because he was lifesize, he could not, in death, be matched with a giant Gladstone, despite the many times that they had faced each other on equal terms across the dispatch boxes of the House of Commons.

A number of busts of varying degrees of interest have been presented to the two Houses from time to time. The most prominently displayed is that of Oliver Cromwell which stands in the Lower Waiting Hall. It came from Lord Northwick's sale and was presented by Charles Wertheimer. There was controversy at the time as to where it should be placed - it even resided for a time in the room of A. J. Balfour. It was said to be the work of Bernini but this now seems to be an unlikely attribution. It sits on a plinth wholly different in character from its Gothic surroundings. Other busts have found their way into various more or less suitable places.

*Mosaics of Saint Andrew, Saint George and Saint Patrick.*

W.H. Smith, Lord Randolph Churchill and Sir Francis Burdett all grace the Members' Staircase where provision was made for three busts. Other busts sit uneasily on a variety of plinths, all alien to their Gothic surroundings. Lady Astor in terracotta has found a corner in the Members' Families Room; Joseph Hume is in the Oriel Room of the House of Commons' Library on a Gothic bracket in the window; Erskine May sits on a wooden Gothic plinth in the Commons' Library.

From time to time committees of Members of both Houses have addressed themselves to the vexed subject of busts. The New Palace was not designed to take such things and no really satisfactory method of display has yet been devised at Westminster.

It is when sculpture is treated as part of the architecture that it is most successful. The New Palace was conceived as a masterpiece of Gothic architecture, therefore the Gothic tradition in sculpture had to be followed if the related works in sculpture were to match their surroundings. Although there was no great continuing tradition, Barry had the good fortune to enjoy the services of John Thomas.

This remarkable man, born at Chalford in Gloucestershire, was left an orphan at the age of thirteen. Apprenticed to a local stone-mason, he later went to Birmingham where his brother was an architect. An early work in the Gothic style in Huntingdon was noticed by Charles Barry, then at work on the Birmingham Grammar School. Barry, at once recognising the great talent of the young sculptor, asked him to execute all the carving both in wood and stone at the new school. Some work for Edward Blore at Crewe Hall and Capesthorne Hall intervened before Barry called upon Thomas to superintend all the stone-carving in the emerging New Palace at Westminster. Superintend he did, but he also found the time and energy to execute the most important parts of the work with his own hands. Thomas was responsible at Westminster for the statues on the north and south fronts, all the panels of arms of the Kings and Queens of England from William the Conqueror to Queen Victoria, together with their supporters. He also executed the statues and the bosses for the Victoria Tower and the bosses in St. Stephen's Hall. In the House of Lords Chamber, the statues of Stephen Langton, Archbishop of Canterbury, and William, Earl of Salisbury are both by Thomas.

Thomas also worked for Isambard Kingdom Brunel making two huge lions for the Britannia Bridge across the Menai Straits. These each weighed eighty tons and were twenty-five feet long. Thomas was responsible for the sculpture on many public buildings. The incredible variety of this man's genius is shown in his work for Prince Albert at Balmoral, the armorials on the Duke of Wellington's funeral car, the great fountain of Castle Howard and sculpture on the Sultan's Palace at Constantinople. Thomas was not only a carver but also an architect. He built Somerleyton for Sir Morton Peto, the great railway contractor, whose partnership was also involved in the construction of the New Palace.

There were other sculptors working at Westminster under the eye of Barry and the superintendence of Thomas. One of these was John Birnie Philip. He was trained at the Government School of design in Somerset House. His first employment was on ornamental sculpture at the New Palace. His best work at Westminster is eight figures of Kings and Queens in the Royal Gallery. Philip's figures also appear at the Foreign Office, at Burlington House and at the Old India Office. His work reached as far afield as Melbourne and Calcutta. His best known work is however the series of great architects and sculptors of the world on the Albert Memorial. There were eighty-seven figures in all, including Barry and Pugin. It is perhaps fitting too that he made the posthumous statue of Colonel Akroyd which stands beside Scott's great All Souls, Haley Hill which dominates Halifax and bankrupted its patron.

Although sadly some of the exterior sculpture on the New Palace has had to be recarved, the new figures have been copied from the originals with meticulous care. Some of these have been set up within the building and thus permanently preserved at Westminster. Others have been disposed of at various times and have been distributed to many parts of the world.

The series of bronze relief panels in the Prince's Chamber were executed by William Theed between 1855 and 1857. Theed was much admired by Prince Albert, who gave him a number of commissions. It was he who made the Prince Consort's death mask for Queen Victoria.

In the Robing Room are a series of bas-reliefs carved in oak by H. H. Armstead in 1870. They depict scenes from the Arthurian Legend and complement the frescoes by Dyce.

The monumental work of John Gibson in the Prince's Chamber should be judged for its effect when viewed from the Royal Gallery with the great north doors flung open as they would be on the occasion of Her Majesty's opening Parliament.

John Gibson, like John Thomas, began life as a stone-mason who soon showed promise as a sculptor. At the age of twenty-seven he went to Rome where he was encouraged by Canova. For the rest of his life he lived and worked mostly in Rome but enjoyed a great reputation in Britain, under the patronage of the Prince Consort. It was not thought fitting that Gibson should produce his monumental group for the New Palace in a studio in Rome. With some difficulty he worked in a place set aside for him within the precincts of the Palace.

The statue of Queen Victoria, accompanied by "Justice" and "Mercy" is often described as Neo-Classical in style. Certainly "Mercy" answers that description. "Justice", however, were she to grasp the hilt of her sword with both hands might pass for a Gothic Saint high up on the exterior

*Statue of the 1st Earl Attlee (1883-1967) in the Members' Lobby, by Ivor Roberts Jones.*

of the Palace. Her Majesty has in her right hand a Classical laurel wreath but in her left she grips firmly a Gothic symbol of authority, the sceptre. She is seated on an eminently Gothic throne, reminiscent of the Coronation chair, although it has a touch of Hawksmoor, as does the west front of Westminster Abbey. The Queen wears a Gothic crown, under which is an expression of youthful authority. Although the figures of "Justice" and "Mercy" have at least once been temporarily removed, at the whim of some committee of noble Lords, Her Majesty has witnessed all of her successor's dignified progress towards the opening of the Imperial Parliament and she is likely to remain in her prominent position.

The larger-than-life size bronze of Richard I, Richard Cœur de Lion, which stands in Old Palace Yard, guarding the entrance to the House of Lords, has had an interesting history. The work of Baron Marochetti, it was exhibited at the Great Exhibition of 1851. It was not one of those statues which found favour with the critics. The striking equestrian bronze stood near the cab-rank, where it was much admired by the drivers. It became even more popular with them and with the public when it was violently attacked by the critics. On its arrival at Westminster the statue stood first in New Palace Yard. It was later removed to the north end of Old Palace Yard. It was intended to match with another statue representing the Black Prince. Had the statue of the Black Prince materialised and had he been placed to the south of the Peers' Entrance, the Embankment traffic would have been confronted with the rear view of a substantial obstruction. This would perhaps have tamed its ardour.

In the very heart of the New Palace, at the foot of the Committee Stairs, where all those who have business in the Palace pass, by day and by night, is the seated figure of its architect. The sculptor J. H. Foley created a memorial in which Sir Charles Barry is seated at work upon the final details of the Victoria Tower. On the wall behind the statue a tablet records Barry's achievement thus *The Palace of Westminster was first built in the 11th century during the reign of Edward the Confessor. The Palace was destroyed by fire on the 16th day of October 1834 in the reign of His Majesty King William the Fourth. The Palace was rebuilt during the years from 1838 to 1852 in the reign of her present Majesty Queen Victoria. The new Palace was designed by Sir Charles Barry, who died in the year 1860 and whose statue was placed below in the year 1865 by public subscription.*

It was the intention of his many friends that Sir Charles should be commemorated looking down the long vista through Westminster Hall and out into New Palace Yard. This position was refused, so it is by accident that Sir Charles sits forever at the very crossroads of public and Parliamentary activity.

The subscribers to the memorial statue (for it was not erected by a grateful Parliament or Government) include many great names of the age:

Banks, Bellamy, Brakspear, Bunning, Burton, Carlisle (Morpeth), Cockerell, Cowper, Crace, Cubitt, Cust, Eastlake, Ferrey, An Humble Friend, Gibson, Grissell, Beresford Hope, Hunt, Kendall, Maclise, Marochetti, Mocatta, Nash, Pennethorne, Peto, Pickersgill, Poynter, Richardson, Roberts, Gilbert Scott, Smirke, Spiers, Tite, Vulliamy, Wolfe, Wyatt and the workmen at Clapham.

*Fireplace in the Prince's Chamber.*

Charles Barry had a clear idea of what he wanted for the windows throughout the Palace. In the Peers Chamber saintly figures of Kings and Queens were to emulate the early Gothic work found in cathedrals. The remainder of the grand interiors would be decorated with heraldry in the Tudor manner.

Barry had to fight off the Commission on two occasions. They favoured glass of the Munich School, which produced windows that looked like paintings. Next Barry had to gain control of the glass in the Peers' Chamber where the Commission landed him with a contractor who was troublesome and far from competent. Barry and Pugin between them managed to obtain a reasonable result from Messrs. Ballantine and Allan. Although that firm actually manufactured the windows, all the drawing had to be done by Pugin. Barry actually had a specimen window made by John Hardman in Birmingham. This specimen would seem to be the only survival from the Lords. A window long stored in the glazier's shop at Westminster was recently examined and discovered to have upon it no fixings of any kind. Clearly this window is a trial or specimen. The subject is William I and that was the subject of the specimen window with which Barry took so much trouble, before Ballantine and Allan were allowed to make anything.

Out of the frustrations experienced in the Lords grew the partnership which produced all the remainder of the nineteenth century stained glass in the Palace. Pugin and Barry persuaded John Hardman in Birmingham to add stained glass to the metalwork which he was already producing for them.

Pugin's experience with William Warrington, (commended by the judging Committee), Thomas Willement and William Wailes confirmed him in his determination to have someone carry out the work as he wished it to be done. Hardman's nephew, John Hardman Powell, was employed at Ramsgate as Pugin's pupil from November 1844. Pugin would do a sketch, Powell would draw it in more detail and then a team of draughtsmen would produce cartoons from which windows could be made. "A scheme for filling the windows of the Great Halls and approaches of the New Palace at Westminster" in Sir Charles Barry's own hand is among the Thomas Greene papers.[7]

"St. Stephen's Hall - Octagon or Central Hall. The four windows are proposed to commemorate by effigies and armorial bearings distinguished persons connected with English History - the effigies will occupy the alternate lights, the intermediate ones being filled with heraldic badges and armorial bearings - by these means an abundance of light will be admitted and yet a rich effect obtained.

Peers' and Commons' corridors leading from the Central Hall to the

*William Theed's bronze panels in the Prince's Chamber (1855-6).*

*William Theed's bronze panels in the Prince's Chamber (1855-6).*

*William Theed's bronze panels in the Prince's Chamber (1855-6).*

two Houses. The small three light windows will contain arms of distinguished Princes such as The Black Prince, John of Gaunt etc. with their proper badges and supporters.

These windows contain effigies in the centre and alternate lights and armorial bearings between them. The effigies will represent the proto-martyr St. Stephen, the Saint commemorated in the original foundation of

*Oak carvings of the Arthurian legend, by H. H. Armstead (1870), in the Robing Room.*

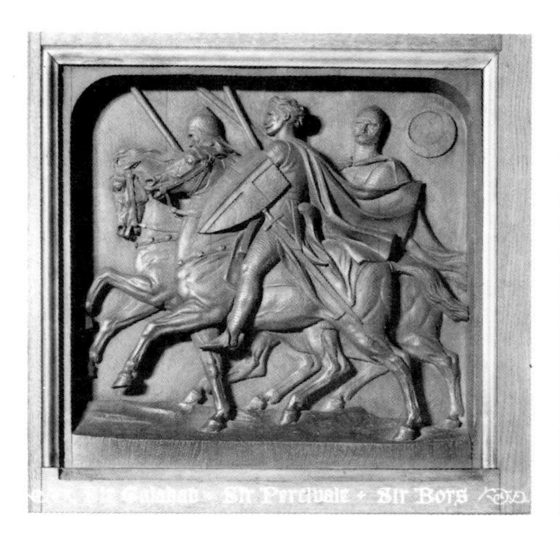
Sir Galahad + Sir Percivale + Sir Bors

Sir Galahad imprisoned by the Tyrant

Sir Galahad's soul borne to Heaven

King Arthur conquering the marvailous

The Knights of the Round Table vowing to seek the Sancgreall

The misadventure of the Adder + Beginning of the Battaile

to Avilion attended by Queenes

the Old Chapel, St. Edmund, St. Edward, St. George etc. and of the Royal Founder his Queen, and the Royal and other distinguished personages who were connected with the creation of the Chapel. Their arms will be introduced in the lights and thus a memorial of this original and famous structure will be perpetuated.

Westminster Hall - South Window. This window will represent a genealogical tree or arrangement of the various Sovereigns or Houses which have inhabited the English Throne from the Conquest to the present time - according to this arrangement each House will occupy an equal number of lights by which the whole window will be entirely filled and due importance be given to our present gracious Sovereign whose arms and badges will occupy a central division.

*Statue of Richard Cœur de Lion by Baron Marochetti in New Palace Yard (1853).*

Throughout the whole of the above arrangement, care will be taken to ensure a sufficient amount of light by the plentiful use of quarry grounds and brilliant tints much broken up so that the lights will be only modified to that tone which is necessary for the due effect of the architecture and the comfort of the spectators. Charles Barry Archt. 29 May 1851."[7]

In November 1851 Barry wrote "Dear Hardman, the glass specimen lights in the Division Corridors are much approved. Pray send up all the stained glass for whatever situation it may be destined without loss of time, so that we may make a show with the fixing of it."[8]

It was Barry's first intention to use effigies and heraldry in both St. Stephen's Hall and the Central Hall. Barry wrote the foregoing before the House of Commons Chamber had been savagely altered. It is possible that some of the glass removed from the upper windows of the Commons found its way into the Central Hall or St. Stephen's Hall. We know also that Barry was prepared at one time to remove the glass from the Peers' Chamber and re-use it in the Royal Gallery, but this was a change which was not made. The Royal Gallery glass might have been taken out altogether had the Prince Consort lived. In the event it was altered by taking out most of the colour. The removal of colour was the fate experienced by other original schemes including the Peers' Corridor and the Commons' Corridor.

Although much glass was put in by Barry and Pugin, much of it suffered alteration and some of it suffered removal or transposition.

"Many of the cartoons for later windows at Westminster were drawn out by Hardman-Powell and eventually Barry was using him extensively for drawings of all kinds, particularly after Pugin's death." In August 1856 Barry writes of "the portion of the House of Commons windows re-used in the windows of the Central Hall" and "I should be glad also to have the cartoon which I arranged with Powell for the further employment of them in St. Stephen's Hall and an account of all the glass you have in store, describing the Arms of which it in part consists."[9] This implies the original plans for the location of the glass had to be changed.

In some cases, when a series was completed, it was found to make the chamber or the corridor too dark and alterations had to be made to lighten the windows. In fact, it is certain that a few years later most of the colour was taken out of many of the windows; a practical step, no doubt, but one which left the heraldry in a very insipid state.

Hardman's chief fixer of glass at Westminster was Mr. J. Bishop. He became a well-known figure and popular at the Palace. It is recalled that at the opening of the Sydenham Crystal Palace, the Police from the House of Lords being in charge of the seating arrangement surrounding the Monarch, put him between the Peers and Peeresses on the grounds that he was a Bishop.

There are a few areas where little change beyond repair seems to have

*The William I stained glass window originally in the House of Lords.*

taken place. There is some fine glass at the entrance to the Serjeant-at-Arm's house in Speaker's Court with the arms of Lord Charles James Fox Russell included. Likewise the former Clerk of the House's residence and the Librarian's former residence each contain original windows, unaltered.

Some of the glass in the internal stone screens which divide the corridors of the principal floor is either original or a careful repair of it.

Hardman's was still in the business of stained glass during and after the 1939-45 War. Mr. Patrick A. Feeny in his article "The Heraldic Glass in the Houses of Parliament" gives a detailed account of the programme of repair which followed after 1945. He also throws light on the early history of much of the glass. Feeny says that at the beginning of the 1939-45 War, the many heraldic windows which the buildings contained were either just removed in time, and in haste, or had to be left to their fate, with disastrous results. This glass had been manufactured almost entirely by the John Hardman studios, mainly between the years 1847 and 1863. Just a hundred years later, in 1947, it was possible for the Ministry of Works to place a contract with the same studios for its repair and restoration. Some four hundred and seven lights, comprising nearly 5,600 square feet of glass, came within the scope of the contract.

"It was known that many of the original cartoons were still in Birmingham, but it is a major task to sort these out and to put aside those which would be needed. Many were in a dilapidated condition, often wrongly named; and some, it was discovered, were specimen cartoons, retained but never used. A detailed contemporary guide-book to the House

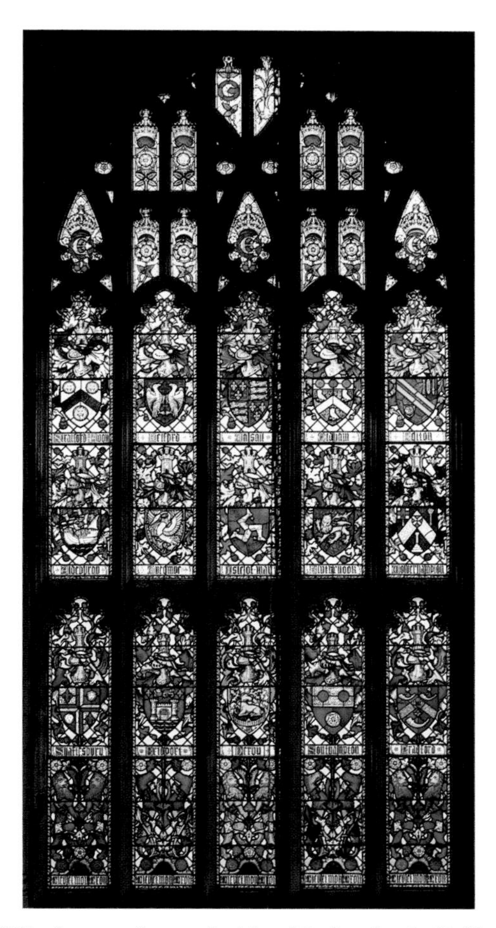

*Window on the south side of St Stephen's Hall.*

*Stained glass in the Corridor from the Central Lobby to the Lords Chamber.*

*Stained glass between the Peers' Staircase and the Prince's Chamber.*

of Parliament, listing the windows and indicating what they contained, would have been invaluable at this stage. But such a book was not available, nor could anyone be found at Westminster with this requisite knowledge."[10] This is an extraordinary statement in view of the existence of guidebooks to the Palace going back to the 1850s and the reference to glass in the Barry volumes of 1849 and 1865.[11]

"Hardman's first task was to restore the ten large windows in St. Stephen's Hall, consisting of some one hundred and fifty shields of Borough, City and Town Arms. Apart from clearing out the background quarries to give more prominence, at the height, to the painted detail, these windows were to be as originally designed." This is of course not strictly correct. The original design, for which we have Pugin's drawings and Barry's statement as to what he intended to do, comprised effigies and arms. No doubt Hardman's restored what existed before the War.

In the Royal Gallery "the original windows were deprived of all their colour some years after they had been installed and the rather drab result of brown and stain called for a change. It was therefore decided, after a specimen window had been tried in place, to compromise by having the shields, at least, in full colour. The remnants redesigned and remade; the new design being based upon the old but with a more lively setting."

In the House of Lords Chamber "an anonymous donor, subsequently identified as the late Lord Kenilworth, had offered £20,000 to defray the cost of this important series. This caused quite a fluttering in the dovecotes as it would certainly be the most interesting part of the glass restoration and a glorious opportunity for the artist chosen, who was to be allowed a reasonably free hand with the design and treatment." Hardman's entered the competition but none of the entrants was acceptable to the selectors. Eventually Mr. Carl Edwards submitted an approved design and the windows were made by Powell of Whitefriars."[10] This series of windows almost overdoes the feeling of brilliantly coloured heraldry against sparkling white background. It would have fitted admirably the kind of Lords' Chamber that Scott would have created by obliterating all the colour and gilding and bleaching the oak.

The windows in the Crypt Chapel were restored exactly as they were originally. In spite of much damage this, happily, was not a difficult matter as the early cartoons were still available and in good condition.

One of the most interesting series of windows followed – those on the Grand Staircase. In the window at the bottom of the stairs is shown the Black Prince in chainmail, with appropriate shields and emblems. The remainder, up the stairs, deal heraldicly with his family and campaigns. The heraldry here was left in its full colour and they are the better windows for that. As usual, though, the glass returned to Hardman's was only a small proportion of the original series and much research and handling was necessary before they were refixed complete.

Hardman's were in possession of "one large roll of cartoons for the great south window in Westminster Hall." Feeny explains how the twenty-seven lights and tracery were originally carried out by Hardman's but the window had been damaged by the explosion of a bomb on the 24th of January 1885, after which the window was repaired using the original drawings. After the Second World War no attempt was made to reinstate the Pugin design because Sir Ninian Comper was asked to design a new window as a War Memorial, to all the many Parliamentarians who had given their lives in the service of their country.

Not all the glass that remained in the Palace at the end of the War was sent up to Hardman's for restoration. Members of both Houses of

*Stained glass in the Lords' Library Corridor.*

*Richard II windows.*

*The Calais-Boulogne windows.*

Parliament were invited to collect souvenirs from the damaged glass. A list of those who signed for quantities of glass was discovered recently in the glazier's shop. A few of those who had signed the book were still alive. None of them could recall what it was they signed for. Nor could anyone recall anything of material significance concerning the state of the glass at the end of the War.

Despite the fear of some that stained glass darkens interiors, there is scope for some cautious experiment. The completion of the lower windows in the Peers' Lobby could do nothing but good to the appearance of that room. The dreary windows in the Central Lobby could either be completely re-worked embodying a little heraldry or alternatively the leaded lights removed altogether and replaced with clear glass set in bronze frames like so much else of the exterior. This would give views of features of the building not normally seen. The Prince's Chamber windows are probably those that are most unworthy of their surroundings. With the John Hardman studios still at work in Birmingham, the Palace could be much enhanced by a revival of stained glass at Westminster.

Some of the windows which Barry asked Pugin to design were illuminated during hours of darkness by gas-jets shining through them from the exterior. Skilful use of floodlighting could produce a fine effect today.

*Á Pugin Weathervane for the New Palace.*

# VIII

## Palace of the Arts

### *Metalwork*

Virtually all the interior metalwork in the New Palace owes its origin to Pugin's fertile imagination and the skilled manufactory of Hardman and Company of Birmingham. There is no metal object, however humble, for which Pugin was unable to produce a Gothic form that was both decorative and functional.

The same care and thought went into a masterpiece like the great brass gates to the House of Lords as into calendars and ink stands for the library or even a door handle for a servant's room. To the practised eye, the Westminster metalwork is instantly recognizable. Even where it has been used in other contemporary buildings it proclaims its origin. There is a robustness about the designs for the New Palace which, unless subtly modified (as was sometimes the case) makes it fit ill into more domestic surroundings. Barry's interiors at Canford, for example, contain woodwork and metalwork which so closely resemble that at Westminster that one might almost be stepping into a lobby of the nineteenth century House of Commons. This work admirably suits a great public school but it was originally part of a great country house.

John Hardman was persuaded into the manufacture of Gothic metalwork by Pugin in 1838. The firm soon began to expand because no one else had thought to venture into the production of work of real scholarship and quality in this field. Hardman's were well established by the time that Pugin was designing metalwork for Westminster.

Much has been made of the so-called archaeological anachronism in Pugin's love of an extensive use of brass. What in fact he did was to broaden its medieval use for the finest things into areas in which iron had been the fashion previously. Bronze occurs in the Middle Ages in the tombs of Kings; brass occurs everywhere at Westminster where it can be effective.

The history of some of the metalwork is well documented. The saga of the brass railing round the Gallery in the Lords Chamber is a classic example. Many changes of mind by Barry involved Pugin in much hard work and Hardman in much abortive expense. All was in position in time for the opening in 1847 at a cost of a little over £2,000. The brass gates to the House of Lords were made for less than £1,000 but with these Pugin had a relatively free hand.

*Detail of Pugin Metalwork.*

It is in the field of light fittings that Pugin's metalwork met its greatest challenge and has suffered its greatest reverse. The New Palace began in the days of oil lamps and candles, lived through the era of gas lighting, and now is lit by electricity. Many of the fittings designed for gas have been converted but many more have disappeared. Much alien metalwork has been imported and some light fittings amount to a defacement of the historic interiors. It is only in recent years that a conscious effort has been made to restore the light fittings in some of the more historic interiors. In some instances it has been possible to bring back, repaired and refurbished, fittings jettisoned to the cellars. The chandeliers in the Peers' Guest Room are an example of this. The eight sconces on the walls are copied from a remaining example found upside-down in the Speaker's House. The four chandeliers in the State Bedroom are exact copies of those in the corner room in the State Apartments. They were made by A.Edward Jones & Co. at the St. Dunstan's works in Birmingham. This firm has inherited the metalwork part of Hardman's.

The best of the modern copies of the nineteenth century brass work are indistinguishable from the originals. However, for every firm capable of producing work of the highest quality, there must have been a dozen who have tried to get away with inferior productions at exorbitant prices. It is sad that so much of the Westminster metalwork was executed after Pugin's death. Some of it shows the influence of his son Edward who joined Hardman's in Birmingham. Together with J. H. Powell, who had become his brother-in-law, they were probably responsible for much of the later and highly elaborate brasswork which abounds in the Speaker's House, the Robing Room, and the Crypt Chapel.

*A key designed by Pugin.*

*Table clock for the Palace of Westminster designed by Pugin (1851).*

Edward Middleton Barry also asked Hardman's to make the iron railings which he designed for New Palace Yard. They are both physically and visually a heavy creation. When it became necessary to extend the railings along Cromwell Green and Speaker's Green, a lighter version of the E. M. Barry railings was devised by Mr. Donald Buttress M.A., Dip. Arch, F.S.A., R.I.B.A. of the Buttress Fuller Partnership.

A recent notable acquisition for the Palace is a unique table clock designed by Pugin and made by Hardman. It is well documented. In a letter of early March 1851, Pugin writes to Hardman, "I send you the clock. There is as much for me to arrange as in a small church. I wish you would not turn clock maker, unless on a great scale. You must do as much of it as you can and leave out what is too costly but I must make a good thing. The four corners are flowers (spring) wheat (summer) grapes (autumn) holly (winter) a beautiful idea showing the passage of time through the seasons. I had written a small ode to accompany the clock but time failed me in transcribing it. It began,

'-how swiftly turn thy timing hands
thou pretty gothic clock
etc. etc. etc."[1]

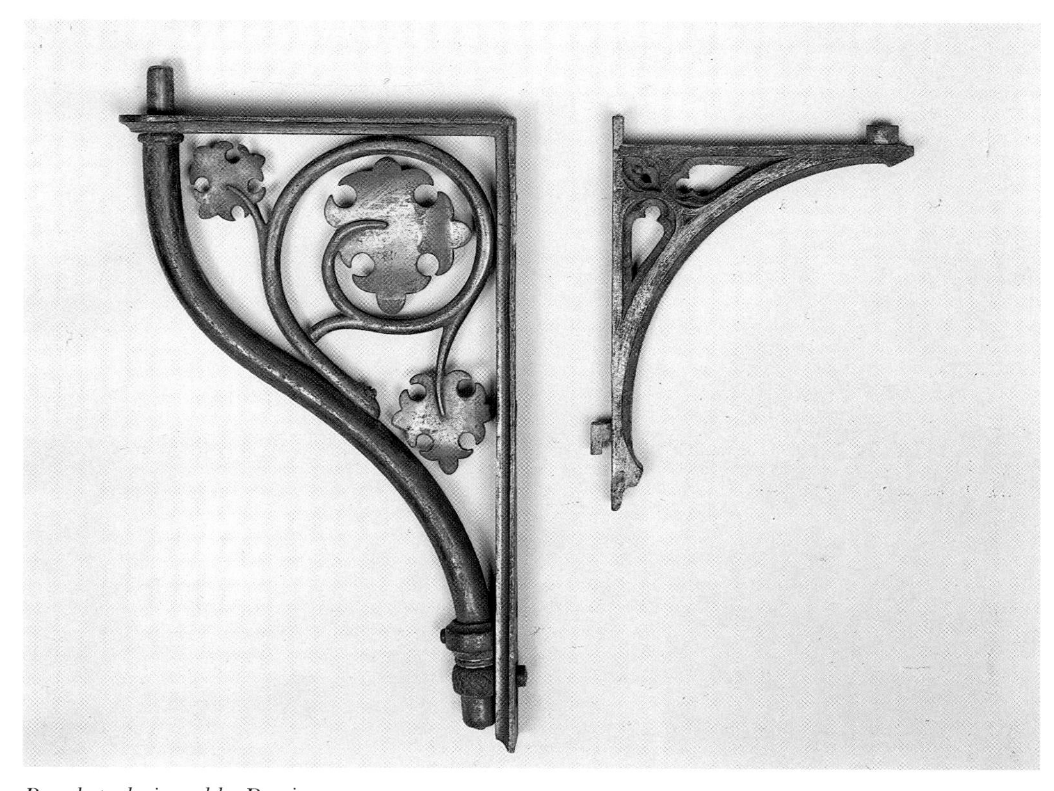

*Brackets designed by Pugin.*

There is also a drawing for the clock in a private collection.

The metalwork which accompanied Giles Gilbert Scott's New House of Commons' Chamber and its surroundings is of the highest quality and design. He followed in the tradition of Pugin in that he demanded that all was special and appropriate to its purpose. Scott's metalwork ranges from the two silver-gilt inkstands with paper racks on the Table of the House (presented by Northern and Southern Rhodesia) to a series of silver-gilt ashtrays, one of which was presented by the Falkland Islands.[2]

Elsewhere Scott's metalwork was all specially designed. The metal grilles in the doors of the Chamber were too subtle. Their hidden sliding catches, the means by which the glass behind could be cleaned, soon worked loose and the grilles fell out. The hinged replacements are a clumsy but efficient substitute. The neighbouring door handles have had a Gothic flavour worked into their sturdy practicality. Scott sidestepped the problem of metal mounts for his furniture by employing wooden handles and concealed hinges.

*A salamander designed by Pugin for the Lords Chamber.*

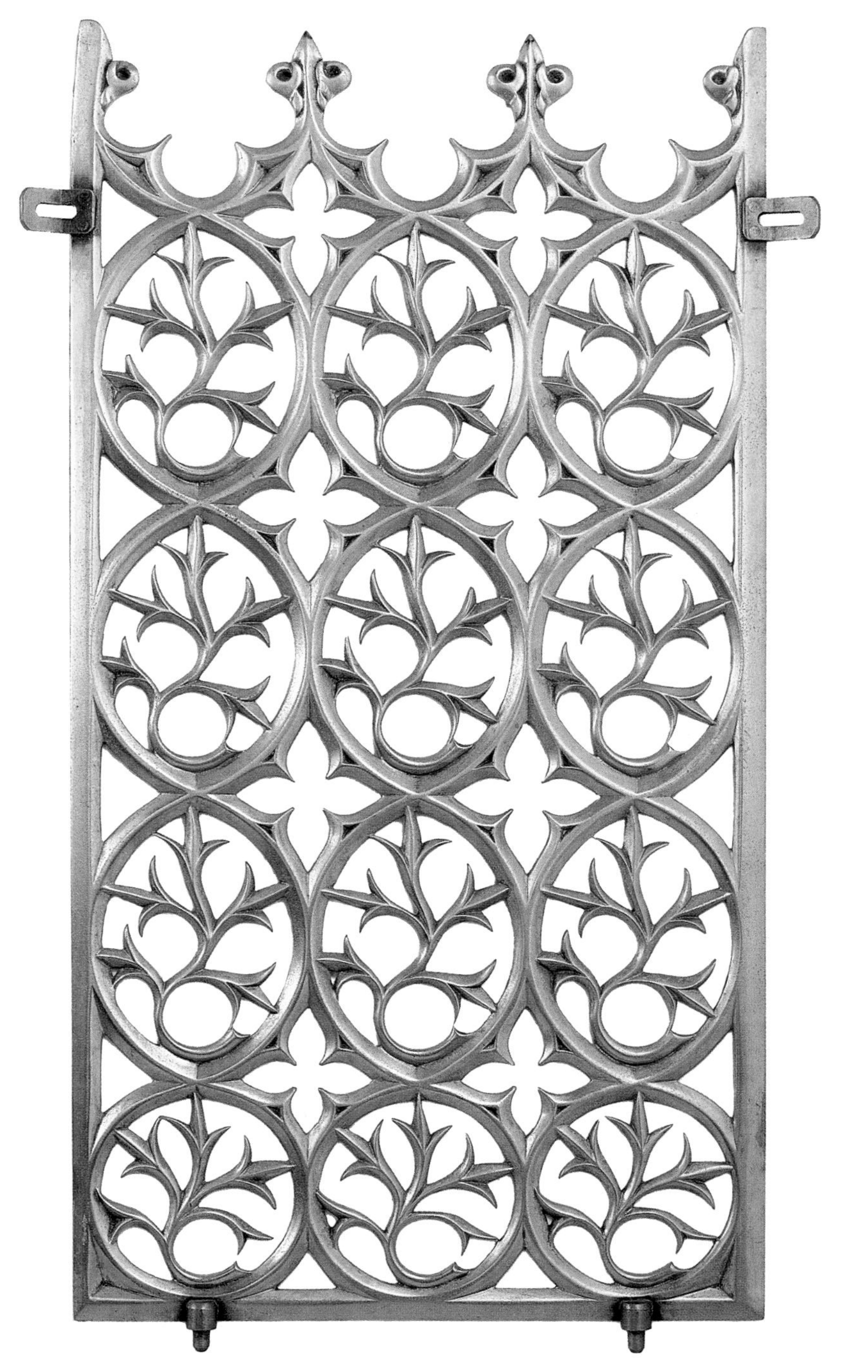

*A door grille designed by Pugin.*

*Tiles designed by Pugin.*

The New Palace contains the finest assemblage of Minton tiles. The floors and staircases of the majority of the public areas were each the subject of an individual scheme carefully worked out by Pugin and mostly executed under his eye. The quality of this original work is the envy even of the present craftsmen at Minton's; under the wing of H. & R. Johnson they have from time to time made substantial numbers of replacements.

The grandest of all the tiled floors is that in the Central Lobby; it is all heraldic and symbolic with huge Gothic inscriptions in white on blue, the most difficult product of the ceramic art. All are in Latin.

"Special attention should be directed to the very beautiful encaustic tile pavement of the Hall with its appropriate inscription, 'Except the Lord keep the House their labour is but lost that build it,' given in the Latin of the Vulgate; unique in its effect and evidencing as do the pavements in this material in different parts of the building, that there is no lack of power in our present manufacturers when their abilities are really called out to vie with the most elaborate and artistic effects of decoration of this kind of former times."[3]

The Lower Waiting Hall, paved also in tiles from the factory of Messrs. Minton, bears the inscriptions, 'Virtue prevails,' and 'Love and Fidelity to our country.'"

*Tiles designed by Pugin, executed by Minton's.*

The encaustic floor tiles were manufactured by the baking together of different coloured clays to produce the patterns. This means that a century or more of wear produces no loss of the design. However, by now, in the most heavily used areas the tiles are wearing out. Minton's have produced new tiles for both the Commons' Corridor and the Peers' Corridor leading off the Central Lobby. The quality has improved with each new order. An area in the south-east corner of the Royal Gallery has also been renewed. Tiles have also been made and stored with a view to tackling other areas which require renewal. It should be possible, by carefully sawing through the joints, to raise individual tiles and replace them with new ones rather than to tear up whole areas as has been the case in the past.

Tiles that have been taken up have been offered to a wide range of Museums thus preserving examples of the Westminster work. A tile rescue programme by the Ironbridge Gorge Museum Trust was mounted in Palace Chambers and adjoining buildings in Bridge Street in 1986, financed by the National Heritage Memorial Fund. These tiles, although they did not relate to the Palace, were of a high quality and interest.

*Lion tile designed by Pugin.*

*Pugin tiles.*

A remarkable feature of many of the Westminster floor tiles is their size. Some tiles are equal in area to four conventional tiles. The lettered inscriptions in white on blue are also of a large size.

In addition to the floors there were areas of wall which were tiled. One of these was the Smoking Room at Terrace level where the tiles exist behind later panelling.

Tiles in fireplaces are of two kinds. Some embellish the hearth; others, often of a large size, form brilliantly colourful surrounds within the stonework. These are particularly prominent in the Peers' Cloakroom, the Robing Room, the Prince's Chamber, and in the Speaker's State Apartments. Here there seems to be no colour with which the makers were unable to cope. A rare shade of green appears with absolute clarity.

Prior to the Minton's renewals, the firm of Carters of Poole made a number of simple tiles for areas in the Crypt Chapel. They used compressed dry materials. Despite the finest brass dies the colours tended to be smudged at the edges and they never succeeded in producing satisfactory results involving blue. It was their brave effort that encouraged the Palace authorities to tackle the floors which had been neglected for so long.

The Victoria and Albert Museum hold a number of coloured designs in Pugin's own hand which were intended for the New Palace. Perry's of Islington have the original blocks for a large number of papers widely used at Westminster. In recent years a number of the original designs have been reprinted. In some cases it has been possible to replace a paper hung in a particular room when it was first created. The many changes in the use of rooms have taxed the ingenuity of those responsible for redecoration. Some remarkable successes are evident as are some less happy attempts at authenticity. Some of the grandest and most successful reprinted papers are the flocks in the Lords Committee Rooms number one to number four. Here the colours and the scale of the pattern are most agreeable. More recently the Peers' Guest Room has been given an impressive but somewhat strident red flock which has yet to mellow.

*A Gothic wallpaper coloured by the author for the Speaker's House.*

*Indian pattern wallpaper in the Royal Gallery.*

The original designs were carefully graded as to size of pattern and grandeur of treatment to suit the status of their surroundings. The larger rooms were intended to have the larger patterns. Some of the larger patterns, if produced in vivid colours, make difficult backgrounds for paintings unless they be of great size. Quite early in the history of the New Palace there were patterns of a small and discreet kind used in the larger rooms presumably in order to provide a more sympathetic background to the pictures. An example of this is a room which began its life as the Painted Chamber or Conference Room. The earliest views of the unaltered room when it had become the Members' Dining Room show quite a small pattern; the St. Stephen's Club illustration of the room shows the same pattern that exists there today.

An interesting group of Pugin designs are derived from "Mr. Barry's idea of introducing badges connected with the history of Westminster Palace."[4] There are a number of these at the Victoria and Albert Museum; some of them exist as samples, none are presently hanging in the Palace. This is a field worthy of exploration. If blocks can be found, or specially made, the designs would form a welcome addition to the better known authentic designs presently being used.

Wallpaper at Westminster is a confusing subject. Many of the Westminster papers have been printed for other people in colours far removed from the originals. A recent scholarly work on the Palace had as its frontispiece a hand-printed paper of a design not definitely identified with the Palace and in colours such that the manufacturers were glad to be rid of a large surplus stock. Papers which look beguiling as patterns sometimes appear very different when actually hung in a room.

*Scott Cuthbertson wallpaper.*

*The Moses Room, looking west.*

*Textiles*

There are a number of designs at the Victoria and Albert Museum, mostly from the Crace Collection acquired in 1908, which would serve either for wallpaper, curtains, carpets or tiles. Some tile designs could serve for wallpapers.

Until recent times, curtains and carpets in the nineteenth century parts of the Palace had strayed far in design from the originals, though crowned portcullisses, roses, and a faintly Gothic flavour prevailed. This is a field in which, resources permitting, much agreeable restoration could take place.

For carpets, a number of designs have been worked up from the original drawings with varying degrees of success. The new carpet for the Lords' Chamber and Prince's Chamber (and the Royal Gallery on State Occasions) is the most recent example at an attempt at authenticity. The next time that it is renewed, the design could be nearer to the original.

A number of geometric designs have been used throughout the two Houses and in some cases in the out-buildings to give a feeling of continuity to the occupants, if not to the architecture.

Pugin was in the business of designing furniture before he set up as a practising architect. By the time he came to design the furniture for the New Palace he had acquired a wide practical experience combined with a knowledge and understanding of the historic examples from which his contemporary work was derived.

The furniture in the New Palace has a strong architectural flavour. It is solidly constructed and has stood the test of time. Not a day goes by in the life of the Palace that furniture somewhere is being moved to accommodate some changed use of a room or some new requirement of a new occupant. It is this fact which has been used as an excuse heretofore for the failure to produce a comprehensive work upon this all important part of the history of the New Palace. The time has surely arrived to pull together the fruits of the labour of at least three living authorities.

As with metalwork so with furniture, Pugin was the inspiration with Barry the controlling influence. There is ample evidence that nothing was actually executed save with Barry's approval.

*A Pugin chest of drawers.*

*A wardrobe designed by Pugin.*

The more important pieces, if not made for the more important places, have in recent years found their way into appropriate surroundings. At the time of the restoration of the Speaker's State Apartments, the retrieval of several clearly identifiable pieces required delicate negotiation. The inmates of rooms to which the Speaker's furniture had migrated were not all immediately generous in their enthusiasm to return it whence it came. A notable exception was Lord Chancellor Hailsham of St. Marylebone. When his Lordship was shown the evidence that the frame surrounding a Lord Chancellor's purse in his own room was in fact Mr. Speaker's firescreen, he immediately authorised its return. The traffic in any case was not all one way. The Salisbury Room in the House of Lords gained a magnificent inlaid octagonal table as a result of the rearrangement. At this time too it was discovered that a great number of walnut single chairs, and some armchairs of the House of Lords' pattern, but made for residences, had become sprinkled about a large number of offices. These were all carefully sorted out.

In the manufacture of furniture, a number of firms were certainly involved. John Webb of Bond Street made the throne for the House of Lords and the accompanying Chairs of State. Webb was also responsible for the Clerk's Table in the House of Lords. The plan of its unusual design is said to resemble a portcullis. The two fine oak octagon tables, of unique design in the Prince's Chamber are also Webb's work.

Webb had a particularly close relationship with Pugin. It is in his work at Westminster that the finest Pugin detail is found. A number of unmarked but particularly grand pieces may well have come from Webb.

Holland and Son were responsible for supplying huge quantities of furniture. The tender document for the Speaker's House has survived together with many of the accompanying drawings. Much of this furniture is in walnut, partly gilded. Although Puginian in feeling it departs in detail from pieces made to Pugin's drawings elsewhere. The Holland drawings are clearly not in Pugin's hand. The poor quality of the design and execution of the Royal Arms on the State Bed would never have passed the eye of the master.

*A wardrobe designed by Pugin, now in the Resident Engineer's flat.*

*Pugin's design for a dressing table for the Speaker's House.*

Gillows were active at Westminster between 1851 and 1856. They stamped their work and many pieces bearing their name exist to this day. Another Bond Street firm, Johnstone and Jeanes, provided furniture for the Palace; examples stamped with their name exist in some quantity, particularly walnut armchairs in various styles. Much of the carcass furniture was supplied by various makers to the Government workshops at Thames Bank where it was fitted with metalwork supplied by Hardman's.

It would be possible, if all the drawings for Westminster furniture were laid out together with all the diary and daybook entries of the architects and the manufacturers and with photographs of all the existing pieces of furniture in the Palace, to make a proper assessment of what was originally made for and installed in the Palace and what now exists.

In addition to the well-documented work of Webb, the extensive supplies by Holland's and Gillows and the lesser contribution of Johnstone and Jeanes, there are a number of important pieces whose authorship is uncertain. An outstanding pair of cabinets dating from the early 1850s and now in the Prime Minister's Room bear no maker's mark. One of them was the subject of a drawing by Richard Norman Shaw. No metalwork is shown on the drawing which suggests that the piece was supplied to the Government workshops and the metal mounts were fitted there. The piece which Shaw drew is not as useful as its pair because it consists of cupboards above and below what might have been a fall-fronted secretaire fitting. The front does not fall but can be entered only by a lifting flap.

The second cabinet is of unusual interest. It has a sloping front which lifts forward to reveal an interior fitted for writing materials. On either side of this piece were originally letterboxes. Messages placed in them fell into a compartment behind the locked doors of the lower section. It would seem possible that this was specially designed to fulfill a procedural necessity in either the Lords or Commons–an application for a question or debate or whatever could be written out on the writing slope and posted into the letter box to be collected with all the others so posted. It seems a fool-proof method of ensuring that all the applications reached a particular place by a particular time (the letter boxes had devices which enabled them to be closed). An official of the House with his key could then remove all the papers from the box below and could conduct the necessary ballot or whatever was required. This second piece, which matches the first in every detail save the design of its central part, languished for many years unloved in the region of what was originally the Upper Committee Floor. It was placed in the Prime Minister's Room at the time of its restoration in the early 1980s. Other fine oak pieces include magnificently fitted partners' desks or library tables in the Libraries of the two Houses. Almost every residence would have had some grand pieces within it. What is now the Home Secretary's Room (formerly the Housekeeper's Room) has a fine sideboard remaining. Another sideboard found its way to the flat of the Resident Engineer in the south front of the House of Lords.

One of the sad results of the change of use of many rooms, particularly residences, has been the removal into storage of pieces no longer required. From time to time stores have a habit of being cleared, their contents sometimes sold. It was thus that the State Bed for the Speaker's House found its way onto the market.

The role of the Craces in the field of furniture is uncertain. It was through this firm that some furniture was ordered. Pugin's request in a postscript to a letter to Crace of November 1850 is significant. "We must have some very simple chairs that will not come very expensive or the Board of Works will be putting in modern things."[5] This probably applies to the single chairs of which there are many hundreds in the Palace in two distinct designs. The "Lords" chair (of which many were made in walnut for residences) is more architectural in detail than the "Commons" chair. It has octagonal legs with Gothic base and capital. There is generally more chamfered work about it and it is more costly to make. The "Commons" chair is equally elegant but simpler in its detail.

Both these designs are reproduced from time to time as occasion demands. Until recently, copies had been made of copies which were copies of copies of the original. This resulted, particularly in the case of "Lords" chairs, in some mean and spindly specimens.

In a number of other fields replacements or additions have been made from time to time and are still being made. Although it is now the practice to copy an authentic example, there are numerous pieces which are poor imitations of the original and some which bear little resemblance to their predecessors.

*Detail of a door panel.*

A notable modern creation are the plain oak stools worked up from the House of Lords' chair design. No plain wooden stools from the nineteenth century have survived within the Palace, if indeed any existed. The modern fabrication fits in well with its surroundings and its sturdy construction should ensure its survival. It might here be stated that much of the furniture of Pugin design made for other buildings departs from the sound designs of the master. Many tables exist which are not properly braced resulting in their uselessness. Others embodying Pugin detail are ill-proportioned and clearly concoctions worked up either from a variety of drawings or from a number of existing sources. From time to time "Pugin pieces" are offered to the Palace. If they are useful and reasonably priced they are purchased. If they are useless and prohibitive, public money is not wasted on their acquisition.

When the House of Commons was destroyed in 1941 much of the finest of Gillows' work perished with it. They had provided the Speaker's Chair and the Table of the House. It is uncertain whether they provided the dispatch boxes but a pair of these designed by Pugin certainly existed. They can be seen clearly on the Table of the House in many of the earlier photographic views. Pugin's drawings for this pair of boxes and a companion pair for the Lords (which do not appear to have been executed) are both in the Royal Institute of British Architects Drawings Collection.

Much of the panelling throughout the Palace is not in its original state. The campaign begun in the days of Lewis Harcourt resulted in the stripping and lightening of nearly all the panelling, doors and accompanying carpentry throughout the Commons. In the Lords some of the woodwork retains some of its original darker colour. The practice of regular stripping and treatment with a sticky solution embodying an element of varnish has not done the woodwork much good anywhere. Similar treatment used to be extended to furniture taken back to the workshops for repair. A more intelligent regime is beginning to emerge. In the Speaker's Private Apartments an interesting finish to the woodwork was obtained long ago by bleaching and rubbing down with wire wool leaving minute rusty stains. The combination of the two treatments has created an appearance of antiquity rather like that achieved by nineteenth century Continental fakers of early Gothic furniture.

The furniture inheritance at Westminster contains a number of pieces no longer required for their original purpose. Chests of drawers can make admirable filing cabinets. Bedside cupboards have been converted to postboxes and one even serves as the receptacle for the declared interests of Members of Parliament. Attempts to Gothicise pieces of equipment, unheard of when the Palace was planned, have met with varying success. The Government Chief Whip of the House of Lords presently enjoys a Gothic oak-panelled refrigerator. Telephone boxes are not all as hideous as

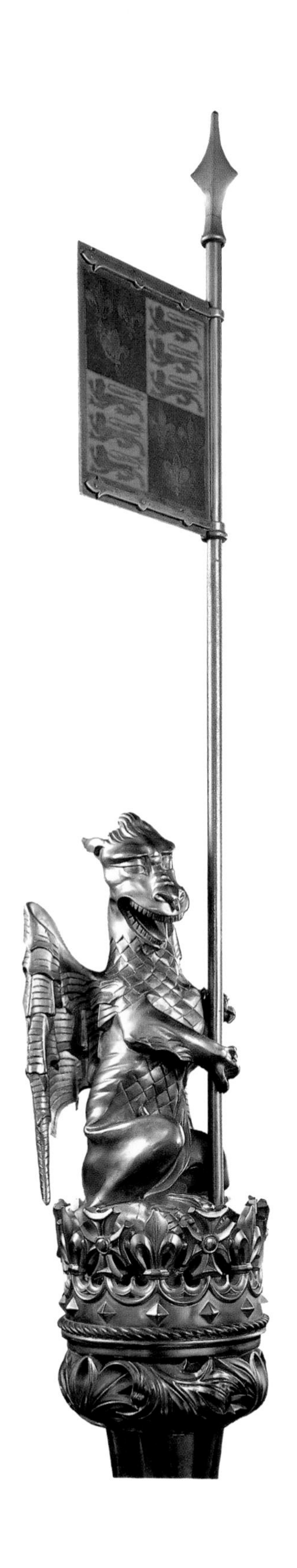

*Heraldic beasts on the Speaker's Staircase.*

those complained about in 1906 but the Royal Parks have not yet progressed beyond hideous plastic plant containers. A marriage would be possible here between their excellent potted palms and some of the plant containers in ceramic and brass which appear in the Medieval Court of the Crystal Palace, designed by Pugin.

Sir Giles Gilbert Scott displayed great ingenuity in the furniture and fittings which he designed to complement his New House of Commons' Chamber. He had the precedent of the Pugin originals as a guide. He was not slow to take up the challenge - umbrella stands, wooden waste paper baskets, oak and bronze table lamps, oak paper racks, and the original letter

*A dispatch box designed by Giles Gilbert Scott.*

*Wood carving by T. H. Kendall in the Members' Dining Room.*

boards in the Members' Lobby (now supplanted by a pair of cunningly devised emplacements with light-up slots for letters and messages - designed by Admiral Sir Alexander Gordon Lennox, K.C.V.O. lately Serjeant-at-Arms). Scott's woodwork is all of the highest quality containing a good deal of hand carved work; it has stood the test of time. Rarely does a Scott table or chair come to pieces unless treated with some violence. This is in sharp contrast to modern things brought in by the Department of the Environment, several generations of which have reached the scrap-heap during the lifetime of the Scott furniture.

Unlike the exclusively oak furniture supplied for the public areas in the nineteenth century, Scott used a variety of woods from the Commonwealth for the fine pieces presented to the New House of Commons by the Commonwealth and Empire.[2] All of these fit agreeably into their surroundings. In each case there is some detail which is symbolic of the nation which made the presentation. The doors of the House of Commons' Chamber presented by India and by Pakistan have an eastern flavour in the carving.

The dispatch boxes on the table of the New House of Commons were presented by New Zealand. Their elaborate metal mounts are of the same quality as Pugin would have demanded for those sadly lost in the fire of 1941. Pugin's boxes were covered with dark green velvet beneath the metalwork. They would have looked quite splendid when new but have become shabby with age and inexpert cleaning. They also had a ring in the centre of the top of the lid which must have got in the way of papers placed upon them by front-bench speakers. Scott skillfully avoided both of these two hazards. His boxes are of buriri wood and their bronze mounts are immune from the clogging "Brasso" dear to every devoted cleaner. In the forty or so years of their existence, they have assumed a worn and mellow appearance, from the myriad hands of the more or less confident front benchers, who have gripped or pounded them, according to their mood. Certainly they give a sense of security to an embattled spokesman facing a hostile House. All other speakers have nothing in front of them but the empty air.

Shortly after the Painted Chamber-Conference Room in the centre of the River Front became the Members' Dining Room, a series of twenty-two magnificent carvings by Thomas Henry Kendall were installed in the upper part of the panelling. These all relate to a Dining Room being representations of birds, animals, fishes and the fruits of the field. Kendall was a nineteenth century Gibbons capable of lively and life-like representations of the works of nature. The study of the interiors, fitting, and equipment of the Palace has been neglected for too long. This would be a rewarding exercise in terms of historical interest and might guarantee the conservation of the treasures for future generation.

Despite the achievements of Prince Albert's Commission, and the fresh impetus produced by the Lords Committee of 1906-7, art was once more a subject for neglect by the end of the Second World War. It was in 1955 that the House of Commons Advisory committee on Works of Art, under the Chairmanship of Viscount Hinchingbrooke, M.P., reported. The committee had looked at what it considered to be the House of Commons part of the Palace. In the section on wall paintings and mosaics they included the Upper Waiting Hall, St. Stephen's Hall, the Central Lobby, the East Corridor and the Committee Stairs, all of which were shared with the House of Lords. The Commons' Corridor only was exclusive to that House.

The committee wrote off as irredeemable the frescoes in the Upper Waiting Hall and suggested that other paintings should be produced and applied over them. What they described as the House of Commons art collection contained "few works of character and artistic merit and emphasis should be placed on obtaining works of art with these qualities." They recommended that the policy of collecting works of art which had some association with the House should be continued but that tapestries and landscapes should also be sought. They published a long list of Parliamentary figures whose portraits should be secured. They believed that the commissioning of portraits of groups of Members should be revived. They stated that "no prospect of carrying out a plan of improvement could rely on loans or gifts of works of art." The Government should therefore make funds available. They asked for a fund of £10,000 or alternatively an annual sum to be made available to an advisory committee of Members. This was eventually done and continues to be the means by which modest works of art can be acquired. The sums involved have (even with the privilege of carry over from one year to another) never amounted to a fund of much more than £5,000.

The constitutional position in the House of Lords is different. Works of art there, and indeed the furnishing and decoration of that part of the Palace, has been the field of the Works of Art Sub-committee, part of the Select Committee structure in the Upper House. They enjoy a smaller annual grant than the Commons for purchases. Under the Chairmanship of the 6th Viscount Hood, Lord Riley and Lord Gibson, progress has been made, particularly with historic restoration. The Lords Committee has been a constant stimulus to those responsible for carrying out the work.

In recent times there have been some notable acquisitions of works of art and artifacts for the Palace.

The great painting by J. R. Herbert, "The Acquittal of the Seven Bishops" was purchased for the House of Lords by the National Heritage Memorial Fund and placed in the Peers' Guest Room. The State Bed made in 1858 for the Speaker's House was rescued and restored by the National Heritage Memorial Fund and placed in a new and better position in the most westerly of the State Apartments. The National Heritage Memorial Fund also purchased, for reinstatement in the Palace, the Chair of State made for Prince Albert at the time of the opening of the House of Lords in 1847. J. R. Herbert's second portrait of A. W. Pugin in its original frame was purchased for the Pugin Room by the National Heritage Memorial Fund. From within the resources of the Crown Suppliers the unique table clock designed by Augustus Welby Pugin was acquired for the Palace. The supplies vote was also used to purchase a large collection of the personal furniture of Augustus Welby Pugin. This was made for his own house at Ramsgate but had found its way to East Hendred in Oxfordshire. It was only the timely intervention of the Crown Suppliers that prevented the dispersal of this collection. It has been installed in the Speaker's House. The Ministry of Works purchased a set of two arm and six single chairs by Pugin from Scarisbrick Hall. Five of the single chairs and one armchair are presently in the Crypt Chapel, the other two are on loan to the Victoria and Albert Museum. The supplies vote was used to purchase a silver soup tureen bearing the arms of Speaker Manners-Sutton, rescued from the fire of 1834. This was added to the collection of silver at the Speaker's House. The Speaker's Art Fund was used to purchase the full-length portrait of John Hatsell, a former Clerk of the House of Commons. This picture was discovered by Mr. Speaker Weatherill and is now in the Speaker's House. The Speaker's Art Fund acquired the portrait of Thomas Greene, M.P., Chairman of Ways and Means, Chairman of the Committee on the House of Commons in 1850 and one of the three Commissioners appointed to secure the completion of the New Palace. The jewelled, gilded brass altar cross (a reliquary cross in the manner of Pugin) on the altar in the Crypt Chapel was presented by Sir Robert Cooke in 1980. Her Majesty the Queen's generous loan of four great paintings by Benjamin West now grace a Lord's Committee Room. A collection of royal portraits from various sources now fill the vacant spaces in the Royal Gallery. A representative collection of paintings of nineteenth century statesmen and other public figures has been hung in the Committee Corridor. A number of these are on loan from the National Portrait Gallery. Other generous private loans have been made for varying periods. No substantial funds exist specificaly to enhance the art collection within the Palace although by a number of temporary expedients and *ad hoc* solutions much has been achieved. The restoration of the eight frescoes in the Upper Waiting Hall may provide the stimulus for further progress.

*Bomb damage to the House of Commons, 10th May 1941.*

# IX

## The Twentieth Century

### *A new House of Commons*

In the World War of 1914-1918 the Palace survived unscathed save for damage to one of the Maclise frescoes in the Royal Gallery from a shell splinter. In the ensuing period, before the resumption of European hostilities in September 1939, substantial stone repairs were carried out to the exterior. Clipsham stone was used to replace the decayed Aston. Although quite durable it weathers to a rough surface not unlike evenly spread brown sugar or a sheet of the coarsest sandpaper. The programme begun in the late 1920s was incomplete at the outbreak of the Second World War.

The Palace sustained much grievous damage before the War was ended, none more serious than the gutting of the Chamber of the House of Commons on the 10th May 1941. This was a Saturday night when the volunteer fire watchers were not at full strength and when a choice had to be made between attempting to save Barry's Chamber or the roof of Westminster Hall. The Hall was saved and the Commons burned.

Immediately after the destruction of their Chamber the Commons met in Church House, Dean's Yard, Westminster. Later they accepted the offer of the House of Lords who resolved that they should vacate their Chamber for the benefit of the Commons. The Lords moved into the Robing Room fitted up as a Temporary Chamber. Here they found the intimate atmosphere most congenial.

On 28th October 1943 the Prime Minister, Mr. Winston Churchill, moved "that a Select Committee be appointed to consider and report upon plans for the rebuilding of the House of Commons and upon such alterations as may be considered desirable while preserving all its essential features." The proposed committee is here told with absolute clarity that they need have no fancy ideas. We cannot do better than quote the actual words of Churchill.

"On the night of 10 May 1941, with one of the last bombs of the last serious raid, our House of Commons was destroyed by the violence of the enemy, and we have now to consider whether we should build it up again, and how, and when. We shape our buildings and afterwards our buildings shape us. Having dwelt and served for more than forty years in the late Chamber, and having derived very great pleasure and advantage therefrom, I, naturally, would like to see it restored in all essentials to its old form, convenience and dignity. I believe that will be the opinion of the great majority of its Members. It is certainly the opinion of His Majesty's Government and we propose to support this resolution to the best of our ability.

There are two main characteristics of the House of Commons which will command the approval and the support of reflective and experienced Members. They will, I have no doubt, sound odd to foreign ears. The first is that its shape should be oblong and not semi-circular. Here is a very potent factor in our political life. The semi-circular assembly, which appeals to political theorists, enables every individual or every group to move round the centre, adopting various shades of pink according as the weather changes. I am a convinced supporter of the party system in preference to the group system. I have seen many earnest and ardent Parliaments destroyed by the group system. The party system is much favoured by the oblong form of Chamber. It is easy for an individual to move through those insensible gradations from Left to Right but the act of crossing the Floor is one which requires serious consideration. I am well informed on this matter, for I have accomplished that difficult process, not only once but twice. Logic is a poor guide compared with custom. Logic which has created in so many countries semi-circular assemblies which have buildings which give to every Member, not only a seat to sit in but often a desk to write at, with a lid to bang, has proved fatal to Parliamentary Government as we know it here in its home and in the land of its birth.

The second characteristic of a Chamber formed on the lines of the House of Commons is that it should not be big enough to contain all its Members at once without over-crowding and that there should be no question of every Member having a separate seat reserved for him. The reason for this has long been a puzzle to uninstructed outsiders and has frequently excited the curiosity and even the criticism of new Members. Yet it is not so difficult to understand if you look at it from a practical point of view. If the House is big enough to contain all its Members, nine-tenths of its Debates will be conducted in the depressing atmosphere of an almost empty or half-empty Chamber. The essence of good House of Commons speaking is the conversational style, the facility for quick, informal interruptions and interchanges. Harangues from a rostrum would be a bad substitute for the conversational style in which so much of our business is done. But the conversational style requires a fairly small space, and there should be on great occasions a sense of crowd and urgency. There should be a sense of the importance of much that is said and a sense that great matters are being decided, there and then, by the House.

We attach immense importance to the survival of Parliamentary democracy. In this country this is one of our war aims. We wish to see our Parliament a strong, easy, flexible instrument of free Debate. For this purpose a small Chamber and a sense of intimacy are indispensable. It is notable that the Parliaments of the British Commonwealth have to a very large extent reproduced our Parliamentary institutions in their form as well as in their spirit, even to the Chair in which the Speakers of the different Assemblies sit. We do not seek to impose our ideas on others; we make no invidious criticisms of other nations. All the same we hold, none the less, tenaciously to them ourselves. The vitality and the authority of the House of Commons and its hold upon an electorate, based upon universal suffrage, depends to no small extent upon its episodes and great moments, even upon its scenes and rows, which, as everyone will agree, are better conducted at close quarters. Destroy that hold which Parliament has upon the public mind and has preserved through all these changing, turbulent times and the living organism of the House of Commons would be greatly impaired. You may have a machine, but the House of Commons is much more than a machine; it has earned and captured and held through long generations the imagination and respect of the British nation. It is not free from shortcomings; they mark all human institutions. Nevertheless, I submit to what is probably not an unfriendly audience on that subject that our House has proved itself capable of adapting itself to every change which the swift pace of modern life has brought upon us. It has a code of its own which everyone knows, and it has means of its own of enforcing those manners and habits which have grown up and have been found to be an essential part of our Parliamentary life.

The House of Commons has lifted our affairs above the mechanical sphere into the human sphere. It thrives on criticism, it is perfectly impervious to newspaper abuse or taunts from any quarter, and it is capable of digesting almost anything or almost any body of gentlemen, whatever be the views with which they arrive. There is no situation to which it cannot address itself with vigour and ingenuity. It is the citadel of British liberty; it is the foundation of our laws; its traditions and its privileges are as lively today as when it broke the arbitrary power of the Crown and substituted that Constitutional Monarchy under which we have enjoyed so many blessings. In this war the House of Commons has proved itself to be a rock upon which an Administration, without losing the confidence of the House, has been able to confront the most terrible emergencies. The House has shown itself able to face the possibility of national destruction with classical composure. It can change Governments, and has changed them by heat of passion. It can sustain Government in long, adverse, disappointing struggles through many dark, grey months and even years until the sun comes out again. I do not know how else this country can be governed other than by the House of Commons playing its part in all its broad freedom in British public life. We have learned - with these so recently confirmed facts around us and before us - not to alter improvidently the physical structures which have enabled so remarkable an organism to carry on its work of banning dictatorships within this island and pursuing and beating into ruin all dictators who have molested us from outside."

Churchill recommended that a committee be appointed to make recommendations on the rebuilding of the House of Commons, then he concluded:

"We owe a great debt to the House of Lords for having placed at our disposal this spacious, splendid hall. We have already expressed in formal Resolution our thanks to them. We do not wish to outstay our welcome. We have been greatly convenienced by our sojourn on these red benches and under this gilded, ornamented, statue-bedecked roof. I express my gratitude and appreciation of what we have received and enjoyed, but,

Mid pleasures and palaces though we may roam,
Be it ever so humble, there's no place like home."[1]

Greenwood, replying for the Labour Opposition, welcomed Churchill's speech and the proposal for the Select Committee. James Maxton, always something of a rebel, thought that the committee should be given a wider mandate. He personally would have liked to see a new House of Commons built twenty miles out of London in good park land complete with its own aerodrome so that communications with the rest of the world would easily be maintained. Viscountess Astor felt that the world after the War would be a different place. "The Prime Minister has always looked backwards more or less. All historians have to look backwards or they would not be historians, the time has come when the House of Commons has to look forward. It might be better to have a circular House." Mr. Tinker, who had sought to intervene in Mr. Churchill's speech, moved an amendment aimed to defer all consideration until the end of the War. He understood that their

*The remains of the House of Commons on 11th May 1941, from the south.*

Lordships were quite happy in the Robing Room and he recalled having seen a thin House looking quite lost in the Lords' Chamber before the fire of 1941. Other Members suggested that extra accommodation might be provided in the course of rebuilding the Chamber and the surrounding area, and the Gallery certainly should be enlarged, "But," said Mr. Butcher (later as Sir Herbert Butcher to be Chairman of the House of Commons Kitchen Committee) "the Gallery should not be so large that the House becomes a place of casual resort and where to spend a quarter of an hour sheltering on a rainy day." Mr. Hanner, the Member for Bilston, likened the pre-war Commons to a Methodist Chapel which compared unfavourably with the glories of the Central Lobby or St. Stephen's Hall. It was he who first suggested that the calcined stone Lobby of the House of Commons should be permanently preserved. He also made some thoughtful architectural observations, gave examples of Classical interiors fitted into Gothic buildings, and he believed that the House should keep an open mind to the idea of having a new Chamber in the Classical style. He did not think that there was any fabric in the entire world that could be taken as an exact model, but he suggested that something in the spirit of Vintners' Hall, one of Wren's great masterpieces of interior architecture, might serve. He also called for a competition.

The debate then degenerated, but there were a number of references to improvements, to the acoustics and ventilation, to the hope that natural light would fall into the reconstructed Chamber and a new Member even suggested that perhaps some kind of automated push-button voting could be installed. Earl Winterton, in a spirited contribution, said that he was not afraid to disagree with great and powerful people and that it would be sensible for the Select Committee to examine the wider uses to which the rest of the Palace should be put in the future. He referred to the amazing anomaly, worthy of a Gilbert and Sullivan opera, concerning the control of this Palace, "The Minister of Works, the Lord Great Chamberlain, you, Mr. Speaker, and the Serjeant-at-Arms, are all so interwoven in the control of this building that nobody knows who is responsible."

Captain Crookshank, Postmaster General, and later Leader of the House of Commons, wound up the debate. He opened by apologising for the absence of the Prime Minister throughout the proceedings. He had a rough time. He was clearly ill-prepared to answer a debate, which had taken a course which he had not anticipated, on the big issue as to whether the Select Committee could look at the Palace as a whole. He stonewalled (no one was better at stonewalling than Captain Crookshank). Mr. Churchill did reappear during the course of this speech and would have sensed the flavour of the complaints. However, the House having voted one hundred and twenty-seven to three in favour of the Prime Minister's motion, it remained to be seen what action the Government would take and who would be put on the Select Committee.[1]

On the 9th December 1943 the House agreed to set up a Select Committee on House of Commons (Rebuilding) consisting of fifteen members. They were Commander Agnew, Mr. Benson, Captain de Chair, Mr. Erskine-Hill, Sir Patrick Hannon, Sir Percy Harris, Mr. Hore-Belisha, Mr. Godfrey Nicholson, Mr. Pethick-Lawrence, Miss Rathbone, Sir Geoffrey Shakespeare, Mr. Bracewell Smith, Mr. Wedderburn, Mr. Wilmot and Earl Winterton. On Thursday 20th of January 1944 it was further ordered "that the committee should have power to invite any specially qualified persons, whom they may select to attend any of their meetings, in an advisory capacity."

This committee, chaired by the energetic Earl Winterton M.P., wasted no time. It reported on the 25th October of the same year. They held twenty-one sittings and examined thirty witnesses and took into account various written communications sent to them. They had the benefit of meetings with Mr. Speaker, the Joint Secretaries to the Treasury, the Clerk of the House, the Serjeant-at-Arms, and the Minister of Works. They were generous in the time devoted to the gentlemen of the Press and could not resist saying that they had taken evidence "in exhaustive detail from the Home, Dominion and Foreign Press."

The specially qualified advisors were headed by Mr. de Normann, Deputy Secretary of the Ministry of Works. He entered the scene on the 4th January and at the next meeting on the 17th he was accompanied by Mr. Mole, Deputy Director of Works, Mr. Adrian Gilbert Scott, Temporary Architect, and Mr. Ramsey, Assistant Director of Works. On 7th February the committee resolved that the Prime Minister, Mr. Lloyd George, the Serjeant-at-Arms, the Clerk of the House of Commons and the Joint Parliamentary Secretaries to the Treasury should be kept informed of progress. On the 14th February the committee divided ayes six, noes six on whether the Gentlemen of the Press should be kept informed of plans which might affect them. The Chairman cast his vote in favour. On the 27th March Mr. Adrian Gilbert Scott was by resolution invited to attend meetings of the committee in an advisory capacity pursuant to the resolution of the House.

Despite strenuous efforts by the more adventurous members of the committee, no changes to the floor of the House were agreed. Substantial extra seating was to be provided for the Press and the public. On the question as to whether up-to-date seating for strangers should be adopted, the committee remembered that wider spacing meant fewer seats and that proposition was rejected unanimously. On the 3rd April Mr. de Normann and Mr. Adrian Gilbert Scott were asked to withdraw from the room, whereupon it was resolved "that the Royal Institute of British Architects be asked to submit the names of three architects for the consideration of the committee." Furthermore, the Clerk of the committee was to be instructed to prepare (in conjunction with the Ministry of Works, that is with the help of Mr. de Normann and Mr. Adrian Gilbert Scott) "instructions to the architect embodying the decisions of the committee." Three weeks later the committee met in the company of Mr. de Normann and Mr. Adrian Gilbert Scott and deliberated. The two advisors then withdrew, whereupon the Committee resolved "that Sir Giles Gilbert Scott, R.A., P.P.R.I.B.A. be selected as the architect to advise the Committee on the rehabilitation of the Commons Chamber in the Palace of Westminster." Mr. de Chair attempted to add the name of Edward Maufe as an additional source of advice. He was unable to get a supporter and his proposition was rejected without a division. De Normann and Adrian Gilbert Scott then returned to the room and at that point it was resolved "that the Institute of Mechanical Engineers and the Institution of Electrical Engineers be asked for three names each from which engineers could be selected by the committee in consultation with the architect." This was to avoid any repetition of the friction between Dr. Reid and Charles Barry. At this meeting it was also resolved "that this committee are of the opinion that no member should approach the appointed architect personally." Lastly it was resolved that the Chairman ascertain from Sir Giles Gilbert Scott whether he could produce sketch plans for the 26th June.

On the 15th May the committee appointed Dr. Oscar Faber as Advisory Engineer. Sir Giles was at the same time requested to prepare sketch plans by the 20th July and a model by October. With Sir Giles Gilbert Scott, Mr. de Normann and Mr. Adrian Gilbert Scott in attendance they accepted the plans of Sir Giles and noted with satisfaction that Sir Giles had agreed to consider certain alterations in detail. On the 18th September they adopted Dr. Oscar Faber's Report, subject to the advice of the Government Chemist. On the 2nd October the architect's design of interior decoration was adopted and most significantly, a proposal "that some provision should be made during the remaining period of planning and during the construction of the Chamber, for contact between the architect and Members of the House, in order that the ideas of Members as to details should be received" was rejected, there being no seconder for the proposal which came from Mr. Godfrey Nicholson. On the 9th October objections advanced by the National Physical Laboratory to the designs of the roof were firmly voted down. On the 23rd October the Report was agreed and ordered by the House to be printed on the 25th. It was left to the architect (in the long appendix) to justify the choice of style. "The design of the wood and stone detail in the old building was not satisfactory and could be considerably improved. The Gothic detail of the old Chamber was lifeless and uninteresting, and the richness was spread evenly over the whole area without relief or contrast. It has been our endeavour to remedy this, with the result that, though still Gothic in style the effect will be entirely different from what existed before." Having castigated the nineteenth century work the Report goes on to admit that some of the basic features had merit.

*The coat of arms of the late Airey Neave D.S.O., O.B.E., M.C., T.D., M.P. over the doors of the House of Commons.*

The false ceiling which Barry was forced to introduce against his will in 1852 was to be echoed in an improved version in which the decoration was concentrated upon the flat central portion. As previously, artificial light was to shine down on the Members when required. The windows on either side of the Chamber could, on occasion, provide sufficient daylight in which case the ceiling appeared to be oak panelled because of the subtle tinting of the glass panels below the lights. There had been an argument with the National Physical Laboratory who wanted the sides to slope at a shallow angle. This would have improved the acoustics in the galleries only and not on the floor of the House. An amplifying system was to be fitted in any case, thus a flatter roof which would spoil the appearance of the Chamber had been discarded. The windows were of a domestic type with no stained glass. The stone screens which had been such a feature of the north and south ends of the old Chamber were retained as an echo of the windows. The carved decoration on the oak woodwork was to be concentrated in horizontal bands. There were to be carved shields in the panelling below the galleries upon which coats of arms could be painted if desired. Those at the ends of the Chamber were in due course embellished with enamelled coats of arms or monograms commemorating Members of the House who were killed in the two World Wars. In 1979, the central shield over the doors of the House by the Bar and directly opposite the Speaker's Chair was, by the direction of Mr. Speaker Thomas, painted with the arms of Airey Neave D.S.O., O.B.E., M.C., T.D., M.P., who was assasinated by Irish terrorists in that year. His name was painted below and his crest placed above the shield, making this a unique commemoration. In the Lords Chamber the coats of arms of the nineteenth century Lord Chancellors (from 1852) have been put in place quite recently: St Leonards, Cranworth, Chelmsford, Campbell, Westbury, Cairns, Hatherly and Lord Selborne. Truro's coat of arms was put up in his own lifetime (1850).

Winston Churchill once more assumed the upper hand in presenting the Report to the House on the 25th January 1945. "I am, personally, extremely gratified to see that the main principles which I ventured to submit to the House eighteen months ago have been confirmed by the committee in such emphatic terms." The Prime Minister must have realised that there was a groundswell of objection to the manner in which the committee had carried out his wishes with such precision, even to the choice of a Gothic architect who had produced detailed proposals within a suprisingly short time. Churchill offered to reconvene the committee to take note of further suggestions. He was, however, anxious that nothing should delay progress with the building. Notwithstanding the vast labour force of some 130,000 men working on urgent war damage repair in London, he felt that a hundred could well be spared to make progress in rebuilding the Chamber. His short speech ended with a stirring passage which resulted in

*The Churchill arch, preserved by Sir Giles Gilbert Scott.*

the preservation of what has come to be known as the Churchill Arch leading from the Members' Lobby into the bar Lobby and the Chamber. The bar referred to would seem to be the place of refreshment which had previously existed off the Members' Lobby and not the Bar of the House.

"I have spoken of the procedure and of the urgency of this matter, and I commend this Report to the House. I will venture to add a suggestion of my own to any which may be made in the Debate. I hope very much that the archway into the Chamber from the Inner Lobby - where the bar used to be - which was smitten by the blast of the explosion, and has acquired an appearance of antiquity that might not have been achieved by the hand of time in centuries, will be preserved intact, as a monument of the ordeal which Westminster has passed through in the Great War, and as a reminder to those who will come centuries after us that they may look back from time to time upon their forbears who

kept the bridge
In the brave days of old."[2]

In the following debate Gothic was attacked and there was an attempt to drag in "who was in charge of the Palace." This proved to be a prelude to much committee activity on the subject.

"I do not agree with Sir Giles's sweeping condemnation of contemporary architecture. I am quite certain there are many good architects, far better judges than I, who do not accept the conclusions of Sir Giles Scott, and who find his design lifeless and dull, as one would expect a design which is a copy of a copy to be. One of these architects wrote the other day, in the *The Architect's Journal* :

'Away with twice two hundred years,
With train and car and aeroplane!
Four centuries have been in vain,
The family motto re-appears,
Return to the historic!
So off with spats and on with spurs,
For come what may, we'll be good sirs,
In keeping with the Gothic.'"

Arthur Duckworth made some memorable comments upon the old Chamber. "The old Chamber was at least remarkable by its very robustness, its exuberance and its vulgarity. I think it probably had a most regrettable influence elsewhere; it was copied and exported to other parts of the world. It made itself felt. It provided, it is true, a setting for many great Parliamentarians, but it did not make them, nor did it really influence them. Fox, Burke, Sheridan, Pitt and others played their part and delivered their great oratory, and raised the reputation of this House to a point that has never been excellent in quite different surroundings. This Chamber which we have been offered will be third-hand Gothic in good taste. It will be a

*The House of Commons rebuilt by Sir Giles Gilbert Scott (1945-50).*

*The Speaker's chair in the House of Commons, by Sir Giles Gilbert Scott.*

prim, anaemic edition of the old Chamber. Will it have any influence anywhere else in the world? Will it ever be said by future generations that it was symbolic and expressive of our times? Even if, finally, no better solution than the present one can be reached, and even if we cannot approve any alternative, I say that to accept this design without any further consideration, without at least inviting other architects to submit their ideas, is to take the easy and defeatist course; it is to accept and admit that we are bankrupt of imagination, aesthetically dead, indifferent to the arts and indifferent to the claims of younger men."

Keeling, Duckworth and twenty-one of their allies went into the Lobby against the Government motion agreeing with the committee in their recommendations. The anti-Goths included Aneurin Bevan, Emanuel Shinwell, (who eventually settled down quite well as a noble lord in Gothic surroundings and lived to be over one hundred), Lord Willoughby de Eresby, and John Dugdale (the owner of Gothick Sezincote where he had obviously had enough of the style, despite enthusiastic commemoration in verse by John Betjeman). Of the one hundred and twenty-one who voted in the Government Lobby more than two dozen eventually migrated to the purer Gothic of the House of Lords.

The Government majority of one hundred was enough to allow the Ministry of Works and Sir Giles Gilbert Scott to get on with the job of creating the new Chamber for the House of Commons without further interruption from the House or any committee. Five years later all was complete.

The rumblings about control of the Palace resulted in the setting up of a joint committee of Lords and Commons to inquire into the accommodation in the Palace. The committee concentrated on the houses and flats occupied by functionaries. Lord Simon, the Lord Chancellor, had occupied for two and a half years the flat which he had now returned to Lord Esmé Gordon Lennox, Secretary to the Lord Great Chamberlain. Lord Simon had had the use of the flat only because Lord Esmé "did not wish to occupy it when the War was rather intense in London" and he wanted it back because the bombing was now over. Brigadier General the Lord Esmé Gordon Lennox K.C.V.O., C.M.G., D.S.O. pointed out that "all the rooms in this building are held by the occupier under a warrant signed by the Lord Great Chamberlain. The only room we do not touch is Mr. Speaker's."

"Would you say the Lord Chancellor had any historical right to reside in the Palace?"

"None at all," retorted Lord Esmé, "The flat the Lord Chancellor is using now was servants' quarters when the Clerk of the Parliaments lived in the House."

This unpromising beginning was followed by a session in which the Serjeant-at-Arms in the House of Commons defended as absolutely essential

*The Aye Lobby, rebuilt by Sir Giles Gilbert Scott (1945-50).*

*The Members' Lobby, House of Commons rebuilt by Sir Giles Gilbert Scott and Adrian Scott (1945-50).*

to his well being the residence of more than twenty rooms which he occupied near the Clock Tower.

Officialdom elsewhere, it appeared, had substantial requirements. The Clerk of the Parliaments wanted his Department to return to the west front where they had a total requirement of from forty to fifty rooms. The Permanent Secretary of the Lord Chancellor's Department put their requirements at some twenty-three rooms situated close together and within easy reach of the House of Lords.

These long and tedious cross-examinations did not throw up any substantial accommodation for the use of individual Members of either House. The Joint Committee fared no better than those who had hoped to tackle the matter in connection with the rebuilding of the Commons Chamber. The Clerk to the Select Committee had written on behalf of a Member who wished to take some measurements in the Palace. He did not presume to write to the Lord Great Chamberlain himself, nor indeed to his exalted Secretary but to an official below him. This official, one Meech, replied; "I am desired by the Secretary of the Lord Great Chamberlain to say he regrets he cannot consent to the taking of measurements in the Palace of Westminster."

In the debate of 25th January 1945 Lord Willoughby de Eresby (who had voted against Gothic) defended his father the Lord Great Chamberlain. "It is almost a general rule of his office that any request is always refused the first time it is made. When it is made the second time, and is a reasonable request, it is always agreed to." Such was the procedure in the House of Lords. In the Commons, the Serjeant-at-Arms, in a memorandum to the committee, claimed that all the accommodation of the House of Commons was occupied and allocated by himself as housekeeper under an Act of the 52nd year of George III. "It is my statutory duty to allocate rooms; I could allocate the whole lot."

The substantial improvements which accompanied the rebuilding of the House of Commons' Chamber quieted for a while the demand for more space for Members at the expense of officials. Scott contrived an additional floor above the Chamber for the benefit of the Clerks Department. Below, two floors, one for Ministers and the other for Members and their secretaries, were at the time much appreciated. Accommodation for the Press was about doubled and their places of refreshment much enhanced.

It was on 26th October 1950 that the Commons returned to their rebuilt Chamber. His Majesty King George VI and Queen Elizabeth came to Westminster Hall, where the Speaker tendered "our most grateful thanks to Your Majesty for having caused the rebuilding, on the same site, of that Chamber in your Palace of Westminster which was allocated for the use of the Commons by your Royal Predecessor, Queen Victoria, nearly a hundred years ago, and which was destroyed by the malice of your enemies in 1941."

His Majesty replied that "the new Chamber has been built as far as possible in the form of the old. There is a traditional intimacy about our legislative Chamber which is very characteristic of Parliamentary life in our land. It suggests a close and almost homely place of discussion and taking counsel, as if it derived some of its virtue from the family circle. I am glad to know that this feature has been preserved in the new building.
I congratulate the architect who designed the Chamber and all the men and women who have taken part in its building and furnishing. Its decorations and fittings are outstanding examples of our skill and craftsmanship in wood and metal and stone."

The ceremony paid gracious tribute to the fact that the House occupied part of His Majesty's Royal Palace of Westminster. The tradition was that following the unfortunate intrusion of his late Majesty King Charles I into a sitting of the House of Commons, no monarch was ever again to set foot in the House. The foundation stone had been laid not by the monarch but by The Speaker, the Rt. Hon Douglas Clifton - Browne M.P. on 26th May 1948.

In March 1960 the Commons again explored the possibilities of providing themselves with better accommodation and amenities.
Mrs. Barbara Castle spoke for an hour urging the House that it was time to implement the proposals of the Stokes Committees. Mr. A. Wedgwood Benn also demanded better facilities; likewise Mr. Gaitskell, who thought that every Member of the House should be entitled to a room. Sir Peter Agnew said this was going too far and Michael Clark Hutchinson confessed that he felt no desire for either a room or a telephone. Sir Hamilton Kerr had long campaigned for a more civilised Smoking Room. He recalled asking a previous Chief Patronage Secretary to make the Smoking Room like a club room with oil paintings and subdued lighting. The response was "Enough, enough, not another word from you. If we make the Smoking Room any more comfortable we shall never get you Back Benchers out of it."

Mr. H. P. G. Channon, the youngest member of the House, intervened because he felt he had a chance of being in the House long enough to enjoy any improvements. He was in favour of moving people who did not have to be close to the Chamber, across the road. On the whole, the Conservative Party were against making any major changes but the Labour Party wanted to get something done. Mr. R. A. Butler, speaking for the Government, undertook to proceed with the proposal that £250,000 be spent on Upper Committee corridors, north and south, where 19,000 square feet would provide space for three hundred desks.

The Bridge Street site was a long term project - it would take three or four years to satisfy local authorities. Alternative schemes focused on filling in court-yards were rejected because they endangered the historic architecture of the Palace.

Following the debate of 31st March 1960 an *ad hoc* committee on House

*The Royal Arms over the door of Sir Giles Gilbert Scott's House of Commons.*

of Commons Accommodation was appointed in order "to consider the proposals to improve the accommodation for Members in the House of Commons set forth in the Minister of Works' statement and, in particular, the proposal to convert the roof space over the Committee Rooms into office accommodation, and to make recommendations." The committee, chaired by Sir James Duncan, reported to Mr. Speaker on 22nd July 1960 that they approved the schemes for Upper Committee Corridor North and South. They also made observations on the possibility of building in New Palace Yard where Sir Charles Barry's original plan for building round New Palace Yard and along to St. Stephen's Entrance might be revived. The Bridge Street site was suitable for an office building.

### *The Bridge Street Site*

The possibility of developing the Bridge Street site to provide additional Parliamentary accommodation was taken up in the Speaker's statement of 21st November 1962 and in the proposals made by Sir William Holford in 1963.

Sir William Holford's outline proposals covered the whole of the site from Bridge Street to Richmond Terrace. They involved the demolition of everything except the two Norman Shaw buildings and the Curtis Green building. On the area now known as the Bridge Street site only one fifth of the site was to be devoted to Parliamentary purposes mainly on the site of the St. Stephen's Club. The meagre provision for the Commons did not find favour with the House.

The Selwyn Lloyd Committee was appointed in 1964 to advise on the perennial problem of increased accommodation for the House of Commons bearing in mind the possible redevelopment of the Palace of Westminster/ Bridge Street area and Holford's recent proposals. The Committee under Selwyn Lloyd's Chairmanship included a future Opposition Chief Whip, Herbert Bowden, a future Minister of Works, Charles Pannell, and a future Minister for the Arts, Paul Channon. They reported on 29th April 1964 that, "They were of the unanimous opinion that the present and future needs of Parliament could be met only by substantial addition to the existing building. It must be consistent with the dignity of Parliament and be an addition of which the nation can be proud. A mere corner of the Bridge Street site, surrounded by shops and offices and connected by an underground passage, would be entirely unsuitable and inadequate." (This is a reference to the Holford proposal).

"The extension should be a part of the Parliamentary precinct and must be seen to be so. For these reasons, in our view, an area extending northwards from New Palace Yard, and including Bridge Street in itself,

*The doors to Sir Giles Gilbert Scott's House of Commons (1945-50).*

*The Members' smoking room, House of Commons.*

should be devoted to the use of Parliament. The front of the building, overlooking New Palace Yard, should be as close as convenient to the line of the existing railings. Since it would thus enclose a third side of New Palace Yard, it should be built in the Gothic style, in order to harmonize with the buildings on the other side, and also to emphasise the fact that it is an integral part of the Parliamentary precinct and in no sense an annexe. This would also enable the floor levels of the existing building on the east side of New Palace Yard to be followed in the new building. Direct internal access to the existing buildings should be provided at all levels."

Rippon repeated the Government's intention to rebuild the Foreign Office (he avoided the use of the word "demolition") and in any case Sir Leslie Martin was producing a scheme for the whole Whitehall area which would be available for the House to study in due course. So ended the debate with the Report approved without a division. The General Election that followed produced a change of administration. No more was heard of the Gothic scheme.

The debate was in reality something of a diversion because several months earlier on the 20th April 1964, the Minister of Public Buildings and Works had appointed Sir Leslie Martin as consultant for the Whitehall area with the brief that he was "to ensure that the various proposals which are under consideration for redevelopment in the Whitehall area are related to each other and have regard to the general architectural character of the area, taking relevant traffic considerations into account." The area for consideration was "centered around Parliament Square, Bridge Street and Whitehall" and the brief specified that "in respect of traffic the surrounding area may have to be brought into consideration."

The redevelopment proposals to be taken into account were specified in the following terms. "The Government have decided to rebuild the Foreign Office block. It is also intended to redevelop the Richmond Terrace/Bridge Street site to provide accommodation for Parliament and for Government Offices. Advice is required on the relationship of a new Parliamentary building to the present precincts of the Palace of Westminster... The consultant should look ahead to the possibility of the eventual redevelopment of other buildings in the area, such as the King Charles Street/Great George Street block of Government Offices and the former War Office building, and the consequences which flow from this."

On the 27th May the Minister had appointed Professor Colin Buchanan to act as a consultant on traffic to assist Sir Leslie Martin. By the 19th July 1965 Martin and Buchanan had produced a substantial Report, *Whitehall - a Plan for the National and Government Centre.* In a statement in the Commons on the same day Charles Pannell, by now the Minister of Public Building and Works, said that "The Government welcome these reports and regard them as the broad framework within which future development of building in

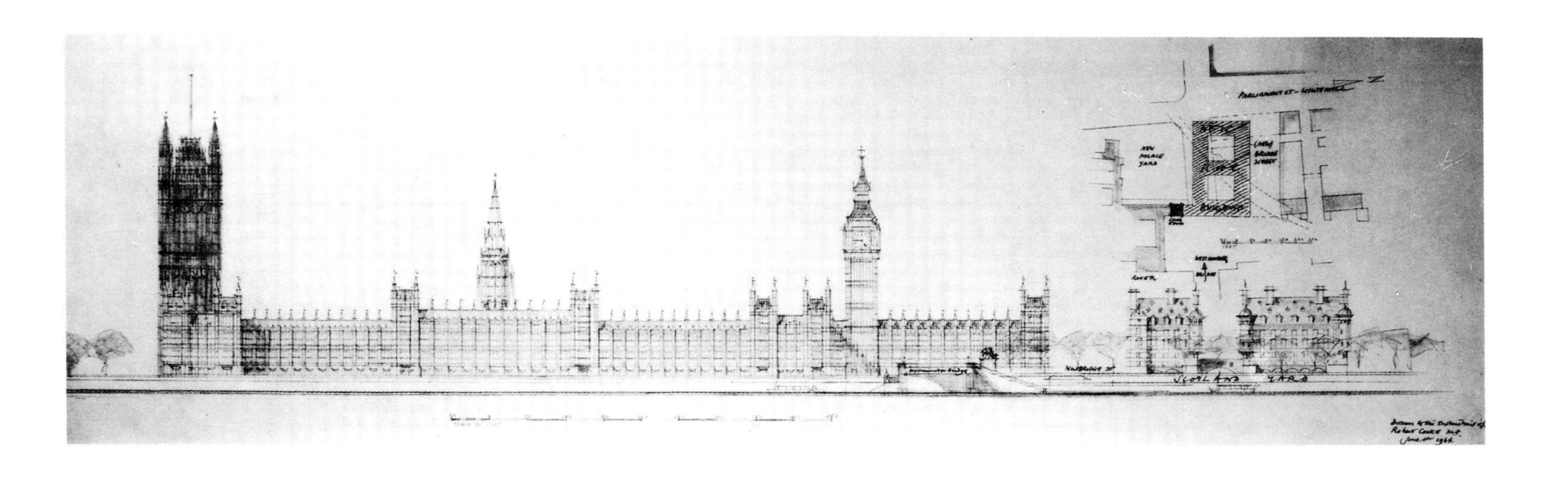


*Top: west elevation of the Palace of Westminster (1964).*
*Below: east elevation (1964).*

Whitehall and Parliament Square areas should take place." He went on to say that in the Government's view the plans put forward in the reports for removing traffic from Parliament Square "must be looked at in the context of London traffic as a whole."

Because the Selwyn Lloyd Committee was, like its predecessor the Duncan Committee, an *ad hoc* affair it did not have the benefit of a printed Report illustrated with plans and drawings. However, a little private enterprise by some of its members produced a pair of elevations and a plan which gave a clear indication of what was intended.

A debate on this subject, on 13th July was opened by Selwyn Lloyd. His was a skillful speech. He pointed out that the committee had been advisory and had no power to make decisions. "It was not our function to examine witnesses about traffic, town planning, cost or architectural style or to pronounce a judgement." He emphasized that there were four experienced Labour Members on the committee, including the Chief Whip, and that the committee was unanimous. He recalled that the Joint Committee of 1944-45 had recognised that the needs of the two Houses could not be met within the existing Palace and that Stokes had firmly stated in 1954 that only by extensive building operations could a long term satisfactory solution be found. Returning to the subject of style, he believed that that was one of the matters which the next House would have to decide. Hoping that the House would accept the Motion to take note of the Report, technical examination could begin forthwith. When pressed on the question of cost Selwyn Lloyd stated that "the question of cost was not for us."

In the vituperative debate which followed, Charles Pannell in characteristic style attacked the indifference shown by Captain Crookshank, who never read the Stokes Report, and R. A. Butler who treated it with the usual casualness with which he treats these things... "We did not get much more from Iain Macleod."

Someone had written to Selwyn Lloyd describing the modern idiom as "self-assertive, aggressive, sub-Christian (shades of Pugin), lacking in love, in reverence, in sense of proportion, in beauty combined with fitness." Pannell then quoted Wren on Westminster Abbey, "I have made a design which will not be very expensive but light, and still in the Gothic form, and of a style with the rest of the structure, which I would strictly adhere to... to deviate from the old form, would be to run into a disagreeable mixture, which no person of good taste could relish." Lord Balniel then quoted Hampton Court at him. Pannell unfortunately had not seen where Wren's work smashed into Wolsey's Tudor and he retreated to argue in favour of an architectural competition. He then switched to an attack on the Lord Great Chamberlain and the misuse of accommodation in the House of Lords by the law departments, but he warned off his honourable friends who were casting covetous eyes on that end of the Palace. "There are rather better people going to the Lords these days - Life Peers - and I think that they must be treated with great respect. They too, will want a room apiece."

Nigel Birch attacked any addition to Barry's Palace as "Barbarous, almost as if someone added a lavatory wing to the Parthenon" and said, "it is quite all right because we intend to build it in the Doric style." He detected "the shuffle and clatter of cloven hooves because there is no doubt that many people are in favour of full-time Members; by their hankering for more committee rooms, they were after a bastard imitation of the American constitution." In the most scholarly speech of the debate, Sir Derek Walker-Smith came down strongly against Gothic. Gothic at Westminster was in any case a result of an accident in that Westminster Hall had survived the fire. Had it not, because of the existing contribution by William Kent, Vardy and Soane, a Classical Parliament House could well have followed. King William IV had presided over the committee which had chosen Barry, claimed Sir Derek. What if his royal predecessor George IV had chosen the architect?. One wonders what sort of building we should be working in today. He recalled Pugin's fanatical intensity which drove him to insanity, a salutary warning to contemporary Parliamentarians against excessive and fanatical zeal. Nikolaus Pevsner and Clough Williams-Ellis were quoted. Gilbert Scott's House of Commons Chamber, thought Sir Derek, was an indication of how difficult it would be to capture the detail of the exterior in any extension.

Few of the succeeding speakers had a friendly word for Gothic and some attacked the Government for proposing the demolition of the Foreign Office. Barbara Castle neatly stated that if the Gothic style is anachronistic, how much more anachronistic is a Gothic form of administration?

Mr. Wedgwood Benn was worried that a Gothic extension would come under the control of the Lord Great Chamberlain. Mr. Rippon side-stepped but Mr. Pannell was clear that a separate building would escape the Lord Great Chamberlain but if it was attached, it would not. Rippon recalled that the results of competitions were frequently unsatisfactory.

The Minister of Public Building and Works announced in the House of Commons that the Government now proposed to take "firm second steps about the architectural arrangements for the three main buildings which will form the first stages of the development. These are the new Parliamentary building and the new Government Offices on the Bridge Street and Richmond Terrace site, and the redevelopment of the Foreign Office site."

For the Parliamentary building in Bridge Street an architect would be selected by means of a competition open to the whole Commonwealth. The Ministry itself would undertake the design of the Government Offices on the Richmond Terrace/Bridge Street site while a distinguished architect in private practice would be commissioned for the new building on the Foreign Office site.

Despite the thorough job done by the two Stokes Committees, modest improvements followed only slowly. The committees did, however, begin the process by which the Commons sought to gain control of their part of the Palace from the Lord Great Chamberlain. This culminated in the agreement announced by the Prime Minister on 23rd May 1965, under which the Speaker (on behalf of the House) was given control of that part of the Palace occupied by the House of Commons. This led to the setting up of the Select Committee on House of Commons (services) whose tasks include advising Mr. Speaker on the allocation of accommodation.

On the 7th December 1965 the Services Committee of the House of Commons was first appointed. On the 26th July 1966 they appointed a New Building Sub-committee to consider what accommodation should be provided in a new Parliamentary building in the Bridge Street area. The committee came to the conclusion that there were insuperable difficulties in linking such a building with the Palace and indeed came to the unanimous view "that the scheme for building a large Parliamentary building on the other side of Bridge Street is founded on a false premise. Members require more accommodation and better working facilities... as near the Chamber as possible." This led them to make an alternative approach.

One idea was to build offices and residences for the House of Lords in Black Rod's garden enabling the Commons to move into the accommodation thus vacated. For a number of reasons it was thought to be "impracticable for the present." An alternative was the completion of the original Barry plan of building round New Palace Yard combined with limited new building and in-filling on the site of the present Palace. This with the transfer of administrative and other functions to a smaller Bridge Street building was ruled out owing to design and aesthetic problems, the high cost of building in the Barry Gothic style, and the limited accommodation which such a scheme would provide. Nonetheless, the Sub-committee asked the Ministry to look again at the idea and to prepare rough outline plans, designs, and models.

The Sub-committee were advised that the catalpa trees, which would need to be removed, were expected not to live for more than a few years. (They survived the building of the underground car-park and flowered abundantly in the summer of 1987).

The Ministry produced a straightforward L-shaped building, stretching from the base of Big Ben round to join Westminster Hall on the present site of the Westminster Hall Committee Room (which would have had to be demolished). It would be four storeys on the Bridge Street side and three on the Parliament Square side. "This limitation of height, lower than that envisaged by Barry, would avoid harm to the main views of the Palace and would preserve the view of the finials and skyline of the main building and the connection with it of Big Ben. The building could also be extended at a

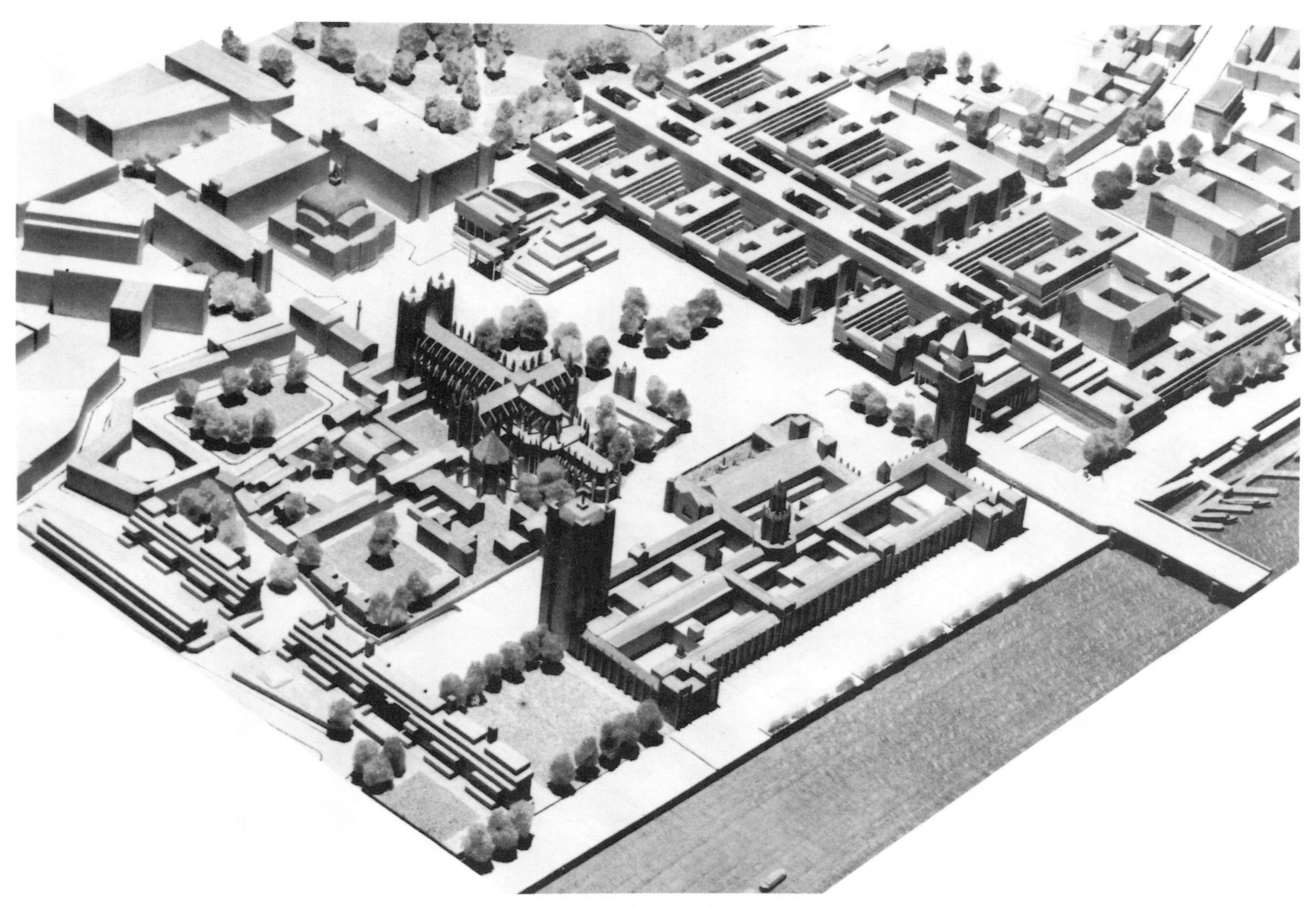

*One scheme for new Parliamentary buildings in the 1960s.*

later date if necessary, along Cromwell Green to St. Stephen's Porch. The present frontage to Cromwell Green does not form part of the original Barry plan for the Palace (having been rebuilt by Pearson after the demolition of Soane's Law Courts in 1884). The models and drawings prepared by the Ministry indicate that later stage building of this part of the site would form a satisfactory completion of the proposed new buildings and would not harm any of the main features of the Palace or the balance with Westminster Abbey opposite.

The building would be in matching stone and of simple design, no attempt being made to copy the Gothic architecture of the Palace, but would have a perpendicular character in sympathy with the existing building."

If it had all been carried out, it would have provided 123,000 square feet at the cost of £1,850,000. This dramatic addition to the Palace would not have satisfied all the contemporary demands. A smaller building would still be required on Bridge Street and a number of schemes for in-filling the Palace would also be required. Those recommended were a new building over the Members' Tea Room in Commons' Court and another in-filling on the east side of Commons' Inner Court. This committee also first mooted the idea of an underground car-park beneath New Palace Yard.

The main committee reported to the House on 27th July 1967 that "in terms of planning of long overdue and essential accommodation, your committee regards these recommendations as worthy of a serious consideration. Since, however, the proposal to build round New Palace Yard raises issues of taste which could override arguments of convenience, they have decided before formulating their final recommendations to attach the Sub-committee's Report as an appendix to this Report and invite discussion on it. The House will in due course no doubt wish to debate these proposals and indicate whether it desires detailed plans to be presented to it for a new building around New Palace Yard."

The Minister told the committee that there were two alternatives only: an entirely new House of Commons on the Bridge Street/ Richmond Terrace site or in Victoria Tower Gardens, or a new Parliamentary building containing offices for Members and administrative staff in Bridge Street as recommended in the Whitehall Plan Report by Sir Leslie Martin in 1965. Because the first alternative would take fifteen or twenty years, cost £20,000,000 or £25,000,000 plus £10,000,000 value of the site, and because it would rule out Government Offices there, the committee rejected it, nor did the Minister recommend it.

Whilst reluctant to agree to a new building north of Bridge Street, evidence from Sir Leslie Martin demonstrated that since the level of the street was above the average level of New Palace Yard, it would be possible, by raising part of the street, to construct a spacious entrance hall to the new building under Bridge Street with a broad entrance direct from New Palace Yard.

Covered access to the Chamber would also be required. The previously suggested covered routes were rejected in favour of two new alternatives both running west of the Clock Tower. One would be beneath the colonnade and Star Court; a lift or escalator would take Members to behind the Speaker's Chair and to the Members' Lobby. Another route would run above a reconstructed colonnade along the side of the Chamber in Star Court giving easy access to both ends of the Chamber without lifts. The committee preferred the route above the colonnade, (which would have destroyed all the stone vaulting and involved its reconstruction.) The site of the new building was to run the entire length of Bridge Street and 200 feet back from there was to be reserved for Parliament. The new building plus the access, which involved raising the street, would be likely to cost £5,000,000 and be ready for occupation within six years of its approval.

On the subject of traffic, the committee advocated a tunnel under the river taking the north-south traffic out of Parliament Square at a cost of between £12,000,000 and £20,000,000. They understood that the Transport Department at the G.L.C. could not give this a high priority but hoped by traffic management to reduce the flow in Bridge Street by twenty per cent.

By the 3rd March 1970, the Services Committee had learned with dismay that there would seem to be no prospect of getting rid of the traffic out of Bridge Street, nor was there any likelihood of the river tunnel being constructed. Further, they were now being asked to set back the building line by twenty feet to allow yet more traffic to flow through it. They were now being asked to decide on a new building without any guarantee of a removal of traffic.

However, because of the need to get ahead and the great need of Parliament for additional accommodation, they recommended an architectural competition for a new building and that immediate consultations should take place with the G.L.C. about schemes for diverting the traffic, the building line to be set back only if it provided an extra area for pedestrians and not for widening the road.

Thus at long last the House of Commons, through its Services Committee fell into line with the Minister's proposal for the architectural competition for a new Parliamentary building. The Commons were pinning their hopes on a proposal that was part of the Whitehall Plan which had by that time many enemies amongst the conservationists. This ambitious proposal involved the wiping out of the Foreign Office, Home Office, Treasury, and everything on the opposite side of Whitehall except the Norman Shaw North building. The proposed new Government Offices which would have resulted from the destruction of Richmond Terrace and everything north of Derby Gate were fiercely attacked by all those interested in amenity. The rebuilding of virtually the whole of the rest of lower Whitehall except No. 10 Downing Street was unlikely ever to become a reality.

Additionally all the Embankment traffic needed to be carried past the River Front of the Palace in a pair of shallow tunnels, the roofs of which would have created a widened terrace (complete on the model with a tasteful shrubbery) to separate Members of the two Houses from members of the public enjoying the new riverside walk.

The architectural competition for a new Parliamentary building launched by the Ministry of Public Buildings and Works was won by Robin Spence and Robin Webster, whose entry was exhibited in Westminster Hall in 1972 along with the runners-up. In a debate of 25th June 1973 Mr. James Prior summed up. "It is difficult to imagine a situation in which there will ever be unanimity. If the second motion is defeated tonight, it is hard to see how any other building will ever find acceptance." On the strength of this the House voted to approve the construction of the proposed new Spence and Webster building, by two hundred and eight votes to one hundred and forty-four. Of those who voted against Spence and Webster there numbered six who were Secretaries of State at the Department of the Environment or its equivalent, two Chairmen of the 1922 committee, two Speakers of the House of Commons and the Father of the House.

The Spence and Webster building had many implacable enemies on aesthetic grounds, although the Royal Fine Arts Commission approved the building provided that about 1 1/2 metres was taken off its height. It was eventually abandoned on grounds of cost which by 16th July 1975 had risen to at least £30 million excluding site costs already incurred. In announcing the termination of the architect's commission the Leader of the House of Commons, Mr. Edward Short, expressed the thanks of the House to the architects for the distinguished work which they had done and undertook that they would be fairly compensated. The architects expressed their thanks for the treatment which they received at the hands of the Department; suitable and final compensation was agreed with them. Mr. Short then stated that the Department would now come forward with plans for the refurbishment of some of the existing buildings on the Bridge Street site.

In 1973 the Department of the Environment and the Services Committee produced a study on the feasibility of providing temporary accommodation in the Bridge Street buildings. One alternative gave the buildings a life of five years, the other a life of twenty years but in neither case would the resulting accommodation have satisfied Members' specific requirements. Moreover, neither project was economical and could not therefore be recommended to the House. Despite two further reappraisals, this view was upheld by the Fifth Report of the Services Committee in 1978 and the Department of the Environment. For twenty years after the War there was a battle between Parliament and the executive over control of Parliamentary accommodation. Since 1965 there was a constant struggle to acquire and fit out further accommodation to meet the growing needs of Parliament.

*The design by Sir Hugh Casson for the Bridge Street Site.*

Always supply lagged behind demand. Any progress has always involved long negotiations with the Treasury and Government Departments.

The two Norman Shaw buildings on the Victoria Embankment to the north of the Clock Tower became available at about this time. The Metropolitan Police abandoned the original building (known as Norman Shaw North) for new offices in Westminster but took over the Curtis Green Building to the north. The south block of 1906, something of a poor relation, was unfit for occupation by Civil Servants. The North block was adapted for Parliamentary use as an award winning scheme by the Department of the Environment for Architectural Heritage Year 1974. The South block was later taken over by the House of Commons subject to a limit of £200,000 worth of improvements. Parliament already occupied the old St. Stephen's Club building on the south-east corner of the Bridge Street site and sundry other buildings nearby, some in better repair than others.

In the Palace itself a number of infilling schemes had been carried out. The east side of Commons Court had been built up for the benefit of the Commons. The ugly intrusion in Star Chamber Court provided further accommodation to the west of the Chamber. Earlier roof schemes at Upper Committee Corridor level had created many small rooms concealed behind the east slope of the River Front, north and south of the central block. Half of these rooms were lit only by skylights, the remainder looked out over the internal courts.

In the Lords, new building on the east side of Peers' Court and the west side of State Officer's Court, together with a cross corridor had provided some relief. The Peers' Dining Room was also enlarged by taking in the Law Lords' Rooms on the north side of Peers' Court.

### *The Landscaping of New Palace Yard*

In their Report of 9th April 1968 the Services Committee recommended, in addition to the construction of a new Parliamentary building on the Bridge Street site, an underground car-park beneath New Palace Yard which could be constructed at a cost of perhaps £250,000, they said. On 8th June 1971, the committee again reported. The proposed new Parliamentary building by Spence and Webster was not due to be completed until the end of 1977. Congestion in New Palace Yard was growing worse each year and the Department of the Environment submitted plans to the committee for an underground car-park which could be completed by the end of 1973. The D.O.E. estimated that for £1.3 million they could provide space for over 500 cars.

The committee thought that the scheme that they proposed would not detract from the architectural merit of the Palace but would improve the setting by creating an attractive landscaped area on the surface of New Palace Yard. The centre should be grassed with a roadway round it. The committee hoped that in addition to the grass the area would be suitably landscaped. This would result in a great aesthetic and amenity gain.

On 9th May 1972 the committee once more addressed themselves to the subject of New Palace Yard. They reported that the cost had risen to slightly under £2 million. They believed the design of New Palace Yard should be decided in relation to that of the New Parliamentary building and they had deferred final consideration of the details until they had examined the outcome of the architectural competition.

On 20th July 1973 the Services Committee returned to the subject of New Palace Yard (the House having voted for the Spence Webster Parliamentary building on 25th June.) They considered what treatment of the surface of the Yard would best harmonise with the architecture of the Palace and with the new Parliamentary building to be erected to the north of Bridge Street.

These were three possible methods of treatment: (a) Central area grassed with a roadway round it. (b) Central area to include reflecting pool and fountain. (c) The entire yard paved with a uniform surface of granite setts, central area separated from roadway by bollards.

The committee agreed with the R.F.A.C. and the Westminster City Council that grass or water would be foreign to the tradition of a large open paved yard. They also agreed with the two bodies that the ramps into and out of the car-park should run east-west rather than north-south. The committee had been told by the D.O.E. that some planting of small trees within the surface of the granite setts would be possible. "The granite setts, unlike the cobbles of the old yard are not rounded but dressed to a comparatively smooth surface and would be comfortable to walk on."

It was at the height of the economic and political crisis which led up to the February election of 1974 that the House debated the Report. On 10th December 1973 a resolution to approve it was defeated by forty-two votes to thirty-five. The proposed landscape was to cost about £110,000 and the total revised estimate for the car-park was £2.5 million.

Several speakers condemned the proposals as dull. A number of uses were suggested for the fenced off part of the yard, these included archaeological displays of items discovered in London; other exhibitions would surely be possible. A couple of tennis courts would also fit in to the middle of the yard. Some Members thought that the price of oil would eventually see the end of the motor car. The granite setts did not meet with universal approval. One Member who had delved deep in the early history of the Palace pointed out that the yard was originally surfaced with mud.

A number of Members urged that granite from their constituencies should be used, whether from Cornwall or Scotland. In winding up the Debate the Minister made the surprising assertion that "there was not sufficient granite available in this country to provide all the granite setts that would be needed "and" we expect to find a Continental source." In an otherwise unconvincing speech he was able to assure the House that an Inspector of Ancient Monuments and an Assistant had been on the site continually since work began in July 1972. Proof had been found that the area of the yard had been a marsh until about 1066. There followed an explanation that the foundations of the mid-fifteenth century fountain built over the site of an earlier fountain had been discovered to contain remains of half of an elaborately decorated marble fountain of about the time of Richard I, thought to have stood originally in or near Old Palace Yard. It was to mark the site of the Tudor fountain and its predecessors on that site that some feature in the central area was proposed.

On 7th May 1974, in their first Report of the new Parliament, the Services Committeee reported that they had been considering the treatment of New Palace Yard as a matter of urgency. They referred back to the attractive landscaped area which had been mentioned in the New Building Report approved in July 1971. It was their conviction that the House no longer wished to retain New Palace Yard as a stark, paved area. Some form of landscaping which would complement the neighbouring buildings of different styles, both existing and proposed, must now be attempted.

"The D.O.E., at the specific request of your committee have produced a scheme which includes, within the central area surrounded by the roadway, a lawn and a pool. This could take the form of a simple hexagonal pool with Portland stone surround to mark the site of the Tudor fountain. There would be a double row of lime trees, the inner row containing fixed seats of Scottish granite. The lime trees would surround the lawn thus forming a shaded walk. Paving is proposed for the lime walk and fan setts for the roadway since these are more appropriate to its shape." There would be a substantial raised curb around the central area incorporating Westmorland slate to match the walls of the car-park ramps. Two pairs of additional trees were to be planted in the north-west and south-west corners of the yard. The lighting of the yard was to continue to be by gas.

The Royal Fine Arts Commission had been consulted and were opposed to the scheme because they believed that the area should remain an open yard. This concept had already been rejected by the House. There was no further debate on the matter. The recommendations of the committee were carried out but not quite as printed. The central area was first covered with a "blue-rug juniper" which did not thrive, then with ivy which eventually grew strongly but was removed by a later committee. The first batch of lime trees were of an inferior variety and were immediately removed and replaced by better ones. The raised walk was first surfaced with a poor effort in Dorset gravel (obtained from Hampshire) and was later covered with a new type of gravel which set like mud-coloured concrete. The seats placed

*Proposal for the car-park entrance arch in New Palace Yard.*

around the inner ring of trees were made of Portland stone, granite being difficult to work and too expensive. The granite setts which the Minister had said were unobtainable in the United Kingdom were to have come from Portugal. However, the nature of the Portuguese regime was offensive to those in political command at Westminster and Scottish granite was demanded. Fortunately, before this was ordered, it was discovered that a canny Scotsman was ordering his granite in from Portugal, ready cut. Eventually some second-hand cobbles (not very comfortable to walk on) were obtained from a disused London market. They were laid by Irish labour.

The fountain pool, placed on the axis through Westminster Hall where the great Tudor fountain shown in Hollar's engraving had once stood, was in the year of Her Majesty's Jubilee adorned with an heraldic sculpture in steel by Mr. Walenty Pytel, resident in Herefordshire and of Polish ancestry. He produced a group symbolic of the continents of the world over which the British Commonwealth and its Parliamentary systems had exerted influence. The lion for Africa, the unicorn for Europe (on the grounds that it was in that continent that the unicorn was last seen), the tiger for Asia. The upper tier consists of a wallaby or kangaroo for Australia, a penguin for Antarctica and an eagle for the Americas. These support a gilded St. Stephen's crown. The pool was inscribed "1952 God Save the Queen 1977" on the south side and on the north side "The Gift of Members of the House of Commons."

Against the background of modest improvements, which always seemed to lag behind demand for space, the House of Commons Services Committee summarized the state of affairs in their Report *New Building for Parliament* on the 23rd May 1978. They looked first at the overcrowded Palace. "The House has virtually exhausted all major possibilities for the provision of additional accommodation within the Palace. The courtyards on either side of the Chamber have been in-filled. Building has been carried out in almost all the roof space which is accessible, yet does not damage the Westminster skyline. Every possible flat roof has temporary huts upon it. There is even a two-storey hut on top of the Noe Lobby which blocks all the windows on the east side of the Chamber."

The committee went on to propose their cautious solution:
(1) "Working conditions for Parliament and those who serve it have failed lamentably to keep pace with the greatly increased and still increasing volume of activity at Westminster. (2) At least five different schemes for major additions to Parliamentary accommodation adjoining the Palace of Westminster have been proposed, examined and abandoned during the last quarter of a century. (3) Hard lessons learnt from past experience have led us to suggest an entirely new approach to the Bridge Street Site. (4) We are mindful that Bridge Street is the most sensitive site in London. It adjoins the most famous and best loved building in the modern world. (5) Under our proposed scheme those buildings on the Bridge Street site which are of real

quality would be retained and restored. The remainder would be replaced to a coherent design from an independent architect, working in partnership with Parliament and government. For this most exacting of tasks we are recommending Sir Hugh Casson, President of the Royal Academy of Arts. (6) We recommend that as soon as a comprehensive scheme has been drawn up it should be submitted to the House for approval." The Report had been deliberately titled *New Building for Parliament* rather than *New Parliamentary Building* .

The committee spelled out in detail their reasons for their choice of architects. "We believe that the man best qualified to advise on the whole project is Sir Hugh Casson, now President of the Royal Academy of Arts. He has long experience in the field of conservation and in dealing with new buildings in historic settings. We have found him to be a man of great energy and enthusiasm with the liveliest of minds. We believe that he will be able to produce a design of real distinction, compatible with its surroundings. Above all we are sure that he will be able to work both with the House and the Department of the Environment to bring the designs for the project to a happy conclusion."

The Motion to approve the Fifth Report was eventually set down for 28th July 1978.[3] It was the last order of the day and it came on seven minutes before the House was due to adjourn at 4 o'clock. However, those who wished to see it passed had persuaded the Government to move that Motions relating to House of Commons Services may be proceeded with at this day's sitting, though opposed, until any hour. Without that Motion, the Report would not have been approved. The author of the Report moved its approval. Three members of committee spoke in support; no one rose to oppose the Motion. The Leader of the House of Commons, Michael Foot, concluded: "Thanks to the way that the hon. gentleman has approached the matter, we now have a better approach than anything we have had before and I express my personal gratitude to him for the way in which he has conducted all that work. The whole House and, therefore, the country owe him a great debt." However, he went on to emphasize that at this stage approval of the Motion would commit the House only to the drawing up of a plan. He expressed the gratitude of the House as a whole to Sir Hugh Casson for the indication of his willingness to assist the House.

Michael Foot recalled that if the will of the House as expressed on 25th June 1973, when it approved the Spence Webster building had prevailed, "We would have committed an outrage on one of the most famous sites in the centre of London. We are proposing to deal with this site over the months and years ahead in a much more sensitive manner. All good architecture should have the quality of good manners. When a new building is to intrude in an area such as Parliament Square, it should do so with some decency and delicacy."

*The Jubilee Fountain, sculpture by Walenty Pytel (1977).*

He could not however resist suggesting a solution of his own. "I have always taken the simple view that the best way to deal with the accommodation problems we have in this House, would be to take over the House of Lords." These remarks did not go unchallenged but Mr. Foot side-stepped that issue by claiming that what was now proposed would not exclude the latter solution.

The Motion was agreed to without a division, as was the proposal that the Select Committee should have power to invite any specially qualified person, whom they may select, to attend any of their meetings in an advisory capacity on any architectural or related matter.

Sir Hugh Casson was duly appointed. By the summer of 1985 his proposals for the Parliament Street block were approved by the commitee and Treasury approval for the finance was being sought in official circles. It was not considered necessary for the House to be further consulted.

One of the most prominent members of the committee, Sir Paul Hawkins, recalled that the only accommodation which he had for his first six months in the House after 1964 was one of the small lockers "strategically placed outside the Dining Room. I was kneeling there trying to put some things inside - I think I had only a bowler hat and some papers - when one of the waitresses came along and, not seeing my feet, went clean over with a whole tray of soup and goodness knows what. After that, I handed my key to the Serjeant-at-Arms and began even more vociferously to demand a filing cabinet. Then came the great occasion when I was allocated a filing cabinet, but it was in the gentlemen's cloakroom and the Serjeant-at-Arms - not the present Serjeant-at-Arms, of course, - did not permit me to allow my secretary to go in there to file my papers. From that moment onwards, I began to take an interest in the services of the House."

Perhaps spurred on by Sir Paul's experiences and encouraged by Mr. Foot's statement that "all good architecture should have the quality of good manners," Sir Hugh Casson wasted no time in producing a feasibility study. This was completed in the middle of the General Election of 1979, thus it was ready for a new and enthusiastic Services Committee.

The new committee, careless of the experience of their predecessors, were not satisfied with a stage-by-stage approach. They put their own gloss upon Sir Hugh's labours and presented at a Press conference their "helter-skelter" approach to the Bridge Street site. Within hours the newspaper headlines read "£100,000,000 Office Plan for Cramped M.P.s." A rival newspaper had "A Palace for M.P.s but it would Cost £120,000,000." This was on Wednesday, December 12, 1979. At Prime Minister's question time the following day the "helter-skelter" scheme was killed stone dead.

In the months that followed, the Services Committee were concerned with the restoration of the Palace. Before any objections could be manufactured, the energetic Secretary of State for the Environment,

*Sir Hugh Casson's design for the Bridge Street site, west elevation.*

Michael Heseltine, set the wheels in motion. By the autumn of 1986 the whole of the exterior of the Palace had been repaired and cleaned with the exception of the Inner Courts, the Central Tower and the Victoria Tower. The same Secretary of State approached the Services Committee with a view to making a start upon the Casson proposals for Bridge Street. A working party consisting of a new building Sub-committee under the Chairmanship of John Silkin (who had been Minister of Public Building), Sir Hugh Casson, officials of the D.O.E. and officers of the House of Commons produced a brief for the Parliament Street block. All the exteriors were to be retained or enhanced. The corner building onto Parliament Square had been savagely altered in its upper floors. The opportunity was here taken to restore the dome which had once graced this Westminster landmark, thus a better balance would be achieved with the massive Treasury building opposite designed by John Brydon (1878). By the autumn of 1986 a start had been made. The remainder of the Bridge Street site was meanwhile the subject of further study, hastened on by the need to demolish Palace Chambers, built partly over the underground railway.

Thus, as the 1980s drew to a close, conservation at Westminster had replaced the wholesale destruction proposed twenty years previously. North of the Bridge Street site Richmond Terrace had been restored with new work behind it carefully blended into the townscape by William Whitfield.

*The river front of the Palace of Westminster during restoration (1986).*

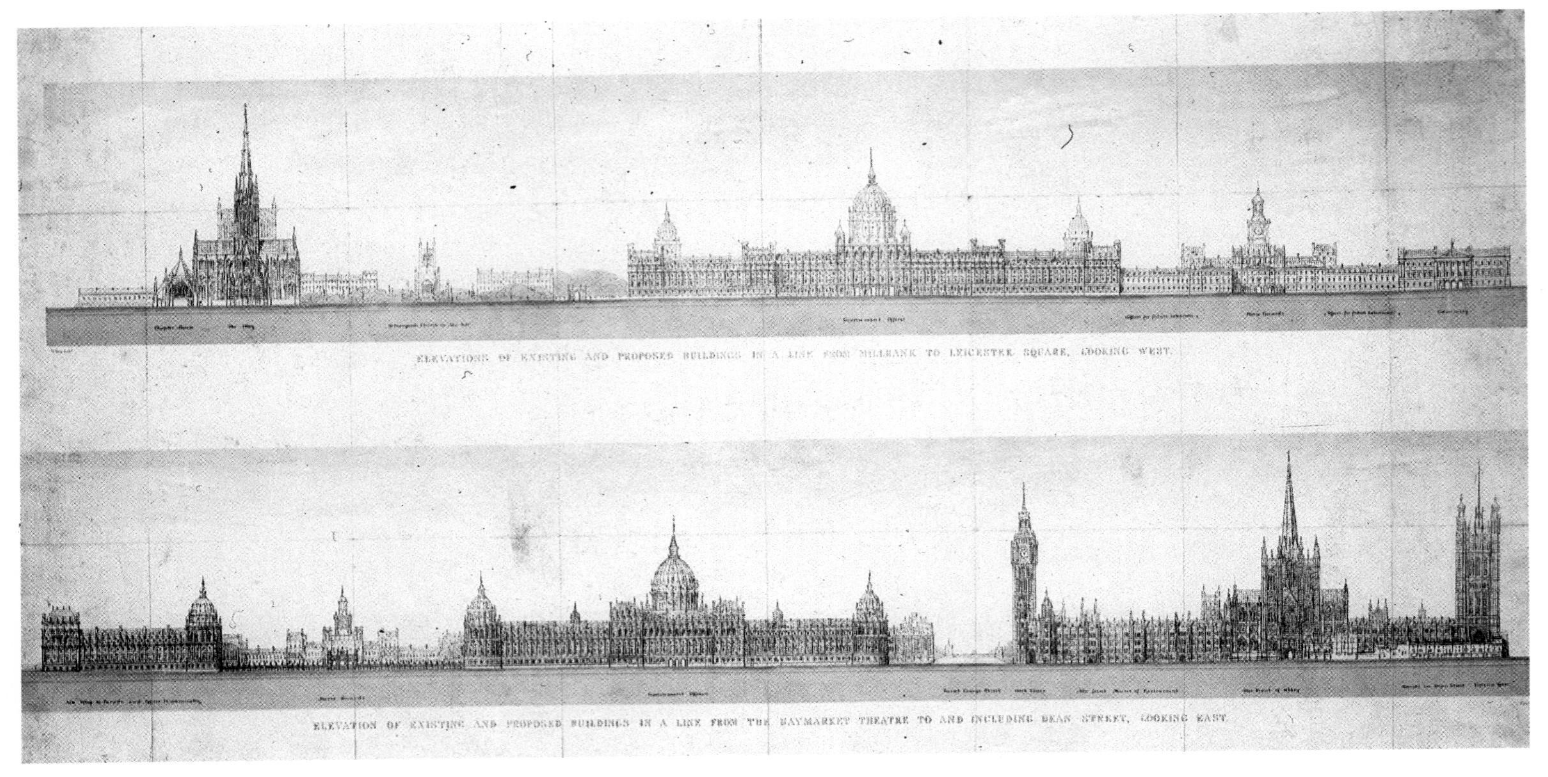


*Sir Charles Barry's proposals for new Government Offices.*

Inigo Jones had planned to cover much of historic Whitehall with his Royal Palace, which included Government Offices. Sir Charles Barry had plans for splendid buildings marching up the Thames to Charing Cross. Had the Curtis Green scheme been completed, everything from Richmond Terrace to the Palace of Westminster would have been reconstructed in the clean lines of his Metropolitan Police building, north of the Norman Shaw blocks.

Centuries of change will now be enshrined in a miscellaneous collection of buildings, few of great distinction but many of interest. Two Georgian houses in Parliament Street serve as a reminder of the Westminster which existed at the time of the building of the New Palace. Indeed it was in a house like these in Bridge Street that Charles Barry was born. The two little houses contain within them remains of earlier structures, the rescue of which was due principally to the dedication of the Comptroller of Her Majesty's Household, Sir Carol Mather, M.P. It was he who by the light of a flickering torch made architectural drawings of historic features which so impressed his colleagues that they insisted upon the retention of the houses.

*Palace of Westminster from the east.*

# Except the Lord Build the House

*Nisi Dominus aedificaverit domum in vanum laboraverunt qui aedificant eam.*

The exhortation from the Psalms which encompasses the Central Lobby is one of many inscriptions in Latin and English to be found all over the New Palace. To its creators the building became something of a religion. Even today the millions who visit London from all over the world frequently mistake the New Palace for Westminster Abbey. In this they may be forgiven, for it is, in the nature of its exterior, a building of greater size and distinction, though it could not have been created without the inspiration of its older partner across the Square.

The Palace has had a sobering effect on the most radical of Parliamentarians yet it has not itself resisted all change. Many new uses have been found for parts created for quite other purposes. The very adaptability of the building has ensured, and will ensure, its continuity as the home of Parliament.

Although great Gothic Parliamentary Palaces deriving from Westminster are limited to Ottawa and more particularly Budapest, there are nineteenth century echoes of Westminster in New South Wales. More recently the Parliamentary procedure of Westminster has resulted in innumerable legislative chambers, resembling to a greater or lesser extent a House of Commons. The "Mother of Parliaments" can boast an architectural progeny throughout the Commonwealth and even elsewhere. The processes which grew up as a result of the architecture of Westminster are capable of evolution. This is proved by the flourishing Inter-Parliamentary Union and Commonwealth Parliamentary Association. Together they embrace every free nation of the world.

We might here dispose of the flattering reference to Westminster made by Adolf Hitler in *Mein Kampf*. "As the Austrian counterpart to the British two-chamber system a Chamber of Deputies and a House of Lords (*Herrenhaus*) were established in Vienna. The Houses themselves, considered as buildings, were somewhat different. When Barry built his palaces, or, as we say, the Houses of Parliament, on the shore of the Thames he could look to the history of the British Empire for the inspiration of his work. In that history he found sufficient material to fill and decorate the 1,200 niches, brackets, and pillars of his magnificent edifice. His statues and paintings made the House of Lords and the House of Commons temples dedicated to the glory of the Nation."[1]

The foregoing was Hitler's excuse to attack the Vienna buildings which could not commemorate any long tradition. "This theatrical shrine of 'Western Democracy' was adorned with the statues and portraits of Greek and Roman statesmen and philosophers. As if it were meant for a symbol of irony, the horses of the quadriga that surmounts the two Houses are pulling apart from one another towards all four quarters of the globe. There could be no better symbol for the kind of activity going on within the walls of that same building."

The adaptability of the New Palace has enabled a number of distinguished new interiors to be created.

### *The Jubilee Room*

In 1974 the northern end of Pearson's addition to Westminster Hall was severely damaged by fire following a terrorist bomb attack. The eastern end of the Grand Committee Room, Westminster Hall, was also damaged.

Advantage was taken in the reconstruciton to create a new Committee room at the north end of the first floor. Various modernistic designs were submitted but the House of Commons Services Committee decided, on advice, to create in this one room something that resembled the parts of the nineteenth century Palace. The work proceeded but slowly and came towards fruition in the year of the Jubilee of Her Majesty Queen Elizabeth II. It was in commemoration of this Jubilee that the room was named. The fireplace which attempts to echo those in other parts of the Palace bears the inscription *1952 Vivat Regina Elizabetta 1977* .

The panelling in this room was made up from materials salvaged from elsewhere in the Palace. The ceiling, all new work, is a cross between the Peers' Dining room and the Moses Room. Some of the decoration was carried out in glass fibre. The gilded bosses are glass fibre casts of examples elsewhere. A consultant, Mr. Ian Grant, prominent in the Victorian Society, designed the pelmets and curtains which accompany the restored Pearson fenestration. The wallpaper is the Gothic lily design on a blue ground.

The six lanterns which illuminate the room are copies of examples found elsewhere and the painting on the north wall is "The Trial of William Wallace in Westminster Hall."[2]

The colour of the woodwork follows that originally used throughout the New Palace, that is a much darker colour than the stripped effect now found throughout much of the Commons end following the activities of Sir Philip Sassoon before the 1939-45 War.

Further works of improvement in 1985 did much to restore the quality of the area below the Grand Committee Room with its fine granite pillars and ribbed vaults. The former stables now provide a modern canteen.

### *The Pugin Room*

In 1979, the former House of Lords Committee Room, which occupies the southern oriel of the central block of the River Front, was dedicated to the memory of Augustus Welby Pugin. To the distinguished stone and woodwork was added a painted ceiling which followed Pugin's design in the companion room belonging to the House of Commons Library. The wall panels were decorated with the grand flock paper now used in the Royal Gallery. The portrait of Pugin by J. R. Herbert has a somewhat similar paper as its background. Herbert's companion picture of the third Mrs. Pugin provides a fine pair; opposite hangs a majestic portrait of Sir Charles Barry. Pugin's great brass chandelier from Alton Towers now hangs in this room. The shields of arms over the door are those of Mr. Speaker Thomas, who opened the room in 1979, and Pugin, Barry and Scott, all of whom have left their mark on the Palace. Mr. Speaker Thomas's crest, of a miner's lamp and daffodil, graces the cresting over a smaller door. The window-seating was cleverly contrived, in a manner of which Pugin could have approved, to provide fine views of the river.

Parliamentary Westminster of the eighteenth century consisted of a mass of miscellaneous and overcrowded buildings, arranged haphazardly around the remains of the Royal Palace. Even before the fire of 1834, a beginning had been made on the clearance of some of the buildings which obscured the north front of Westminster Hall. Further improvements were planned. The New Palace, as it emerged, towered over the many streets of modest houses which ran up to it from all sides. This presented our ancestors with a dilemma. There were grand plans for sweeping away all of the past, including even St. Margaret's Church. So many vested interests were involved that such dreams stood little chance of realisation in Britain. London is different from Paris or Berlin. Even in the City, Sir Christopher Wren did not wholly succeed, despite the inheritance of a vast area cleared by the Great Fire.

The surroundings of the New Palace changed only slowly. The houses

*The Jubilee Room.*

*The Pugin Room.*

along the south side of Bridge Street stood beside New Palace Yard until the 1860s. The north side of the street was gradually Victorianised as was the east side of Parliament Street, where two only of the Georgian houses now remain.

Whitehall was widened as it reached Parliament Square, by the demolition of the west side of Parliament Street. At this time the parallel King Street disappeared, and eventually the north side of Great George Street was engulfed by Brydon's Treasury building, running down to St. James's Park, completed in the 1920s. The south side of this street yet retains one eighteenth century house beyond the Royal Institution of Chartered Surveyors, which now forms part of the west side of the enlarged square.

South of the New Palace, part of Abingdon Street had to be sacrificed for the enlarged site upon which Barry built. Eventually, Victoria Tower Gardens and a widened Millbank replaced that which remained. Some houses on the west side of Abingdon Street survived until after the Second World War. They were demolished to build the Abingdon Street car-park, roofed over with a garden embellished with a Henry Moore sculpture.

St. Margaret's, stripped of the buildings which encumbered its east end and north side, survived to receive a spectacular restoration for which Mr. Speaker Weatherill and many willing allies collected the money.

The layout of Parliament Square was the subject of a number of alterations in the nineteenth century. Further improvements were made in the twentieth. Nineteenth century statues have been joined by statues of Field Marshal Jan Smuts and the Rt. Hon. Sir Winston Churchill. He faces the scene of so many of his Parliamentary battles. One planned embellishment to this historic Square, which would have happened but for the warnings of the railway engineers, was the erection opposite the entrance to New Palace Yard of Cleopatra's Needle - a wooden replica was even put up to try the effect.

An even more dramatic proposition which would have dwarfed the New Palace was proposed for the area between the Abbey and Great College Street.

J. P. Seddon and E. B. Lamb's "Imperial Monumental Halls and Tower" of 1904, had as its prototype the Valhalla on the edge of the Danube created by the King of Bavaria. Westminster Abbey was uncomfortably full of monuments by the middle of the nineteenth century, when there were a great number of schemes to build a national shrine centred on the area running south from the Chapter House. George Gilbert Scott had in mind a wide and lofty cloister of great length in which could be housed the more offensive monuments from the Abbey. A Royal Commission in 1891 suggested taking over part of Westminster School but this did not find favour. Henry Yates Thompson, the benefactor who built the art school at Harrow, offered £38,000 but nothing came of that. Dr. David Woolfe suggested a huge pyramid in Hyde Park. It was possibly the awfulness of this scheme that inspired Seddon and Harvey and later Seddon and Lamb to design the Imperial Monumental Halls with a tower 550 feet high (100 feet higher than the Victoria Tower). The great cloister of Westminster Abbey was to be linked to a reception hall in the base of the Tower. Galleries for monuments were to fill the inside of the Tower which was designed to have an open ambulatory below the belfry at the top. The Great Monumental Hall extended 192 feet to Great College Street ending in a double transept 157 feet long. All around the walls there were to be spaces for monuments to eminent men and women of the British Empire.

More recently, one of the designs entered for the competition for the New Parliamentary Building (won by Spence and Webster) was a giant tower like a gas-holder topped with a Gothic dome. It was accompanied by a text which might have puzzled a Parliamentary Committee, had that entry ever reached their eyes.

The south-west corner of Parliament Square has seen many changes in the last two hundred years. Where is now the Queen Elizabeth II Conference Centre was for long the Westminster Hospital. The Middlesex Guildhall, just to the east, took its final form of Art Nouveau Gothic at the beginning of the twentieth century. Where is now the Methodist Central Hall was once the Royal Aquarium and a theatre, which for a time was run by Lily Langtry. Monolithic buildings at the beginning of Victoria Street have replaced Abbey House on the north side, once a fine hotel, and a not uninteresting office block to the south.

Parliament Square, long the centre of important activity, became with the construction of the Thames Embankment, a tiresome obstruction to an ever increasing flow of north-south traffic. The historic accident of a nearby bridge of ample proportions, added to the congestion. Various schemes for relief have been mentioned in Chapter IX, but nothing is at present in prospect.

The Embankment north of the Clock Tower might have provided the setting for an unexpected companion to the homes of Parliament and Government, in the form of an opera house.

Colonel Mapleson, an operatic impressario, planned to build the finest opera house in the world on the Embankment close to Westminster Bridge, on the site of what is now Norman Shaw North. Work began in 1875 when excavations 50 feet deep were required to find firm foundations. Constant pumping was needed before they could be completed at an outlay of more than £30,000. The outside walls were in due course completed, but the money required to roof the building was not forthcoming, so for lack of £10,000 the building was demolished in 1880 at a cost of £3,000. Ten years later, Norman Shaw used the site and there are still traces of the opera house to be found in the basement of Norman Shaw's building.

The National Opera House was to have been a rival to La Scala, Milan, both in size and magnificence with its own underground station and a subterranean passage to the Houses of Parliament. There were to have been rooms for the artists providing such recreations as Turkish Baths and billiard tables. Resident medical attention was to have been available for artists who became indisposed. From Westminster Pier close by, a houseboat could take the whole company on river rehearsals.

It is interesting to speculate what effect an adjoining opera house would have had upon attendances in the Chamber of the House of Commons.

The south end of Whitehall, which would have been obliterated if the plans by Martin and Buchanan had been carried out, contains several fine and significant relics of nineteenth century public building. The old Home Office on the west side runs into Scott's Italianate Foreign Office, with its memorable front onto the Park. The old Treasury, north of the entrance to Downing Street, is not quite what it seems. Charles Barry reorganised an incomplete Classical elevation which ran up to the remains of the Tudor Whitehall Palace of Henry VIII. All is now obscured from the street but relics of the sixteenth century are buried within. A little of the exterior can be seen just to the east of 10 Downing Street.

The east side of Whitehall, still known as Parliament Street, contains the much restored Richmond Terrace, at the south of which has been added the Richmond Yard scheme by William Whitfield.

*The National Opera House.*

All of the grand clearances and complete rebuilding schemes for Whitehall, from Inigo Jones to Martin and Buchanan, have come to nothing. In times of optimism and opulence there have been some fine new proposals, but invariably they have shrunk, either through economic necessity or change of fashion.

On the south bank of the Thames, opposite the River Front of the New Palace, Barry planned the fourth side of a great Gothic square flanked by a pair of bridges in similar style. The Venetian pavilions of Florence Nightingale's St. Thomas's Hospital eventually claimed this splendid site. the northern-most block fell victim to the Second World War, as did part of its neighbour. A plan for the complete rebuilding of St. Thomas's, set back discreetly from the water's edge and obscured by trees, was shown to Parliament in 1962. The central part of the present Hospital, faced with green slate, dates from this scheme. The vast intrusive, white-tiled excrescence which actually now dominates the northern end of the site was never shown to Parliament. The remains of the Nightingale Hospital are now being conscientiously restored. Perhaps one day all will be reinstated. With a little ingenuity the restored Hospital buildings could have provided a home for the European Parliament. When this proposition was put to the Prime Minister who led Britain into Europe, he reacted enigmatically.

The many architectural relics of the past which have survived to serve a modern Parliament are matched by a number of picturesque but emminently practical Great Offices of State. Their titles have been part of the scene since the Middle Ages and they retain the more significant of their duties.

Of the high public functionaries, whose official duties connect them with the Houses of Parliament, and who have residences or offices in the Palace, the principal is the Lord Great Chamberlain of England, the hereditary Governor of the Palace of Westminster.

"To this great officer (writes the accurate compiler of *The Laws of Honour* ) belongs livery and lodgings in the Royal Court, and certain fees due from each Archbishop or Bishop when they perform their homage or fealty to the Sovereign, and from all the Peers of the Realm at their creation, or doing their homage of fealty; and at the coronation of every King or Queen claims forty ells of crimson velvet for his own robes, as also on the Coronation Day, before the King rises, to bring his apparel, and after he is by him dressed, the bed and all furniture of the Chamber is his fees, with all the King's apparel that he wears on that day: he carries the gloves and linen used by the King at the Coronation, likewise the sword and scabbard, and the gold to be offered by the King, with the robe royal and crown, and to put them on; and to serve the King that day before and after dinner with water to wash his hands, and to have the basin and towel for his fees.

*Lord Hailsham of St. Marylebone, painted by Derek Hill (1984).*

To him belongs the care of providing all things in the House of Lords during the time of Parliament to which he has an apartment near the Lords House.

He has the Government of the whole Palace of Westminster; he also issues forth his warrants for the preparing, fitting and furnishing of Westminster Hall against Coronations and trials of Peers or others tried by Peers in Parliament.

It is in his breast to dispose of the Sword of State to what Lord he pleases, to be carried before the King or Queen when they come to Parliament; and goes on the right hand of the sword next to the King's or Queen's person, and the Lord Marshal on the left. Upon all solemn occasions, the keys of Westminster, and the keys of the Court of Wards, and Court of Requests are delivered to him."

The Lord Great Chamberlain is no longer the subject of attack by those who seek to struggle for control of the Palace. His duties are presently confined to waiting upon Her Majesty at Westminster, but in all matters Ceremonial he is active and indispensible. No Head of State could receive an adequate welcome at Westminster without the presence of the Lord Great Chamberlain and those who serve him.

In Westminster Hall, the First Commissioner of Works claims equal status with the Lord Great Chamberlain. On royal occasions they walk together in procession. Until the 1960s they walked backwards down the steps, as the Sovereign left the Hall. This proved too stern a task for the then First Commissioner but not for the eighty year old Marquess of Cholmondeley. Since that time, that part of the ceremonial has been abandoned.

Although the relationship between the Lord Great Chamberlain and Black Rod has changed over the years, it is still Black Rod who summons the Commons to Her Majesty's presence in the Parliament Chamber. The picturesque nineteenth century description of the office omits the arduous day to day management of the domestic side of their Lordship's activities for which Black Rod and his supporters are responsible.

"The Gentlemen Usher of the Black Rod has the charge of the chamber in which the Peers sit during the session of Parliament: he is sent to summons the Members of the House of Commons to the presence of the King or Queen on state occasions in the House of Lords. He is called Black Rod, from the black staff or rod, about three feet long, tipt with silver, and gilt with the King's arms at one end, and a lion couchant at the other end, and a gilt knob in the middle, which he carries in his hand: he is always a person of quality, and born the King's subject, and if not a knight, is made one upon admission to this office, and hath his office by patent; the first grant of it beginnning in the reign of King Henry VIII.

Before the sitting of Parliament he observes the Lord Great Chamberlain's directions, in taking care that the House be fitted with all things for the reception of the King and those who sit there.

His employment also is to introduce Lords into that House. And after that House is sat, he hath employments concerning the commitment of delinquents, etc."

All those who serve in the Palace have but one aim, and that is to secure the smooth running of the two Houses of Parliament. The Lord Chancellor occupies a position of somewhat greater antiquity than that of Mr. Speaker. More than a hundred years ago it was said that:

"The Lord High Chancellor performs all matters which appertain to the Speaker of the House of Lords, and sits upon the woolsack, with the Great Seal of England constantly before him.

He is the inlarger, explainer, interpreter, or pronouncer of the King's commands or pleasure; and that which is further observable, of seventy-two officers under his jurisdiction, more than forty-four of them are employed in Parliamentary concerns; either upon its summoning or during its sitting. And as his warrant is the second warrant that gives life to a Parliament, and vivacity to its continuance by sessions and recesses, so he gives the second fiat to its dissolution. He hath also an apartment near the Lords House for himself to retire to, and for his Serjeant-at-Arms and others of his attendants."

Perhaps one can detect here a somewhat defensive reference to the size of his staff. The ratio of functionaries to legislators has long been a matter of controversy. The Lord Chanceller himself, however, has the use only of a most modest residence within the Palace.

The House of Commons Library has its origins in the time of Mr. Speaker Abbott, (1802-1817). The first Librarian, Benjamin Spiller, was allocated a room between the Smoking Room and Bellamy's Coffee Room. Bellamy's responsibilities included the care of the Library Room, hence the erroneous tradition that it was with Bellamy that the Library began. In fact, it was the distracting proximity of Bellamy's catering activities that persuaded the Select Committee of 1825 to make proper provision for the Library and its growing collections. Sir John Soane was thwarted in his first intentions for a new Library by the immovable Clerk of the House, John Henry Ley. Nonetheless, he contrived a fine room, fifty five feet long by twenty three feet wide and thirteen feet six inches high. Described as the "Best and most agreeable room in London,"[3] it was in a Gothic style. The Librarian at this time was the famous Thomas Vardon. During part of his long reign, he had a capable young assistant, Erskine May. May graduated to the Clerkship of the House of Commons, in which office he produced his *Parliamentary Practice*. This bible of Parliamentary precedent and procedure has since enjoyed worldwide influence. Although the Commons' Library was more severely damaged than the Lords' in the Great Conflagration of 1834, it was given the finest rooms on the River Front of the New Palace. It has grown in size and influence ever since. The services which it can provide are many and various. Additional to the enlightenment of Members of both Houses of Parliament, it has been charged with the responsibility of educating the public in the mysteries of Parliament.

The influence of Sir Robert Peel upon the architecture of Westminster is matched by the ever present vigilance of the Police Force, which he created. The Police who serve the Palace have to tread a delicate path. They do not have the power to arrest Members of either House within the precincts, but they are charged with the maintenance of good order among all those who have business there. They have to combine the virtues of "Dixon of Dock Green" when dealing with the worried and the lost who seek the help of their Member, with the sterner task of combating the terrorist whose attack may take any form. The Police are today capable of greater skills of protection and detection than the celebrated nineteenth century Inspecter Denning could ever have dreamed. The Police at Westminster present what is fashionably described as a "low profile" but can be relied upon to appear with alacrity whenever they are needed. It was a Policeman who saved the Crypt Chapel from destruction in the nineteenth century. Those who have sought to attack the Palace or its inmates, either through ignorance or malevolent intent have invariably soon found themselves in the arms of the Law.

First came the struggle for control and then the struggle for possession. More recent has been the nearly insatiable demand for more and more of the facilities necessary to support a Legislature determined to equip itself for effective control of the Executive.

The relentless advance of technological aids may soon mean that the New Palace is once more dominated by the Members of the two Houses in their two Chambers. All that supports them could be agreeably dispersed, through what Churchill called "the benefits of modern science."

Hidden away over what used to be the Members' Entrance to the House of Commons is an exhortation to a less frantic Parliamentary life:

"He that hath knowledge spareth his words."

# Appendices

## Appendix A: Architect's report as to internal decorations, addition to building, and local improvements

*Westminster, 22nd February, 1843*

Sir,

As presiding over Her Majesty's Commissioners for encouraging the Fine Arts in connexion with the rebuilding of the new Houses of Parliament, I venture to address your Royal Highness, and, in compliance with the instructions of the Commission, to offer the following suggestions relative to the internal finishings and decorations of the new Houses of Parliament, the completion of the exterior, and the local improvements which are in my opinion necessary to give full effect to the new building; and by way of illustration of the remarks which I have to make on these subjects, I beg to transmit the accompanying plan of the principal floor of the new building, a general plan of part of Westminster, in which the new building is shown in connexion with various improvements proposed to be made in its locality, and two drawings relating to Westminster Bridge.

With reference to the interior of the new Houses of Parliament generally, I would suggest that the walls of the several halls, galleries, and corridors of approach, as well as the various public apartments throughout the building, should be decorated with paintings having reference to events in the history of the country; and that those paintings should be placed in compartments formed by such a suitable arrangement of the architectural design of the interior as will best promote their effective union with the arts of sculpture and architecture. With this view I should consider it to be of the utmost importance that the paintings should be wholly free from gloss on the surface, so that they may be perfectly seen and fully understood from all points of view. That all other portions of the plain surfaces of the walls should be covered with suitable architectonic decoration or diapered enrichment in colour, occasionally heightened with gold, and blended with armorial bearings, badges, cognizances, and other heraldic insignia, emblazoned in their proper colours. That such of the halls as are groined should have their vaults decorated in a similar manner, with the addition occasionally of subjects or works of arts so interwoven with the diapered ground as not to disturb the harmony or the effect of the architectonic decorations generally, or interfere with the elementary features of the architectural composition. That such of the ceilings as are flat should be formed into compartments by moulded ribs, enriched with carved heraldic and Tudor decorations. That these ceilings should be relieved by positive colour and gilding, and occasionally by gold grounds with diaper enrichments, legends, and heraldic devices in colour. That the screens, pillars, corbels, niches, dressings of the windows, and other architectural decorations, should be painted to harmonize with the paintings and diapered decorations of the walls generally, and be occasionally relieved with positive colour and gilding. That the door-jambs and fire-places should be constructed of British marbles, of suitable quality and colour, highly polished, and occasionally relieved by colour and gilding in their mouldings and sculptural enrichments.

That the floors of the several halls, galleries, and corridors, should be formed of encaustic tiles, bearing heraldic decorations and other enrichments in colours, laid in margins and compartments, in combination with polished British marbles; and that the same description of marbles should also be employed for the steps of the several staircases.

That the walls to the height of from 8 to 10 feet should be lined with oak framing, containing shields with armorial bearings emblazoned in their proper colours, and an oak seat should in all cases be placed against such framing. That the windows of the several halls, galleries, and corridors, should be glazed doubly, for the purpose of tempering the light and preventing the direct rays of the sun from interfering with the effect of the internal decorations generally. For this purpose the outer glazing is proposed to be of ground glass, in single plates, and the inner glazing of an ornamental design in metal, filled with stained glass, bearing arms and other heraldic insignia in their proper colours; but so arranged as that the ground, which I should recommend to be of a warm yellowish tint, covered with a running foliage or diaper, and occasionally relieved by legends in black letters, should predominate, in order that so much light only may be excluded as may be thought desirable to do away with either a garish or cold effect upon the paintings and decorations generally. Practically, I consider that the double glazing will be of essential service in carrying out the system of warming and ventilating proposed to be adopted in the building generally; which system renders it unnecessary that the windows in those portions of the building above referred to should be made to open, so that all prejudicial effects upon the paintings and other decorations which might be caused by the dampness and impurity of the atmosphere, and much practical inconvenience and probably unsightliness in the means that would be necessary to adopt for the opening and shutting casements, would be avoided.

That in order to promote the art of sculpture, and its effective union with painting and architecture, I would propose that in the halls, galleries, and corridors, statues might be employed for the purpose of dividing the paintings on the walls. By this arrangement a rich effect of perspective and a due subordination of the several arts to each other would be obtained. The statues suggested should in my opinion be of marble, of the colour of polished alabaster, and be raised upon lofty and suitable pedestals, placed close to the wall in niches, surmounted by enriched canopies; but the niches should be shallow, so that the statues may be as well seen laterally as in front.

The architectural decorations of these niches might be painted of such colours as will give the best effect to the adjoining paintings, being relieved in parts by positive colour and gilding; and the backs of them might be painted in dark colours, such as chocolate, crimson, or blue, or they might be of gold, for the purpose of giving effect to the statues.

Having thus described the views I entertain as to the character of the decorations of the interior generally, I now proceed to notice in detail the special decorations and arrangements which I would propose for the several halls, galleries, and principal apartments.

*Westminster Hall*

I would propose that Westminster Hall, which is 239 feet long, 68 feet wide and 90 feet high, should be made the depository, as in former times, for all trophies obtained in wars with foreign nations. These trophies might be so arranged above the paintings on the walls and in the roof as to have a very striking and interesting effect.

I would further suggest that pedestals, twenty in number, answering to the position of the principal ribs of the roof, should be placed so as to form a central avenue 30 feet in width, from the north entrance-door to St. Stephen's porch, for statues of the most celebrated British statesmen whose public services have been commemorated by monuments erected at the public expense, as well as for present and future statesmen whose services may be considered by Parliament to merit a similar tribute to their memories.

The statues (twenty-six in number) which have been already proposed to be placed against the walls between the pictures, I would suggest should be those of naval and military commanders.

The subjects of the paintings on the walls, twenty-eight in number, 16 feet in length and 10 feet in height, might relate to the most splendid warlike achievements of English history, both by sea and land, which, as well as the statues that are proposed to divide them, might be arranged chronologically.

To give due effect to these suggested decorations, it is proposed that the light should be considerably increased by an enlargement of the dormer windows in the roof, by which also that extraordinary and beautiful piece of decorative carpentry of the fourteenth century may be seen to much greater advantage than has ever yet been the case.

This noble Hall, certainly the most slendid of its style in the world, thus decorated by the union of painting, sculpture, and architecture, and aided by the arts of decoration as suggested, it is presumed would present a most striking appearance, and be an object of great national interest.

*St. Stephen's Hall*

I would suggest that this Hall, which will be 90 feet long, 30 feet wide and 50 feet high, and have a stone-groined ceiling, should be appropriated to the reception of paintings commemorative of great domestic events in British history, and statues of celebrated statesmen of past, present, and future times. The paintings may be ten in number, 15 feet long and 10 feet high, and twelve statues would be required as a frame to them. In the upper part of the Hall, thirty niches will be provided for statues of eminent men of the naval, military, and civil services of the country.

*The Central Hall*

This Hall will be an octagon of 60 feet in diameter and 50 feet high, covered with a groined ceiling in stone. As each side will be wholly occupied by windows and arched openings of access, paintings cannot form any part of its decoration. It may, however, with good effect, be extensively decorated with sculpture. In the centre of the pavement might be placed a statue of Her present Most Gracious Majesty, upon a rich pedestal of British marble, highly polished, and relieved in parts by gold and colour. The niches in the walls and screens might be filled with statues of Her Majesty's ancestors, in chronological order, even up to the period of the heptarchy. In front of the eight clustered pillars in the angles of the Hall might be placed, with good effect, sedent statues of some of the great lawgivers of antiquity.

*The Victoria Gallery*

This Gallery will be 130 feet long, 45 feet wide, and 50 feet high, with a flat ceiling, and will admit of both paintings and sculpture. The subjects of the paintings on the walls, sixteen in number which may be 12 feet long and 10 feet high, might fill the central niches at the ends of the Hall; and the other niches, as well as the pedestals between the paintings, might be occupied by statues of Her Majesty's ancestors. These statues might with good effect be of bronze, either partially or wholly gilt.

*Corridors of Access throughout the Building*

The principal Corridors of access to the various apartments of the building will be 12 feet wide, their ceilings will be flat, and they will generally be lighted from windows near the ceiling. Their walls might be decorated with portraits as well as with paintings, illustrative of some of the most remarkable events in the history of the country, or in the lives of its most eminent personages. For this purpose about 2600 feet in length of wall, by a height of about 7 feet, may be appropriated on the principal floor; 900 feet in length, by a height of about 7 feet, on the one-pair floor; and about 400 feet, by the same height, on the two-pair floor. These paintings may be divided into subjects at pleasure, by margins or borders or architectonic decoration, in accordance with the style of the building.

*The House of Lords*

This House will be 93 feet long, 45 feet wide, and 50 feet high, and will have a flat ceiling in panels. As the fittings for the accommodation required for the business of the House, together with the windows which are necessary for duly lighting it, leave little space of plain wall, paintings cannot, with good effect, form any part of its decoration. Niches, however, will be provided, which might be filled with statues of royal personages. The architectural details of the ceiling may be enriched and relieved with gold and colour, and the windows filled with stained glass, as before described. The whole of the fittings are proposed to be of oak, with appropriate carvings. The throne will be highly enriched and relieved by colour and gilding, and the back lined with cloth of gold, containing the royal arms emblazoned in their proper colours.

*The House of Commons*

This House will be 83 feet long, 46 feet wide, and 50 feet high, and will have a flat ceiling. It is proposed to be finished in the same style as the House of Lords, but with less enrichment, and less of colour and gold in its decorations. The nature of its design, and the extent of the fittings for the accommodation required, will not admit of the aid of either painting or sculpture.

*The Queen's Robing Room*

This room will be 38 feet long, 35 feet wide and 20 feet high, and have a flat ceiling in panels, richly moulded and carved, and relieved with gold, covered with a diaper enrichment, and blended with legends, genealogical devices, badges, cognizances, and other heraldic insignia, &c. in colour.

The wall-fittings of the room are proposed to be of oak, richly carved and moulded, and enriched with heraldic and other decorations in positive colour, relieved with gold. Compartments will be formed in the wall-framing, which might be filled with paintings referring to events in British history in which the sovereign has personally taken a conspicuous part, or with other appropriate subjects.

*The Anti-Room or Guard Room*

This Room, which adjoins the Queen's robing-room, will be 38 feet by 38 feet and 20 feet high. The ceiling will be of oak, with characteristic decorations. Oak framing, 8 feet high, with heraldic decorations, and a seat at the foot of it, will line the room. The walls are proposed to be covered with representations of battle-scenes and pageants of English history, in which an opportunity will be afforded of displaying the warlike costumes of its several periods.

*The Conference Hall*

This Hall, which is in the centre of the front towards the river, will be 54 feet long, 28 feet wide, and 20 feet high and will have a flat ceiling. The walls are proposed to be lined with oak framing to a height of about 6 feet, above which they might be covered with paintings representing celebrated state trials, and extraordinary sittings of Parliament, conferences, &c.

*As to the Apartments Appropriated to the Private and Public Uses of Each House*

These Rooms consist of libraries, refreshment-rooms, robing-rooms, state officers' rooms, and committee rooms.

Nine rooms are appropriated to libraries, six of which are 50 feet long and 28 feet wide; two are 33 feet long and 28 feet wide; and one is 32 feet long and 23 feet wide. The refreshment rooms are four in number, of which one is 60 feet long and 18 feet wide; two are 28 feet long and 18 feet wide; and one is 34 feet long and 18 feet wide. The robing-rooms for the the archbishops and bishops are three in number, of the respective sizes of 30 feet by 20 feet, 20 feet square, and 16 feet square. The robing and other rooms for state officers are seventeen in number, averaging in size about 24 feet by 18 feet. The committee-rooms are thirty-five in number. On the principal floor, five of them will be 37 feet long by 28 feet wide; two, 35 feet by 26 feet; and one, 32 feet by 23 feet. On the one-pair floor, two will be 42 feet long and 33 feet wide; one, 54 feet by 28 feet; four, 36 feet; by 28 feet; ten, 34 feet by 28 feet; and two, 34 feet by 22 feet; and on the two-pair floor the number will be eight, averaging in size 28 feet by 20 feet. The whole of these rooms are about 20 feet in height, with the exception of those on the two-pair floor, which will be about 14 feet high, and will be lighted by windows of the usual height from the floor.

The ceilings will be flat, and formed into panels by moulded and carved riobs, relieved by characteristic and suitable carvings.

The floors are to be of oak, with borders and inlays.

The fire-places and door-jambs are proposed to be of British marbles, highly polished. The doors, frontispieces, linings of walls, and fittings, will also be of oak. In some of the rooms it is proposed that the wall-framing should be carried to the height of six or eight feet, in others that it should be of the full height of the room, and with panels for paintings, portraits, &c.

The plain surfaces of the walls might be covered with paintings of historical events, and the panels in the wainscoting might contain portraits of celebrated personages in British history.

The architectural details, both in stone and plaster, might be painted in positive colours, occasionally relieved by gilding; and the armorial bearings, badges, and other heraldic insignia, which will enrich the wood-framing, might also be relieved with gold and colour.

*The Speaker's Residence*

This Residence being designed for state purposes, might also be adorned with paintings. The style of its finishings, fittings, and decorations, will be in accordance with the best examples of the Tudor period.

Its principal rooms for purposes of state are as follows: - A reception-room, 34 feet by 23 feet; a library, 34 feet by 23 feet; a dining-room, 45 feet by 24 feet; a drawing-room, 38 feet by 22 feet; and a corridor of communication, 8 feet wide, surrounding an internal court.

With respect to any further encouragement of the Fine Arts in the exterior of the building, I am not aware of any opportunities that offer, as arrangements have already been made for all the architectonic or conventional sculpture that will be required to adorn the several elevations. Equestrian statues of sovereigns in bronze might however be placed, with considerable effect, in the proposed quadrangle of New Palace Yard, the Speaker's quadrangle, and the royal court.

I have now described, in general terms, the whole of those portions of the building that might, I think, with propriety and effect, be adorned with works of art, and the arts of decoration; but, in making the several suggestions which have occurred to me, I should wish it to be understood that I have merely stated my own views on the subject, as far as I have hitherto been able to consider it in its general bearings, and with a view to show how the objects for which the commission has been established may, if desired, be carried out in the decorations of the new building to their greatest extent. I should not, however, wish to be strictly confined in all cases to the adoption even of my own suggestions, as upon a more mature consideration of the subject in detail hereafter, when the shell of the building is completed, I may be induced to vary and modify some of the views which I entertain at present, and which, I fear, I have but imperfectly communicated in this paper.

*As to the Completion of the Exterior*

It has ever been considered by me a great defect in my design for the new Houses of Parliament that it does not comprise a front of a sufficient length towards the Abbey, particularly as the building will perhaps be better, and more generally, seen on that side than upon any other. This was impossible, owing to the broken outline of the site with which I had to deal. I propose, therefore, that an addition should be made to the building (which upon the accompanying plan is coloured orange), for the purpose of enclosing New Palace Yard, and thus of obtaining the desired front. This addition would be in accordance with the plan of the ancient palace of Westminster, in which the Hall was formerly placed in a quadrangle, where, in consequence of its low level, it must have been seen and approached, as it would ever be under such circumstances, to the best advantage. The proposed addition would, in my opinion, be of considerable importance as regards the increased accommodation and convenience that it would afford in addition to what is already provided for in the new building, as hitherto proposed.

It has long been a subject of serious complaint and reproach, that the present law courts are most inconveniently restricted in their arrangements and accommodation. If it should be determined to retain the Courts at Westminster, the proposed addition would admit of the means of removing this cause of complaint; it would also afford accommodation for places of refreshment for the public, for which no provision has been made in the new building; also for Royal Commissions and other occasional purposes required by Government, and now hired most inconveniently, in various parts of the town, at a considerable amount of rental; or for such of the Government offices as may, without inconvenience, be detached from the rest, such as for instance the Office of Woods, or for a Record Office, and chambers or residences for public officers. It will also afford the opportunity of making an imposing principal entrance to the entire edifice, at the angle of Bridge Street and St. Margaret's Street; a feature which is at present required, and which would add considerably not only to the effect of the building, but also to its security in times of public commotion.

Of the several local improvements indicated in the accompanying plan, none in my opinion is of greater and more pressing importance than that which I have to suggest in respect of Westminster Bridge. The anomaly of the size, outline, and character of that bridge, considered as it must ever be from its proximity as an adjunct to the new Houses of Parliament, must have forcibly struck every one who has passed over or under it since the new building has risen into importance; and the steep and dangerous acclivities of the roadway, as well as its want of width for the traffic that passes over it, have constantly been a subject of public complaint.

In order, therefore, to remove these serious objections, I propose that the superstructure of the bridge should be rebuilt upon the old foundations, which are now in course of being repaired and extended under the able superintendence of Messrs. Walker and Burgess. As it is, in my opinion, of the utmost importance both as regards the effect of the new Houses of Parliament, when viewed from the bridge, and the convenience of the public in passing over it, that the roadway should be made on the lowest possible level, I would recommend that the form of the arches of the new bridge should be painted, by which great facility would be afforded for accomplishing that very important object, namely, by materially reducing the thickness of the crown of the arches within what is considered necessary for arches of the circular form. I am induced also to recommend this form of arch on account of another very important practical advantage which it offers, namely, the elevation of its springing above the level of high water, by which the water-way through the bridge will be the same at all times of tide; whereas at present the spandrils of the arches offer an impediment to the water-way at high water nearly equal to one-twentieth of its sectional area, occasioning rapid currents, with a considerable fall, and sometimes much danger to craft in passing through the bridge under the influence of high winds. I consider it also of the greatest importance, in an artistic point of view, not only that the bridge should be materially lowered, but that it should be made to accord with the architecture of the new Houses of Parliament, in order that both in composition as well as style the ensemble should be harmonious and effective. Upon a rough estimate which I have formed of the cost of the new superstructure, I am satisfied it could be erected for about £120,000. beyond the cost which it will be necessary to incur to carry out Messrs. Walker and Burgess's design for widening the present bridge to the extent proposed.

With the view of illustrating the several suggestions which I have made on this subject, I venture to submit the accompanying design for a new superstructure; but in so doing I wish it to be clearly understood that I have no desire whatever to interfere with the employment of the engineers who are now engaged upon the repair and extension of the foundations of the present bridge; who, having so ably commenced the work, should in my opinion be left to complete it.

I leave this subject, therefore, in the hands of the Commissioners, in the hope that they will at their earliest convenience, if they should think fit, make a formal and urgent communication to the Government in accordance with the views which I have now laid before them, particularly as an early decision is of great importance, in order that the works now in hand may not be proceeded with further than is necessary to carry out those views, if they should be ultimately adopted.

Next in importance to the rebuilding of the superstructure of Westminster Bridge is the formation of the proposed lines of embankment on both sides of the river, from Vauxhall to London Bridges, as suggested by Messrs. Walker and Burgess in their late Report on the subject to the Government and the Corporation of the City of London.

In the accompanying plan I have shown so much of those lines of embankment as more immediately affect the new Houses of Parliament and their locality. As there would doubtless be serious objections to a public road upon the embankment on the north side of the river, I confine my observations to the southern side, where, if a road could be obtained, it would afford a succession of fine views of London, and the best situation for views of the principal front of the new Houses of Parliament. Having maturely considered the subject, I think it would be practicable to obtain a public road of ample width, upon arches, from the termini of the South Eastern and Dover and the Brighton Railroads at the foot of London Bridge, to the terminus of the South Western Railway at Vauxhall.

The road might be raised upon arches to a level that would coincide with the levels of the roadways of the several bridges which it would intersect, by which means the waterside frontages of the several wharfs need not be interfered with in any material degree; indeed, the extend of such frontages might, by the means of docks of convenient form and size, be very considerably increased, and the archways might to a great extent be appropriated, if desired, to warehouses and other purposes of trade. By extending the archways to a sufficient depth to the south of this road, a frontage for building might also be obtained, particularly opposite Privy Gardens and the new Houses of Parliament, where, if the houses were designed in masses, with reference to architectural effect, they would form an agreeable and striking view from the north side of the river, and effectually screen the present low and mean display of unpicturesque buildings on the Surrey side. The proposed houses, from being raised to a considerable elevation, would have a fine command of the river and the principal public buildings of the metropolis; and having, in addition to these advantages, a southern aspect, would form very agreeable residences, such as would probably yield a very considerable return for the capital expended upon it; and, when effected, would not only form one of the most striking improvements of an ornamental character of which the metropolis is susceptible, but would materially conduce to the convenience, the comfort, and recreation of the public. It would also perhaps render unnecessary the line of road that has been projected from the termini of the railroads at the foot of London Bridge through Southwark to the foot of Westminster Bridge, for the convenience of the west-end of the town; as the distance to that part of London would be materially shortened by taking the proposed embankment road, and passing over Waterloo Bridge.

The other local improvements indicated in the accompanying plan relate to an enlargement of the spaces immediately contiguous to the new Houses of Parliament, and an improvement of the approaches.

Old Palace Yard is proposed to be considerably increased in size by the demolition of the houses which now occupy that site, as well as the houses on both sides of Abingdon Street, by which means a fine area for the convenience of state processions, and the carriages of peers and others attending the House of Lords, as well as a spacious landing place adjoining the river, would be obtained. The Victoria Tower, as well as the south and west fronts of the building, would thus be displayed to the best advantage. The Chapter-house would be laid open to public view, and, if restored, would form a striking feature in conjunction with the Abbey; and a considerable extent of new building frontage that would be obtained by this alteration might be occupied by houses of importance in a style of architecture in harmony with the Abbey and the new Houses of Parliament, by which a grand and imposing effect as a whole would be produced. As one means of improving the approaches, I propose that the noble width of street at Whitehall should be extended southwards, by the removal of the houses between Parliament Street and King Street, by which the Abbey would be wholly exposed to view as far as Whitehall Chapel. The houses on the north side of King Street should be removed for the purpose of substituting houses or public buildings, if required, of an imposing sytle of architecture. Millbank Street is proposed to be widened and improved, in order to make it a convenient and effective approach from Millbank Road to the Victoria Tower and Old Palace Yard. Tothill Street is also proposed to be widened and improved, in order that it may be made an equally convenient and striking approach to the Abbey, the Houses of Parliament, and Whitehall, from the west end of the town. Saint Margaret's Church, if suffered to remain in its present position, should be improved in its external decoration, in order that it may not disgrace, as it now does, the noble pile of the Abbey, which rises above it.

I have thus enumerated all the principal improvements which I should wish to see effected in the locality of the great work in which I am engaged; and, although I have thought it right thus to place on record my views upon the subject, I am aware that a considerable time must elapse before they could all be effected, if approved.

I trust, however, I may hope to see accomplished, at no distant period, the rebuilding of the superstructure of Westminster Bridge, the embankments of the river, the enclosure of new Palace Yard, and the enlargement of Old Palace Yard; which, in my estimation, are improvements of the utmost importance, whether as regards the beauty of the metropolis, the effect of the new Houses of Parliament, or the convenience, as well as the enjoyment, of the public.

I have the honour to be, With the greatest respect, Your Royal Highness's most obedient and humble servant,

CHARLES BARRY

To His Royal Highness Prince Albert, K.G.

Source: Appendix No. 1 *The Second Report of the Commissioners on the Fine Arts* (1844)

# Appendix B: Letter from Charles Barry to Lord Duncannon 3rd October 1839

Foley-place 3rd October 1839.

My Lord,

The time is now arrived when it is desirable to decide upon the system to be adopted for warming, lighting, and ventilating the intended New Houses of Parliament, as it is of great importance that every preparation should be made for the purpose in the progress of the intended buildings, so as to avoid considerable expense, and probably dissatisfaction hereafter. I should therefore wish to be put in communication with, or be empowered to apply to such persons as have distinguished themselves in that department of science, in order that a general system may at once be devised to meet the objects in view, that will not interfere in any degree, if it be possible, with the convenience or beauty of the intended building. Dr. Reid, who is well known to your Lordship, and whose success in warming and ventilating the present House of Commons is generally acknowledged, and Mr. Oldham, who has long been employed in the mechanical departments of the Banks of England and Ireland, which have been warmed and ventilated by him upon a new system with great success, are both persons who in all respects are eminently qualified to be employed upon this business; but as Dr. Reid is a resident of Edinburgh, and does not profess to be thoroughly acquainted with the practical details of building and machinery, and as Mr. Oldham's official appointment at the Bank of England would prevent him from giving up much of his time to the execution of the work that may be necessary, I should wish also to have the further assistance of a practical engineer who has specially turned his attention to the subject, and whose duty should be to direct, superintend, and be responsible for the proper execution of all the works that may be requisite in carrying out the details of the system that may be agreed upon. For this office I beg to recommend Mr. Manby, of Great George-street, Westminster, who has long acted as the agent for Mr. Price's patent system of warming by hot water, in which capacity he has been employed at the British Museum, and many other public buildings, as well as at several of my own private works, in directing and superintending the application of that patent with great success.

I have the honour to be, my Lord, your very faithful and obedient servant,

CHARLES BARRY

Source: *The Second Report of the Committee of the House of Commons to consider the present state of Westminster Bridge and the New Palace of Westminster* (1846)

# Appendix C
# The Diary of Charles Barry Junior (1846-47)

*"I begin this book with the hope and intention of keeping a more regular and systematic diary than heretofore, the practice I believe to be most beneficial from inducing oneself to review one's own actions, by exercising thought on other men and things and by enabling one to express habitually and concisely one's views of events.*

*Father has I hope recovered his attack and though I fear is not strong is almost well again in all but temper which must show I fear that all is not right in health."*

Saturday, 31st January 1846

*"The House of Lords at the motion of the Marquiss of Clanricarde has appointed the New Houses Committee but I think as there was a perfect understanding that the new House of Lords would not be ready till next session, that father will not be much annoyed, I think their Lordship's enquiry will be turned on Dr. Reid who I trust will meet the exposure he deserves."*

Sunday, 15th February 1846

*"Father with Mr. Wolfe arranging his weapons of attack towards Dr. Reid in readiness for coming before the Committee on the subject, that in the Lords having been moved by Lord Clanricarde and which meets the first time on the 17th next and that in the Commons is to be moved for tomorrow by Sir Robert Inglis.*

*Was all day engaged in packing and arranging drawings of NHP. The number of plans is very great. Father was engaged in preparing evidence for the Lords Committee to be held tomorrow, but at 10:00 p.m. o'clock came a notice that it was put off till Monday next. Father is sorry as he wishes the thing knocked off as soon as possible..."*

Sunday, 22nd February 1846

*"Father read over to me the heads of what he intends to put before the Lords and Commons Committee tomorrow respecting Reid's malpractices....Meeson has drawn up a very good opening statement taking two isolated parts of the building, the House of Lords and the River Front."*

Tuesday, 24th February 1846

*"Father had a satisfactory meeting of the Committee yesterday. He opened his case with a statement of one or two facts showing that Dr. Reid's ignorance of construction of building, his vacillation and want of system. After seventeen hours sitting, their Lordships hastily adjourned after having asked the Doctor a few questions apparently having heard enough to give them matter for reflection."*

Tuesday, 3rd March 1846

*"Went over to see Messrs. Ballantine and Allans' first attempt at stained glass in the House of Lords - it is beastly - the cartoon ... does not appear at all well drawn and the colours are abominable. The red is no red but orange, the blue bad and the yellow fit for waterclosets only. There is a great want of ... white and the figures, so I told father, I had found... too fat for the size of the height - saw Grissell who called on father to tell him what I think will not take him wholly unprepared as he like me has heard it rumoured before that he and Peto had dissolved partnership. What this will lead to I know not. I think on the whole it will be good. It will preclude Grissell having anything to do with railways."*

Wednesday, 4th March 1846

*"Was all the afternoon in attendance on father looking up old letters from the Office of Woods in 1839/40/41 to see if Dr. Reid is then notified to father as the appointed ventilator of the NHP and to see if father is anywhere distinctly ordered to act with him as such, but the whole affair seems to have been done so slovenly that no such order is to be found...Father did so but recommends that any detailed report and drawings showing his whole system should be furnished forthwith by Dr. Reid. This has never been done...*

*Pugin came in the evening to... father as to stained glass. He will not see anything wrong proportionally in the cartoons but abominates the glass."*

Thursday, 5th March 1846

*"Father attended Commons Committee this day. Sir R. Inglis in the Chair but came home cruelly hurt and annoyed by the conduct of the former... Father terribly annoyed at all this and declares he will not stand it, that he will roundly tell them that if they do not place confidence in what he says and does, they had better find someone else to carry on the building. ...With the Lords... so far he has got on well and I fancy must prove his case with all men of good common sense...If Committees really understood the ...they are called on to decide they would find matter for wonder rather than for censure in the progress. But this is one of the evils of Parliamentary supervision that judges in nine cases out of ten do not and cannot understand the cases they are called on to decide."*

Tuesday, 10th March 1846

*"Found that the Committee sat this day but were wholly occupied in examining Dr. Reid and therefore did not call father at all."*

Wednesday, 11th March 1846

*"He is in terribly low spirits today. He has seen at the Office of Woods an evident desire to uphold that humbug Reid and hardly knows whom to depend on himself...constantly by such things as this business of Reid and by Committees of foolish wise men to destract and occupy his thoughts - the cruel disappointment of which I really believe would kill him, and going on in this way will also wear him out so that either way I fear and anticipate with anxiety the end of it all."*

Thursday, 12th March 1846

*"At Thames Bank, measuring all the afternoon, Sir Edward Cust came then while I was there and I accompanied him over the place. He seemed much delighted with what he saw, especially with the ingenuity of the carving machines (Jordans, which were occupied at the time on the Victoria Gallery spandrels, two roof beams and in the various wall panelling). I think he is one of father's oldest and trusty friends.*

*Had occasion to go this evening at nine o'clock to the works - it was a glorious moonlight night and its effect on the River Front and the south return was the most superb I can conceive. I stood involuntarily in admiration for some time on the dam - the only thing I can compare its effect to, is a most beautifully drawn pencil drawing - there was all the softness and all the deep effects of light and shade, the detail, the richness without being so distinct in itself as unduly to attract the eye which I think it does in the strong light of day, it is indeed a gorgeous monument."*

Thursday, 26th March 1846

*"He heard Dr. Reid seems to have been made to confess that in almost every case when he has applied his system he has been unfortunate or unssuccessful...*

*There is an article in this morning's Quarterly Review quizzing Reid and his whole system, indeed all things seem tending to the inevitable conclusion of his humbug and incompetency."*

Tuesday, 31st March 1846

*"The House of Lords at a standstill for Dr. Reid. The House of Commons nearly up to the wall plate, Palace Yard Front to top of second floor windows and the works generally active."*

Thursday, 2nd April 1846

*"Went up today for father with Mr. Quarm to Thames Bank to... the state of preparation of the joinery fittings, more particularly for the House of Peers and its adjuncts. An address has been moved in the House of Peers by the Chairman of the Committee on progress, Lord Clanricarde to Her Majesty praying her to issue orders that the works beb forthwith completed. This was opposed by Lord Canning, Chief Commissioner of Woods, etc., on the plea that it was interfering with Government in dealing with its servants, and by the Duke of Wellington on the same ground. The Duke at the same time advising that the question be dropped as it was the intention of Government to adopt immediate measures to expedite the business - the motion was dropped and a message sent to the Commons... there the matter rests till after Easter. Anyway there will certainly be a great pressure this year to get much of the woodworks belonging to the Peers House... fixed... To do this will require great energy and I will give my constant efforts to attain this end. Quarm also is full of the necessity of acting promptly..."*

Thursday, 5th April 1846

*"After breakfast today father called Alfred and me into his rooms and intimated to us that he had been compelled by a train of events to contemplate the probability of his taking a very extreme course and one that would probably materially influence our future prospects viz his resignation of his post as the architect to the New Palace at Westminster. He had, he said, been driven ... to this in consequence of what took place yesterday - Lord Canning, the Chief Commissioner, had summoned both him and Dr. Reid at the same hour and confronted them both which was neither considerate nor courteous as they had as he knew not...met for long and he had told them both: "that the Government could not suffer any further delay in consequence of their disagreement and that unless they could either separately or conjointly by Monday submit a proposition by which they could act together it would become his duty to take steps for the future expedition of the work that would be disagreeable to both." Father said that if this (as he thought it did) meant that the Government expected him to again act with Dr. Reid on the old footing he could not, nor would not consent but would immediately resign...*

Friday, 17th April 1846

*"The Government have resolved to appoint a tribunal with unlimited powers to deal with summarily any point at issue between father and Dr. Reid connected with ventilation etc....committee rooms on second floor, river front, being fitted up temporarily. ... and lighted thoroughly, having fitted up temporarily and the walls and ceilings, arches white washed and the windows filled with thick square sashes, floors laid down rough. It will not do to make them too comfortable and handsome as they will with difficulty give them up ..."*

Monday, 2nd June 1846

*"... Made arrangements for curing the smoking propensities of many of the rooms they smoke as consequence of Quarms want of judgment in taking the smoke of twenty flues 9 by 14 into void horizontally 14 by 14. They must all have separate vents. I think it is Quarms characteristic and I do not think it was a well judged step to make him anything but a Clerk of Works; in that he was excellent. But he is rather above himself now, as I fear."*

24th June 1846

*"Dined alone with father at six. He has attended what will probably be the final meeting of the Lords Committee on the new Palace and building, and they have indicated... to him orders to proceed immediately with fitting up permanently the House of Lords for next session (independently) entirely of the doctor. This is glorious news and father is of course delighted."*

7th July 1846

*"The report of the referees Hardwick, Stephenson and Graham appears in today's Times and a pretty strong report against Reid. They declare that his system is non-scientific, requiring too much attention, that though possibly practicable, it is by no means advisable, that it is incompatible with a fire proof building and that they recommend that when much modified it should only be applied to the Houses proper... This is very good and as the Peers have already turned the doctor out of their House and libraries, there will nothing be left for him but the Commons House and its adjuncts..."*

Monday, 31st August 1846

*"Went to Cheadle with Pugin to see his new Roman Catholic Church there."*

Monday, 21st September 1846

*"Up at seven and this is my twenty-third birthday. A solemn reflection it is that I have been thus long in the world and have already so much time to account for. Father being in better spirits - to enjoy the day - returned at eight to see an experimental lighting by gas of the new House of Peers. It looks very grand and the colours appear even better by artificial light than by daylight. Mr. Dyce's fresco also shows very well and proves the superiority of fresco over oil painting or such mural decorations - bed at eleven."*

Saturday, 26th September 1846

*"Went at 9.00 with Mr. Wolfe, father and Alfred, to see a further trial of lighting re House of Peers - came to the decided conclusion that if it is possible to get light enough it is far the most agreeable mode to have it chiefly from above or about half the entire height or twenty feet from the floor. Two standard candelabra will necessarily be required at the sides of the Throne to light it as with its projecting canopies it will appear a dark mass if all the light is above it. The House looks as well if not better by artificial than it does by daylight. Tried experiments as to its excellencies for hearing and speaking most satisfactory to be heard plainly from one end to the other is no effort to the speaker."*

The height of the chandeliers in the Lords Chamber was

altered for the purpose of permanent television lighting in 1986. At the same time the size of the pendant glass globes was enlarged and the power of the bulbs within them increased. The chandeliers were "skyed" to give a better view of the frescoes. The great chandelier in the Central Lobby was also "skyed" to give a better view of the indifferent mosaics placed therein, but it was lowered to a more reasonable level in the 1970s.

Tuesday, 29th September 1846

*"Father, Mr. Wolfe and I went at nine to see a further experimental lighting of House of Peers. Double the number of burners... that there were last time but certainly without producing twice the lighting effect - I think however there was...enough light. The burners were disposed thus: (here a little sketch), the actual place being a portion of the Gallery framing and the niche between windows. The effect was I think too scattered. The two branches did not seem to make...as was intended... Father however saw enough to come to his determination."*

This system of lighting is clearly shown in the Joseph Nash watercolour. The effect was spectacular, the glare considerable and the heat intolerable.

It was not long before these lights, which also existed in the Prince's Chamber, were replaced by a different system of lighting suspended from the ceiling, shown in another view by Joseph Nash. It was this system, compounding the damage already done by the previous arrangement, that roasted the ceiling. The use of the space above as a route for the escape of heated effluvia of various kinds so damaged the ceiling that by the 1980s much of its structure was approaching disintegration. 15

Monday, 5th October 1846

*"Went with Edward who commences his professional life today to Mr. Wayatt, the new master, to see him started..."*

Saturday, 17th October 1846

*"Again engaged preparing work for father to take to Ramsgate for the fittings of the House of Commons which is now in hand there. He left for Ramsgate at four and a half."*

Wednesday, 21st October 1846

*"Attended morning service at the Abbey...Called at Thames Bank to put in hand the corridor ceilings alterations at NHP."*

Sunday, 25th October 1846

*"Ramsgate, a most miserable day - cold, windy and perpetual rain. Attended Morning Devotion at St. George's Church with mother, Emily and Edward. Prayers, very properly read by Curate, and we had an excellent sermon...from the Vicar, Mr. Harcey, but this last was much spoilt by an unnatural voice which the poor man has and which he strains to a painful degree... The building built some years since by Mr. Kendall and by him styled Gothic is below criticism, is in fact execrable - went on the pier between the showers in the afternoon and saw various vessels towed in, in distress, by the harbour steam tugs. A vessel was washed on the pier head last week and three of the crew out of five were drowned - they were Frenchmen and Roman Catholics. Therefore Mr. Pugin whose house is on the cliff above with the bodies washing ashore gave them burial with all the solemnities of the Roman Church in the cloister attached to the church he is erecting close to his house. This was very generous and at the time politic of him and created great sensation in the place. Dined at five and mother gave us some music in the evening."*

Monday, 26th October 1846

*"Ramsgate. Caught a severe cold yesterday on the pier in the wet...*

*Visited Mr. Pugin in his true Gothic house built by himself on the cliff above the town. A complete survival it is of the old Gothic gentleman's house, unique and complete in all its appointments. Uninviting and indeed I think ugly outside, but inside quite correct. Rooms all lined with wood, low ribbed wood ceilings, painted in heraldry, old quaint stone emblazened chimney pieces, bay windows, deep window recesses, and fine window drapery. Wallpaper above the wainscoat all has been made on purpose and is characteristic and good in effect. His living rooms consist of a small but quaint hall, parlour, library, dining-room, with a fine projecting chimney piece and chimney corner seats and a small but tasteful chapel with all the decorations and appointments belonging to the Romish ritual - this is only for domestic prayers - there is a tower attached to the house from the top of which the French coast and a long sweep of the English shore can be clearly seen. He is building just detached from the house but close to it a school, church, ecclesiastical library with cloister, and priest house all in good keeping all at his own expense...May God stir up a like spirit among us also and prompt us to offer him freely of our substance for His honour, and thus pray to the knowledge of Him in this world. Dined at six, my cold being very troublesome, retired early...*

*Perhaps also God may allow my eyes to be cured before long when I shall be better able to attend to work."*

Saturday, 21st November 1846

*"At Westminster at nine. Found poor father terribly annoyed and cut up by a letter received from Lord Morpeth saying that he thought that Reid must be again let in to ventilate the House of Commons in which he had many friends and much favour. I had really hoped that he had been dismissed finally, and it is this finding that he cannot depend on the action of the Government being final that disturbs father so much. He did not sleep all night for thinking of it. He feels I fear inclined to bring matters to an issue by being firm in his expressed determination to give up rather than work with Reid. This I trust he will not do... I therefore hope that father may really be induced to consider the possibility of letting Reid have the House of Commons... Making stipulation however that some third person of real science and common-sense (which the Doctor either has not or will not show) in whom both father and Reid shall have confidence, shall be appointed by Government to communicate wth both parties if such a one can be found..."*

Monday, 23rd November 1846

*"Father is happily I find inclined to make matters sweet if possible with respect to Dr. Reid - with Lord Morpeth's wishes but will strongly protest against his being admitted on his former footing at the works."*

Wednesday, 25th November 1846

*"He set off to visit Sir Robert Peel by invitation for a few days at Drayton Manor. Took with him various subjects of interest to the public and him, the Horseguards designs, those for Westminster Bridge, Wellington's statue pedestal, Record Office and Law Courts, etc. Continues that day with discussions with Professor Faraday over*

*ventilation at new House of Lords and the lighting - he trusts far more to the action of gravity for inducing a circulation of air in the House. The entry air being colder and heavier than that going out...He approves of the whole apparatus fully theoretically and believes it will be successful practically."*

Sir Robert Peel (Prime Minister from 1834 - 1835 and from 1841-1846) was, over many years, a steadfast and influential supporter of Charles Barry. Lord Palmerston (Prime Minister 1855-1858 and 1859-1865) carefully distanced himself from controversy over the New Palace. Benjamin Disraeli (Prime Minister 1852, 1858-1859, 1866-1868, 1874-1880) although a member of the circle who had embarked upon the great Gothic Adventure could not resist the opportunity to make witty speeches and writings at the architect's expense.

Thursday, 17th December 1846

*"Went to the works. Much has been done in my short absence towards fitting the House for the Peers' next session. Discovered with some anxiety the cracks indicating a settlement which has lately caused anxieties to father and well it may be so. They are in the south return over the archway out of the Royal Court southward...breaking all stones in the way and string course, ashlar, the parapet, ...I fear Mr. Wolfe's hypothesis of the cause is the true one. Appears that the weight of the great Tower drags the building attached with it and this is most serious as the Tower is not a quarter of its... height and the heaviest part is that to come,...Why was the Tower bonded with the building and not allowed to settle if it would?...*

*... the cracks in the south return, they are indeed most serious and doubly so if the Tower be the cause. I am half induced to fancy and hope that they are really due to the fact that a part of th is south front, including the Tower form part of the present contract, and whereas that part towards the east was in another contract so there were two years difference in the two foundations."*

*"Goodbye 1846. Evening passed reading aloud Dombey & Sons, No. 2."*

Friday, 1st January 1847

*"Up at seven and a half. A happy new year to all dear to me and praise to God for all His blessings past and present."*

Saturday, 23rd January 1847

*"At 2 :00 p.m. went with Emily and Caroline Green to see the Queen's chair for the Throne in the new House of Lords, making at Webbs, Bond Street. It is most gorgeous and satisfactory. The chair ... too for Prince Albert and the Prince of Wales are very fine. They are beautifully made."*

Thursday, 4th February 1847

*"Called on Vulliamy as to NHP clocks..."*

Tuesday, 2nd March 1847

*"Mr. Claudit called on me at half past nine and we went over the works of the New Palace together chiefly with the intention of selecting spots from which Daguerreotype views might be taken. He was much struck with what he saw and thought that many most excellent pictures might be made.*

*He was most civil to me, advising me to practise for my purpose with the Talbot type, not the Daguerreotype and offering to teach me everything."*

Wednesday, 3rd March 1847

*"Accompanied Cust and friends to House of Lords. Visited Thomas's studio to see my marble font. It is coming out beautifully. Called on Mr. Page and obtained the tracings of Emperor's views of front NHP which he ought to have returned long since."*

Tsar Nicholas I called the new Palace *un rêve en pierre* when he was shown round the incomplete building by Charles Barry in June 1844. As a result of this historic occasion, Barry presented the Tsar with a principal floor plan, a small group of architectural details for the River Front and two watercolours by Thomas Allom. These were sent to St. Petersburg where they have remained ever since. They were recently tracked down by the combined researches of Mrs. Alexandra Wedgwood and Mr. Richard Ware of the House of Commons Library. Mrs Wedgwood travelled to Leningrad to see the Tsar's drawings. Photographs of the watercolours may be seen at the House of Lords Record Office. On the occasion of the visit to Westminster by Mikhail Gorbachev, Mr. Speaker Weatherill mentioned the Tsar's drawings to him and permission was later granted for the reproduction of the watercolours in this book.

The watercolours show a dramatic Central Tower such as might have been required for Dr. Reid's more extravagant ventilating processes. The Clock Tower appears in two different guises, neither of which were executed. Charles Barry's proposed enclosure of New Palace Yard with its great gateway is also clearly visible.

Wednesday, 10th March 1847

*"At work all day preparing sections of House of Lords to assist Faraday in his intended lecture at Royal Institution on the ventilation."*

Wednesday, 14th April 1847

*"I cannot keep my journal regularly. All this week I am so much taken up with preparations for my departure for Italy that I have time for nothing else. During the Easter Parliamentary recess the arrangements have all been made for the occupation of the new House of Lords tomorrow but without any ceremony. The day after the adjournment of the House, Tuesday before Easter, the old House was completely gutted leaving only the bare walls and ceiling and all is now refurnished as a temporary access to the new House.*

*The new House is gorgeous in the extreme and marvellous and really comfortable with all its magnificence - when lighted up it like a fairy dream and is well described in the terms which have been applied to it. "Stone and wood music" the Queen and Prince Albert came this morning incognito and were shown all things by father. She was evidently much pleased and was very affable. She stayed 1 1/4 hours. All is now finished for tomorrow's opening."*

Thursday, 15th April 1847

*"The House of Lords was open for business this day at 4 o'clock and many were the tones and characters of admiring phrases applied to it, albeit there was also many objections and cavilling. However, what seems most important, indeed serious, is that the voice is not apparently well heard in the vast size of the place, many of the speakers being very indistinctly heard. There was moreover such an intolerable row and talking below the Bar and at the throne that the wonder was that any could be heard. Nevertheless, the governor was much vexed and made himself rather miserable in the evening..."*

Source: House of Lords Record Office, reproduced by kind permission of Mrs P. B. Stanley-Evans.

# Appendix D: Mr. Goldsworthy Gurney's Report on the ventilation of the House of Commons (1852)

In obedience to the Order of your Honourable House, dated the 12th day of March 1852, I beg to Report, That I am investigating the arrangements for the warming, ventilating, and lighting the New House of Commons; and, having been given to understand by several Members that it would be acceptable to The House that I should make a First Report on the state of the Ventilation as early as possible, I beg further to Report as follows:

That, although I have been interrupted in my investigations, and thereby prevented from making them as full and complete as I could have wished, I have seen sufficient to satisfy myself of the causes of the great inconvenience experienced at this moment.

That I find the atmosphere of the House in a dessicated and oppressive state, and subject to constant disturbance from initial and retrograde currents passing in all directions, as if at random, and apparently without control, producing direct draughts in particular parts of the House, and oppression in others. I also find that from the same want of proper control, offensive vapours and effluvia (emanating from contaminated sources) are drawn into the House.

That most of these evils can be corrected by a simple arrangement, and at an expense comparatively trivial, and although this is a common-sense question, yet it would be difficult to demonstrate it on paper unaccompanied by actual experiment, or to explain the facts and conditions on which this conclusion is arrived at. And inasmuch as on former occasions an unfair advantage has, I think, been taken of the statements and evidence which I have given from time to time, and portions of my plans have been adopted without consulting me, I am induced to ask permission to refrain from entering into details at present.

The principles of ventilation which have been recommended by me, and, to the best of my belief, acted upon in the Chamber of Deputies at Paris, and now in operation in the Courts of Exchequer and Commons Pleas in Westminster Hall (which courts were previously unsatisfactorily ventilated by a similar arrangement to that now applied to this House), and their success in every Court of Judicature, and other places in the provinces to which they have been extended, afford sufficient evidence (in addition to what I have seen in this House) to justify me in saying, that if the House be placed under the control of the Office of Works for a short time, I would pledge myself, with their assistance, to remove all the material evils that at present exist, at a very trifling expense; and at the expiration of such control, to restore the ventilation, if required, to its present state, within the space of a few hours.

Of course it will be understood that this Report applies only to the House itself, and not to the entire building.

GOLDSWORTHY GURNEY

5 April 1852

# Appendix E: Mr. William Molesworth's Report on the ventilation and lighting of the House of Commons (1853)

The Committee reports, that the alterations that have been made in the mode of ventilating the House have been in accordance with a Report presented to the Board of Works by Mr. Meeson, and have had the cognizance and sanction of the Committee. They consist principally in covering with lead that portion of the perforated floor which is usually walked upon, to prevent dust being carried upwards, and to obviate also the inconvenience felt from currents of air; in substituting openings for free admission of air in all available positions in the risers of steps and gangways; in cleansing, raising, and putting in good order the air channels or the vaults, &c.; in fixing screens for purifying and moistening the air; in laying on water, and making arrangements for washing, moistening and cooling the channels and chambers; in examining and cleansing the drains; in improving and putting in order the steam-boilers, and the apparatus connected therewith; and in making provision for a certain supply of air from the ceiling.

The ventilation of the House has been interfered with during the progress of the alterations required for the introduction of the system of lighting of Mr. Gurney, and much dust has necessarily been made by workmen constantly employed nearly up to the hour of The House meeting.

The Lighting of Dr. Reid has been removed, and the present system substituted by Mr. Gurney, under the direction of the Chief Commissioner.

Members of the House will be competent to judge of the quality of the Lighting; but there are other considerations connected with this part of the subject, viz., the heat produced by the combustion of so large a quantity of gas as is required to attain the transmission of sufficient light through the ground-glass panels, the effect of the heat on the House by radiation downwards from the roof, and also on the ventilating arrangments, which will have the careful attention of the Committee.

The charge of the Lighting and Ventilation is now entirely under the control of Mr. Meeson, but he is not empowered to make any alterations in the arrangements without the sanction of the Chief Commissioner of Works.

WILLIAM MOLESWORTH
(Chairman)

# Appendix F: A description of the Maclise Frescoes in the Royal Gallery

1. *Interview Between Wellington and Blücher After the Battle of Waterloo (Fresco by D. Maclise Esq., R.A.)*

This picture is executed upon one of the large compartments, which are forty feet long, of the Royal Gallery in the Palace of Westminster. Nearly in the centre of the work is placed the Duke, mounted upon his horse, Copenhagen; Blucher, also mounted, grasps the hand of Wellington with characteristic force and fervour, his eager, resolute face, with his grizzled moustache, his grey hair and keen grey eyes hard, strong and grim - show beneath the Prussian travelling cap he wears. He has just moved his horse to go, and yet again pulls him up to clasp the victor's hand, whose work he is now about to finish; for it has been settled between the Generals that the pursuit should be taken up by the Prussians, while the tired and war-worn English rested upon the field of battle. Tired and war-worn is the Duke; calmer, more resolute and still than the demonstrative Prussian. The composition forms itself in great masses, very skilfully designed to emphasize this central group of the Duke and General, and, without obviously declaring the art employed to that end, resolving itself into sections which are subservient to a grand whole. We see along the back of the picture the English cavalry pursuing the artillery and waggon-train down a hill and upon its rising crest. Immediately behind the heads of the Generals is the name of the inn, "La Belle Alliance", appropriately written upon a board fixed against the side of the house. The ruined roof, the torn walls, the slow wreaths of smoke that rise through the denuded rafters, the deserted dove-house, whose inmates the war has frightened away, are all signs of the havoc that has been going on, and even yet not ceased as the flying artillery shows.

Like two wings of the composition, on either side of the Generals is grouped the Staff of each. On the Prussian side, next to Blucher, ride Gneisneau, the commander to whom the pursuit was given, with white plumes in his hat, Nostitz, Bulow - an old, yellow man, in a blue coat loaded with orders, - Zeithen, and others; amongst them a Brunswick officer, with the skull and cross-bones on his shako, and nearest to the front, mounted upon a magnificent white horse, rides Sir Hussey Vivian (Lord Vivian) in a hussar's dress. On the Duke's side is a group of officers, few, indeed, of note, seeing that most of the heroes of the fight had been rendered *hors de combat* before the meeting took place. Just behind the Duke are General Somerset and Lord Arthur Hill (Lord Sandys), and between them is seen the face of the Hon. Henry Percy, who bore home the despatches and the captured eagles. A few of the 2nd Life Guards and the Royal Horse Guards Blue, in the blue or red uniforms of each corps, such as the fortunes of the day had left in their saddles, to form the Duke's escort, make up this wing of the composition. Some of them cheer, waving their sabres; one bears an eagle, and another the shot-torn banner of his regiment. The shakos, helmets and bearskins worn by each body respectively, have been grouped and got together by the artist with wonderful skill, so that they fall into harmonious masses of fine composition.

No part of this extraordinary picture deserves more unqualified admiration than the grouping of the horses, with the immense variety of their actions and even their expressions. Solid, alive, vital, as it were equine, and magnificently drawn and grouped are these animals. The steed Blucher is mounted upon is full of the fire of his fierce master, and seems bent upon dashing off. Wellington's famous animal, Copenhagen, stands with gingerly delicacy and grace amongst the slain; his glossy flank seems to twitch and his grave eye to look commiseratingly about. Hardly inferior to these are the black horses of the English Guards, which form a mass of solid colour gravely contrasting with the lighter bays mounting the Prussians on the other side, to which last the most magnificently painted white horse ridden by General Vivian forms a luminous central point of brilliant colour that will win the admiration and delight of every spectator.

This horse of General Vivian's is a very important element of the composition, not only by centralizing and illuminating the whole of that side of the composition by its colour and brilliant treatment, but by its action connecting the upper group of riders with the line of wounded and slain men lying upon the ground athwart the front of the picutre. The animal snuffs at the face of a Carabineer, whose breath has gone for ever. Beside this Carabineer lies a wounded Englishman; next is a French Cuirassier, and then a Highlander, who, having been wounded in the arm, has had a tourniquet applied to it. He is a piper, and has blown his instrument with his last breath; for the surgeon, who left the tourniquet upon his limb, will find, indeed, more pressing cases to attend to, seeing that he has gone beyond the reach of human ministration. There he is left, with outstretched arms and fingers strained and rigid; beside him, fallen from his grasp, lie the pipes he will never blow more, and the steel-hilted claymore that failed to save him from the winged Death. Above are two Irishmen frantically cheering their victorious countryman the Duke, and waving their caps; these are Connaught Rangers. Next, beyond this, is a group about a captured gun, over which lies a French Artillery officer's body, just as he died to defend his command, and a Cuirassier dead upon the ground before the muzzle; the gun-carriage has been shattered, and the gun itself indented by English shot. Below lies an English colour-sergeant, disabled by a wound in his leg, which a hospital orderly bandages up. This is an Englishman; and his face, confessing but not succumbing to pain, is finely expressive.

On the other side of the composition, behind the Duke, are several groups; a Highlander, a Foot-guard and a Fusilier carry of the body of a youth of twenty-two years of age: - this is the "young, gallant Howard", mentioned with grief by Byron. He has been struck down just at the end of the battle, and leaves a young widow and unborn child to mourn the terrible war. The faces of his attendants, full of tender commiseration, are perfectly expressive and apt. Upon the ground lies an English General Officer, wounded in the breast, attended by a Light Dragoon, a Foot-guard and a drummer. Nearer the centre, three of the Life Guards, whose contorted faces show the pain the effort costs them, brandish their sabres and cheer. Their trumpeter lies dead in the front, his silver instrument battered by a musket ball, its embroidered, beard-like banner across his knees. Quite in the centre, and seen between the horse's legs, lie more of the wounded and the dead. Removed from this, and at the extreme left of the picture, is the wounded white horse of a Cuirassier, vainly striving to rise from under his master's body, which thrown almost from the saddle, lies athwart the carcass of another horse, whose eyes are just glazing in death. Against the margin of the picture lies a tall Enniskillen Dragoon, badly wounded, his helmet off, attended by a comrade. On a gun above these lies a dying Hanoverian, to whose lips a priest holds the crucifix, with wondrous earnestness of expression, - a companion holds up the heavy head. A Sister of Mercy and a Vivandiere regard the scene; the last, hardened but commiserating, holds a glass of spirits for the dying man, taken from her barrel. Behind her and upon the frame of the gun is placed a knapsack filled with crosses, jewels and gew-gaws torn from the slain; these a round-headed infant, the woman's child, plays with. All about the field are scattered arms, stove-in drums, broken musical instruments, spentshot and shattered shell.

Source: *The Anthenaeum* 2 November 1861, pp. 585-6.

2. *The Death of Nelson (by D. Maclise Esq., R. A.)*

In this picture Mr. Maclise has cast himself as wholly and heartily into his naval task as he did into that with the military theme. The scale of both, life-size, on a space of forty-five feet long by twelve-feet high, is the same; they form the largest single portions of the wall-pictures to be produced by him in the Royal Gallery - a hall set apart for his hands alone to decorate. Anxious as before to produce a permanent and eminently characteristic record of the scenes, the painter has not only availed himself of existing portraits of men engaged in the battles, but studied and portrayed every detail of manners, costume and arms of the period in question. So happily has he done this, and so vigorous are the pictures, that their subjects and motives impress the spectator before he learns that such and such were the buttons, plumes and head-dresses of the one, or the guns, rigging, pigtails and cutlasses of the other. An artist recognises in both that admirable generalisation which is consistent with the utmost elaboration of detail; and while it renders the number on a soldier's button, gives the texture, lustre and minutest character of the thing, even to those on its stamped ornamentation, yet does not make the same distinct in the picture. To deal with the masses of blue supplied by the sailors' dresses in the new subject has been a difficulty far beyond that of the red coats of the former one. Mr. Maclise has hardly been recognised as a colourist; indeed, excepting some phases in the "Hamlet", he has seldom aimed at that quality. In "The Death of Nelson", the very difficulty referred to has stimulated him to an unwonted success, and, considering, the whole nature of the task, no one will deny its value herein.

Mindful of the architectonic character of his task, the artist has placed his principal incident in the centre of his picture, and ably led the eye to that point by its colour, and giving a strong note of white in the lower part of Nelson's dress, in contrast with his deep blue coat. Not less guiding the eye to the same point is the concentration of the action of the principal group upon the wounded hero, who, half-raised from the deck, and supported in the lap and arms of Captain Hardy, lies back, with an expression of subdued suffering; while the surgeon, Dr. Beattie, heedfully raises the right arm of his patient, for it was on that side he was wounded, and, with his own disengaged hand, approaches the hole the ball has made in the upper part of the coat-breast. The lower limbs of Nelson are drawn up on the deck, his empty coat-sleeve buttoned up in the usual way. Between the surgeon's and Nelson's faces appears the handsome countenance of a Lieutenant of Marines, named Ram, who was present on the occasion, and seems here full of anxious grief.

Nelson, just before dying, asked, "How many flags have we taken, Hardy?" Mr. Maclise has followed the suggestion thus given, and placed a sailor in the fore part of this group, supposed to have come towards the Admiral at the moment before he fell, bearing the ensign of a captured ship. This man kneels, his glorious charge forgotten in view of the stricken commander's danger; his face, no less than those before mentioned, is admirably wrought. Around the group thus described, a host of minor incidents appear. The bustle and uproar of a battle, at sea even more than on land, cause some occurrences within arm's reach to be beyond notice, while others, more distant, to which attention is driven, are potent to interest. News at such a time does not always travel swiftly; at Trafalgar it was not until the end of the action that Nelson's fall was known through the ship; he himself, when carried below, spread his handkerchief over the orders on his coat, hiding them so far as possible to conceal the fact. Availing himself of this slow spread of news, the artist has shown us, in the double-ranked men forming a gun's crew in the background, one who has seen the event heedfully speaking behind his hand to his next comrade, and telling the secret the officers strove to hide: the next, or third, of this rank, a stolid fellow, has seen nothing, and thinks of nothing, but waits, with folded arms, for the word of command to haul the cannon inboard, after the discharge. The captain of the piece sights along its tube, taking aim, and, with stooping back, notes his mark in the near side of the *Redoutable,* the *Victory's* antagonist.

Nelson fell on the spot of the *Victory's* deck which is now marked with a brass plate. Mr Maclise proved that, by an odd coincidence, his finished pictures and the actual deck so marked are identical in size. Thus, six feet from the marked spot is the ship's companion-way or ladder leading below: such will be the distance in the picture from the same opening, down which two sailors, naked to the waist, and full of earnest care for a younger wounded comrade, are carrying him. The elder man's face, showing him old enough to be father to the poor fellow, is a perfect study of expression, very moving to the spectator in its honest sorrow that does not weep. This incident occurs a little to the spectator's left, and consequently, nearer the bow of the ship than the place of Nelson's fall. Immediately behind it stand the crew of a gun at their quarters, three on each side, its captain on the left: thus near, these men have seen the Admiral wounded; but true in discipline, they keep their posts, with diverse expressions of emotion. Nothing can exceed the variety in this quality the picture shows. The artist is a master of expression, and so felicitous in dealing with it that nowhere do we get the slightest stain of melodrama or attitudinizing, although the circumstances might well lead ordinary designers into those follies. It is impossible to look at the crews of the above-mentioned guns, still less at that which appears still further on our right, and fail to admire the power shown in rendering many personalities and varieties of human expressions among individuals of one common class engaged in a common office.

Between the two guns spoken of is seen a naked negro pointing out to a marine the man of the *Redoutable* who shot the Admiral; the soldier takes aim with his musket at him. Next to these going forward, come two marine officers looking through telescopes for signals from some other ship of the English Fleet. Returning aft now, we come upon the steps that lead to the poop, ascending and descending which are marines and soldiers, some bearing wounded men. Upon the poop deck itself is, with others, the young midshipman who shot the Admiral's slayer; the last being a mizen-top man of the *Redoutable.* It is related that the English sharpshooters during the rest of the fight kept their eyes so effectually on this part of the enemy's rigging that none came down alive, and of those that did not attempt to descend the whole were slain; some of their bodies hung, arms and heads downwards, over the sides of their little stronghold. The midshipman with eager face watches among the knot of French sailors for his man.

Seen under this poop as a gallery is the covered part of the quarter deck, and just beneath the last-named group is a third gun and its crew, the captain of which pulls the lanyard or string of its flint lock, with the true professional upward jerk of his fist. An incident so apparently barren of interest as this of a gun's discharge, has been rendered peculiarly effective by the genius, skill and care of the artist. The men keep their ranks, some quite at home and indifferent, some interested but steady; one, a stalwart fair faced youth in his first battle, leans a little forward to watch through the port-hole the effect of the shot. Mindful of what we said respecting the artist's heedful study of costume, let us here exemplify its working. It was thought that the carronades of Nelson's time had long ago been melted into new fashions, but after much search one was discovered in some half-forgotten corner of the dockyard, furbished-up, re-fitted with its proper breaching or rope tackle, its appropriate flint lock and carriage; this Mr Maclise has painted most heedfully, and the thing is a record for all time of singular interest. Many things have become quite obsolete since the great Admiral's day; before the use of percussion caps flint locks for cannon vanished, with them the horn of priming powder the captain of each gun wore slung by a belt across his body. Flint-locks were very fallible, and in the hurry of action not easily got to rights; on such failures, a common fuse was employed, for safety in using which each gun was furnished with a bucket, full of water, and fitted with a perforated cover, into which the burning end of the fuse could be placed after use in discharging the piece. With powder and cartridges about, and magazines open, such precautions were essential. Such a bucket stands here at the breech of this gun. Round about are many old-fashioned weapons, chain-shot, shot neatly bound up with rope to form the fearful grape, ramrods, sponges, screws, handspikes etc. Facing us, and as if drawn inboard from the port side of the ship on which we stand, is a gun being sponged out by its crew; the captain, a weather-beaten fellow, strong and rough as a north-easter, stands with his thumb on the vent; a rosy, but powder-smirched boy, all heedless of death, runs along with a cartridge for this piece in his arms.

Proceeding now to the other end of the picture, passing the wounded Nelson and his friends, we come upon various excellently portrayed groups. A man, shot in the chest, is tended by comrades; one staunches the blood, - another, an old negro with a red handkerchief round his head, brings brandy in a glass. More to the right of these (forward) are three sailors mightily pulling on the main-topsail halyard, with the purpose of clearing the rigging of falling spars or ropes. Across the deck and on the bulwarks are the hammock nettings, forming a sort of fortress of ropes and iron stanchions lined with the men's bedding, within which much of the work of a ship in action and all the scene before us takes place. Here are more men, living, wounded, and dead. Thus far we have described the human element of this noble picture. Alongside of Nelson's ship are visible the three masts of the *Redoutable.* Showing beyond the rigging of both ships entangled with and borne aloft by that of the *Victory,* is an upper yard, with its sail attached, of her antagonist. Shot away, and thundering down upon her deck, is one of the Frenchman's masts, its head and top.

Source: *The Athenaeum* 7 March 1863, pp. 335-6.

# Appendix G: Statement of expenditure on the works of art in the Palace of Westminster 1862-1900 (1907)

| Work | | 1863-4. | 1864-5. | 1865-6. | 1866-7. | 1867-8. | 1868-9. | 1869-70. | 1871-2. | 1879-80. | 1898-9. | 1899-00. | Total |
|---|---|---|---|---|---|---|---|---|---|---|---|---|---|
| | | £ | £ | £ | £ | £ | £ | £ | £ | £ | £ | £ | £ |
| * Statues of Monarchs | Charles I. (Thornycroft) | 400 | – | 400 | – | – | – | – | – | – | – | – | 400 |
| | Charles II. (Weekes) | – | – | – | – | – | – | – | – | – | – | – | 400 |
| | James I. (Thornycroft) | 400 | – | – | – | – | – | – | – | – | – | – | 400 |
| | Mary II. (Munro) | 400 | – | – | – | – | 400 | – | – | – | – | – | 800 |
| | William III. (Wollner) | 400 | – | – | 400 | – | – | – | – | – | – | – | 800 |
| | George IV. (Theed) | – | – | – | 400 | – | – | – | – | – | – | – | 400 |
| | William IV. (Theed) | – | – | – | 400 | – | – | – | – | – | – | – | 400 |
| * Moses descending with the Tables of Law to the Israelites. (Herbert) | | 1,300 | 1,500 | – | – | – | – | – | – | – | – | 4,300 | |
| * Expulsion of the Fellows of a College of Oxford. (Cope) | | 300 | – | – | – | – | – | – | – | – | – | – | 300 |
| * Landing of Charles II. at Dover. (Ward.) | | 300 | – | – | – | – | – | – | – | – | – | – | 300 |
| * Train Bands of London setting out to relieve Gloucester. (Cope.) | | – | – | 400 | – | – | – | – | – | – | – | – | 400 |
| * Death of Nelson. (Maclise.) | | – | – | 3,250 | – | – | – | – | – | – | – | – | 3,250 |
| * Speaker Lenthall asserting the Privileges of the House of commons. (Cope.) | | – | – | – | †1,300 | – | – | – | – | – | – | – | 1,300 |
| Battle of Ascalon. (Marochette.) Bas Relief. Statue of Richard Cœur de Lion | | – | – | – | 750 | – | – | – | – | – | – | – | 750 |
| * Acquittal of the Seven Bishops. (Ward.) | | – | – | – | 600 | ††800 | – | – | – | – | – | – | 1,400 |
| * Judgment of Daniel. (Herbert.) | | – | – | – | – | 1,000 | 1,000 | – | – | 1,000 | – | – | 3,000 |
| * Monk declaring for a Free Parliament. (Ward.) | | – | – | – | – | 600 | – | – | – | – | – | – | 600 |
| * Lords, &c., presenting the Crown to William and Mary. (Ward.) | | – | – | – | – | 600 | – | – | – | – | – | – | 600 |
| * Meeting of Wellington and Blucher. (Maclise.) | | – | – | – | – | – | 1,500 | – | – | – | – | – | 1,500 |
| "St. George." Mosaic in the Central Hall. (Poynter.) | | – | – | – | – | – | – | 665 | – | – | – | – | 665 |
| "St. David." Mosaic in the Central Hall. (Poynter.) | | – | – | – | – | – | – | – | – | – | 924 | 3 | 927 |
| Renovation and repair of Frescoes | | 158 | 195 | 193 | 199 | 374 | 75 | 31 | 68 | – | – | – | 1,293 |
| | | 3,658 | 1,695 | 5,743 | 4,049 | 3,374 | 2,975 | 696 | 68 | 1,000 | 924 | 3 | 24,185 |

* These works, though completed and paid for subsequently, were executed under agreements concluded previously to the dissolution of the Fine Arts Commission.
† This amount also includes balance for completion of seven other pictures.
†† This amount also includes balance for completion of eight pictures.
Source: Report from the Select Committee of the House of Lords (1907).

# Appendix H: The gifts of the Commonwealth (1950)

Aden - Members' Writing Room table. Australia - Speaker's Chair in Australian black bean. Bahamas - Minister's writing desk and chair. Barbados - Minister's writing desk and chair. Bermuda - Two triple silver gilt inkstands. Botswana - One silver gilt ashtray. British Honduras - Minister's writing desk and chair and Royal Coat of Arms. Canada - Table of the House in Canadian oak. Ceylon - Serjeant-at-Arms's chair. Cyprus - Member's Writing Room table. Dominica - One silver gilt inkstand. Falkland Islands - One silver gilt ashtray. Fiji - One silver gilt inkstand. The Gambia - Two silver gilt inkstands. Ghana - Minister's writing desk and chair. Gilbraltar - Two oak table lamps with bronze shades. Grenada - One silver gilt inkstand. Guernsey - Minister's writing desk and three chairs. Guyana - Four triple silver gilt inkstands. Hong Kong - One triple silver gilt inkstand. India - Entrance doors to Chamber. Isle of Man - One silver gilt inkstand and two silver gilt ashtrays for Prime Minister's Conference Room. Jamaica - Bar of the House in bronze. Jersey - Minister's writing desk and chair and silver gilt inkstand. Kenya - Minister's writing desk and chair. Leeward Islands - Six oak table lamps with bronze shades. Lesotho - Two silver gilt ashtrays. Malawi - One triple silver gilt inkstand and one silver gilt ashtray. Malta - Three silver gilt ashtrays. Mauritius - Minister's writing desk and chair. Newfoundland - Six chairs for Prime Minister's Conference room. New Zealand - Two dispatch boxes in pururi. Nigeria - Furniture for Aye Division Lobby in iroko. Northern Ireland - Two clocks and division clock for the Chamber. Pakistan - Entrance doors to Chamber. Rhodesia - Two silver gilt inkstands with paper racks. Sabah - One table and five chairs for interview room. St. Helena - One Chairman's chair for Prime Minister's Conference Room. St. Lucia - One silver gilt ashtray. St. Vincent - One silver gilt ashtray. Seychelles - Minister's writing desk and chair. Sierra Leone - Minister's writing desk and chair. Singapore - One table and five chairs for interview room. South Africa - Three chairs for Clerks at the Table. Swaziland - One silver gilt ashtray. Tanganyika - One table and five chairs for interview room. Trinidad and Tobago - Minister's writing desk and chair. Uganda - Furniture for No Division Lobby in mvule. Zambia - Two pairs of bronze brackets for the Mace. Zanzibar - One silver gilt ashtray.

## Notes to Chapter I

1 Walter Besant, *Westminster* (1897), pp. 18-19.
2 Henry T. Ryde, *Illustrations of the New Palace of Westminster*, Second series, (1865).
3 Frederick Mackenzie, *The Architectural Antiquities of the Collegiate Chapel of St. Stephen Westminster* (1844).
4 Yevele's contract was for a tomb for the King and Queen, to cost £250 and to be completed by Michaelmas 1397. If the tomb met with the King's approval Yevele was to receive a bonus of £20. In January 1374/5 he had stood surety for the ship Margarete of Wareham which was carrying two tombs of marble for the Earl of Arundel and his deceased wife, also a great stone for the Bishop of Winchester.
5 Indenture, P.R.O. E101/473/21. L. F. Salzman, *Building in England down to 1540* (1952), p. 472.
6 W. Beckford, *Recollections of an Excursion to the Monasteries of Alcobaca and Batalha* (1835), pp. 82-87.
7 A. C. Pugin, *Specimens of Gothic Architecture* vol. i (1821-3), note to plates on Westminster Hall, pp. 21-22.
8 Lord Herbert of Cherbury, *The Life and Reign of King Henry VIII* (1683), p. 13.
9 28 Henry VIII, Chapter XII.
10 E. W. Brayley and John Britton, *The History of the Ancient Palace and Late Houses of Parliament at Westminster* (1836), p. 352.

## Notes to Chapter II

1 *The Journal of the House of Commons*. 5-9 November 1605, 21-23 January 1606.
2 G. Chowdhavay-Best, "The Colours of The Two Houses of Parliament at Westminster," *Notes and Queries* vol. 214 March 1969, p. 89.
3 For this report etc., see H. M. Colvin (ed.), *The history of the Kings' Works,* vol. v (1977), pp. 402-6.
4 Sir John Prestwich, *Prestwich's Respublica* (1787), pp. 3-23.
5 E. W. Brayley and John Britton, *The History of the Ancient Palace at Westminster* (1836), pp. 455-6.

## Notes to Chapter III

1 "Report on House of Commons Buildings" (1833), in J. Britton, *A Collection of Prints, Sketches and Drawings Illustrative of Westminster Hall, The Painted Chamber, The Late Houses of Parliament and Other Buildings Constituting the Ancient Palace of Westminster* (1834).
2 O. C. Williams, *Life and Letters of John Rickman* (1911), p. 110.
3 Benjamin Ferrey, *Recollections of A. N. Welby Pugin* (1831), pp. 32-33.
4 J. Britton. *Graphic Illustrations with Historical Descriptive Accounts of Toddington, Gloucestershire, the Seat of Lord Sudeley* (1840), p. 27.
5 A. W. N. Pugin to E. J. Willson, 6 November 1834. Fowler Collection, Johns Hopkins University.
6 Alfred Barry *The Life and Works of Sir Charles Barry* (1867), p. 4.
7 *Ibid.* p. 5.
8 *Ibid.* p. 5.
9 *Ibid.* p. 145.
10 *The Spectator* 25 October (1834), p. 1013.
11 *The Westminster Review* vol. xxii (1835), pp. 163-172.
12 *Parliamentary Paper* 262.
13 *Fraser's Magazine* vol. vii (1833), p. 602.
14 Alfred Barry, *op. cit.* p. 146.
15 J. Britton, *op. cit.* p. 35. Among the subscribers are listed: C. Barry, Esq., R.A. Architect, London, The Hon. Sir Edward Cust, G. Vivian, Esq., Claverton House, E. W. Brayley (Britton's collaborator at Westminster), Sir Francis Chantrey, Decimus Burton, T. Cubitt, T. Hopper, C. J. Richardson, P. F. Robinson, E. J. Willson, among the architectural profession. Members of

Parliament - H. T. Hope, James Morrison of Fonthill, Joseph Neeld of Grittleton and ominously Dr. Reid of Edinburgh.

16 Richard Tennyson was a surgeon who married an heiress, Mary Clayton, a descendant of the medieval family of D'Eyncourt. Their son George augmented the family fortune, establishing himself as a country gentleman at Bayons in Lincolnshire, a house of medieval origin. Being anxious to found a dynasty based on distinguished ancestry, he disinherited his eldest son, another George, whom he regarded as unsuitable material and a drunkard. He brought up eleven children in slum-like conditions. One of the children, however, became the most famous of all Tennysons and a Peer of the Realm, not through politics but poetry. The favoured heir was George's second son, Charles. He inherited Bayons in 1835 and christened himself Tennyson D'Eyncourt. It was now necessary to create the architectural background to support a dynasty.

17 Alfred Barry, *op. cit.* p. 132.

18 Alfred Barrry, *op. cit.* pp. 196-197.

19 *The Report of the Commissioners appointed by His Majesty to examine and report on the plans which might be offered by the competitors for rebuilding the Houses of Parliament.* 29 February 1836.

20 J. Britton, *op. cit.* p. 46.

21 *Report of the Commissioners* 29 February 1836, Q. 59-393.

## Notes to Chapter IV

1 Alfred Barry, *The Life and Works of Sir Charles Barry* (1867), p. 197.

2 He later became a Member of Parliament and developed the Somerleyton Estate in Suffolk. Here John Thomas, the sculptor at the New Palace turned architect, created a fantastic house embracing a winter garden 100 feet square. The house yet survives. Peto found himself in financial difficulties and sold Somerleyton in 1863 to Francis Crossley, a fellow Parliamentarian. Crossley, created a baronet in 1863, was a member of the famous Halifax family. His son became the first Lord Somerleyton in 1916. He served as Lord in Waiting between 1918 and 1924. The third Baron was appointed a non-political Lord in Waiting to Her Majesty the Queen in 1978 in which capacity he has accompanied many Heads of State on their visits to the Palace of Westminster.

3 *The Illustrated London News* 2 June 1860.

4 For Barry's Report, see Appendix A.

5 For a list of the subjects of the pictures see Chapter VII.

6 *Diary of Charles Barry* (1846 -47). By kind permission of Mrs. P. B. Stanley Evans. See Appendix C.

7 Alfred Barry, *The Architect of the New Palace at Westminster. A Reply to the Statements of Mr. E. Pugin,* (1868) p. 53.

8 *Ibid.* p. 39.

9 *The Illustrated London News*, 30 September (1843).

10 Lord Sudeley, *Observations on the Plans for the New Houses of Parliament by one of the Commissioners Appointed by the Crown in the Year 1835 to Examine the Designs.* Issued anonymously (1844).

11 *Ibid.* p.18.

12 Authority for this information is based on a drawing signed by Barry, 1844. PRO Works 29/112.

13 For Barry's letter to Lord Duncannon see Appendix B

14 *Select Committee on Westminster Bridge and New Palace*, evidence of 5 March 1847, Q256-260.

15 Alfred Barry, *The Life and Works of Sir Charles Barry* (1867), pp. 247-8.

16 Reproduced by gracious permission of Her Majesty The Queen.

17 John Wolfe, Manuscript notes on the life and works of Sir Charles Barry. R.I.B.A. WO5/1/2/1/(lvi-).

18 Henry T. Ryde, *Illustrations of the New Palace of Westminster*, First series (1849), unnumbered pages.

19 Alfred Barry, *The Life and Works of Sir Charles Barry*, (1867), p. 199.

20 Charles Barry Junior, "Some Description of the mechanical scaffolding used at the New Palace of Westminster, particularly in reference to the three main towers of the building." *Proceedings of the RIBA* , 15 June 1857, p. 156.

21 In the Middle Ages such places would have been preserved for the images of the Saints. In the Lords Chamber, although there are two archbishops represented, the remainder are

powerful political figures whose descendants yet sit below them.

22 For details of the restoration of the ceiling in the 1980s see Clive Aslet, "The House of Lords ceiling restored," *Country Life* 8th November 1984, pp. 1354-58, also Donald Insall, "Restoration of the Lords' ceiling at the Palace of Westminster," read to the Royal Society of Arts, 5 February 1986.

23 *Architectural History* , vol. xxvii (1984), pp. 59-73.

24 The description of the House of Lords is from Henry T. Ryde, *Illustrations of the New Palace of Westminster*, First series (1849).

25 *The Illustrated London News* 8 May 1847.

## Notes to Chapter V

1 Later exchanges revealed that the seats for visitors in the new House numbered 53 only.

2 John Wolfe, Manuscript notes on the life and works of Sir Charles Barry. R.I.B.A. WOJ/1/1/1.

3 George Basevi (1794 - 1845), took a cruel delight in Disraeli's successive failures to enter the House of Commons. The Basevis refused point blank to help with his financial difficulties. Dizzy, however, had the laugh on all of them when he was elected for Maidstone. The unfortunate George met his death by falling off one of the greatest Gothic buildings in the United Kingdom, Ely Cathedral. He built most of Belgrave Square. His country houses include Gatcombe Park, Glos. for David Ricardo.

4 Henry T. Ryde, *Illustrations of the New Palace at Westminster* , First series (1849), pp. 11 - 14.

5 First Report Select Committee on Ventilation and Lighting of House, 6th April 1852. For Goldsworthy Gurney's Report of 1852. See Appendix D, and Molesworth's Report (1853), Appendix E.

6 Henry T. Ryde, *Ibid.*

7 *Ibid.* p. 10b.

8 *Ibid.* p. 10b.

9 *Ibid.* p. 13b.

10 Alfred Barry, *The Life and Works of Sir Charles Barry* (1867), p. 341.

## Notes to Chapter VI

1 Henry T. Ryde, *Illustrations of the New Palace of Westminster*, Second series (1865), unnumbered pages.

2 *Ibid.* unnumbered pages.

3 The scene represented occurred at the small cabaret on the causeway between Waterloo and Genappe, at about nine o'clock in the evening of the 18th June 1815. It has been said that the heroes did not meet here; that may be, but certainly they were together and parted here; and Lord Sandys (at that time Lord Arthur Hill) who saw them on horseback at that spot, and whose portrait is introduced in the picture, narrated the circumstance to Mr. Maclise.

4 Lord Nelson was pacing the quarter-deck with Hardy, and as he turned from the main-mast in the direction of "the companion ladder, a ball fired from the mizen top of 'The Redoubtable' struck him in the left shoulder and he fell upon the deck on the spot now marked by a brass plate inscribed *Here Nelson Fell* . The shattered yard arm suspended in the rigging of 'The Victory' represents an incident which occurred during the engagement, and by means of this the enemy at one time attempted to board the ship. In both these pictures the artist has adhered to facts as far as he could, in the accessories and in the incidents which are introduced."

5 Henry T. Ryde, *Illustrations of the New Palace of Westminster* , Second series (1865), unnumbered pages.

6 *Report on the Ventilation of the House of Commons* (1886).

7 *Report from the Select Committee of the House of Lords on the Palace of Westminster*, 10 July 1907, Q1010-1228.

## Notes to Chapter VII

1 For a full description of the Maclise frescoes "Trafalgar: The Death of Nelson" and "Waterloo: The Meeting of Wellington and Blücher," see Appendix F. Also Chapter VI.
2 Henry T. Ryde, *Illustrations of the New Palace of Westminster*, First series (1849), p. 62.
3 *Report from the Select Committee of the House of Lords on the Palace of Westminster* 10th July 1907.
4 See Appendix G.
5 Sir Henry Newbolt, *The Building of Britain. A series of Historical paintings in St. Stephen's Hall, Westminster, described by Sir Henry Newbolt* (1930), pp. 2-3.
6 Committee document containing the plan, unnumbered, undated series of plans and donations. Each plate entitled "New Palace at Westminster." Tinted areas showing positions for works of art, inscribed on flyleaf in a contemporary hand. "Plans of rooms in the New Houses of Parliament showing where there may be opportunities of introducing pictures, frescoes, or other works of art." Day and Son, Lithographer to the Queen. Author's Collection. Photographs in House of Lords Record Office.
7 Greene 2/21. House of Lords Record Office.
8 Letter Barry to Hardman, November 1851. Quoted in Patrick A. Feeny, "The Heraldic Glass in the Houses of Parliament," *Journal of the British Society of Master Glass - Painters* vol. xii, No. 2, 1956-57, p. 143.
9 Letter Barry to Hardman, August 1856. *Ibid*, p. 144.
10 Patrick A. Feeny, p. 146.
11 Henry T. Ryde, *Illustrations of the New Palace of Westminster* First series (1849), Second series (1865).

## Notes to Chapter VIII

1 Letter Pugin to Hardman, early March 1851. In a private collection. Copy in the House of Lords Record Office.
2 See Appendix H for a list of the gifts of the Commonwealth.
3 *New Palace of Westminster Guide* (1856), p. 43.
4 Letter Pugin to Crace, 3rd January 1851. Crace Ms PUG 8/3 R.I.B.A. Drawings Collection.
5 Letter Pugin to Crace, November 1850. Crace Ms PUG 7/66 R.I.B.A. Drawings Collection.

## Notes to Chapter IX

1 Churchill Speech, House of Commons Rebuilding, *House of Commons Hansard*, 28 October 1943, cols. 403-410.
2 *House of Commons Hansard*, 25 January 1945.
3 The mover of the Motion on 28 July 1978 was R. Cooke, who had been Chairman of the Committee referred to by Mr. Foot and others in the debate.

## Notes to Chapter X

1 Adolf Hitler, *Mein Kampf* (1930), p. 75.
2 This picture belongs to the Guildhall Art Collection, London.
3 J. Gore (ed.), *Creevey's Life and Times* (1934), p. 347.

# Bibliography


Adkins, Kathleen (ed.), *The Travel Diaries of Sir Charles Barry 1817-1820* (Privately printed 1986).

Arts Council of Great Britain, *Daniel Maclise 1806-1870* (1972).

Aslet, Clive, "The House of Lords ceiling restored" *Country Life* 8 November 1984 also "The Speaker's House, Palace of Westminster" *Country Life* 13 November 1986.

Barker, Felix, *Riverside Highway: The Evening News Plan* (Associated Newspaper Publications 1956) also Barker, Felix and Hyde, Ralph, *London. As it might have been* (John Murray 1982).

Barry, Rev. Alfred, *The Life and Works of Sir Charles Barry* (John Murray 1867) also *The Architect of the New Palace at Westminster, A Reply to the Pamphlet by E. W. Pugin Esq.* (1868).

Barry, Sir Charles, *Desk Diary 1845* Manuscript, R.I.B.A. Drawings Collection.

Barry, Charles Junior, *Diaries 1846-47*. Private collection; transcript House of Lords Record Office also "Some description of the mechanical scaffolding used at the Palace of Westminster," *Proceedings of the R.I.B.A.* 15 June 1857.

Barry, E. M., "An Account of the New Palace at Westminster and the Progress of Building the Same," *Transactions of the R.I.B.A.* vol. viii (1858).

Bayley, Stephen, *The Albert Memorial: the monument in its social and architectural context* (Scolar Press 1981)

Bond, Maurice (ed.), *Works of Art in the House of Lords* (H.M.S.O. 1980).

Brayley, E. W. and Britton, J., *The History of the Ancient Palace and Late Houses of Parliament at Westminster* (John Weale 1836).

Britton, J., *A collection of prints, sketches and drawings illustrative of Westminster Hall, Painted Chamber, the late Houses of Parliament and other buildings constituting the Ancient Palace of Westminster* (1834) also *Graphic Illustrations with Historical and Descriptive Accounts of Toddington, Gloucestershire, the seat of Lord Sudeley* (1840).

*Catalogue of cartoons sent for exhibition in Westminster Hall* (1843).

*Catalogue of the designs offered for the New Houses of Parliament* (1826).

*Catalogue of the designs offered for the New Houses of Parliament, now exhibiting in the National Gallery* (1836).

Cescinsky, Herbert and Gribble, E., *Early English Furniture and Woodwork* 2 vols (G. Routledge and Sons 1922).

Chancellor, E. B., "The New Westminster: the vision of Sir Charles Barry," *Architectural Review* vol 61 (1927).

Clark, Kenneth (Baron Clark), *The Gothic Revival* (Constable 1950).

Cocks, Sir T. G. Barnett, *Mid-Victorian masterpiece: The story of an institution unable to put its own house in order* (Hutchinson 1977).

Colvin, H. M. (ed.), *The History of the Kings Works* vol. v 1660-1782 (H.M.S.O. 1976).

Cormack, Patrick, M.P., *Westminster Palace and Parliament* (Warne 1981).

Crook, J. Mordaunt and Port, M.H., *The History of the Kings Works* vol. vi 1782-1851 (H.M.S.O. 1973).

Dart, J., *Westmonasterium* 2 vols (1723).

Darwin, John, *The Triumphs of Big Ben* (Robert Hale 1986).

Ferrey, B., *Recollections of A. N. Welby Pugin* (1861).

Ferriday, Peter, *Lord Grimthorpe 1816-1905* (John Murray 1957).

Girouard, M., *The Victorian Country House* (Yale U. P. 1979) also *The Return to Camelot* (Yale U. P. 1981).

*The Graphic* (1872-1880).

Gullick, T. J., *A Descriptive Handbook for the National Pictures in the Westminster Palace* (1865).

Harvey, John T., *Henry Yevele c. 1320-1400* (Batsford 1944) also *Gothic England* (Batsford 1947).

Hastings, Maurice, *Parliament House* (Architectural Press 1950) also *St. Stephen's Chapel* (University Press, Cambridge 1955).

Hennessy, James Pope, *The Houses of Parliament* (Joseph 1975).

Hopper, Thomas, *Designs for the Houses of Parliament* (1842).

*The Houses of Parliament. A description of the Houses of Lords and Commons in the New Palace of Westminster. A handbook guide for Visitors* (1850).

Hunting, Penelope, *Royal Westminster* (R.I.C.S. 1981).

*Illustrated London News* (1842-1882).

Insall, Donald, "Restoration of the Lords ceiling at the Palace of Westminster," *Proceedings of the Royal Society of Arts* 5 February 1986.

Lindsay, Sir Martin, *The House of Commons* (Collins 1947).

Mackenzie, Frederick, *Architectural Antiquities of the Collegiate Chapel of St. Stephen, Westminster* (1844).

Newbolt, Sir Henry, *The Building of Britain. A Series of Historical Paintings in St. Stephen's Hall, Westminster, described by Sir Henry Newbolt* (T. Nelson and Sons 1927).

Oswald, Arthur, "The Speakers' House, Westminster," *Country Life* 30 November 1951.

Palace of Westminster: *Catalogue and Guide to the New Palace of Westminster* (1852, 1854, 1856, 1861, 1862, 1916, 1950).

*Parliamentary Papers and Committee Papers* (1840-) House of Lords Record Office.

Pevsner, Sir Nikolaus, *The Buildings of England. London I. The Cities of London and Westminster* (Penguin 1952, 1962).

Port, M. H. (ed.), *The Houses of Parliament* (Yale U. P. 1976).

Pugin, A. C., *Specimens of Gothic Architecture* (1821).

Pugin, E. W., *Who was the Art Architect of the Houses of Parliament?* (1867) also *Notes on the Reply of the Rev. A. Barry to the "Infatuated Statements" made by E. W. Pugin on the Houses of Parliament etc.* (1868).

*Reports of the Fine Arts Commissioners* Parliamentary Papers 1842 (412) xxv, 1843 (499) xxiv, 1844 (585) xxxi, 1845 (671) xxvii, 1846 (685) xxiv, 1846 (749) xxiv, 1847 (862) xxxiii, 1849 (1009) xxii, 1850 (1180) xxiii, 1854 (1829) xix, 1857-8 (2425) xxiv, 1861 (2806) xxxii, 1863 (3141) xvi.

Richardson, J., *The Eglinton Tournament* (Colnaghi and Puckle 1843).

Ryde, Henry T., *Illustrations of the New Palace of Westminster*, First series (1849), Second series (1865).

Saunders, Hilary St. G., *Westminster Hall* (Michael Joseph 1951).

Stamp, Gavin, *The Changing Metropolis* (Viking 1984).

Stanton, Phoebe, *Pugin* (Thames and Hudson 1971).

Steindl, Imre, *Le palais du Parliament Hongrois* (1909).

Stevens, Ann, *The woodcarvers of Warwick* (no date).

Stow, John, *Survey of London* (1598), revised by J. Strype (1720, 1754).

Summerson, Sir John, *Sir John Soane* (Art and Technics 1952).

Thornton, Peter, *The Furniture in the House of Lords* (H.M.S.O. 1973).

Wainwright, Clive, "A.W.N. Pugin's Early Furniture," *Connoisseur* vol. cxci (1976), pp. 3-11.

Walker, R. J. B., *Catalogue of Paintings in the Palace of Westminster* (1962).

Wedgwood, Alexandra, *Catalogue of the RIBA Collection of Pugin Family Drawings* (Gregg International 1977) also *Rebuilding the Houses of Parliament: drawings from the Kennedy albums and the Thomas Greene papers* (H.L.R.O. 1984), also *A. W. N. Pugin and the Pugin Family. Catalogue of Architectural Drawings in the Victoria and Albert Museum* (Victoria and Albert Museum 1985).

Westlake, H. F., *St. Margaret's Westminster: the church of the House of Commons* (1914).

Wolfe, John L., *Notes on the life and work of Sir Charles Barry* Manuscript, R.I.B.A.

Wright, Arnold and Smith, Philip, *Parliament Past and Present* 2 vols (Hutchinson 1902-1903).

# INDEX

Abbreviation: NHP (New Houses of Parliament)
Pl. (Plate)

Note: The entries are followed by page numbers.
The page number after Pl. indicates the page number of the illustration

# Sources of Illustrations

The Clerk of the Record and the staff of the House of Lords Record Office, also the House of Commons Library must be thanked for their assistance. Among the many archivists, curators and librarians who have kindly given their time and help, I especially thank Mr. Stephen Croad of the National Monuments Record, Mr. Robert Elwall of the Royal Institute of British Architects, Dr. M. Foster of the Public Record Office, Miss Phillis Rogers, Curator of Works of Art in the Palace of Westminster and Mr. Malcolm Hay the Assistant Curator, Mr. John Steedman, Librarian of the PSA Photographic Unit. I also thank Mr. Wyn Lewis O.B.E., Mr. John Darwin, Mr. Graham Goode and Mr. David Kempton for their help. I am most particularly grateful to Mrs. Alexander Wedgwood, the authority on Pugin's drawings for her advice. Lord Winterbottom kindly contributed information about Brangwyn.

*Robert Cooke*

Reproduced by gracious permission of Her Majesty The Queen. Copyright reserved, 22, 45, 120, 294.

Controller of Her Majesty's Stationery Office (Crown Copyright), 21, 26, 38, 44, 45, 55, 57, 62, 63, 65, 70, 73, 77, 78, 79, 95, 99, 100, 136, 140, 141, 143, 149, 154, 158, 165, 166, 167, 173, 174, 175, 179, 188-93, 205, 210, 211, 213, 232, 233, 254, 257, 258, 260, 261, 263, 264, 265, 267, 273, 275, 277, 278, 279, 280, 281, 289-93, 310, 316, 317, 321, 322, 323, 324, 336, 341, 373 and front cover.

Ashmolean Museum Oxford, 27.

Vicar of St. Andrew's, Toddington , 85.

Birmingham Public Libraries, 123, 168, 170, 196, 249, 251, 252.

The British Architectural Library, R.I.B.A. London, 88, 96-7, 199, 200, 219.

The British Library, 28, 82.

The Broadlands Collection (by permission of Lord Romsey), 185.

Syndics of Cambridge University Library, 14, 17.

The Casson Condor Partnership, 369, 378.

The Central Office of Information (Crown Copyright), 376.

City of Westminster Libraries Archives Department, 58.

Mr. William Drummond, 64.

The Provost and Fellows of Eton College, Derek Hill, 392.

Mrs. P. B. Stanley-Evans, 105.

Mr. Christopher Gibbs, 124.
Mr. Mark girouard, 84.

The Graphic, 390.

The Guildhall Library, City of London, 87.

The Clerk of the Records, House of Lords Record Office (Historical Collection), 33.

The Illustrated London News Picture Library, 124, 138, 144, 146, 152, 162, 171, 182-3, 231

Mr. Peter Jackson, 40.

The National Portrait Gallery, London, 51, 110, 181

The N.S.P.C.C. and Mrs. Gilly Rayner, the frontispiece.

The Public Record Office, 34-5 (E101/473/21), 325 (Works 29/2581).

The Royal Commission on the Historical Monuments of England, 36, 195, 222, 223, 225, 226, 296-7, 298-9, 301, 302, 303

The Trustees of Sir John Soane's Museum, 49.

Tapisserie de Bayeux (avec autorisation spéciale de la ville de Bayeux), 18, 19.

The Town Mayor and Councillors of Tewkesbury, 117.

The Director of the Research Museum of the U.S.S.R. Academy of Arts, Leningrad, 128, 172, back cover.

The Board of Trustees of the Victoria and Albert Museum, 60.

The Dean and Chapter of Westminster, 31.

*Photographs taken by:*

Geremy Butler, 68, 90, 91, 96-7, 103, 105, 106, 109, 112, 115, 121, 122, 131, 161, 163, 176, 178, 199, 200, 203, 208, 219, 234, 235, 237, 245, 271, 282, 308, 309, 314, 315, 361, 365, 380.

A. C. Cooper, 187, 216, 220, 227, 228, 241, 285, 287, 306, 308, 311, 312, 313, 314, 315, 318, 319, 320, 327, 329, 330, 331, 345, 347, 349, 350, 352, 353, 356, 358, 359, 379, 382, 386, 387.

Patrick Cooke, 85.

La Goelette, Paris, 25.

Godfrey New, 49, 87.

Posers Photography Tewkesbury, 117.